WINDOW SEAT
ON THE WORLD

WINDOW
SEAT
ON THE
WORLD

MY TRAVELS WITH
THE SECRETARY OF STATE

———

GLEN JOHNSON

DISRUPTION
BOOKS

Austin   New York

The opinions and characterizations in this book are those of the author and do not necessarily represent official positions of the United States Government.

Published by Disruption Books
Austin, TX, and New York, NY
www.disruptionbooks.com

For ordering information or special discounts for bulk purchases, please contact Disruption Books at info@disruptionbooks.com.

Print ISBN: 978-1-63331-039-1
eBook ISBN: 978-1-63331-040-7

First Edition

For my wife, Cathy.

She raised two successful boys while I built a career,
relished the chances to share in my professional adventures,
and gave me confidence on the campaign trail and diplomatic circuit
because she always had things under control at home
—even while soaring as a real estate broker.

I wouldn't have lived a happy and complete life if
I hadn't noticed her slipping extra cheese onto my Big Beef burgers
during her Friendly's days . . .

CONTENTS

Window seat view of Mount Fuji, Honshu, Japan, August 8, 2015.

AN UNDERSTANDING OF THE ANCIENT
AND, TO OUTSIDERS, MYSTERIOUS ORGANIZATION,
AS IT WAS TO ME WHEN I JOINED IT, REQUIRES A LOOK
AT ITS WORK AND AT THOSE WHO DID IT.

—DEAN ACHESON, *Present at the Creation*

PROLOGUE

MOST OF THE PEOPLE on our plane were asleep as the sun rose on July 1, 2013, and with good reason. John Kerry was amid a marathon trip typical of his frenetic four-year tenure as secretary of State.

We sweated through 105-degree heat in Qatar for a multinational meeting about the civil war in Syria. We flew on for our annual Strategic and Economic Dialogue with India. Then we doubled back to consult with Saudi, Kuwaiti, Jordanian, Palestinian, and Israeli officials as Middle East peace talks sputtered.

Our final stop was the nation-state of Brunei for a meeting of the Association of Southeast Asian Nations.

Getting to Asia from Israel required an overnight flight, wiping out the travel team as we neared two weeks on the road.

Nonetheless, I was awake and looking out the window next to my seat when Kerry came running down the aisle, waving to me and calling my name. I gave chase as he returned to his cabin.

"Look outside the window," he said, pointing his finger at the panes beside his desk. "You can see the Mekong's headwaters."

I came around the desk, looked forward of the wing, and sure enough, there they were: the outlines of the Vam Co Dong River and other tributaries of the mighty Mekong River. Each sparkled against the dark countryside as a brilliant sun illuminated their twists and turns.

With the map on a nearby big-screen TV showing most of Indochina, the secretary became tour guide while recalling a central part of his biography: his Navy service during the Vietnam War.

"That's the main Mekong," he said, tracing his long index finger down the map. "And that's the Saigon River," he said, turning to another ribbon of blue. "I worked out of here for a while, down in here," he said, pointing to what is now known as Ho Chi Minh City. It formerly was Saigon, South Vietnam.

Moving his finger southwest along the coast, he said, "Then we went down here and through these rivers, then we went down on this river," pointing to the Bô Đê.

"We got a lot of action down there," he added, almost matter-of-factly.

The map abruptly disappeared from the screen, replaced by a page of flight statistics that had rotated into view. They showed our plane was at 37,000 feet, with another hour and thirty-eight minutes until landing.

It's possible to recount the conversation at length because I had pulled out my iPhone and started snapping pictures as Kerry looked out the windows. When he walked over to the map, I switched to video mode, because the moment had hit me like a thunderbolt.

I was alongside John Kerry as we flew over the place that had come to define him as a man and a politician, and I was the lone pupil for a tutorial about his service.

A place only in my mind was now before my eyes, and the person for whom it meant so much was standing in front of me, telling me his story.

It was moments just like these that would make the grind of my four years in the State Department worth it.

I'd had a similar experience during our first trip abroad. We were in Berlin and Kerry announced he wanted to take a walk outside. I was sitting in a staff meeting, and most of our security team had already turned in for the night.

But as their radios crackled with the change in plans, everyone came running out of their hotel rooms. The guards threw on their clothes and shoes and earpieces and gun holsters as "Fenway"—the secretary's security code name—headed for the exit.

The scramble paid off.

We walked into the square overlooking the Brandenburg Gate, the former portal between East and West Germany. It was the same spot through which a twelve-year-old Kerry famously rode his bike during the Cold War, before thinking the better of it and turning around to go home.

His father, a US diplomat at the time, was apoplectic about how close his son had come to causing an international crisis. He responded by yanking his diplomatic passport. The story became legend as Kerry told it throughout his 2004 presidential campaign, and that near-mythic tale had now come to life in 2013.

Kerry pulled out his cellphone to take a picture of the Gate. I pulled out my own cellphone to take a picture of him taking his picture.

Most around him thought he was just playing tourist, but I was struck by the history of the moment.

Less than five months later, flying over Vietnam, I had that feeling again.

Throughout my prior work as a reporter, "John Kerry" and "Vietnam" had become almost synonymous to me. I'd heard and read much about the decorated service that sparked admiration, as well as the subsequent antiwar protests triggering condemnation.

I was dockside at Boston Harbor during Kerry's 1996 reelection campaign when retired Admiral Elmo Zumwalt, who commanded all US Navy forces in Vietnam, defended the then senator. A *Boston Globe* columnist had raised the specter of him committing a war crime in 1969 while recounting how Lieutenant Kerry chased down and killed a Viet Cong soldier who tried to destroy him and his Swift Boat crew with a shoulder-fired rocket.

Likewise, I was sitting at the FleetCenter in Boston when the secretary began his 2004 presidential nomination acceptance speech by snapping a salute and declaring, "I'm John Kerry, and I'm reporting for duty."

And I witnessed the remainder of the race, as the campaign team for President George W. Bush shredded his war record with attacks by the "Swift Boat Veterans for Truth" and other critics. They accused Kerry, a Silver and Bronze Star winner, of embellishing his war record. They also said the recipient of three Purple Hearts was two-faced for opposing a war in which he once fought.

Now, as a part of his State Department team, I would make four trips to Vietnam alongside Kerry. Each of them was infused with that personal history, but all were emblematic of the possibilities he pursued elsewhere in the world while serving as secretary of State—his final job in public service.

While Kerry had traveled to Vietnam seventeen times as a senator, he hadn't been back in more than a decade when he accompanied Bill Clinton as the first president to visit since Richard Nixon.[1]

He would visit for the first time as secretary of State in December 2013, during the last trip of his first year in office.

His focus was on educational and environmental issues, the latter to be highlighted by a sail back up the Mekong.

I'd first laid eyes on the river early one morning, from seven miles overhead.

OUR FIRST STOP THAT December was Ho Chi Minh City (HCMC), which had been the capital of South Vietnam when it was known as Saigon. You could still see grassed-over bomb craters surrounding the airport, and revetments where American F-4 Phantom fighters had been parked near the runways.

HCMC is described by some as the Vietnamese version of New York, electric with energy and commerce. The people are notably friendly—especially to the Americans who were their wartime allies.

If that analogy holds, then Hanoi—in the former North Vietnam, and now capital of the unified country—would be considered its Washington. Hanoi is home to the Communist Party and political leaderships, both operating from mustard yellow buildings flying a national flag with a simple red field and a solitary gold star in the center. In the middle of the city is the tomb where their revolutionary leader, Ho Chi Minh, lies embalmed for public viewing to this day.

Ho's gilded bust sits in every leader's office, usually above the throne-like seats where the Communist officials greet their visitors.

We cleaned up at our hotel before a quick tour downtown preceding a series of meetings and an official dinner. Our informal host was Tom Vallely, a Massachusetts native and Marine veteran of Vietnam who'd become friends with Kerry during the antiwar movement. "Tommy" had a sobering distinction: he was the only member of his unit not killed or wounded in the war.

Now he was head of Harvard University's Vietnam program.

Vallely led the secretary across the street from the InterContinental Hotel and past an overwhelming sight: a road full of motorbikes lined up at a stoplight. They looked like they were anxiously awaiting the start of a motocross race. The only thing restraining them was a police officer dressed in a khaki uniform holding up a baton, silently transmitting the message to wait.

Our destination was the Notre-Dame Cathedral, a Catholic sanctuary harking back to Vietnam's French colonial days. The secretary attended Mass, offering tangible support for religious institutions in a country that, officially, does not recognize religion.

Afterward, Vallely turned the party around and pointed out an apartment building at 18 Gia Long Street. One of the last helicopters evacuating US citizens and desperate South Vietnamese took off from its famously flat roof after the fall of Saigon to the North Vietnamese.

Like Dealey Plaza in Dallas or Red Square in Moscow, it's a spot you instantly know from the history books despite having never seen it in person.

Following his meetings, the secretary paid a nighttime visit to the US consulate in Ho Chi Minh City. He thanked a group of elderly Vietnamese who'd worked in the now-shuttered Saigon embassy and remained faithful to their American employer, even as war enveloped the city.

They now sat in the front row, some in wheelchairs.

"You are the ones really defining this new relationship in modern terms, as Vietnam goes through this enormous transformation. I can't tell you how much of a transformation it is," Kerry said. "None of these big, tall buildings were here twenty years ago. And now there are—40 percent of the country is under the age of twenty-five, a young country for whom the war is ancient history."[2]

We left the consulate and went to a restaurant for dinner, a meal becoming less formal with each round of Tiger beers. With the group loosened up, the secretary suggested we visit one of his old haunts, the Rex Hotel.

It was a wartime crossroads for journalists covering the fighting, soldiers on liberty, and Vietnamese looking to make money off everyone.

THE REX HAS A famous rooftop bar overlooking Ho Chi Minh Square, a promenade running up from the Saigon River to City Hall. The hotel sat beside a traffic circle where motorbikes from all directions converged on a single loop. It collected them, circulated them, and spat them out a different path.

During our next trip to Vietnam, we'd return to find—much to our dismay—that the circle had been replaced with traffic lights and a standard four-way intersection. The city government changed the landscape while building a subway underneath to alleviate the traffic.

Secretary Kerry sat in the middle of a long table as the waiters brought aqua-colored cocktails and rounds of beer served in chilled mugs. Joining him was Assistant Secretary of State for East Asian and Pacific Affairs Danny Russel, who'd evolved into an Asia expert after first visiting Japan to study karate in a dojo.

At one point, the secretary got up and started to walk around, looking at the stage where a guitar player and his group sat framed by a pair of Rex trademarks: romping elephants and an Aladdin-like crown. He moved over to the bar, running his hand across its surface and silently taking the measure of its layout. He then went back to the balcony overlooking the traffic rotary, watching its whirl of lights and motion.

During his remarks to the elderly Vietnamese at the consulate, Kerry foreshadowed what he seemed to be feeling at that moment:

We would sit up there, and we were having a beer, which we couldn't have normally where we were, and you'd look out at the flares all around the city. And every so often you'd hear this b-r-r-r-r-t of gunfire from what we called "Puff the Magic Dragon," that was flying around, which was a C-130 that would shoot. It was really eerie. I can't tell you how totally bizarre it was to be sitting on top of a hotel, having a beer, sitting around, talking with people—a lot of press people used to hang out there—while all around you, you would be seeing and hearing the sounds of a war. And that was the sort of strangeness and duality of that period of time.[3]

I was the State Department's official travel photographer, so I surreptitiously took pictures as the secretary remembered those moments from visits long ago. There were occasions such as this on each of our trips to Vietnam: times when John Kerry would go quiet and relive something none of us had been around to experience.

Each time, I tried to recede into the surroundings, working to capture but not interrupt it.

The following day, the group boarded a pair of propeller planes for the flight south to Cà Mau, a staging area for our trip up the Mekong Delta. The secretary wanted to call attention to the region's environmental challenges and the Lower Mekong Initiative. It tries to prevent actions upstream— such as river damming and pollution runoff—that can harm people living downstream.

Those men, women, and children depend on rice grown in flooded fields, and protein from the fish and shrimp in the rivers and nearby sea.

Our flight took us from the chaos and modernity of the city to the tranquility and simplicity of the countryside. We flew through thick clouds and over rice paddies and shrimp ponds. The latter were outlined by retaining walls and stirred with water fountains providing oxygen to farmed shellfish destined for the United States and other markets.

After we landed, our motorcade passed houses with tin walls displaying the ever-present Vietnamese flag. Despite the remoteness, kids wore jerseys from their favorite British and Spanish pro soccer teams.

When we boarded our boat to head upstream, Secretary Kerry took up a spot at the center of the bridge. It let him survey the landscape and get a fresh breeze in his face through the open cockpit.

At one point, we passed under a bridge. He looked over and said, "I remember going under that," referring to his Swift Boat patrols. Another moment, he pointed to the heavy canopy of mango and banana trees covering the riverbanks and said he and his crew never knew when the leaves of the trees would begin to shred, as hidden Viet Cong soldiers began firing at them with .50-caliber machine guns.

When we finally reached our turnaround point, the Kien Vang Market Pier, the secretary disembarked to deliver an environmental speech. A sampan cut through the water as he spoke.

"That river is a global asset, a treasure that belongs to the region," he said. "Sharing data and best practices in an open and cooperative dialogue will help ensure that many resources of the Mekong continue to benefit people not just in one country, not just in the country where the waters come first, but in every country that touches this great river."[4]

Afterward, Kerry met a group of Vietnamese girls from a nearby school, many dressed in flowing white dresses. He talked to them about how the United States and Vietnam were moving past their war history and into a new future based on economic and educational cooperation.

As sound as the trip was thematically and in execution, you could tell it really didn't satisfy the Boss. It was clear he wanted to push upstream to the sites of his combat service, not as the lieutenant he once was, but as the secretary of State he'd become.

That would have to wait.

———

OUR SECOND TRIP TO Vietnam came more than a year later, in early August 2015, as the secretary visited to commemorate the twentieth anniversary of US–Vietnamese diplomatic relations. John Kerry had worked with his Senate colleague John McCain, a fellow Navy veteran of Vietnam and former prisoner of war, to normalize relations in 1995.

The centerpiece of the secretary's 2015 trip was a major speech about the transformation of the relationship during the prior two decades. Among those in the audience was Vietnamese foreign minister Phạm Bình Minh, who also served as the country's deputy prime minister.

By the numbers alone, the change truly was remarkable: In 1995, there were fewer than sixty thousand annual American visitors to Vietnam. By 2015, the number had grown to five hundred thousand. In 1995, fewer than eight hundred Vietnamese students studied in the United States. By 2015, there were seventeen thousand. In 1995, trade between the two countries was valued at $451 million. By 2015, it totaled more than $36 billion.[5]

During his speech, the secretary said:

> Vietnam and our shared journey from conflict to friendship crosses my mind frequently as I grapple with the complex challenges that we face in the world today—from strife in the Middle East to the dangers of violent extremism with Daesh, Boko Haram, al-Shabaab, and dozens of other violent extremists, and also even the dangers of the march of technology with cyber intrusion and potential of cyber warfare. That we are standing here today celebrating 20 years of normalized relations is proof that we are not doomed merely to repeat the mistakes that we have made in the past. We have the ability to overcome great bitterness, and to substitute trust for suspicion and replace enmity with respect. The United States and Vietnam have again proven that former adversaries really can become partners, even in the complex world that we face today. And as much as that achievement matters to us, it is also a profound and timely lesson to the rest of the world.[6]

After the speech, Secretary Kerry went for dinner at a Hanoi restaurant. He sat with Ted Osius, the US ambassador to Vietnam, and three friends and fellow Vietnam veterans from Massachusetts: Vallely, David Thorne, and Chris Gregory. Joining them was Francis Zwenig, who'd been Kerry's administrative assistant and staff director of the Select Committee on POW/MIA Affairs.

Now gray-haired, the onetime soldiers ate and told war stories in the capital of the former North Vietnam, the city where McCain had spent his five years as a prisoner of war.

I took several photos for their scrapbooks and then waited outside.

Our third trip to Vietnam came the following year, in May 2016. We visited Hanoi and Ho Chi Minh City alongside President Obama.

The good news for us staffers was that when the secretary accompanied the president, he was incorporated with the White House delegation. The State Department crew was left with little to do but wait at the hotel.

Most of us slept or gingerly explored the surrounding neighborhood. You never wanted to be left behind, and you never wanted to cause a diplomatic incident by being caught in the wrong place at the wrong time. As tempting as the local delicacies may be, you also had to be careful about what you ate on the street.

Our plane was no place to end up sick.

One item on our own schedule was an interview with Margaret Brennan, a CBS News correspondent who covered the State Department. She'd asked to speak with the secretary in Vietnam for a biographical piece she was preparing for *CBS Sunday Morning*.

During the interview, conducted in Hanoi at dusk on a shiny scarlet bridge over a lake leading to the Ngoc Son Temple, she asked Kerry how serving in Vietnam had affected him.

He said, "[It] gave me a sense of understanding how people in positions of responsibility, when they look at something, misunderstand it and mistake what's happening, and make the decisions that cost lives, put people's lives at risk, puts America at risk."[7]

Critics had accused him of duplicity, noting he opposed the Vietnam War after fighting in it. They also complained about such proclamations after he voted in Congress to authorize the Iraq War in 2002 but later opposed it.

As both a US senator and secretary of State, Kerry explained he had voted to give President Bush the authority to wage war in Iraq, but only after he'd been promised the administration would exhaust all possible avenues to avoid it. Kerry complained the president hadn't kept that promise and, instead, had rushed to battle.

Kerry's opinion of Vietnam, meanwhile, changed after what he saw during his combat tours.

The irony of the Swift Boat Veterans attacks is that Kerry had seen combat, unlike his opponents in the 2004 presidential campaign.

John Kerry and George W. Bush were at Yale University at the same time; but when they graduated, they took divergent paths. Kerry entered the Navy and volunteered to skipper a Swift Boat on the Mekong Delta. Bush joined the Texas Air National Guard and flew training missions over the Gulf of Mexico.

Bush's running mate, Vice President Dick Cheney, got five draft deferments. He later told *The Washington Post*: "I had other priorities in the 60's than military service."[8]

Nonetheless, he and Bush were able to turn the Vietnam War into Kerry's Waterloo.

That whole episode remains, to me, one of the most egregious misrepresentations of duty and honor and service that's transpired in American politics, because it was committed to the advantage of a president and vice president who'd each found ways to avoid the same risks Kerry confronted head-on.

Brennan asked the secretary if the attacks had taken on an extra "sting" because of his continued connection to Vietnam.

"What took on a sting were the lies," he said. "I mean, just rank, unbelievably contrived, totally out-of-whole-cloth lies, which were proved again and again were lies, but which people were repeating again and again."[9]

———————

AFTER OUR STOP IN Hanoi, we flew south along the Vietnamese coast. One member of our traveling party, Kerry's dinner companion David Thorne, pointed out Da Nang, where he'd served during the war.

Thorne was the leader of a State Department economic development team, but he had a unique stature with the secretary, particularly when it came to Vietnam.

The two had been classmates and soccer teammates at Yale. They were reluctant to confirm it, but they also were members of the secretive Skull and Bones Society that counted President Bush and his father, former President George H. W. Bush, among its members.

John Kerry and David Thorne decided as college juniors to join the Navy after graduation, and each finished his military career a combat veteran.

The secretary went on to marry Thorne's twin sister, Julia, and the couple had two daughters, Alexandra and Vanessa, before divorcing in 1988.

Despite that split, the friendship between John Kerry and David Thorne endured, and Kerry recommended in 2009 that President Obama nominate Thorne to be US ambassador to Italy.

Thorne had grown up in Italy after President Dwight D. Eisenhower picked his father, Landon, to work in the country as administrator of the Marshall Plan. Thorne became fluent in Italian and later ran his father's newspaper, the *Rome Daily American*, during what amounted to two decades in the country.[10]

Thorne was at the bottom of the steps at Ciampino Airport in Rome when Kerry's plane pulled to a stop during our first trip abroad in February 2013. The secretary smiled and shot him a trigger-finger greeting as he descended the stairs. The two now-diplomats hugged as an Italian honor guard saluted them both.

When his ambassadorship ended, David Thorne came into the State Department fold as senior adviser. In truth, he truly was an ambassador without portfolio. As one of the secretary's closest friends, he went places and said things others would not. He also was a moderating influence, whether traveling with Kerry, walking with him between offices in the Harry S Truman Building, or sitting next to him at restaurants around the world.

If someone needed to speak truth to power, David Thorne could always do it. He was a constant for the secretary of State, tying together his past and present, his personal and professional lives.

Our group landed in Ho Chi Minh City just before President Obama, who was making his first visit to Vietnam.

The scene confronting us was overwhelming.

There were thousands of people lining the streets along the entire route from the airport to the hotel downtown. They were more than a dozen deep and cheered loudly as our motorcade passed. Some thought they were waving at the president, who was about a half hour behind us, but it was clear when the secretary took a walk later that he was tremendously popular in his own right.

As we crossed intersections or waited at traffic lights during our walk, people recognized the towering man with the thick head of hair. "Kerry," they yelled, as they cheered and waved enthusiastically.

When we reached the Saigon River, the secretary told me about his first visit. He brought his Swift Boat to the same spot for repairs, docked it at a pier still there, and was picked up by a US Intelligence officer who'd been a buddy in language school. The pal was waiting with a motorbike and a bottle of Champagne, and they set out to tour the city before Kerry rejoined his crew and sailed away.

As we walked, the secretary remarked about the futility of the war: "All that pain, suffering, and killing—and look at it forty years later," he said.[11]

By the time we'd walked along the river and up the promenade past the Rex and City Hall, both of us were soaked through our suits from the humidity. We went back to the hotel, put on bathrobes, and immediately sent our jackets and pants out for dry-cleaning. It was the only way to save them.

That evening, the secretary addressed the White House traveling press corps at the request of President Obama's staff. He spoke again about his own service in the country and the changes that had occurred since the late 1960s.

"I have to tell you that for many years I have looked forward to a time when people would hear the word 'Vietnam' or the name 'Vietnam' and think more of a country than a conflict," he said. "And with President Obama's visit this week, with the crowds that we saw along the street today, the remarkably warm and generous welcome, the unbelievable excitement of people that we are here with a president of the United States at this moment is absolutely palpable, and I think it is a demarcation point."[12]

Kerry added: "This is a prime example of the way in which the United States has been able to forge a new relationship out of the ashes of war and to create real peace."[13]

The secretary later headed back to the Rex Hotel for beers and cigars with his staff and another special guest. This time it was former US senator Bob Kerrey.

Like the secretary, the Nebraskan had been a Vietnam vet; but the former Navy SEAL left badly wounded after losing part of a leg in a battle just three months into his first combat tour. His bravery earned him the Medal of Honor.

Again I found myself with another pinch-me moment in Vietnam: the secretary of State sitting with a fellow decorated veteran back in a country where they had both once fought. Bob Kerrey had fended off his own war-crime accusations for the deaths in a village raid he led, but there also was no denying he'd displayed heroism on the battlefield.

The former senator and past president of the New School in New York City was in Vietnam for a ceremony the following day encapsulating the essence of what John Kerry had tried to do in the country since returning as a civilian.

Vallely and his Harvard colleague Ben Wilkinson had worked for years to develop a truly independent university in Vietnam. Pivoting off the success of the Fulbright Scholarship program, which had let many top-level Vietnamese officials study in the United States before returning home, the Fulbright University Vietnam was conceived as a place to provide a similar education within Vietnam itself.

Kerry marked various waypoints toward the university's creation during his four years as secretary of State, but a ceremony on May 25, 2016, was the most significant. Government leaders planned to hand over an operating license to university officials—the veritable keys to the car.

"The single smartest investment we can make in the next generation is education, and that's what we are doing here today," Kerry said during the handover ceremony.[14]

Noting there were 22 million people under the age of fifteen in Vietnam, he added: "The decisions that they make now and the education that they receive now—not in 10 years, but today—will have a pivotal impact on this country's future and that of the region itself."[15]

The secretary closed by saying, "Folks, it took us 20 years to normalize and almost 20 more to move from healing to building. Think of what we can accomplish in the next 20 years."[16]

OUR LAST TRIP TO Vietnam was our most momentous for a variety of reasons, not the least of which was that it came in January 2017 during our final trip abroad.

First, the flight in was another of those overnight affairs with another of those sunrise spectacles. This time, the secretary and I were back in his cabin, but not to see the Mekong Delta. Instead, we looked out at Mount Everest—the highest peak on Earth—as we flew along the southern edge of the Himalayas.

He snapped pictures with his iPad. I did the same with my professional cameras.

Then, after we landed, Tommy Vallely and Ben Wilkinson were there again, but this time with a new sidekick: Ed Miller, a Dartmouth history professor specializing in the Vietnam War. He came to the country at Vallely's request because he'd located maps depicting southern Vietnam during the time the secretary had served in the war.

Over dinner, the secretary ran his fingers over those maps. He retraced his routes up the region's rivers and tributaries, pinpointing the sites of some of his more ferocious battles.

The plan was to return to the most famous of them all, the place where he chased down that Viet Cong soldier with the shoulder-fired rocket launcher.

For not just John Kerry but also those who'd covered his career and come to know him over the years, the last visit to Vietnam was to conclude with the ultimate step back into history.

We departed from Ho Chi Minh City with practiced efficiency. The group again split in two and boarded yet another pair of propeller planes. The cityscape turned to countryside on the flight south, and again we deplaned in Cà Mau.

We even drove past the same tin houses and Communist flags, to the same dock from which we departed in 2013 for that environmental speech.

xxiv PROLOGUE

This time, though, the secretary quickly left the boat's bridge and instead stood in a hull opening near the bow. The spot allowed him to lean back on the doorframe and survey the muddy waters of the Bai Hap River as his hair flapped in the rushing wind.

Memories came back to the secretary in bits and pieces, with him again recalling a bridge or turn but especially a village we passed. Ed Miller came forward with his maps and Kerry unfolded them on his lap, struggling to hold down their corners in the breeze.

Unable to sleep the night before, the secretary spent time on Google Earth, searching the contours of the rivers and the recesses of his memory. He called back to the United States, speaking with his Swift Boat turret gunner and asking for his recollections of the area where they got into the firefight.

Then came the moment hours later on the boat when the secretary looked into the riverbanks and back into time, all the way to the moment of the battle. He pointed to the shore, and we realized he'd navigated himself back to the spot of that infamous firefight. To us, it was a thicket of vegetation. To him, it was the place where he almost lost his life.

We bobbed in the water for several minutes as the moment sank in. The secretary stood silently, looking across the water's edge to a small clearing and the jungle beyond.

Kerry had told us over some of those boozy dinners in Vietnam how he'd worried about the safety of the crew as the firing began, and how that prompted his unconventional decision to turn the Swift Boat, *PCF-94*, directly toward the fire.

Steering the boat from broadside to head-on narrowed its profile and let its commanding officer make a beeline to their attackers.

When the boat beached, Lieutenant Kerry jumped off, M-16 in hand, and chased a man who tried to disappear into the thicket with his rocket launcher.

When the soldier stopped and turned back to face him, the lieutenant fired. The soldier fell, dead.

During the 1996 Massachusetts Senate campaign, then *Boston Globe* columnist David Warsh questioned whether Kerry had delivered the "coup de grace" to a soldier already wounded by another member of his crew—a potential war crime. Some of the Swift Boat Veterans for Truth and other 2004 campaign critics also suggested the Viet Cong soldier may have actually been a boy, which would be another pox on his killing.

Kerry had disputed such assertions whenever they were made, but they may have ended up costing him the presidency. He was left to take solace in his own integrity, the citations justifying his combat decorations, and the memories held for decades by him and his crew.

But now, in 2016, the rest of us on the boat with him had a chance to see the spot previously known only to them.

———

WE MOTORED BACK TO the dock in Cà Mau just as we had in 2013; but this time, Vallely and Wilkinson had a surprise for Kerry.

Working with local Vietnamese officials and the US consulate in Ho Chi Minh City, they'd found a shrimp and crab farmer who said he'd been a Viet Cong soldier whose unit regularly attacked US Navy Swift Boats during the Vietnam War.

Not only had now-seventy-year-old Vo Ban Tam seen action in the region where Lieutenant Kerry had fought, but he said some of it had been on the banks of the Bai Hap River. Some of it, in fact, during the battle on February 29, 1969, when the lieutenant beached his boat and shot the Viet Cong soldier.

Vo Ban Tam said that person was his comrade.

"He was a good soldier," Vo told Kerry, providing facts that fleshed out a fleeting memory held by Kerry and his crew.

Vo explained the soldier had been twenty-four years old—not a teenager but, in fact, just two years younger than Kerry was at the time. He also specialized in firing the B-40 rocket launcher, but his weapon apparently jammed that day.

Vo didn't claim his comrade's death was a war crime. His casual demeanor suggested he accepted his killing as the possibility they all had faced in war.

It took a second for it to seep in.

The truth had been put to lies that had dogged John Kerry since he stood up to oppose the war in which he'd fought.

For someone who'd followed his career, I was witness to the moment fiction was displaced by fact, allegation and innuendo elbowed aside by reality.

I realized the magnitude of this revelation and clicked away with my camera, trying to preserve the scene for posterity.

As Kerry asked questions, Ben Wilkinson—who'd lived in Vietnam as a child—translated, an American uttering the words Vo Ban Tam rattled off in Vietnamese. Wilkinson's lips were a portal to the past, and we all traveled back in time with each word he spoke.

When Kerry asked if he knew the soldier's name, Vo said yes.

"Ba Thanh," he said.

It was the moment the secretary learned the identity of the person he had killed.

Kerry later described the moment as "weird" and "a little surreal," but he was cautious at accepting Vo's story. It subsided with each successive question. He asked his former opponent about Ba Thanh. He asked about their unit's tactics. He asked about the unit's assessment of their opponents.

Despite the crowd surrounding them, it was two men in isolation, speaking soldier to soldier.

Vo Ban Tam said with a bit of bravado that he and his fellow Viet Cong could hear the throaty Swift Boats coming from three thousand feet away, more than enough time to take aim at their thin aluminum hulls.

He said the boats, which chugged more than sped along, often missed their targets with their own heavy-duty guns.

"We were guerrillas," Vo said. "We were never where you were shooting."

Kerry smiled at the comment. It may have been true, but there was at least once when his shot hit its mark.

The secretary chose not to contest the point, saying instead, "I'm glad we're both alive."

After chatting for just over ten minutes, the two shook with both of their hands. Kerry placed one of his commemorative secretary of State Challenge Coins in Vo's palm.

He then turned and walked back to his motorcade for the drive to the airport and the start of his return flight. We gave him some space as our plane flew away from Vietnam for the last time.

The headlines the next day captured the juxtaposition of the moment, with *The Washington Post*'s putting it in sharpest relief.

It read: "Back on the Mekong Delta, John Kerry Meets a Man Who Once Tried to Kill Him and Finds Exoneration."[17]

Veteran State Department correspondent Carol Morello, who'd accompanied us up the river and then listened to Vo Ban Tam, wrote: "Up until that moment, all Kerry knew was that he had shot a Viet Cong soldier. Suddenly, the soldier took shape as a man, with a name and a set of skills that he had used against Kerry and his crew."[18]

Her report was picked up by *The Boston Globe* and printed for Kerry's family, friends, neighbors, and longtime constituents to read back in his hometown.

His last trip to Vietnam as secretary of State had provided the final chapter in a life of public service beginning nearly fifty years earlier, with his first visit to the country as a Navy lieutenant.

John Kerry could go home again, his duty to his country—and himself—now complete.

Countries visited by the author,
1962–2012

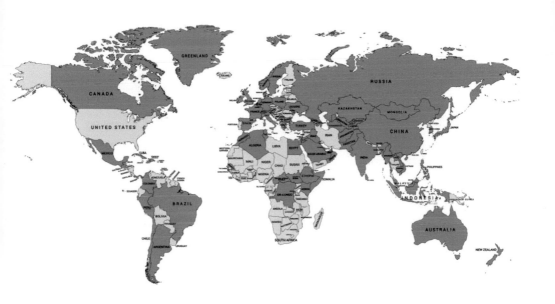

Countries visited by the author,
2013–2017

1

HER NAME WAS
ANNE SMEDINGHOFF

JOHN KERRY HAD BEEN shot at in a war, had been vilified during a bitter campaign for president, and for nearly thirty years, had endured the indignities accompanying the privileges of politics.

None of that could ease the gut-wrenching moment he now faced.

"I need the room, please, folks," he told his staff—one member sobbing—shortly after arriving at Andrews Air Force Base on April 6, 2013.[19]

The secretary of State and his traveling party were about to set off on their third trip together. It was an eleven-day, 23,000-mile, around-the-world journey that would take them to Turkey, Israel, the United Kingdom, the Republic of Korea, China, and Japan. They'd then make a refueling stop in Alaska before their final leg back to Washington, DC.

But first, Kerry sought the privacy of a conference room in the Distinguished Visitors Lounge for what he later said was "no more painful conversation in the world."[20]

Hours earlier and on the opposite side of the globe, a suicide bomber had steered a car filled with explosives toward a group of American servicemen and diplomats in Afghanistan's southern Zabul province. The group was in Qalat to drop off books at a local school.

The vehicle-borne IED killed three American soldiers, an Afghan interpreter, and a twenty-five-year-old State Department Foreign Service officer named Anne Smedinghoff.

Another FSO named Kelly Hunt was seriously wounded, along with an Afghan who worked for the US embassy in Kabul, Abbas Kamwand.

Now Kerry had to make a call to the Chicago suburb of River Forest, Illinois. It was his duty to tell Tom and Mary Beth Smedinghoff their daughter, the second of their four children, had died serving her country.

Smedinghoff was the first diplomat killed in the line of duty since US ambassador to Libya Christopher Stevens. He and three others died on September 11, 2012, during an attack on a US diplomatic outpost in Benghazi, Libya.

As the secretary sat alone in the conference room, speaking over the telephone to the Smedinghoffs, the veteran Foreign Service officer who'd been crying—despite not knowing Anne Smedinghoff personally—explained why her eyes were red and tears trickled down her cheeks.

"It could have been any one of us," she said.[21]

In this instance, the claim wasn't melodramatic: less than two weeks earlier, Kerry had visited Kabul for meetings with Afghan president Hamid Karzai, US ambassador James Cunningham, and Marine Corps General Joseph F. Dunford Jr., who commanded the international military mission in Afghanistan.

A young woman had been chosen by embassy officials to escort Kerry to his meetings, a plum job known as control officer. The honor and responsibility, a sign of an employee on the rise, had been given to a diplomat named Anne Smedinghoff.

With her Ray-Ban Aviators on her nose and trademark scarf around her neck, Smedinghoff was captured in a photograph as she walked behind Kerry after a job fair with female Afghan entrepreneurs. The event would endure as one of the secretary's favorites during his four years in office.

Now, eleven days later, Anne Smedinghoff was dead.

Following his call to her parents and an overnight flight to Turkey, the secretary expressed his feelings during a news conference in Istanbul.

"I want to emphasize that Anne was everything that is right about our Foreign Service. She was smart and capable, committed to our country," Kerry said. "She was someone who worked hard and put her life on the line so that others could live a better life."[22]

The comments underscored the secretary's personal connection to the diplomatic corps. And they enunciated the very real dangers its members confront on behalf of their countrymen and their international partners.

On the day he entered the State Department for the first time as secretary, February 4, 2013, John Kerry climbed a set of steps in the flag-decked main lobby so he could address his new coworkers. He repeated a comment made the month before during his confirmation hearing: "I said that the

Senate is in my blood," he told the packed lobby, "but it is also true that the Foreign Service is in my genes."[23]

He explained that not only had his father, Richard, been a State Department Foreign Service officer, but his sister Peggy had worked most of her professional life at the US Mission to the United Nations.

His wife, Teresa, had done some translating for the UN early in her own career, and Kerry himself had spent twenty-eight years on the Senate Foreign Relations Committee, the last four as its chairman. The committee helps oversee the State Department.

On this first day, though, the secretary found a unique way to underscore this link to his new staff.

He reached into his pocket and pulled out the Diplomatic Passport—Number 2927—he'd received as a child when he accompanied his father to Berlin for his inaugural assignment abroad.

The first stamp was from 1954 and the city of Le Havre, France, where the Kerry family had landed after a six-day sail across the Atlantic Ocean aboard the SS *America*. The secretary said:

> That was a great adventure and I will tell you: 57 years later today, this is another great adventure. . . . Here, we can do the best of things that you can do in government. That's what excites me. We get to try to make our nation safer. We get to try to make peace in the world, a world where there is far too much conflict and far too much killing. There are alternatives. We get to lift people out of poverty. We get to try to cure disease. We get to try to empower people with human rights. We get to speak to those who have no voice. We get to talk about empowering people through our ideals, and through those ideals hopefully they can change their lives.[24]

With almost childlike wonderment, he added: "That's as good as it gets. And I'm proud to be part of it with you. So, now, let's get to work."[25]

The sense of grief and frustration Kerry later felt over Smedinghoff's senseless death returned after each of the string of terrorist attacks from Paris to Bali that blotted his term.

The secretary said repeatedly that members of ISIS and other terrorist groups offered no positive vision for the world, only the specter of death for those who disagreed with them.

The tragedy of Smedinghoff's being killed, as she distributed a means of enlightenment, only underscored the gulf between advancement and retrenchment.

Kerry labeled it "a stark contrast for all of the world to see between two very different sets of values."[26]

––––––––––

UNLESS THEY'VE LOST A passport abroad, most Americans have little appreciation for the reach and scope of the US Department of State, or the perils faced by its employees.

It's the most forward-deployed and far-flung element of the US government. And although its workers get some protection from the United States and foreign governments, they don't carry weapons like soldiers and Marines and must rely on their personal demeanor in many situations.

It was the first federal agency formed, when President George Washington signed legislation to create the Department of Foreign Affairs on July 27, 1789. Two months later, another bill changed its name to the Department of State.

Around the same time, President Washington appointed a fellow Founding Father—Thomas Jefferson—to be the first secretary of State. Jefferson had been serving in Paris as minister to France, helping establish his new nation's initial relationships abroad.

For its first decade, the State Department was headquartered in Philadelphia, then the capital of the country. In 1800, the State Department and the capital itself moved to Washington, thanks partly to a backroom deal cut between Secretary Jefferson and Alexander Hamilton. It gained wide attention in 2015 through the Broadway musical *Hamilton* and its song, "The Room Where It Happens."

Behind closed doors, Hamilton got Jefferson and another Founder, James Madison, to support legislation under which southern states would help northern ones pay off their debts. In return, Hamilton pledged to support moving the capital south.

The State Department eventually moved to its current location, 2201 C Street, N.W., west of the White House and north of the Lincoln Memorial, when it took occupancy of an art deco structure intended for the War Department. "Foggy Bottom," a shorthand reference derived from the name of the surrounding neighborhood, became the country's diplomatic headquarters.

In 1960, an addition expanded the original building to 1.4 million square feet. The building, also referred to as "Main State," was formally renamed in September 2000 as the Harry S Truman Building in honor of the thirty-third president, who enacted the Marshall Plan.

Today, HST houses more than eight thousand workers—a fraction of the nearly seventy thousand State Department employees worldwide.

Some of the rest work in nearby buildings in Washington and Virginia or offices in major cities across the United States. But the vast number serve overseas, spread across 285 embassies, consulates, or other installations in almost every place on the globe.

Everywhere they're located is a little bit of the United States, endowed with diplomatic privileges, demarcated by the Stars and Stripes overhead, and representing a piece of home for Americans abroad—sometimes down to the hometown beers in the fridge or the US-style electrical outlets in the wall.

In fact, all the components for the current US embassy in Beijing—its walls, windows, roof, and furnishings—were shipped to China in diplomatically protected cargo containers. They were then assembled onsite by American contractors.

The reason? To inhibit the Chinese from installing eavesdropping devices.

An embassy is typically placed in a nation's capital, such as the one in Ankara, Turkey. A consulate is usually placed in another major city, like the one in the tourist hot spot of Istanbul.

The embassy in Paris, on the edge of the Place de la Concorde, is where the US ambassador to France works. It offers him or her easy access to the nearby Élysée Palace, where the French president lives and works, and the Quai d'Orsay, a building across the Seine River housing the office of the French foreign minister.

Yet with so many Americans visiting France, especially in the summer, there also are six consulates in the country: Bordeaux, Lyon, Marseille, Rennes, Strasbourg, and Toulouse.

In other less-traveled parts of the world, there may be just one diplomatic outpost for an entire country. The US embassy in Dhaka, Bangladesh, is an example.

While embassies are the seat of local diplomatic relations for the United States abroad, they also are home to workers from other agencies within the United States government. Some have offices for Commerce and Treasury Department employees, as well as FBI agents who work with local law enforcement officials.

Host-nation governments may monitor the comings and goings at the gate, believing the United States also places personnel from intelligence agencies in embassies, under the cover of diplomats.

Embassies represent a huge investment and asset for the United States government because they're sovereign territory in countries around the world. When you step into one, you're governed not by local law but US rules and regulations. A host nation can't step foot inside uninvited, and it has the obligation to protect the facility—as it would expect the US government to do with its own embassy in Washington or its consulates around the United States.

The workers within an embassy must attend their share of social functions, mixing with the host-nation government officials and leaders of local industry at cocktail parties as part of their jobs; but they also have more routine work to do for their country.

Consular Affairs officials interview locals and issue visas to those seeking to come to the United States. They also can resolve that moment of panic that strikes Americans abroad who lose their passport. After an interview, they can reissue one on the spot.

Economic officers work to promote US business abroad and to ease access to US markets for foreign enterprises seeking to do business back in the United States.

All employees, no matter their specialty, have a responsibility to take what they've learned abroad and send their findings back to their colleagues at Main State. Their information is shared not only within the State Department but also across the US government.

These reports come back to Washington in the form of emails or "cables," formal dispatches whose name stems from the electronic wires that used to transmit teletype messages back home. They're usually relayed to various agencies or Congress after being repackaged to answer specific questions.

In this sense, embassies and consulates are not only forward-deployed physical assets of the United States but also forward-deployed listening posts.

Some of that listening generates intelligence in the cloak-and-dagger sense, but much of it also provides more generic insight to the executive and legislative branches of government. It may be about who in a certain country is on the rise politically, what business may be wanting to work within or seek investment from the United States, or which nations need a little TLC from the president or others in an administration.

During Secretary Kerry's time at the State Department, a young French-man named Emmanuel Macron rose from deputy to the French president to economic minister to the leader of an opposition party. He became president of France himself little more than three months after Kerry left office.

His ascent was dutifully reported in cables sent from Embassy Paris and handled back in Washington by a staff whose department has an organization all its own.

———————

OF THE SEVENTY THOUSAND State Department employees overall, the vast majority of them aren't Americans. Some forty-five thousand are locally employed staff (LES), foreign nationals like those South Vietnamese in Saigon who temper their allegiance to their home country so they can work on behalf of the United States government.

Some might serve as interpreters. Others may manage the motor pool or handle clerical work. Still other LESs use their contacts to brief US officials on local customs or expedite them through the nearby airport.

And some are like Mustafa Akarsu.

He was a Turk and Muslim manning an outer checkpoint at the US embassy in Ankara on February 1, 2013. That was when a man wearing a trench coat attempted to enter but instead detonated a suicide bomb beneath his garment when Akarsu wouldn't let him inside.

The death resonated especially with John Kerry, since it occurred the day he was sworn in as secretary of State. Three days later, after beginning his first day in the office with his speech in the Truman Building's main lobby, Kerry traveled across the Potomac River to the headquarters of the Diplomatic Security Service.

Agents there replayed surveillance video of the attacker's approach and the ensuing explosion.

The bomber looked like an average person dressed in a hat who had come to the embassy for help—until he was rebuffed.

The video stream of the encounter instantly turned into a random smattering of pixels.

"Americans who serve overseas are blessed to never serve alone," Kerry said on March 1, 2013, while addressing Akarsu's family and US staff members in Turkey.[27]

The secretary had stopped by to dedicate a fountain on the embassy grounds in memory of the slain guard.

"Local employees around the world commit themselves to building strong and lasting relationships between their home countries and the United States, and they often serve for decades with loyalty and with devotion," Kerry said. "You are the sturdy backbone that holds together the kind of mission that we are engaged in, and we are enormously grateful to you for that."[28]

Whenever the secretary addressed the staff at an embassy, he usually asked the local staffers to raise their hands. Then he asked for a round of applause from their American guests.

He was equally proud of everyone at an embassy, and he often gave them all a promotion of sorts during what was called a meet-and-greet.

"Every single one of you, whether you're doing an interview in a consulate and you get tired doing it because you got too many people to process every day—you're the face of America," he said at Embassy Moscow in May 2013. "In many cases, you may be the only government official people ever meet. You'll be the impression, and you'll be the ambassador of our country."[29]

The next largest group of employees within the State Department is what most people would classically think of as diplomats: the 13,000-member Foreign Service.

These are college-educated men and women who fill out a detailed application and then submit to grueling written tests and oral interviews for a spot in an "A-100" class for beginner diplomats.

In the past, the saying was that the typical Foreign Service officer was "male, pale, and Yale." That recalled the early days of the State Department, when the staff was either in the Diplomatic Service, providing support to ambassadors, or the Consular Service, helping promote US trade abroad.

The complexion of the ranks began to change early in the twentieth century, when Lucile Atcherson passed an exam with the third-highest score in her group. On December 5, 1922, she was appointed as a secretary in the Diplomatic Service.

Today, women account for about 40 percent of the Foreign Service. Nonetheless, they hold only about one-third of what are deemed Chief of Mission posts, the rank of either ambassador or consul general.[30]

The Foreign Service also continues to struggle with diversity, with African Americans comprising 9 percent of its specialists, Hispanics 7 percent, and Asians just over 6 percent.[31]

Congress and the Department have developed programs to recruit minorities in exchange for guaranteeing them slots in the Foreign Service, and Secretary Kerry repeatedly emphasized the need to diversify the ranks.

He was especially proud that for much of his term, one of the Department's two deputy secretaries was a woman (Heather Higginbottom), as were four of the six undersecretaries (Wendy Sherman, Cathy Novelli, Sarah Sewell, and Rose Gottemoeller). The same was true for five of the six regional assistant secretaries (Linda Thomas-Greenfield, Victoria Nuland, Anne Patterson, Nisha Biswal, and Roberta Jacobson).

"In order to represent the United States to the world, the Department of State must have a workforce that reflects the rich composition of its citizenry," the secretary said in a statement issued during his tenure. "The skills, knowledge, perspectives, ideas, and experiences of all of its employees contribute to the vitality and success of the global mission."[32]

While concerns about diversity within the Foreign Service linger, Kerry came to office after a series of minorities and women served as secretary of State—akin to the titular FSO.

On January 23, 1997, Madeleine Albright became "Madame Secretary," after President Bill Clinton appointed her to be the first woman to hold the job.

She was succeeded in January 2001 by former Army General Colin Powell, whom President George W. Bush named as the first African American secretary. Secretary Powell himself was succeeded in January 2005 by Condoleezza Rice, an African American woman who'd previously served as President Bush's national security adviser.

Secretary Rice, in turn, was succeeded in January 2009 by Hillary Clinton, a former first lady and US senator from New York who accepted the post after losing the 2008 Democratic presidential nomination to Barack Obama.

All that prompted Kerry to jokingly ask during his Harry Truman arrival ceremony: "Can a man actually run the State Department?"[33]

He added, to laughter, "As the saying goes, I have big heels to fill."[34]

The final segment of the State Department staff is the Civil Service. At 11,000 strong, its men and women are the permanent bureaucracy keeping the agency running, regardless of who—or which political party—is in charge.

They are part of the 2 million-person civilian workforce within the federal government that makes it the largest single employer in the country.

They're largely hired through a competitive process, and oftentimes they handle the backroom functions necessary to keep any enterprise operating, from payroll and accounting to human resources.

The nature of the State Department bureaucracy underscores the challenge confronting any secretary when he or she assumes office.

When a new president is sworn in on Inauguration Day, they walk into an empty White House and get to fill the East and West wings with political loyalists. In cabinet agencies such as the State Department, there's a large workforce that's already there and will stay well beyond its new leadership.

In Kerry's case, he was the first member of the Obama administration's second-term State Department leadership team to be sworn in. He was administered the oath of office on February 1, 2013, during a private ceremony in the ornate Senate Foreign Relations Committee Room in the US Capitol.

Two days later, on February 3, 2013, seven staffers—Chief of Staff David Wade, Deputy Chief of Staff Bill Danvers, Scheduler Julie Wirkkala, Speechwriter Stephen Krupin, Senior Aides Matt Summers and Jason Meininger, and I, the deputy assistant secretary for strategic communications—took the same oath as their boss.

The following morning, this Kerry team began working atop a Department organization ten thousand times larger than it.

Turning that massive enterprise the way a new secretary wanted was akin to making the proverbial course correction aboard an aircraft carrier.

––––––––––

ANYONE TALKING ABOUT THE State Department is loath to forget the US Agency for International Development.

While it's an independent agency, it coordinates closely with State, receives its overall foreign policy guidance from the secretary, and is led by an administrator with the rank equivalent of a deputy secretary of state.

Since the George W. Bush administration, the administrator has served concurrently as the director of foreign assistance, ensuring US foreign aid is used effectively to meet the country's foreign policy goals.[35]

Another class of employees mistakenly considered distinct from the rest of the State Department is the Diplomatic Security Service (DS). It's the leading US law enforcement organization abroad and is responsible for protecting the country's diplomats and diplomatic missions. It also protects foreign dignitaries visiting the United States.

Each September, virtually its entire 2,000-agent workforce is brought to New York City to provide bodyguard service to foreign ministers and other dignitaries attending the United Nations General Assembly week.

The US Secret Service is responsible for protecting the heads of state; DS has pretty much everyone else.

Agents on protective duty, such as those who guard the secretary around the clock both home and abroad, are often confused for and labeled "Secret Service" because of the radio earpieces and sunglasses both types of agents wear.

Many DS agents, though, will tell you their jobs are more professionally satisfying.

First, they're not just State Department employees but members of the Foreign Service. They qualify for the same language, educational, and other professional development received by other Foreign Service members.

They also say their work is far more diverse than that of Secret Service agents.

While both do investigations—financial fraud for the Secret Service, visa fraud for DS—the relative smallness of the Diplomatic Security Service means its people do more, and far earlier in their careers. There are, quite simply, fewer staffers to go around.

Some agents work on physical security. DS, in fact, is credited with developing things like the drop-down driveway barriers and protective sidewalk bollards now ringing government and military installations worldwide.

Other agents counteract eavesdropping, while still others rotate through the SWAT-style Mobile Security Detachment teams. They're deployed to high-threat areas to protect dignitaries or help evacuate diplomats.

And after a short training period, even the most junior DS agents organize individual stops on the secretary's travel itinerary. They're responsible for negotiating with host nations, and they serve as the point of contact between the US government and local law enforcement agencies.

In Secretary Kerry's case, agents in Amsterdam once had to jump on a train to Paris, arrange a motorcade, and secure an entire hotel after he decided during a flight home from Saudi Arabia that he needed to divert to France.

Agents who skied or rode bikes also found themselves tapped for special duty protecting their sports-loving boss as he relaxed on nights, weekends, or on vacations.

DS is a law enforcement Swiss Army knife.

*S*o how does a former reporter become an official photographer? And for
the secretary of State, no less?

Necessity.

As deputy assistant secretary for strategic communications, I had to
approve all images of Secretary Kerry. I quickly found the photographs
submitted to my office varied too widely in quality—best when coming
from a major embassy, less so if a post was too small to have someone
handy with a camera.

We couldn't live with the inconsistency because these pictures were
intended to be the backbone of the Department's website and social media
feeds.

I've had a lifelong interest in photography, starting by taking photos
of a Little League team that I developed in a friend's darkroom. When my
younger son wrestled in high school, I took pictures of him and his teammates during hundreds of matches.

I also took personal pictures with a pocket-sized Canon ELPH during
the five presidential campaigns I covered; and I shot behind-the-scenes
photos with my cellphone at both The Boston Globe and the early days at
the State Department.

One of those photos went viral within The Building: that February
2013 shot of John Kerry using his own cellphone to take a picture of Brandenburg Gate, the scene of his infamous childhood bike ride.

I decided to ask the State Department Public Affairs Office if there was
any extra equipment lying around. It turns out there was: a professional
Nikon D3 camera that was dirty and in need of a lot of TLC.

I cleaned it up and later sent it to Nikon for a factory refurbish-
ment. Ultimately, I prevailed on the State Department to upgrade to a
pair of top-of-the-line Nikon D4s cameras. I paired them with the Holy
Trinity of lenses: a 14–24mm wide angle, a 24–70mm zoom, and a
70–200mm zoom.

From there, I taught myself how to operate the cameras and a flash I
also got, and to edit my photos with Adobe Lightroom. Using my reporter's training, I sent them back to the State Department from a MacBook

Pro using a Wi-Fi card. The good folks at the Office of Digital Engagement were on call 24/7 to post them real-time.

The work ended up dovetailing with my regular Department duties. At home and wearing my strategic communications hat, I'd help plan our trips and our overall media engagement. On the road, I was able to focus on this different job.

In the end, I took well over 100,000 pictures. I also accompanied Kerry everywhere he went, from the office of Pope Francis to center ice for a puck drop at Madison Square Garden, from the Kremlin and No. 10 Downing Street to a helicopter flying over Antarctica.

I also snapped him in his barren office before his farewell remarks.

My goal was to leave him—and history—with the best and most complete photo archive of any secretary of State.

Secretary Kerry studies Leonardo's Last Supper
in Milan, Italy, on October 17, 2015.

(Top) A return to Brandenburg Gate.
(Bottom) Perfect frame at UN Mission, New York City.

(Top) A good luck sign at Andrews Air Force Base. (Bottom) Sunset over St. Peter's Basilica in Rome.

———

THE BULK OF THE State Department is organized into regional and specialty offices labeled with acronyms underpinning "State-Speak."

"S" is the singular letter meant to designate the secretary of State. Staffers would often refer to him by that title alone, and his helpers as "S Staff."

"D" is for the deputy secretary, and like characters in a James Bond movie, other officials had singular labels, such as "P" for the powerful undersecretary for political affairs, or "M" for the all-knowing undersecretary for management.

No, there wasn't a "Q."

The most prominent acronyms apply to various diplomatic regions—the geographical divisions for how the bulk of the State Department is organized.

"EUR" stands for European and Eurasian Affairs and is the grande dame of them all. It covers a sweeping area of old Europe, from our first ally of France through Russia and down to the Asian steppingstone of Turkey.

"EAP" stands for East Asian and Pacific Affairs. It deals with China, Japan, and Korea, and includes the region extending through the South Pacific to Australia and New Zealand.

"NEA" is for Near Eastern Affairs and covers Egypt, home to the largest Arab population in the world, as well as Israel, Jordan, and Persian Gulf states such as Saudi Arabia.

"AF" is short for African Affairs, covering the continent of Africa and the chaotic governance of many of its countries.

"SCA" stands for South and Central Asian Affairs. It covers, most prominently, India and the surrounding area.

"WHA" is Western Hemisphere Affairs. It covers the territory north to south from Canada through Central America and South America.

The geographical divisions are not pure, since many secretaries of State have created special envoy positions for unique situations.

For example, Nisha Biswal, the SCA assistant secretary for Secretary Kerry, did not deal with matters in Afghanistan and Pakistan—two huge countries in her stomping grounds of South Central Asia. Instead, those two were handled by "SRAP," the special representative for Afghanistan and Pakistan. That was because of unique issues related to post-9/11 antiterrorist efforts.

NEA also didn't have oversight of the Middle East peace process. Instead, it fell to "SEIPN," the special envoy for Israeli–Palestinian negotiations.

That was because of the complexity of negotiations between the Israelis and Palestinians, as well as the time and attention required for talks between the two parties.

In the sort of caste system pervading State, EUR is considered the primo assignment for both young and old Department staffers.

Foreign Service officers feel lucky if they can spend their first tours issuing visas in the Consular Affairs office at Embassy London or Paris. Senior officers often use their bidding clout to win coveted spots in Old World capitals as they finish their careers.

AF and WHA, meanwhile, often beg for attention. It's a product of their perceived lack of impact on global affairs or, in the case of WHA, familiarity bred by proximity to such major trading partners as Canada and Mexico.

EAP received a boost in attention under the Obama administration, thanks to the administration's so-called Pivot to Asia.

The diplomatic and economic shift acknowledged the continued importance of Europe in world affairs, but it also recognized China had the world's No. 2 economy; and Asian countries like Vietnam, the Philippines, and Indonesia were emerging as economic powerhouses of their own.

They also were allies in need of help against Chinese encroachment.

Foreign Service officers bid for their assignments, with the likelihood of them getting their pick increasing with each year of service and through the network they build during that time.

First-tour officers often end up in less desirable posts, a dues-paying exercise. Better posts come with more time in the Service. The typical tour in either spot lasts three years, after which the officers rotate to a new post. Sometimes it's in their same region, but oftentimes it's not—a structural way of preventing an officer from becoming too comfortable with their host country or a particular region in the world.

That often means they spend time between assignments back in the United States, learning a new language as a full-time student at the Foreign Service Institute. That's the continuing education campus for diplomats, military officers, and other government officials in Arlington, Virginia.

Someone learning Mandarin could be there for as many as eighteen months before being sent to an onward assignment in China.

After either six years abroad or back in the United States, FSOs are expected to come home or head overseas. Most try to serve overseas assignments while their children are young or after they've left home for college. A six-year stint in the United States is often saved for the high school years, when parents want to keep adolescents in just one school or near their grandparents.

Officers can accelerate the process, or their prospects for landing a plum future post, by serving special Unaccompanied tours. These are typically one-year stints in dangerous places such as Kabul or Baghdad.

Each is considered a hardship post because officers can't be accompanied by their family members while serving in those locations. The separation is eased with three months of vacation over the course of the yearlong assignment.

The State Department also covers all the officers' housing and meal expenses while they're hunkered down within walled compounds, such as those in Kabul's Diplomatic Quarter or Baghdad's Green Zone.

———

FOR ALL THE RISKS and hardships faced by Foreign Service officers, there are plenty of rewards that make the State Department consistently ranked as one of the top places to work within the United States government.

For example, officers get free language training. For students attending the Foreign Service Institute, it's a full-time job, meaning their only demand from 9 a.m. to 5 p.m. is to study a foreign language.

Officers living abroad also get free housing and free education for their children, as well as free or cheap domestic help. FSOs are known to flip through binders of various US-owned homes around the world, looking at pictures to choose their future accommodations.

The fact that the government covers most normal expenses allows officers to rent out their homes back in the States, and to bank what they'd normally spend on rent or mortgage payments while they live abroad in free housing. And their children often attend highly rated international schools akin to private academies.

The inducements are so rich, Foreign Service officers usually do better financially living abroad than at home.

The State Department eases their transition in either direction by covering their moving expenses. It also gives them vacation allowances, letting them pack and unpack on either end without having to go to work.

The three-year tours, the constant requirement to move up or out of the hierarchy, and the need to court future bosses create a unique culture within the State Department.

You can barely walk down a hall in Main State without hearing a worker rattling off their entire acronym-filled résumé to a colleague. Acquaintances are often introduced by their geographical pedigree: "Glen, this is Mike. We started together in EUR before he went to WHA, and I went to EAP. Now we work together in SRAP."

In addition, the relatively short duration of assignments, and the need to find a next posting, can inhibit worker productivity.

People end up worrying more about their careers than their jobs.

The first year in a three-year assignment is typically devoted to learning the job. The second is spent actually doing it. The third year is focused on looking for the next assignment and readying to move to it.

Members of Kerry's senior staff felt this acutely when it came to dealing with members of the Line. This is a highly selective team that travels in advance of the secretary and sets up his hotels, motorcades, and official meetings.

No sooner had a Line member learned how to arrange a room, organize a news conference, or place flags than they were heading off to their next assignment. That meant spending time each year training a new group of Line officers—and sometimes correcting the same mistakes before the new members learned the old lessons.

It also meant that when the secretary's staff found a particularly adept Line officer, we tried to find a way to ensure they were sent on the most demanding advance trips. We also explored ways to extend their service.

We didn't want to keep reinventing the wheel.

State Department culture is also infused with vertical envy.

The secretary and his team work at the top of The Building. Accordingly, employees seek to work in or gain favor with those stationed on "the 7th Floor."

A top official at the Foreign Service Institute once told a meeting of Kerry-era employees they had to understand the perception of the State Department bureaucracy they were commanding.

"They are scared of you," she said of her colleagues.[36]

She went on the explain that employees in this "caste system" would embrace members of Team Kerry to the degree they were perceived as close to the 7th Floor, or "how close you rotate to the sun," in another analogy she used.

While she defended her explanation by saying, "You need to understand the culture people are working in," it left some newcomers shaking their heads at the fickleness of the relationship.[37]

Another senior State Department official once chuckled as he offered his own description of his colleagues in the Foreign Service. He made the comment as we discussed our annual senior staff retreat and the Chiefs of Mission Conference, when all ambassadors and chiefs of mission are brought back to the State Department to ensure everyone's diplomacy is in sync.

"We're like border collies," the official told me. "Incredibly smart and take direction well, but if we're left to our own devices, we end up digging in the garden or knocking over the flower pots."[38]

Spring is a particularly angst-ridden time in the Department, because it's when annual evaluations—employee evaluation reports, or EERs—are filled out. These performance reviews are the basis for promotions and upward assignments, so they command an inordinate amount of attention.

Workers actually fill out their own reviews, prompting many to exude a healthy respect for their work. In one employee-focused newsletter, *The Daily Demarche*, the writer joked that some reports contain phrases like "When Dick is not walking on water, he is busy turning it into wine."[39]

Supervisors must review and comment on the EERs, knowing what they say can make or break an employee.

After employees bid on their next assignment, potential bosses review their résumés and EERs and make final decisions about whether to bring them onto their team.

One veteran Foreign Service officer who worked with the S staff described the death knell for any applicant: when a potential boss emails a colleague who'd previously been the applicant's supervisor and asks for their opinion of him or her.

If the colleague writes back, "Can I give you a call?" the conversation is largely unnecessary. The potential boss knows their colleague doesn't want to put their criticism in a written document like an email.

On the flip side, there's State-Speak for those destined to get the assignments they want.

First, they get a "kiss," meaning an informal acknowledgment they're likely to get the job. That's followed by a "handshake," the term meaning the job is theirs but for the formal paperwork. Officers are frequently seen hugging their friends after they've gotten their kiss or handshake.

Most officers are deserving of what they get.

Despite the perks, the job requires long hours of work, often far away from their hometown friends and family. An FSO's kids can be uprooted like Army brats, and their family forced to flee on a moment's notice if a host nation's security situation deteriorates.

They're targets for foreign intelligence agents and harassment by unfriendly host governments. A car being driven by a Defense Department attaché, who works in an embassy, was buzzed by a Russian Hind helicopter that flew just feet over its hood as he and his State Department colleagues drove between Murmansk and Pechenga, Russia, in July 2016.[40]

Many FSOs work their way up the ladder, steadily building expertise over the years in a given geographical or subject-matter area. They're the go-to contacts for a president, secretary, or member of Congress seeking a quick answer. And they can be founts of wisdom for families in need.

Once during John Kerry's term, two young women from Massachusetts were killed in a horrific traffic accident during a flight layover in the United Arab Emirates. Their car split in two after it hit a light pole while they rode with two men they'd met on their plane from the United States.

The local police called the US embassy to report their deaths, and an FSO sat in the morgue with their bodies until their families arrived days later. The US ambassador to the UAE wept as she spoke to me about the violent nature of the accident and the dedication of her staff members.

Another time, I saw a longtime Civil Service employee carefully placing china creamer pots in a microwave oven for a few seconds before a bilateral meeting in the Secretary's Conference Room on the 7th Floor.

When I asked him why, Ken Matthews, who once played college basketball at North Carolina State for famed coach Jim Valvano, explained he didn't want the guests' milk to curdle when they poured it in their coffee.

The career goal for Foreign Service officers, the Top Guns of the State Department, is to land a chief of mission assignment as either an ambassador or a consul general.

An ambassador runs an embassy and is the chief US contact for a host government and its leader. A consul general runs a consulate and is similarly atop the food chain, although just for a geographic region in a country.

Ambassadors live in a "CMR," or Chief of Mission Residence. Their top FSO assistant, the deputy chief of mission, lives in a DCM residence.

Both places are the unspoken gems of Foreign Service life.

The Chief of Mission Residence in Paris is a gilded structure just doors from the Élysée Palace, where the president of France lives. The one in Rome is called Villa Taverna and has exquisite gardens and a vast wine cellar. The CMR in London, called Winfield House, borders Regents Park and has the second-largest yard in the English capital.

The first is across town—the backyard at Buckingham Palace.

The beauty of these homes, many bought decades ago at pennies on the dollar, is why a president often awards such ambassadorships to key political supporters. It's payback for helping them raise money for their campaign or supporting them when others felt they were political long shots.

Not all great CMRs go to presidential patrons, though. The one in the Cubanacan neighborhood of Havana largely fell off the radar while the United States had no diplomatic relations with Cuba.

That meant the chief of mission job went to a Foreign Service officer subsequently entitled to live in a two-story mansion covered in coral limestone, decked with marble floors, and accented with a pool and tennis court on grounds stretching for five acres. Local lore is it was intended to be a winter White House for President Franklin Delano Roosevelt.

Some Foreign Service officers winced when President Obama normalized relations with Cuba and then stayed at the CMR while he and his family visited the island in March 2016.

They were happy with the policy, but guessed future presidents would realize the quality of the posting and its home—more than half the size of the White House—and reserve the ambassadorship in the future for a donor rather than a career diplomat.[41]

SECRETARY KERRY'S CONNECTION TO the Foreign Service and the lingering emotions following the Benghazi attack prompted him to pay close attention to diplomatic security throughout his tenure.

He vowed to do all he could to avoid a repeat of that tragedy, and started nearly every day's 8:30 a.m. senior staff meeting by asking his undersecretary for management, Patrick Kennedy, about the safety and security of US missions and diplomats serving abroad.

Kennedy himself had a special sensitivity to the questions, having overseen embassy security as M for Secretary Clinton.

Kennedy was revered within the State Department for his mastery of the budget process and seeming ability to get anything done, but he became a Republican bogeyman following the Benghazi attack.

He was accused of ignoring requests for additional security resources from Ambassador Chris Stevens before the attack, and then protecting Clinton during congressional investigations that followed. He also was a focal point for investigations into her use of a private email server while at the State Department.

Despite his emphasis on employee and outpost safety, Kerry regularly conceded he couldn't eliminate all risks. That was especially true when diplomats stepped "outside the wire" and worked directly with locals living beyond embassy and consulate gates.

Famed World War II journalist Edward R. Murrow, who later went on to head the US Information Agency, once underscored the necessity of such expeditionary work.

"The real crucial link in the international exchange," he said, "is the last three feet, which is bridged by personal contact, one person talking to another."[42]

Anne Smedinghoff's first steps toward those final three feet began with her choice of Johns Hopkins University in Baltimore as a college and international relations as her major.

As she neared her senior year, a friend encouraged her to take the Foreign Service exam. She did and saw the application process through, including a day of tough interviews in May 2009. Her friend opted instead to head to the Peace Corps, a common feeder for the State Department.

Smedinghoff spent the summer after her graduation riding a bike four thousand miles across the country to raise money for charity. In December 2009, she received a letter confirming her acceptance into an A-100 class beginning the following February.

She arrived during a 2010 storm dubbed "Snowmageddon" for the eighteen to thirty-two inches it deposited across the region. The city was paralyzed by one of the top five snowstorms to hit the area since government record keeping.

Smedinghoff graduated from the Foreign Service Institute and, in August 2010, lucked into her first choice for her stint as a Consular Affairs officer in Caracas. She used her Spanish-speaking skill while interviewing Venezuelans seeking visas.

Less than two years later, Smedinghoff put in for an assignment she felt was more vital to US foreign policy interests: a slot as a Public Diplomacy officer at the US embassy in Kabul. By April 2012, she'd been selected. In July 2012, she reported for duty.

"She seemed very comfortable sort of operating in a foreign culture, just getting around day to day and navigating the logistics," Tom Smedinghoff said of his daughter during an interview with the *Chicago Tribune* after her death.[43]

Service in an Unaccompanied posting such as Kabul can be challenging, even for those like Anne Smedinghoff, who didn't have a spouse or children.

FSOs spend virtually all day, every day in a walled compound, their routines subject to change if a siren blasts out a "duck-and-cover" alarm. More senior people live in apartments, while others are housed in so-called hooches: stacks of shipping containers outfitted with a desk, TV, bed, and bathroom.

The closet contains a Kevlar helmet and flak jacket, while illustrations taped to the walls explain the meanings of the different alarms and the most direct routes to safety bunkers.

There is free food, as well as decent gyms, a pool, and a bar ringed with protective sandbags affectionately called The Duck and Cover.

The close quarters force people training for an annual marathon to run repeated circles around the inside of the compound walls. They also create extremely tight bonds between coworkers who spend virtually all waking hours together.

Smedinghoff engendered such endearment from her colleagues, despite being just twenty-five years old and only two years into the Foreign Service.

"Everyone will tell you that Anne Smedinghoff was a rising star in the Foreign Service, and that she was smart, savvy, and strategic. All of that is true. But Anne was also witty, irreverent, and stylish," one friend, Stephenie Foster, told me. "She was virtually never still and strode across the embassy compound with both flair and purpose."[44]

Secretary Kerry's first visit to Kabul followed earlier stops in Israel, where he joined President Obama on an official visit, and Jordan, a friendly Arab nation the secretary viewed as pivotal in a task assigned to him by the president: renewing peace talks between the Israelis and Palestinians.

Amman, the capital of Jordan, also served as the staging area for trips by the secretary to Baghdad, as well as across the snowy peaks of Afghanistan en route to Kabul.

A short helicopter flight later, the secretary landed in an Afghan soccer field used as a heliport for the International Security Assistance Force. He was greeted by General Dunford, a fellow Bostonian who commanded the NATO-led ISAF military force.

The two rode in an armored convoy across the street to the US embassy, where Kerry set up shop in the living quarters of Ambassador Cunningham. A big focus of his meetings was the ongoing number of US troops in Afghanistan, something President Obama had pledged to cut.

Smedinghoff led the way for each of the secretary's movements, as she would the following day through the women's job fair and the helo flight back to Kabul International Airport.

She smiled as she posed for a photo in front of the secretary's plane before he took off on March 27, 2016, for France and the return flight to Washington.

Eleven days later, she was walking with the group in Qalat when she was killed by the suicide driver's bomb.

The news reached Kerry as he motorcaded to Andrews Air Force Base for his next trip, that first around-the-world journey to Turkey and onward through Japan.

"Everything that our country stands for, everything we stand for, is embodied in what Anne Smedinghoff stood for," Kerry later told the staff at the US consulate in Istanbul.[45]

Recognizing the sacrifices they all were making, he added: "It is important for us to be able to help to bring stability and rule of law and alternatives to this kind of nihilistic violence that simply destroys and steals lives without offering any other constructive purpose whatsoever."[46]

Kerry reprised his role as the Department's chief consoler just over a week later when he asked that his plane make a stop at O'Hare International Airport in Chicago while he wrapped up the round-the-world trip beginning with the news of Smedinghoff's death.

When the plane rolled to a stop, the normal group of Air Force security officers stayed onboard, instead of going down to the tarmac. The same was true of the Diplomatic Security Service agents, who usually formed a ring around the secretary wherever he went.

Instead, Kerry walked down the steps alone, greeted by a lone airport official. The two went across the tarmac to a small building on the outskirts of the otherwise busy airport.

The secretary was already filled with sadness and disbelief, but as his plane crossed Canada, I knocked on the door of his cabin and told him to turn the TV to CNN. When he did, he saw the news of the twin bombings back home at the Boston Marathon.

Now the secretary was walking into a building in Illinois where Tom and Mary Beth Smedinghoff were waiting with their surviving children.

The secretary wanted to see them to personally offer his condolences on their loss.

After nearly an hour with the family, he called for me to join the group inside the building. The Smedinghoffs had accepted his offer to take a group picture, which he asked me to snap with a family camera.

When I entered the room, I felt like an intruder. All I could say was "Sorry."

After his goodbyes, Kerry walked back to his plane, climbed the steps under a dark gray sky, and took off for his flight home.

He'd later tell us staffers the Smedinghoffs were "just a regular, good ol' hard-core American family with solid values."[47]

I was reminded of our visit more than a year later, as I walked down a hall inside the Harry S Truman Building.

There, coming in the opposite direction, was a woman with wavy black hair, dark eyebrows, and a face I remembered from that moment in Chicago.

The woman was Regina Smedinghoff, Anne's younger sister. She'd followed in her sibling's footsteps and now worked at the State Department.

Her focus? Advancing women's issues around the globe.

It was the same goal of that job fair in Kabul the secretary so loved, held the day he and we on his team said goodbye to Anne Smedinghoff, flew out of Afghanistan, and left our control officer behind to resume her normal duties at the embassy—and across those crucial last three feet.

Anne Smedinghoff

IF YOU WOULD LIKE to perpetuate Anne's work, you can make a donation in her memory to four causes endorsed by her parents, Tom and Mary Beth Smedinghoff:

The Anne Smedinghoff Scholarship
Fenwick High School, 505 Washington Blvd., Oak Park, IL 60302

Coordinated by Fenwick High School, her alma mater, it provides $2,000 in tuition assistance for a rising senior "with an interest in international relations and/or public service."

The Anne Smedinghoff Memorial Fund
krieger.jhu.edu/giving

Coordinated by her college, Johns Hopkins University, it "provides financial support to students wishing to pursue activities in the area of international development or diplomacy."

The Afghan Girls Financial Assistance Fund
www.agfaf.org

Established within the Community Foundation of New Jersey, AGFAF "helps young Afghan women, who are committed to working for gender equality and improving life in Afghanistan, pursue and finance educational opportunities in the United States."

The School of Leadership Afghanistan
www.sola-afghanistan.org

SOLA provides a safe boarding school in Kabul for middle- and high-school women from around Afghanistan as they pursue the national curriculum. The Smedinghoffs added this to their list of favored causes after meeting its founder.

2

WELCOME
TO BLAIR HOUSE

SECRETARY KERRY TOOK ON his fair share of challenges during his four years in office, but he used to tell a joke about one of the vexing aspects of diplomacy.

"What's the difference between a protocol person and a terrorist?" he'd say.

While an audience grasped for the answer, the secretary would smile and explain, "You can occasionally negotiate with a terrorist."

If there's a lifeblood to formal diplomacy, it's protocol: the set of rules and procedures structuring matters of governance and diplomacy. If those rules aren't ironclad, as Kerry suggested, they're certainly rigid—as are the people who enforce them.

And as obnoxious as that may be for people who just want to get something done, it also has its benefits.

That's why protocol is crucial to diplomacy.

Protocol provides the structure for conducting a negotiation. It lets participants avoid land mines preventing a conversation from even starting. And its rigidity gives a ready-made excuse when you have to resolve a problem.

If someone doesn't want to sit next to someone else, the host can explain the seating arrangement is alphabetical or is based on the length of their countries' diplomatic relationship.

Making decisions through objective criteria or a set of traditions avoids accusations of subjectivity or favoritism.

"Protocol is not an end in and of itself. Rather, it is a means by which people of all cultures can relate to each other," says the Foreign Service Institute's "Protocol for the Modern Diplomat." "Protocol is, in effect, the frame for the picture rather than the content of it."[48]

The dictates of protocol are vast. They cover elements of basic manners: how to properly greet someone, when to arrive and depart a party, and how and when to convey your thanks. They also encompass everything from who hosts a meeting to where it's held and who sits at what spot along a table.

The people about to be posted abroad as a US ambassador go to a special finishing school in Virginia where one major focus is protocol.

Because protocol underpins diplomacy, the chief enforcer in the United States—the Office of the Chief of Protocol—is located within the Department of State. And in a nod to its importance, the person who serves as chief of Protocol is given the rank of ambassador.

During most of John Kerry's term as secretary of State, the job was held by Pete Selfridge. He learned the trade as a campaign advance man for both Kerry's 2004 presidential bid and President Obama's 2008 White House campaign. He went on to serve as White House deputy director of advance during Obama's first term.

During the second term, Ambassador Selfridge's hand was often the first a foreign leader shook when he or she stepped off the plane at Andrews Air Force Base. Even before that greeting, his team would have worked with the visitor's staff to settle on accommodations, a schedule, entertainment, and how to address any personal needs, such as food allergies or pillow preferences.

The Protocol Office oversees a dignitary's arrival at the White House and State Department, escorts guests to meetings with the president and secretary of State, seats and feeds those who accompany them, and leads the visitors back to their cars and on to their next event.

In between, the Protocol Office addresses myriad details, including whether and how to exchange gifts, and precisely which one should be given by the US government. The president and secretary of State travel with a trunk filled with spare gifts of all sizes and costs to prevent being caught empty-handed if a host surprises them.

Protocol staffers also serve as bouncers at the door of a meeting room, and select what food should be served to security guards and staff members left waiting in a holding room.

The Office and its impeccably dressed, exceptionally well-mannered staff also accompany the president and vice president on their own foreign trips, ensuring everything goes off without issue.

Selfridge could often be seen backstage, briefing President Obama with a diagram of a room or pointing him down a red carpet and toward his seat.

When an event was under way, he'd stand in a corner, scanning the room and looking for problems or guests in need of something. And when he wasn't at work, Selfridge and his wife, Parita Shah, spent many nights attending functions at embassies on behalf of the US government.

On one level, he was a professional party-thrower and partygoer.

As with the Diplomatic Security Service, the Protocol Office's Super Bowl takes place every September, when diplomats from around the world converge on New York City for the annual United Nations General Assembly meeting.

Selfridge and the staff would handle arrangements not only for all of President Obama's events during his two or three days in the city but also for those involving Vice President Biden and Secretary Kerry.

The secretary used to label the flurry of meetings—sometimes more than sixty-five of his own in just five or six days—as "speed-dating." In that construct, Protocol staffers were the matchmakers.

When one meeting ended, Kerry would step into a waiting room to make a call or speak with his aides. The Protocol team would step in and swap out the flags, name cards, water glasses, and snack trays.

They'd then readmit the press, lead the secretary to his designated greeting spot, and introduce the next guest and his team, one by one.

Once everyone was seated, Protocol would lead the media out and supervise the waitstaff as they poured fresh coffee or other beverages.

Only after the participants were settled would the Protocol staff leave the room and close the doors behind them. They'd enter only if someone needed to pass a note to one of the meeting participants or if the waiters had to refresh the drinks.

When the time allotted expired, a Protocol staffer would softly knock on the doors and open them, indicating it was time to move on to the next meeting.

———

IF THE WHITE HOUSE is the ultimate venue the Protocol staff has at its disposal, Blair House is a close second option.

Located across Pennsylvania Avenue from the White House, Blair House is the president's official guesthouse. It's overseen, though, by the chief of Protocol and the State Department.

"House" is a misnomer, because four adjoining buildings actually make up Blair House: Blair House, Lee House, Peter Parker House, and 704 Jackson

Place. They're connected internally and run from Lee House—immediately to the left of the pale yellow Blair House—around the corner to the east, before ending at 704 Jackson Place.[49] It overlooks Lafayette Park.

All told, Blair House measures 70,000 square feet—bigger than the White House—and has 119 rooms. They include fourteen bedrooms and thirty-five bathrooms. The house even includes a beauty salon that's staffed when a guest is in residence.

President Truman largely lived and worked out of Blair House while the White House was renovated from 1948 to 1952.

The Lincoln Room just off the front door is a tribute to President Abraham Lincoln. It includes a portrait over the fireplace that the sixteenth president sat for just weeks before his assassination.[50] Randy Bumgardner, the Tennessean who long managed Blair House, would say the detail in the Edward Dalton Marchant painting provides a near-photograph of President Lincoln just before his death.

The Treaty Room in the Peter Parker House—named for the physician who originally owned it—has a twenty-two-seat mahogany table.[51]

Incoming presidents move into the house five days before their inauguration, and the families of deceased presidents usually stay there while they are in Washington for funeral or memorial services.

Heads of state are allowed to stay in Blair House during official visits to the United States. If two visitors of equal rank are in Washington at the same time, neither is invited to stay in Blair House to avoid favoring one over the other.

The rule is rooted in—what else?—protocol.

Secretary Kerry used Blair House for several large meetings related to the Middle East peace process, and several one-on-one conversations with visiting leaders.

Unbeknown to many Americans, the stodgy State Department also has its own version of Blair House. Called the Diplomatic Reception Rooms, they're spread across the eighth floor of the Harry S Truman Building. They represent the country's effort to provide an awe-inspiring setting for formal diplomatic events.

The forty-two rooms house portions of a five-thousand-item collection of American paintings and furnishings, and each is designed to evoke a period or place in US history from 1750 to 1825.[52]

The collection is worth an estimated $150 million. It includes antique silver shaped by Paul Revere for John Adams, the original *Spirit of America* painting, and an architectural desk used by Thomas Jefferson.

Perhaps its most famous piece is another desk, the one on which the Treaty of Paris was signed to end the Revolutionary War. Secretary Kerry regularly ended tours of the rooms at the desk, explaining to his foreign guests its importance in US history.

The rooms were privately financed and are privately endowed with the goal of matching the spectacular settings Old World governments offer for diplomatic events. Without the gilding of the Diplomatic Reception Rooms, the Truman Building would be little more than a sterile block of offices.

When people enter the Diplomatic Reception Rooms, they're often stunned. That was the case for us original members of the Kerry staff who, shortly after taking our oath in February 2013, were given a tour of the eighth floor by curator Marcee Craighill.

With a theatrical flair, she spoke of the rooms and their accompanying art collections, spinning around to point out objects of note while raising and lowering her voice to hold her audience.

Like Kerry, Craighill finished at the Treaty of Paris desk. When she revealed its history, it overwhelmed me and reinforced the weight of the responsibility I'd just assumed on behalf of the country.

The biggest of the Diplomatic Reception Rooms is named for Benjamin Franklin, who first lobbied within Europe for an independent United States and then was the new country's first diplomat as ambassador to France.

With its floor-to-ceiling columns, banks of windows, and massive scale, the Ben Franklin Room gives off a stately air. In the center of its ceiling is the Great Seal of the United States, a badge with an eagle holding arrows in one talon and an olive branch in the other. That crest is stamped on certain official US documents to prove their authenticity.[53]

It's displayed so prominently in the room because, like Blair House, it's administered by the secretary of State.

Kerry would regularly point to Franklin's portrait, hanging on the room's eastern wall, as he regaled his audiences with a recap of the Founding Father's colorful life—filled with wine and song.

"He liked to have a really good time, folks," the secretary said in May 2015 as he hosted a reception in the room for members of the Arctic Council. "And he didn't spare the booze, and while he was in Paris he led a life that clearly meant that had he lived today and been nominated, he would never have been confirmed for office."[54]

The BFR is the venue for larger gatherings, such as the biennial Strategic Dialogues that take place between the United States and select governments.

It's also the scene for larger ambassadorial swearings-in. And it's the site of the Department's annual string of Christmas parties for staff, diplomats, and the press corps, as well as its annual Fourth of July party for foreign ambassadors to the United States.

The guests at that party relish the chance to eat all types of American food and then to head outside to a balcony, where they get an unobstructed view of the National Mall during the annual Washington fireworks display.

In addition, the Ben Franklin Room is the place for State Lunches, hosted by the State Department for visiting heads of state. They're typically on the afternoon before the evening the guest of honor attends a State Dinner at the White House.

The room is also the venue for the annual Kennedy Center Honors Dinner.

That gathering is held each December to recognize artists from across the American entertainment spectrum. During Secretary Kerry's tenure, they included guitarist Carlos Santana, actor Tom Hanks, and singers Mavis Staples and James Taylor.[55]

———

FOR JOHN KERRY, ONE of the most important events to occur in the room during his four years was his own swearing-in ceremony.

Although he'd already been officially sworn in behind closed doors at the US Capitol on February 1, 2013, the secretary invited his family and friends for a public celebration in the Ben Franklin Room on February 6, 2013. Vice President Joe Biden ceremonially administered the oath while Teresa Heinz Kerry held the Bible for her husband.

"You know, it's not the first time John has taken an oath," the vice president said. "The first time John took the oath to his country was in 1966, as a young naval officer. On that day in '66, he swore an oath to his nation, an oath that has animated his entire life, from the Mekong Delta to the Foreign Relations Committee to be standing here with all of you in this room today."[56]

As I stood and listened to the vice president, he put into words what I'd instinctively felt when Kerry called me in a newsroom in January 2013 and offered me the career-changing experience of a job on his State Department staff.

John Kerry had enjoyed a life of personal privilege, attending private grade schools and then one of the finest colleges in the world, Yale University. He spent part of summers at his mother's family home on the Brittany Coast in France and others at a family reserve on Naushon Island, near Martha's Vineyard.

His life also had an unmistakable "Forrest Gump" quality to it, inevitably putting him in proximity to momentous events.

He once went sailing off Newport, Rhode Island, with President John F. Kennedy. He was in San Francisco for Navy training during the "Summer of Love" in 1967. His ship returned to Los Angeles the night Robert F. Kennedy was fatally shot after winning the 1968 Democratic primary. A picture that later hung in his office showed him with former Beatle John Lennon at an antiwar rally in Central Park. The president at the time, Richard Nixon, was heard on one of his infamous White House tapes remarking about his charisma and how to undermine him.

When it came down to the choices he made in his professional life, though, John Kerry chose public service.

A year before graduating from Yale in 1966, he decided to join the US Navy and serve in the Vietnam War. After his first stint aboard the USS *Gridley*, a guided-missile cruiser, he sought a more harrowing assignment as the skipper of a Patrol Craft Fast, the so-called Swift Boats.

When Kerry returned, disillusioned by the war, he took a leadership role with the Vietnam Veterans Against the War. He sought to end the fighting in Southeast Asia, in part through his nationally televised testimony in 1971 before the Senate Foreign Relations Committee.

He famously said then, "How do you ask a man to be the last man to die for a mistake?"

After running for Congress and losing, Kerry went to Boston College Law School and worked as a prosecutor in a district attorney's office.

He later ran for lieutenant governor of Massachusetts before taking a shot in 1984 at an open US Senate seat. He was a member of the upper chamber of Congress until he resigned to become secretary of State.

He served some facet of the state or federal government continually from his college graduation to his nominal retirement.

Until he was tapped to be secretary, my most intimate contact with John Kerry had come as I reported on the run-up to his 2004 presidential campaign.

I'd chased him across the country from 2001 to 2003 as he courted donors and built a campaign staff, almost person by person from venture capitalist Mark Gorenberg in San Francisco to political activists John and Jackie Norris in Des Moines, Iowa. During one visit to the Bay Area, he commandeered a rented car and drove me over to Treasure Island to show me where he had trained in 1967 to deploy on the *Gridley*.

I was at Marshall University in Huntington, West Virginia, on March 16, 2004, when Candidate Kerry made one of the biggest blunders of his campaign. He disputed suggestions he didn't support supplemental funding for military operations in Afghanistan and Iraq by telling a crowd, "I actually did vote for the $87 billion before I voted against it."

President Bush and his campaign seized on the remark as evidence of Kerry's tendency to flip-flop on major policy issues. Vice President Dick Cheney and campaign strategist Karl Rove also hammered the theme, while other critics derided the French-speaking Kerry for his interest in foreign affairs and "continental" air.

Then House Majority Leader Tom Delay used to bring down the house at Republican events starting his speeches by saying, "'Hi!,' or as John Kerry might say, 'Bonjour!'"

Then Commerce Secretary Don Evans once derided Kerry by saying, "He looks French."[57]

Secretary Kerry had just attended a lunch at the Hotel Seehof in Davos, Switzerland, when he motioned to me and senior aide Jason Meininger and told us to join him on a walk.

We headed across the street to the St. Theodul Kirche, a small, sandstone-colored sanctuary with a flame-like crimson dome.

We walked through a reception room and then had to duck down—with the six-foot-four secretary of State leading the way—to get through a Hobbit-sized entry into the main part of the church.

When we did, I was overwhelmed by the heavy wooden beams on the ceiling and the simple wood pews running from front to back.

I wasn't surprised we did this little diversion; John Kerry was endlessly curious everywhere we went. But after looking up, down, and around, the secretary told me and Meininger why this place was different.

He recalled being a young boy when his father took him into the solitude of that very church to tell him about the death of an aunt.

She was the first person the younger Kerry knew who had died.

Meininger and I said nothing and simply listened as he unexpectedly replayed this most personal of moments.

After one more silent look around, Kerry headed out. He ducked back under the low doorframe and paused on the other side to write a message in the guest book for this family sanctuary.

Everyone who traveled with him never knew what to expect, no matter where we went.

John Kerry points to the spot where he learned a childhood lesson.

As a reporter, I frequently wrote about Kerry's preference for nuance and his proclivity for arguing both sides of an issue. But I never understood the derision over his interest in the world or his active engagement in foreign policy.

When John Kerry took the lead at the State Department, I knew it was the meeting of man and moment. If ever there was a job for him, secretary of State was it—perhaps even more than president.

Kerry himself would regularly admit as much during our four years together.

He argued that secretary of State is a unique post because it offers the chance to focus on a single subject—foreign affairs—without the usual demands of politicking, chief among them fundraising or reelection campaigns.

In fact, State Department officials are prohibited by the Hatch Act from engaging in many of the usual forms of political activity. Officially named "An Act to Prevent Pernicious Political Activities," it prohibits public campaigning by members of the executive branch.

"It's one of the best jobs in the world," Kerry told CBS News during an interview in September 2016 as he prepared to leave office.[58]

"This is a fascinating job because it's an opportunity to actually have an impact on challenges that make a difference in life and death, that for the long run can make a difference for our kids," he added.[59]

Around the same time, a reporter from Britain's Sky News asked the secretary whether he felt he could have more influence on the world in his current job than he may have had as president of the United States.

That concrete comparison prompted a quick reply.

"No, I think that the president of the United States is obviously the most powerful position in our country, certainly, and one of the most powerful in the world, if not the," the secretary said.[60]

In perhaps the greatest irony of his four years in office, many of the things that had been demerits during his own run for the presidency in 2004 proved to be assets in the job he landed nine years later.

During our first trip abroad, from London to Doha, Qatar, it quickly became clear that Kerry didn't have to be introduced to many world leaders. Most, it turned out, were old acquaintances.

Regardless of the subject at hand, whether it be Russian aggression in Eastern Europe or Chinese expansion in the South China Sea, Kerry had become versed in it as a senator, as the chairman of the Foreign Relations Committee, or as a first-term foreign affairs emissary for President Obama.

That French-speaking ability? A huge plus. French is the official language of diplomacy—all signs at the United Nations are French first, English second—and French is spoken in far more places around the world than France.

Crowds would light up in central Africa and Southeast Asia when the secretary would greet them in their native French. His schoolboy studies in Switzerland and Norway also acquitted him well when he'd offer up phrases in German or Norwegian—even his Mozambique-born wife's native Portuguese—while traveling the world.

You can't overstate how such fluency combats the image of the ugly American abroad.

Kerry's command of French also proved useful, sadly, when he visited Paris and Brussels following their terrorist attacks. In each, he offered condolences—in French—on behalf of President Obama and the American people. It had special resonance with the locals.

Meanwhile, while John Kerry can be excitable, he more often exudes a level-headedness that's extremely valuable for a diplomat.

In April 2016, as we stood in the apartment that Lyndon Baines Johnson had used while visiting his presidential library at the University of Texas at Austin, the secretary said, "One of the things diplomacy requires is patience."[61]

He explained that quality was underscored for him in the 1960s, when the United States was rocked by a succession of assassinations: President Kennedy, Martin Luther King Jr., and Bobby Kennedy. It could have deflated political activists, he said, but it ended up spurring them to greater action.

I'd often think of this as I considered the possibility that Susan Rice might have served as President Obama's second-term secretary of State, instead of John Kerry.

She'd served as US ambassador to the United Nations during the president's first term, but her expected ascent to secretary was thwarted in September 2012. Rice was tapped for a series of television interviews and suggested the deadly attack on the US diplomatic compound in Benghazi was the result of a spontaneous attack, sparked by the violent reaction to an anti-Muslim video released earlier in Cairo.[62]

Subsequent investigation showed the attack—which killed Ambassador Chris Stevens and three others—was planned, and Stevens had previously requested extra security at the compound he was visiting.

Congressional Republicans pilloried Ambassador Rice over her initial explanation, effectively preventing her from being confirmed as secretary of State. That prompted her to remove her name from consideration. President Obama picked her instead to be his second-term national security adviser.

While Secretary Kerry would go on to have weekly meetings with President Obama, Rice became the day-to-day link between the White House and the military and diplomatic establishments.

She wasn't shy about calling out foreign officials or the secretary if they didn't agree with her views.

"You Palestinians," she was once quoted by *The New Republic* as saying to Palestinian Authority chief negotiator Saeb Arakat, "can never see the fucking big picture."[63]

That temper, belying her doctorate from Oxford and background as a management consultant at McKinsey & Company, contrasted with the modulated manner of Kerry, who was twenty years older than Rice.

While John Kerry would later be criticized for being a secretary of State who was too optimistic in his world view and too willing to hear out his adversaries, his military and political backgrounds, prior relationships, and patience left him well suited for the job when he assumed office.

As President Obama said when he announced his nomination as secretary, Kerry was "not going to need a lot of on-the-job training."[64]

And with no disparagement intended toward Susan Rice, Vice President Biden acknowledged as much before he asked him to raise his right hand so he could administer the final oath the onetime Lieutenant Kerry would take in public service: "John, it's now your time," the vice president said during that ceremony in the State Department's prestigious Ben Franklin Room. "And this moment, as I said, in the history of our country and the management of our foreign policy, I can honestly think of no man or woman whose hands I'd rather that responsibility be in than John Kerry."[65]

3

WELCOME ABOARD

BY ALMOST ANY INDEX, the twenty-first century is the most connected in world history.

You can capture an instant with Snapchat, share a moment on Facebook, and speak face-to-face for hours using Skype and FaceTime. If you're the US government, you also can connect leaders around the world using encrypted Secure phones and videoconference equipment.

While Secretary Kerry carried an iPad everywhere he went for four years, when it came to diplomacy, he was decidedly old school.

He made clear—through his words and the mileage he racked up—his belief that diplomacy was best conducted through a face-to-face conversation.

"I've got to feel it out," he told his senior staff the morning of February 21, 2013, three days before he set out on the first trip of his term. "That's what this trip is all about."[66]

That inaugural trip included visits with longtime allies in the United Kingdom, Germany, and France, but after further stops in Italy and Turkey, the secretary continued to Egypt, Saudi Arabia, the United Arab Emirates, and Qatar.

All four nations would be pivotal if Arab states were ever to offer Israel a peace extending across the Middle East. The secretary wanted to meet their leaders immediately to get input for the administration's final stab at brokering peace between Israel and the Palestinians.

Over the ensuing four years, Kerry became the most traveled secretary of State in history while working out a power-sharing agreement in Afghanistan, convincing Iran to get rid of its nuclear weapons program, developing a counter-ISIS coalition, and brokering climate change agreements, including the 2015 Paris accord.

No matter the challenge, the secretary's impulse wasn't just to pick up the phone. It was to get on the plane.

"The only way for me to manage this is face-to-face," he told his senior aides in December 2014, explaining why he was headed to Rome for yet another conversation with Israeli Prime Minister Benjamin Netanyahu.[67]

A reporter had picked up on his style in October 2013, barely eight months into his tenure.

"The 69-year-old former senator and 2004 Democratic US presidential nominee made an unannounced visit to Kabul last week for one-on-one talks with (Afghanistan) President Hamid Karzai, after scrapping plans to visit the Philippines due to a typhoon," wrote Reuters Diplomatic Correspondent Lesley Wroughton. "The personal touch seemed to work with Karzai. The pair reached a preliminary deal that would keep some US forces in Afghanistan beyond a 2014 deadline."[68]

Wroughton went on to quote an unnamed senior State Department official who said, "He decided that making this trip, spending the time, rolling up his sleeves, and doing personal diplomacy, which you all know he enjoys doing, was important."

The secretary's peripatetic nature was nothing new.

Once while he was in a meeting, we staffers killed time by watching a replay of his 1971 appearance on *60 Minutes*. That interview came after a twenty-seven-year-old John Kerry had burst onto the national scene with his antiwar testimony before the US Senate.

In providing background about Kerry and his then-wife, Julia, CBS correspondent Morley Safer told viewers, "The Kerrys have a house in Waltham, Massachusetts, but they are rarely there. He is almost continually on the road, speaking on behalf of the veterans."[69]

Everyone nodded at the affirmation of a lifestyle they were sharing forty years later.

KERRY WASN'T THE FIRST secretary ribbed or criticized for his penchant for travel.

Carly Fiorina, the former chief executive officer of Hewlett-Packard Co. and a 2016 Republican presidential candidate, chastised Hillary Clinton when she was seeking the Democratic presidential nomination that same year.

At the time, Clinton held the record for the most destinations visited by a secretary of State—a total of 112.

"Like Hillary Clinton, I, too, have traveled hundreds of thousands of miles around the globe. But unlike her, I have actually accomplished something," Fiorina said in January 2015, while addressing the Iowa Freedom Summit in Des Moines, Iowa. "Mrs. Clinton, flying is an activity, not an accomplishment."[70]

Some opponents made similar comments about Kerry even before he surpassed Condoleezza Rice for most miles traveled by a secretary, which had been 1.059 million. Secretary Kerry exceeded that in April 2016 and ended up with 1.41 million in total. That equaled fifty-seven times around the world.

He never matched Secretary Clinton for destinations visited, hitting ninety-one countries—some twenty-one fewer than she. That was largely because Kerry spent extended periods in a handful of places, such as Jerusalem for the Middle East peace talks, Vienna for the Iran deal, and Paris during its 2015 climate change conference.

On that final point, some critics needled Kerry by saying if he really cared about the environment, he'd spend less time on his carbon-emitting airplane.

Whenever I heard these criticisms—not all unjustified—I thought back to one of my earliest conversations with him.

At that time, he said he wasn't interested in breaking any records as secretary, only in what he termed "purpose-driven" travel.

He defined this publicly on August 31, 2016, before an audience at the India Institute of Technology–Delhi in New Delhi. A student had asked him about surpassing the record for most miles traveled.

"I honestly am not counting countries, or miles for that matter," Kerry said. "We're going where we think we need to go when we need to go and trying to make things happen."[71]

A month later, as he began a series of exit interviews to review his time as secretary, he elaborated in response to a question from CNN.

"I go to Nigeria because it is vital that Nigeria be able to beat Boko Haram, an ISIL adjunct, and it's vital that Nigeria be able to build better governance and stronger ability to deliver to its citizens," the secretary said. "Similarly in Somalia, I went to Mogadishu because it's important for us to beat al-Shabaab, which is another violent terrorist group that threatens stability. And so each of these, all of my trips are connected to really trying to make us safer."[72]

In fact, Kerry said repeatedly his voluminous travel stemmed from him holding his job at a unique time in world history.

And he explained that wasn't just a product of events occurring during his four years in office, but a social and political transformation coinciding with the rise of technology—especially smartphones and social media.

I remember once motorcading through the poverty-stricken Solomon Islands, passing children who lacked clothing while they played next to signs in the roadside vegetation hawking smartphones and high-speed data plans. People would stand at unpaved intersections, using their phones to shoot video of us driving by.

The secretary argued technology gave much to people but had an unexpected effect. It showed them what they didn't have by letting them see how people lived elsewhere in the world.

"It is a huge benefit, but also a disrupter in terms of economies and lifestyles," Kerry said.

He told the IIT students in New Delhi that technology "moves change at a pace that different places have difficulties keeping up with. In many places there is a clash of culture, of religion, of local mores with modernity itself. . . . And, so, governing is harder. It is harder today to build consensus around an issue than it used to be."[73]

When he was a child, Kerry recalled, a president could deliver a speech that was covered by three or four national television networks. The following day, everyone stood around the office water cooler and talked about what they'd heard.

As an adult, he lived in a world with a fractured media landscape and specialty news channels, letting viewers select the viewpoint for the information they received.

Consensus was a casualty of proliferation. And that lack of unity bred social and political unrest around the world, especially with low-tech, individualized broadcasting made possible by YouTube.

———

EXACERBATING THINGS, THE SECRETARY of State doesn't have the luxury of focusing on just one region, hot spot, or issue—unlike some of his European or Asian counterparts.

US engagement around the world is expected, if not a necessity.

"The nature of this job now is you've got to have a lot of balls in the air," Kerry said on November 12, 2013, while addressing a meeting of his assistant secretaries and other top State Department leaders.

He'd just returned from a 23,000-mile trip taking him to Egypt, Saudi Arabia, Poland, Israel, Jordan, Switzerland, and the United Arab Emirates.[74]

The secretary would frequently lead his listeners on a virtual trip around the world. He'd "stop" in Africa, where he would discuss US efforts to stop an Ebola outbreak; the South China Sea, where the country sought to limit Chinese efforts to impinge on the freedom of navigation; Ukraine, where the United States and its European allies worked to keep Russia from moving West after it seized Crimea and separatists took control of the eastern part of the country; and Yemen, where he tried to broker a cease-fire between opposing forces in a proxy war between Saudi Arabia and Iran.

"I think if you measure all of American history, there has never been a moment where the United States is more engaged, in more places, simultaneously, on as significant a number of complicated issues, as we are today—and with impact," Kerry said in September 2016, after ticking through the list at a forum sponsored by The Atlantic and Aspen Institute.[75]

The secretary's belief in personal diplomacy inspired a "Hometown Diplomacy" series that ran throughout his four years. It was a pet project of mine and developed a template: invite foreign leaders to Boston, embrace them with drinks or dinner in the secretary's home, take them to a cultural attraction, and hold meetings in a venue far removed from the formalities of the nation's capital.

"Literally, some of the most candid and productive conversations that I have had have been over a good meal in somebody's country," Kerry said once while addressing an event celebrating the State Department's culinary diplomacy efforts. "A little good wine doesn't hurt, either," he added.[76]

During the first Hometown Diplomacy visit, Kerry hosted British foreign secretary Philip Hammond in October 2014 during his first official trip to the United States. The two delivered speeches at the Wind Technology Testing Center in Boston's Charlestown neighborhood, toured the USS *Constitution*, and stopped by the secretary's former cookie shop in Quincy Marketplace: Kilvert & Forbes.

A week later, Kerry welcomed Chinese state councilor Yang Jiechi for lunch at Legal Sea Food's Harborside restaurant and a tour of the John Adams Historical Site in Quincy, Massachusetts. Another time, the secretary and his wife had Japanese prime minister Shinzo Abe and his wife, Akie, for dinner at their townhouse on Beacon Hill.

Australian foreign minister Julie Bishop, an avid runner, was given a tour of the Boston Marathon finish line and offered a special advance screening of the movie *In the Heart of the Sea*—a Nantucket whaling adventure starring Australian actor Chris Hemsworth.

The final invitees, a group of European foreign ministers, climbed a spiral staircase from the secretary's private office to the roof deck of his townhouse, where they posed for a photo together against the setting sun and Boston skyline. Earlier, they held meetings at Tufts University, home of the Fletcher School of International Law and Diplomacy, and took a cruise around Boston Harbor.

Most of the meetings were conducted without neckties, and all of them engendered goodwill between the participants and among their staffs. The 2014 China meeting, in particular, was credited with igniting cooperation between the two countries on climate change that led to passage of the 2015 Paris accord.[77]

In mid-February 2015, the secretary was invigorated after hosting the Mexican and Canadian foreign ministers in Boston for the annual North American Trilateral Meeting.

They met at historic Faneuil Hall, walked down a snowy street for clam chowder and lobster rolls at the Union Oyster House, and then sat in a sky-box and watched a Boston Bruins game. The secretary's counterparts wore black-and-gold Bruins team jerseys he gave them, heresy for the Canadian foreign minister John Baird.

"It really works to break it down, make it less official," Kerry told a meeting of assistant secretaries and other senior State Department leaders.

THE PRIMACY SECRETARY KERRY placed on personal interaction was rooted in his sense of human nature.

"Everybody comes from somewhere," he told CNN in that September 2016 exit interview. "They come from a background, they have parents, they have families, they have aspirations, they like to laugh and live a life—most of them—that's decent and safe. And you need to see another person in another country through their eyes and get to know them a little bit and talk to them and find out where common ground might be. I don't think anybody had to be an enemy. I've never met a child two and a half years old who hates anybody. Hate is taught."[78]

The secretary expanded on the theme in October 2015 as he addressed students at Harvard University.

One asked how he assessed Russian president Vladimir Putin as a negotiator, and what were his main insights from negotiating with him.

"President Putin has very, very strong ideas about the ways in which he perceives Russia to have been either wronged or threatened over the course of these last most recent years. And as you know, he famously has lamented the fall of the Soviet Union as a great geostrategic loss," Kerry said. "I think a very important part of diplomacy is listening and making sure you hear what's really beneath the other person's, leader's complaints or perceptions, and not allowing yourself to get distracted by the daily din and screed of the 24-hour talk circuit and politics and particularly in a presidential year."[79]

He added: "I think that there's no room for hubris in diplomacy. It's an invitation to disaster."[80]

Besides the patience and understanding permeating his diplomatic style, the secretary exuded optimism. It was a facet of his personality I hadn't fully appreciated before working for him.

"I will say also that while sometimes things look bleak and difficult, there's opportunity in everything, and you have to find the opportunity, you have to work to do that with creative leadership," he said in July 2016. He spoke in Luxembourg City, Luxembourg, as he and the country's foreign minister, Jean Asselborn, reacted to the recent Brexit vote.

"I am absolutely confident that if people approach this thoughtfully, studiously, soberly, with creativity, there is a way to find strength out of whatever we do ahead," Kerry said.[81]

The secretary conceded that his approach and style—an aptitude for globe-trotting and an iron constitution at the negotiating table—had its critics. Some accused him of naiveté or self-delusion.

Israeli defense minister Moshe Ya'alon famously refused to confirm or deny his exasperation with Kerry's relentless Middle East peace efforts, after being quoted in January 2014 as saying the secretary was "obsessive" and "messianic" in leading the negotiations.[82]

Ya'alon supposedly added: "The only thing that can 'save' us is for John Kerry to win his Nobel Prize and leave us alone."[83]

The secretary remained undeterred.

"I've read people say, 'Kerry thinks that if he talks at them long enough, he can persuade.' I don't believe that," he told CNN. "There's a ripeness to diplomacy, there's a ripeness to any negotiation, actually, any negotiation. And if the other side, if their interests can't be met in a way that also meets your interest, you're never going to have a deal."[84]

The interviewer asked if he feared failure, which I felt often set him apart from the more risk-averse Secretary Clinton. She was always worried about preserving herself for her future presidential campaign.

Kerry dismissed the thought. He was on the opposite side of any such calculus. Having a job he loved toward the end of his career liberated him to act as he felt was best.

I admired his willingness to take a risk.

"Why worry about failure?" Kerry said on CNN. "I lost the presidency of the United States, so you can't lose anything much bigger than that. And what it taught me is, 'Don't worry about it.' If you have the opportunity to get things done, go get them done."[85]

While the secretary was self-deprecating, I can say without equivocation there were certain things that wouldn't have happened but for his presence and drive.

One was the power-sharing agreement in Afghanistan he negotiated over several visits between rivals Ashraf Ghani and Abdullah Abdullah (he adopted the same last name as his first).

Abdullah accused Ghani's backers of rigging a June 2014 national runoff election, a charge Ghani denied.

Amid fears of a possible civil war, the secretary met with each man individually in the US ambassador's residence in Kabul, and with them together and their small group of advisers in a downstairs meeting room—several rounds each.

Finally, he reached an agreement in principle in July 2014, and Abdullah waited nervously as Ghani walked into the ambassador's apartment and embraced his former foe.

A gasp went up from reporters attending a subsequent news conference when Kerry announced both men had agreed to an audit of each and every one of the 8 million ballots cast in the runoff. They also promised that Abdullah would have an important role in the new government, even if Ghani's tentative victory were affirmed.[86]

Ghani ended up winning the audit, and Kerry finalized the deal with Abdullah in September 2014. Despite occasional friction, Ghani remained president—with Abdullah as Afghanistan's chief executive officer—even after the secretary finished his term in January 2017.[87]

In January 2016, Kerry also visited Nigeria amid election recriminations between President Goodluck Jonathan and his challenger, retired

Major-General Muhammadu Buhari. He urged both candidates to accept the outcome of their contentious race—regardless of the winner.

They both followed through on their pledge even after Buhari staged an upset and Jonathan became the country's first incumbent president to lose reelection.

The secretary returned to the central African nation on May 29, 2016, to attend President Buhari's inauguration and commemorate the peaceful transition.

"He told the party in government then, and those of us in opposition, to behave ourselves, and we did," President Buhari said of Kerry two years later.[88]

In addition, Kerry distinguished himself in October 2016 by being one of the only—and certainly the most high-profile—foreign ministers to attend a climate change meeting in Kigali, Rwanda.

Attendees from 170 nations ended up adopting a legally binding agreement aimed at reducing the use of hydrofluorocarbons, chemicals in air-conditioners and refrigerators that could raise the Earth's atmospheric temperature.

The New York Times reported the following day, "The talks in Kigali, the capital of Rwanda, did not draw the same spotlight as the climate change accord forged in Paris last year. But the outcome could have an equal or even greater impact on efforts to slow the heating of the planet."[89]

Kerry walked from room to room, meeting with any wavering delegations. Low-level technical experts were stunned at one evening session when the US secretary of State walked into their meeting, listened to their discussion, and then deferentially asked if he could address the group.

Negotiations continued late into a Friday night before the final deal was sealed at 7 a.m. on Saturday.

By that time, John Kerry was already flying on to different meetings in Switzerland and the United Kingdom.

———

AFTER SECRETARY KERRY LANDED at Andrews Air Force Base in March 2013 to complete his first trip abroad, then State Department spokesperson Toria Nuland asked me how I enjoyed our eleven-day, eleven-city, 16,000-mile inaugural journey.

I told her it was exhilarating, if exhausting.

"Good," she replied as we rolled our luggage back across the airport tarmac. "Now be ready to do it forty more times."[90]

I got her point, but she was a little bit off.

In the end, we took 109 overseas trips. That didn't include domestic jaunts to New York City for UN meetings or places like Austin, Texas, where the secretary delivered a speech about climate change.

No matter the numbers, there was mind-numbing routine to our trips that simultaneously comforted the travelers while leaving them feeling like they were on a merry-go-round.

It's no small irony that "Ferris Wheel" was the code name the Diplomatic Security Service gave to the plane carrying the secretary of State. It's much like "Air Force One" is the call sign for the aircraft carrying the president of the United States.

The DS agents would radio to colleagues on the ground, "Ferris Wheel, wheels up," each time we took off, and "Ferris Wheel, wheels down," each time we landed.

I sent my wife, kids, and a few other relatives that same "wheels up/wheels down" message each time, so they knew where we were and that we were safely moving about on our journey.

We went on all those trips for a variety of factors.

Some were prompted by tradition: the first stop for any new secretary usually is the UK, our mother country, or Canada and Mexico, the two countries with which the United States shares a border.

Others were dictated by fixtures on the diplomatic calendar, such as NATO meetings held twice a year in Brussels.

Others were requested by ambassadors. They might ask for a secretarial visit if they faced a thorny problem or if his presence would add a grace note for a host country's special occasion. That might be a momentous national anniversary or a presidential inauguration, like the one we attended in Nigeria.

Still others were driven by crisis management, like the condolence visits Kerry paid after terrorist attacks.

Another segment of our travel was directed by the White House, including an extended stay in Bali when the president canceled his own visit to Indonesia because of a government shutdown back home. The secretary was there for preparatory meetings and was told to remain as a stand-in for President Obama.

A final category was trips prompted by the secretary's interests or priorities. That accounted for the bulk of our travel.

An "interests" trip included a November 2016 visit to our seventh continent—Antarctica—so Secretary Kerry could see and learn firsthand about the effects of climate change. A "priorities" trip included his numerous stops in the Middle East for peace talks, or cities across Switzerland as he drove toward the Iranian nuclear agreement.

Whether a trip was a need-to-do or want-to-do venture, the request for travel set off a chain of action within the State Department. Most immediately, it triggered the production of reams of paper including briefers about the countries being visited and biographies of the meeting attendees.

The paperwork and tentative schedule were then discussed during a series of planning meetings held in one of two conference rooms on the 7th Floor at the Harry S Truman Building.

Kerry occasionally popped his head in, looking for someone. He'd inevitably be shocked by the twenty or so people sitting around the table, with more looking on from the backbenches.

"It takes *all* these people to plan my trip?" he'd say, eliciting laughter.

The numbers in part stemmed from the complexity of secretarial travel.

Wherever a secretary of State goes, the US Air Force has to fly him, so a liaison to the 89th Air Wing at Andrews is at the meeting. The secretary also is under twenty-four-hour protection by DS, so the security team has to hear about plans and make arrangements for agents to meet and escort him at each destination. The Line has to book hotels and meet with the host government to plan out the specifics of each stop and meeting. A medical officer began traveling regularly with Kerry after he had a bike accident and broke his leg in May 2015. The Pentagon and State Department also had an arrangement where the assistant to the chairman of the Joint Chiefs of Staff would travel with the secretary, in case there was a crisis or he needed instant advice about military programs or capabilities.

Other seats at the meeting were taken by subject-matter experts for different stops, and representatives of the different three-letter regional offices whose territory we'd visit as we progressed around the world.

Finally, there were people like me, members of the secretary's direct staff. We were charged with ensuring a trip advanced the administration's public policy priorities and achieved Kerry's personal goals.

We also made it our priority to expose him to the local community and culture, and ensure that people in the places we visited—and the folks back home—got a sense of him as a person. In Mongolia, this meant going to an outdoor cultural fair, where he watched men wrestle in loincloths and children race across the tundra on horseback. In Abu Dhabi, we took a tour of the massive Sheikh Zayed Grand Mosque.

We'd all also aim to meet with the local embassy staff at each stop to thank them for their service and work on our trip. (They'd celebrate our departure with their own "wheels-up" party.)

Our Public Affairs staffers would listen to each of these elements and offer insights about how much time reporters might need to file their stories at a specific destination, and how to sequence the events to ensure maximum media coverage of the secretary's activities.

The constant tension between "The Building" and the secretary's staff was over how to make a trip work for him, rather than all the other people around the table claiming equities in a specific stop.

The strain between must-dos and nice-to-dos was constant in devising a trip schedule. So too was our attempt—and "attempt" is the right word—to make a trip survivable.

Quite often, we'd build an itinerary calling for us to take off in the morning and fly east, letting us land in Europe or elsewhere as night fell. The theory was we could get some sleep and start our meetings fresh the next day.

Quite often, though, Secretary Kerry would nix this while reviewing the final proposed schedule. He'd ask that we depart at night and arrive in time to work in the morning.

"We'll sleep on the plane," would say the only person aboard with a bed. The groans would go up from everyone else who'd be required to nap in a chair.

Many times we'd work Monday through Friday in Washington and then depart for Andrews on Friday evening, while everybody else in the capital was heading out for happy hour or home to watch Netflix. We'd take an overnight flight to Europe and upon landing, work Saturday and Sunday. Then we'd roll straight into the next workweek wherever we were in the world.

This cycle could sometimes go for two or nearly three weeks, meaning we not only worked every day, but we also missed the weekends when people in the civilian world recharged.

And all this came while moving back and forth across multiple time zones.

The stress and jet lag strained everyone involved, from DS agents who had to leapfrog from city to city to the pilots who flew us, from staffers who started work a couple hours before Secretary Kerry awoke to those of us who didn't finish until after he went to bed.

I gained about thirty pounds, lost muscle tone, and ended up with a kidney stone. The doctor attributed it to dehydration from our constant flying. My eyes also were perpetually bloodshot from the dryness. The staffer who traveled second-most to me developed a bad back from all the sitting on our airplane. He needed physical therapy for months after finishing his job.

At regular intervals, Kerry would vow a more humane schedule, but the pace never subsided. Toward the end of our four years, he lamented the toll on all of us and on his family.

"While I wish I could come and stay for longer, the press of the current conflicts and the business that we have makes it extremely difficult to stay anywhere very long," he said on August 2016 during a visit to the Edward M. Kennedy Center in Dhaka, Bangladesh. "Just ask my kids and my wife."[91]

He expanded on the theme in another of his exit interviews, this one in September 2016 with CBS News: "It is tough on my family, and I am very grateful to my family for putting up with this," he said, using words that rang especially true to me. "They've given me a gift of being able to do this job and try to do it well. And they realize it's for a finite period of time, and you go at it. It's a privilege."[92]

EACH OF OUR TRIPS started with "bag call": a deadline for depositing luggage in an office on the 7th Floor at Main State. That was often eight or more hours before wheels up. This buffer gave the Grand Master of the State Department, Senior Support Specialist George Rowland, enough time to deliver the bags to the airport, have them swept for explosives, and place them in the belly of our plane.

Two hours before departing on an outbound flight from Washington, we'd assemble on C Street in front of the Truman Building and board a caravan of black vans for the ride to Andrews. We'd drive past groups of unknowing tourists and teams playing flag football or softball on the National Mall. Depending on traffic, the trip could take twenty minutes or an hour.

A security guard at the Main Gate of Joint Base Andrews, the official name for Andrews Air Force Base, would check IDs before waving us onto the grounds. The vans would park, and we'd get out at a terminal used by armed service members catching rides on military planes. It also housed the Distinguished Visitors Lounge.

The lounge represents the military's best effort at a VIP staging area. Its chairs, couches, and conference rooms could be occupied at any time by members of Congress, generals heading off on a trip, or staff like us awaiting the arrival of a cabinet member for a Special Air Mission flight.

The lounge is run by Air Force Protocol Officers who are unfailingly polite and work to ease the downtime. They provide an urn of coffee (requested donation: $1 per cup), a vat of ice water, and Otis Spunkmeyer cookies for sale.

Their desk sits beneath a radar screen showing either the inbound or outbound flights for Andrews. Across the room, a television displays cable news. The walls are lined with photos of various presidents coming and going from the airport.

A favorite of mine was a shot of President George W. Bush waving directly at the camera from the top of the front stairs to Air Force One. It was snapped from the top of the rear stairs by Eric Draper, a former colleague of mine at the Associated Press who went on to serve as the chief White House photographer during Bush's presidency. The picture captured a mischievous smile by a person I'd come to know well while covering his 2000 presidential campaign.

Another wall is lined with photos of the Andrews Protocol Staff; and one more has a cluster of portraits seen in all military facilities: the president, the secretary of Defense, and the local base commander.

A sliding door leads from the lounge to a sidewalk. That path leads to a black iron gate. Beyond that is the concrete tarmac and a waiting plane. Or make that planes.

The 89th Air Wing's primary client is the president, and it prides itself on a 100 percent service record for him. There would be huge repercussions if they had to cancel a flight on Air Force One because of a mechanical failure.

To ensure the president or a Distinguished Visitor, known as a "DV," is never stranded, the 89th always has a primary and backup plane ready for departure. That includes a second set of pilots sitting at the ready in the spare plane.

If the primary plane has a problem, everyone can transfer to the backup and takeoff. Shifting over all the luggage and food takes about ninety minutes, which happened to us once when a ground crew member banged the door while backing away the boarding stairs.

The flight crew wasn't completely confident in the door seal and didn't want a pressurization problem in flight, so they opted to fly on the backup. We passengers endorsed the move, despite the delay.

If an identical plane wasn't available to serve as the backup, the 89th would at least have a smaller aircraft at the ready. If we had to fly on that plane, a senior staffer would slash the passenger manifest on the spot, a cold calculation leaving some would-be travelers behind.

The backup plane doesn't travel in tandem with the secretary of State, even though the spare to Air Force One follows the president on all his foreign trips to prevent him from being stranded overseas.

For all the miles we flew and impromptu or improvised trips we took, the 89th Air Wing provided stellar service to Secretary Kerry. We suffered few flight delays and our plane broke down only twice, once in Vienna and another time in Honolulu. Each time, the secretary was able to get home on a commercial airliner.

Kerry's most common complaints were about the age of and communications faults with our aircraft. He said they inhibited him from speaking with the White House or his counterparts as we flew around the world, and the dated amenities kept his staff from getting proper rest.

He'd get especially agitated when we landed in cities hosting major conferences and our nearly twenty-year-old aircraft pulled up next to the brand-new planes used by many of his fellow foreign ministers.

Most of those planes were wide-body aircraft with intercontinental range and sleeper seats for the staff. Ours was a single-aisle plane originally designed for domestic flights and outfitted with chairs that no more than reclined.

After one trip in March 2014, which had been interrupted by numerous dropped calls, we landed back at Andrews and found the Air Force officer in charge of the 89th Air Wing waiting for the secretary at the bottom of the airplane steps.

Kerry descended and said to him, "Colonel, we still had comms problems."

The colonel nodded and replied, "Yes, sir, I heard. I can assure you, you have the attention of everyone on the base."[93]

The secretary reached over and grabbed his elbow, as if to reassure him.

As a civilian, it was a graphic example of a military leader taking responsibility for his command. But it also showed two government officials working out a problem professionally.

Despite his technological grievances, Kerry always made sure to laud our different flight crews—giving members his commemorative Challenge Coin, buying them other souvenirs, celebrating their birthdays and military promotions and retirements, and once posing for photos with a pilot and his family after he completed his final flight in the Air Force.

The secretary held a valid multiengine pilot's license until his work at the State Department prevented him from renewing it, and the airplane junkie would often sit in a cockpit jump seat for special takeoffs and landings.

The crew reciprocated his generosity, asking leaders of the 89th Air Wing for permission to remove the secretary of State seal from our plane after his final flight in January 2017.

They presented it to Secretary Kerry as he took a parting photo with the group.

————

WE FLEW PRIMARILY ON one of four identical airplanes, all Boeing 757s known in the Air Force as the C-32.

The planes were outfitted the same, with only their call sign changing depending on the DV aboard. When it was the vice president, the plane was known as "Air Force Two." When it was the first lady, it was "Brightstar." When it was a cabinet member, the chairman of the Joint Chiefs, or attendees on a CODEL (or congressional delegation trip), the plane was known to air traffic controllers as "SAM," short for "Special Air Mission."

DS preferred their special "Ferris Wheel" moniker for the secretary's specific plane.

While the planes had the same exterior, number of engines, and paint jobs, we could tell them apart by their unique numbers. That number was on the tail, just below the American flag painted where an airline name or logo usually appeared on a commercial jetliner.

The sight of a particular tail number could produce sighs of relief or groans of anxiety. While each of the planes offered the same amenities, some were better than others at Internet speed or phone reliability. The Air Force was addressing this as Secretary Kerry finished his term, installing new communications equipment in each plane.

Kerry's hope for their swift replacement never materialized, though. The Joint Chiefs representative traveling with us once inquired about how long the C-32s were slated to remain in service.

The answer was 2031.[94]

Each plane has a capacity of seventy-two people. Commercial models of the same aircraft, the 757-200, seat about two hundred, depending on configuration. The rough allocation of space on the C-32s is twenty-six passengers for the Air Force and forty-six for the traveling party, with slight fluctuations depending on the needs of each.

The Air Force allotment always includes four pilots. That's two sets of captains and first officers who fly in rotating pairs, taking mandatory rest when it's not their turn at the controls. The redundancy and rest allows the pilots to fly a DV for up to twenty-four hours.

The remainder of the crew includes flight attendants, security guards, communications operators, and a pair of aircraft mechanics.

The rest of the space on the plane is reserved for the DV and his traveling party. In our case, that included a press corps whose size fluctuated depending on our destination and the attendant media interest. We sometimes traveled with as few as three reporters and several times with as many as nineteen.

*T*wo places we never told our families we were visiting in advance were Baghdad and Kabul.

Secretary Kerry rides in an Embassy Air Chinook helicopter while flying from Kabul International Airport to ISAF headquarters in Afghanistan on April 9, 2016.

(Top) Arriving in Baghdad, Iraq. (Middle) Flying over Saddam's parade ground.
(Bottom) An escort at ISAF Headquarters in Kabul.

Because of the threat of an attack on a high-profile official like Secretary Kerry, the reporters who traveled with us also couldn't reveal our destination until we were wheels down.

When we flew to Iraq, the Air Force didn't want to use our blue-and-white C-32 with "United States of America" on the side, fearing it might be targeted with a shoulder-fired missile or high-caliber rifle shot.

Instead, we'd fly in aboard a plain gray C-17, indistinguishable from the other military cargo planes servicing Baghdad International Airport. The planes can also take evasive maneuvers on takeoff or landing, if necessary.

After landing in Baghdad, we'd board a group of helicopters for the flight downtown to Embassy Baghdad. The choppers were known as "Embassy Air" and were flown by State Department contractors, almost all of them former military.

We'd fly over the former Camp Liberty, a large home to US forces during Operation Iraqi Freedom, and along the infamous "Route Irish," a seven-and-a-half-mile gauntlet between the airport and the Green Zone.

We could also see pockmarked palaces once used by President Saddam Hussein.

I'd sit knee to knee with John Kerry so I could take photos of him as he surveyed the scene from an open door.

There was nothing between us and the ground—several thousand feet below—except for a mesh seat and a lone seat belt strap buckled across our waist.

We'd eventually descend over the Tigris River before landing at the embassy heliport. On the flight out, we'd get a view of Saddam's former parade ground just outside the compound. I immediately recognized the crossed swords next to his reviewing stand.

Afghanistan was considered as dangerous as Iraq, but we were able to take our regular plane into Kabul International Airport because of the large military presence supplied by the International Security Assistance Force.

We'd land and taxi over to a tarmac where another group of helicopters would be waiting. While ISAF Headquarters was only three miles away via Airport Road, traveling by motorcade was considered too dangerous.

Instead, we flew.

Our first visit, our helicopters belonged to the US Army, complete with a door gunner. Amid an ensuing troop drawdown, though, we'd board private helos again flown by Embassy Air contractors.

We'd travel in a line like a string of Christmas lights and land in pairs. Passengers on the first two would disembark before their helos made way for the next group of helicopters.

As we flew in or out of Kabul, I was often struck by the juxtaposition: we sat inside a modern aluminum cylinder, cradled in leather seats with fresh food cooking in the galley and a flight attendant walking by, asking if we wanted a drink.

Meanwhile, outside my window were forbidding snow capped peaks and endless dusty expanses.

As we got closer and closer to Kabul, we'd see small mud villages—a group of homes and a pen filled with livestock.

They were only a few thousand feet away, but we were worlds apart.

Addressing US troops in Afghanistan.

Typically, our travel party included the secretary's senior staff; the trip director; members of The Line to arrange calls, process paperwork, and produce the daily schedule; the Joint Chiefs representative and his aide; subject-matter and regional experts; Diplomatic Security agents; and, finally, a representative from the White House, almost always a member of the National Security Council staff.

This person walked a tenuous line, traveling with the secretary and being privy to his thoughts, while also reporting directly back to the White House to ensure he stayed on message—or got back on it. The military aide was in the same position, spending a lot of time with the secretary but responsible for writing reports solely for the benefit of the chairman of the Joint Chiefs.

Secretary Kerry could be remarkably blunt with the NSC and Pentagon representatives about issues and personnel, sometimes to the chagrin of his own staff. After all, these people traveled with us not primarily for him but their own bosses.

It was one team, but people had different loyalties.

Senior staffers and special guests boarded the airplane through a door just in front of the left wing. More junior staffers and the media used stairs and a door at the tail. This differentiation stemmed not only from protocol hierarchy but practicality.

The entire plane is known as a "SCIF," or Sensitive Compartmented Information Facility. The most sensitive, Top Secret material can be discussed and stored on the aircraft, which remains under twenty-four-hour armed guard wherever it travels. It's a flying State Department 7th Floor or White House Situation Room.

Because such classified information is handled in the staff section of the plane, the media isn't allowed to walk through it. That prevents inadvertent disclosure, either by a reporter seeing a paper or overhearing a conversation.

The general rule on the planes is that people can't walk forward of their own cabin but are free to walk back as far as they want. This had the effect of restraining the press corps, since the only thing behind their seats was the rear galley.

The Air Force occupies the front of the plane, everything from the staff boarding door in front of the wing up to the cockpit at the nose.

Immediately to the rear of that boarding door is the DV cabin, a private space with a couch that folds into a queen bed, a desk with a pair of swiveling captain's chairs facing forward and backward, and a private bathroom and changing area. The dignitary can select a movie or travel map that plays only on the television in their cabin.

Immediately aft of the DV cabin is an eight-seat conference area. There's a table on each side of the aisle, and two first-class-sized seats facing forward at each table and a pair facing backward.

Next is the senior staff cabin. It has twelve first-class-sized seats, six on each side of the aisle, arranged in three rows of two. There's a pair of lavatories after the seats, as well as an alcove containing a computer printer.

The rest of the plane has a passenger compartment and a galley in the tail. About half the seats are first-class-sized while the remainder are regular, three-abreast coach chairs.

This section was used by the media and Public Affairs staff, Diplomatic Security agents, and Air Force personnel who didn't fit in the forward cabin or who wanted a place to stretch out and sleep when space permitted.

Reporters reimbursed the government for each leg on a trip, with their seat costing the same as a coach airline fare for a given route. The media had a most diplomatic way for allocating whatever first-class seats might be left after the government traveling party had been seated.

They'd write numbers on a piece of paper, cut it up, and place them in a hat. A reporter picking 1 would look at a map of the plane and have first choice of the empty seats. The person with 2 would go second, and so on. The drawing always produced cheers or howls of protest in the Andrews DV lounge, especially if the lottery organizer had the good fortune of drawing the best seat.

Those complaints were also heard at the end of some trips, when reporters might lose the more spacious seats. Sometimes the State Department reclaimed spots so it could give a lift home to guards or staffers who'd worked at the secretary's final stop.

A reporter could go from the comfort of a first-class seat to the middle one in a three-person row, occasionally on days lasting up to thirty-eight hours, such as when we flew home from Asia.

I chose to sit on the inside of the last row on the right side of the senior staff cabin, even though my staff rank and attendance on virtually every trip would have let me to sit further forward.

I picked that spot because it let me recline without bothering anyone, lean against the side of the plane as I slept, and gain some extra storage in the bulkhead behind me while keeping my cameras accessible in the footwell in front.

With three panes of glass situated directly below the words *United* and *States* painted outside on the fuselage, it became my window seat on the world.

———

WHEN WE GOT WORD at Andrews that Secretary Kerry had left the State Department or his home en route to the airport, the traveling party would move from the DV Lounge to the airplane. We'd find name cards identifying the occupant of each seat.

Many passengers would be dressed casually, hoping to sleep on the flight or at least not wrinkle their work clothes. Those of us who typically wore suits would change just before takeoff, hanging up our jacket and slacks during the flight and switching into jeans and a sweatshirt or other comfortable attire.

I often didn't change until after the secretary arrived at Andrews, because if I wasn't riding with him to the airport, I'd disembark from the plane and snap photos of his arrival. I wanted to look professional for the occasion.

His limousine would be led by an Air Force security vehicle and followed by an SUV filled with DS agents. Sometimes that would be trailed by a van carrying the most senior staff members, in the event they had to remain at the office until the secretary departed for the airport.

The motorcade would make a sweeping left-hand arc across the tarmac as it reached the plane, stopping when the secretary's limousine reached the foot of the boarding stairs. He'd hop out, say hello to a uniformed Protocol Officer standing at attention, and then pose for any photos. Sometimes they were with State Department workers who came out to see the departure, other times with people who were retiring or rotating to a new assignment.

Secretary Kerry would then climb the stairs alone, allowing the traveling media to get a shot of him setting out on a journey. At the top of the stairs, he'd turn around and wave goodbye before ducking his head inside the door. We'd sometimes chuckle when it was just me and my camera on the tarmac.

He waved out of habit, but I was the only recipient of his bon voyage.

The new secretary was so excited to start his first trip in February 2013 that he neglected the traditional wave and went straight on the plane, prompting a needle in the story written by Matt Viser of the hometown *Boston*

Globe. During our final trip in January 2017, I joked that John Kerry had finally gotten the hang of it, compiling a series of snapshots of him waving goodbye at every stop.

Whatever he did on the stairs outside, once the secretary was aboard the plane, the tempo quickened.

DS agents would scramble up the stairs, carrying any remaining bags and rushing to their seats. An Air Force ground crew would back away the stairs while the pilots started the right engine, located on the opposite side of the plane. Once the stairs were clear, the flight attendants would shut the front and rear doors. The pilots would then start the left-side engine.

When both engines were up to speed, the plane started moving and the clock began ticking. We typically took off within ten minutes, often less. This ability to depart whenever we wanted was one of the biggest benefits of traveling in a government aircraft, far different than being restricted to the schedule of a commercial jetliner.

The US Air Force also has an uncanny ability to predict arrival times, often down to the minute. It's quite a feat when your destination is an ocean away and the projected arrival is eight or nine hours later. Nonetheless, more often than not, we'd land in another country and roll to a stop at the precise minute scheduled.

Kerry had an equal skill as a quick-change artist. After boarding the plane, he'd disappear into his cabin in his suit and tie and emerge several minutes later in what became a flight uniform: compression socks, jeans, and blue-and-white Yale University hoodie. Sometimes he'd swap in an orange sweatshirt with a Southwestern-style trim, but usually he showed his pride in his undergraduate alma mater.

Once the plane reached ten thousand feet, the pilots would turn off the seatbelt sign and everyone was free to move about the cabin. That sparked all kinds of activity.

The staff had access to air-to-ground telephones, as well as Internet service. This was both a blessing and a curse, because you could work almost anytime, anywhere—and you had no excuse for not working almost anytime, anywhere.

The worst situation was in Asia, when we'd be ready to sleep just as Washington was waking up, twelve hours behind us. We'd often have to answer questions or listen in to meetings while our body clocks were saying it was time to turn in for the day.

In flight, The Line would use its airphones and Secure and Unsecure computers to organize the secretary's phone calls, check in with the advance officer at our destination, and make final adjustments to our schedule.

Toward the end of a flight, they'd put a colored cover page on top of a stack of pages and staple together our daily schedule.

This pocket-sized "mini" was our guidebook, telling everyone where to be and when, as well as which vehicle to sit in and any miscellaneous notes about local customs or dos and don'ts. Secretary Kerry consulted this schedule but refused to be beholden to it, letting meetings run over if necessary and then seeking to make up time elsewhere.

He'd often get exasperated if we interrupted while trying to get him back on track. He felt the purpose of his trip was to attend the meetings he scheduled, not to race from destination to destination without regard for the progress he might be making in a particular conversation.

In that sense, the schedule became a guideline rather than a dictate.

The tension for us staffers was rooted in our focus on the entirety of a trip, not just each stop. Running late in one place risked offending those waiting at our next destination. And if we got too far behind schedule, we faced the very real risk of not getting to where we needed to be before the flight crew's duty-day expired.

One time in Afghanistan, we raced out of a news conference after the government power-sharing agreement was announced, needing to be wheels up by midnight if we hoped to reach Paris by the end of the crew-clock.

We started our takeoff roll at 12:00:30 a.m.

Several times, the aircraft commander had to call back to Andrews and get special dispensation to go twenty or so minutes beyond the deadline.

It was never a position we wanted to put the crew in, because the military had strict safety protocols. They were tightened further after Commerce Secretary Ron Brown died in 1996 when his Air Force plane crashed in Croatia.

Besides The Line officers beginning their work, takeoff prompted others to read briefing books, intelligence updates, or newspapers and magazines they hadn't had time to peruse back home.

During the course of our four years, I also gained a healthy respect for the market that had emerged for on-demand content. Often before our trips, staffers would use the Wi-Fi at their homes or in the Andrews DV Lounge to load up on movies and television series from iTunes, Hulu, or

Netflix. Once aloft, you could walk down the aisle and see almost everyone looking at a laptop, iPad, or iPhone. Some would be working, but many would be watching whatever they downloaded and laughing as they listened via their headphones. One of our DS agents continually cracked me up, showing incredible stamina by playing the Candy Crush video game for eight or more hours straight.

Kerry would also use our ascent to come back and greet the press, if he hadn't before takeoff. Sometimes, he'd talk on the record, giving them some meat for the stories they'd write in flight. Quite often, he'd speak off the record, providing anonymous background and context so the reporters would understand his thinking as he traveled between his meetings.

The flight crew also got to work immediately after takeoff. Some of the flight attendants took drink orders and others put on aprons and made final preparations in the galley to serve whatever meal was appropriate for the time of day.

On this front, the Air Force aimed for first class-treatment. Food was served on trays carrying a real plate and a metal fork and knife. They were accompanied by a garnish of some fashion, a roll and butter, and a small pair of glass salt and pepper shakers. The napkins were not paper but linen, a fresh cloth for each meal.

The menu was selected in advance by the trip director and purchased in bulk by the Air Force at places like Costco. The flight attendants would cook many items in advance—a favorite crew member named Juan took great pride in his Bolognese sauce—and then freeze what wasn't immediately needed until later in the trip. It would be stored in a luggage hold, packed in coolers lined with dry ice. The crew was able to keep ice cubes cold this way for weeks.

The general rule was that the crew transported everything we might need for a trip, including extra meals should we expand our itinerary. The Air Force tries to avoid shopping overseas because it increases the risk of causing food poisoning in the traveling party. The effect was that as a trip went on, we were served fewer and fewer fresh items like fruit and salads. Instead, we got more and more reheated dishes pulled from the dry ice.

A hallmark of virtually every trip was the 89th Air Wing's famous turkey taco salad. It's little more than ground turkey and spices, mounded on a bed of nacho chips. But it was served in a bowl, accompanied by an array of guacamole, pico de gallo sauce, and sour cream, along with a mini-loaf of jalapeño cornbread.

There was a stir each time the flight attendants started delivering turkey taco salad from the rear galley. Everyone doctored it up to their liking.

The director for the secretary's final trip, Jonathan Mennuti, made sure to include it in the meal rotation.

When Mennuti asked when the Air Force should serve it, the answer was a no-brainer: the last supper.

Secretary Kerry, who like all DVs was always given the option to have a special meal like pasta or shrimp, devoured it alongside the rest of us.

———

AFTER A MEAL AND a drink, most everyone would plot a sleep strategy based on the schedule we'd keep after landing. If we were heading straight to the hotel for the night, people would stay up on the plane and work or watch a movie. If we were landing and going directly to a meeting, everyone would try to sleep before our arrival.

Some people could fall asleep no matter the place or time of day. Others needed help to reset their body clock. I went au naturel for the first two years, simply forcing myself to sleep or at least close my eyes when the situation warranted. But as we reached the halfway point in our term, I asked my doctor about sleeping pills. He said it was entirely appropriate to pop an Ambien if I absolutely, positively had to get to sleep.

That often was the case on our overnight flights to Europe, even if we left Washington after dark. The trip to London or Paris was often no more than eight hours. Factoring in the time to take off, change clothes, and then wake up, change back, and prepare for arrival, there often was little more than four or five hours in the middle of the flight for sleep.

In those cases, I'd pop a pill, put on my eye mask and noise-canceling headphones, wrap myself up in a velour blanket I bought at Target for eighteen dollars, and lean against an inflatable pillow so I could go to sleep. I am convinced that beyond the pill, the difference-maker for me was a seven-dollar folding stool I got at Ikea.

I carried that stool and my blanket in the garment bag I'd bring to store my suit during a flight. When I unfolded the stool in my footwell, it transformed my reclining chair into a semi-sleeper seat with a footrest.

Even with the occasional pill, I had a tough time sleeping on the plane for more than four hours at a stretch. Often I had photos to process, or I simply found the view out my window to be engrossing. It usually was like a movie reel playing before my eyes.

One of my favorite flights was a daytime trip from Israel to any of several destinations in Europe. We'd depart from Ben Gurion International Airport, cross the Israeli coast above Tel Aviv, and climb out over the Mediterranean Sea before turning north. The route would typically take us over the Greek Isles, so I'd use Google Maps to pinpoint the specific islands along the way.

Santorini has such a distinctive hooked harbor I came to know it by heart.

We'd then fly north over the Adriatic Sea, with the heel of the Italian boot off the left side of the plane and the coastline of Albania, Montenegro, and Croatia in the distance outside my windows on the right.

We'd cross back over land to the west of Venice before heading north over the Italian and Swiss Alps. From there, we would fly over Bavaria, the French countryside, or the ship-filled English Channel.

Some of my other favorite flights were over Africa and the South Pacific, where heat and humidity built tremendous cloud formations. These would look spectacular at sunset. I created a folder on my laptop called "Clouds" to save the best of my cloud-formation shots. Once I asked my friends on Facebook to pick their favorite of four South Pacific shots I snapped.

They were so stunning they almost didn't look real.

Another favorite scene came at early morning as we flew into Japan. I was looking out the window at the bluish pre-dawn haze when the wingtip rose for a turn. That gave me an unobstructed view of Mt. Fuji, shrouded in the fog. I grabbed my camera and squeezed off several frames. My Facebook friends furiously Liked it.

Another time I was looking out the window when someone on the opposite side of the plane called over. I jumped across the aisle and looked out to see a Swiss Air Force F/A-18 fighter jet flying alongside us. It was so close you could clearly see the pilot. He soon dipped the right wing and flew beneath the belly of our plane, returning to view back on the right side of the aircraft.

I got a good look and took some photos before the pilot pushed the stick hard to the right, tilting the left wing upward and peeling his jet off in a big sweeping turn.

The local air force used our flights over Switzerland for escort duty or to practice intercepting hostile aircraft, but we were told they had to give advance notice after one approach caused alarm for the passengers flying on a plane carrying first lady Michelle Obama.

On still other flights, we saw the Eiffel Tower, the Thames River, the island of Malta, and the Great Pyramids while landing in Cairo.

We crossed the equator ten times during Secretary Kerry's four years in office, each time shifting from summer to winter or vice versa. We also took fourteen trips that went fully around the world.

On one trip, we flew back and forth between Muscat, Oman, and Beijing four times in a week: once from Muscat to Beijing as we headed to China for meetings, once for a round trip as we briefly left China for a meeting in the Omani capital, and then a fourth time to refuel in Muscat after departing Beijing for the last time.

I took a picture of the flight map each time to document our ping-ponging across the Arabian Sea, India, Southeast Asia, and Chinese countryside.

As a typical flight neared its end, I almost always changed from my casual clothes back into my business suit. Because I entered and departed the plane from the forward door, and because I took photos of the secretary's arrival and departure in my capacity as official travel photographer, I always wanted to look presentable as we came and went.

Not only did that mean wearing a suit and tie, but also leather-soled business shoes. This somehow felt appropriate to me: We were representatives of the United States of America, and I felt a responsibility to look as professional as possible. I couldn't imagine doing so in a pair of rubber-soled shoes, so I went old school and took repeated advantage of Johnston & Murphy's $125 shoe resoling program.

Because I needed to change my clothes, and because there were up to forty-five people using two bathrooms (the forty-sixth passenger, Secretary Kerry, had his own), my routine was to wake up at least two hours before our scheduled arrival time.

That let me snap out of my haze, wet my hair, and clean up in the lavatory with a washcloth and minitowel I packed in my carry-on. I'd then get redressed in a space not much bigger than a phone booth. By the fourth year, I dropped most of the pretense and would often simply strip down to my underwear while changing clothes in the alcove between the bathrooms and the computer printer.

I did it when no one was looking, but by then everyone was pretty much family. I just didn't have the patience to wait for a bathroom to open, or to try to take off or put on clothes while my elbows smashed against the walls. I could do it all faster and easier just outside in my little private spot.

I remember Elise Labott, CNN's global affairs correspondent, once catching a colleague as he stood out in the open, his chest bare as he changed shirts. She was aghast at the sight.

"Have we no dignity?" she asked with a mix of seriousness and humor.[95]

While I'd never gotten naked like my colleague, or ventured beyond the privacy of my little alcove, I remember thinking to myself, "Nope. Not anymore."

––––––––

ONCE WE HAD LANDED and come to a stop, the DS agents would race down the rear stairs, carrying equipment for themselves or colleagues waiting on the ground. The press would also deplane from the back. Our goal was to give the television and still camera operators enough time to set up so they were ready to capture the secretary walking out the forward door and down the steps.

Invariably there'd be a greeting party, usually including a Protocol Officer from the host nation and the local US ambassador. Sometimes they'd give the secretary flowers or ask him to participate in a coffee or tea ceremony.

Then he'd head to his limousine while we all raced to our respective cars. For the first half of the term, I rode in what was labeled Staff Van 1. For the last two years, I usually rode in the spare limousine, a backup SUV that typically traveled just in front of or two cars behind the secretary's own.

This left me less distance to run after taking his airport arrival photos, and more time to get out and get positioned for any shots as he got to his next destination.

No matter where we went, we traveled in a long motorcade that included the secretary, security personnel, the staff, and any host government officials. People sat in vehicles as assigned by manifests printed in the scheduling mini. Friendships often developed during repeated long car rides together.

In some cities, such as Berlin, the police would literally shut down every intersection to let our motorcade pass without traffic or stoplights. In places like Cairo, we once had to slam on the brakes in the middle of a highway as a donkey cart strayed into the lane being used by the motorcade.

Once, in India, there was chaos when a pair of dogs tried to dart across the road just as we passed. The mother made it but the puppy got clipped, prompting our driver to break the cardinal rule of motorcade travel: never stop for anything.

The agent driving the spare limo slammed on the brakes and tried to swerve to avoid the puppy, setting off a chain reaction ending when the secretary's limo was struck from behind by the SUV carrying his DS agents.

Kerry was unhurt, but it was an embarrassment to the Diplomatic Security Service.

We never saw the agent who braked for the dogs on another of our trips.

I always felt—across reporting about five presidential campaigns and working four years in the State Department—that traveling in motorcades was the most dangerous thing we did.

I usually had the benefit of a professional DS driver in the spare limo, since we might have to jump out at a moment's notice so the secretary could hop in if there was a problem with his own vehicle. But almost all of the other cars in the motorcade were operated by civilian volunteers or an embassy's locally employed staff. Many did not have the experience or training to safely travel at high speed so close to other vehicles.

Furthering the danger was the harrowing practice of driving "counter-flow." That was when the whole motorcade would cross over the center line and travel opposite the normal flow of traffic. Sometimes, this was planned in advance and the oncoming lanes were empty. Often, it was not, such as when we hit a traffic jam in the direction we were headed. The police at the front of the caravan would make a spot decision and then drive head on at the cars approaching on the other side of the road.

They'd use their lights, sirens, and, sometimes, frantic arm motions to clear everyone out of the way.

After a while, counter-flow became just another fact of our travel experience, even though it was like something out of *The Fast and the Furious*. In fact, when I got home from a trip, I sometimes had to check myself from going counter-flow when the traffic in front of me stalled, but I saw open road in the other direction.

My wife's cousin, Vic Palumbo, especially loved the term *counter-flow*, and thought its practice captured the urgency of our travels to hot spots around the world.

For all our time in motorcades—on either side of the median—I took it as a blessing when we finished our term with little more than the dog incident on our record.

A vehicle in a motorcade carrying Samantha Power, the US ambassador to the United Nations, struck and killed a child who darted out into the road as she visited Cameroon in April 2016.[96]

Power was aghast at that accident and went back to apologize to his family. The ambassador, a mother of two, was heartbroken.

Most often, even if we had meetings scheduled after we landed in a new city, our motorcade went straight to the hotel so Secretary Kerry could make a quick stop to freshen up. Unlike Air Force One, his plane didn't have a shower, so he could have hat head in his meetings if we didn't set aside time for a bathroom break.

Sometimes we in the staff could also grab a quick shower, but often we couldn't because we had to get ready for our next stop. We'd end up wearing the same clothes for forty-eight hours.

After this pit stop, everyone would get back in their respective vehicles and set off for the rest of the stops on our schedule. At the end of the day, we'd go to the airport for our outbound flight or back to the hotel for some sleep.

The State Department was practiced at streamlining the hotel check-in process, sending ahead a staffer who registered most everyone in advance. We'd get steered through the lobby and toward a waiting elevator, ride up to a designated floor, and then pointed down the hall to our rooms. We'd find a nametag and key taped to the door of the only private space we'd have on a trip.

Uncle Sam paid the room charge, but we were responsible for any incidentals.

The State Department set up a full office for us at each hotel stop, complete with phones and computers and printers and other office equipment. There were file folders with each staffer's name for messages and the next day's mini, and Secure spaces for us to speak or read printed materials.

All of this area was protected by a Marine Security Guard detachment. Its members are based in Quantico, Virginia, and compete for the slots. The guards must be single, due to the heavy travel, and willing to head overseas at a moment's notice.

It was always a relief to land in an unfamiliar place but be greeted by a "Hello, sir," whenever I headed for the office in our hotel.

I'd look over and see a clean-cut Marine smiling at me—even as they made sure I was on the list for authorized entry.

Fortunately for us, each trip ended as it began: we'd fly back into Andrews, the secretary would head home in his motorcade, and we staff members would board our respective vans for the ride back to the State Department.

I originally would call for a cab once we got there, but with the advent of Uber, we all became practiced at syncing our request for a vehicle with our estimated arrival time back at HST.

It was funny to watch people surreptitiously requesting a car as they engaged in a silent battle with their fellow travelers for what could be a limited number of drivers near the State Department.

My strategy was always to place my iPhone on mute and order my car as we rounded the Tidal Basin and headed toward the Washington Monument.

That would leave the perfect amount of time for our van and my Uber driver to reach C Street at the same moment.

Many times, though, I wasn't in the staff van, because I'd jumped back in the spare limo or in a separate staff van to accompany Secretary Kerry to his office or an appointment downtown.

Oftentimes, we'd work for a couple of more hours, even though we'd already had a full day in Europe and then flown eight or more hours back across the Atlantic.

The pace was relentless and didn't end until January 18, 2017, when we took our final flight from Basel, Switzerland, to Andrews Air Force Base. The secretary had been in Switzerland to deliver parting remarks at the World Economic Forum in Davos.

Kerry often lamented our long absences from the State Department, but they were an outgrowth of his belief in personal diplomacy and the many things he sought to accomplish while he had what he felt was the privilege of being secretary of State.

"I Ii, I'm John Kerry," he said on September 16, 2016, as he looked at Undersecretary of State for Political Affairs Tom Shannon after being away from Washington for fifteen days. Our travels had taken us to Sweden and China.

"I'm embarrassed," Kerry said, before correcting himself. "No, I'm not embarrassed. We got a lot done."[97]

4

THE BALLET OF
THE BILAT

THE FUNDAMENTAL BUILDING BLOCK of diplomacy is the bilateral meeting. As its name denotes, it's a conversation between the principals from two countries.

From 2013 to 2017, the United States was represented by Secretary of State John Kerry. He had some consistent counterparts, including Sergey Lavrov, the Russian foreign minister and longest-serving G-20 chief diplomat. Others rotated in and out with changes in their home governments.

Italy had six different foreign ministers as its ruling coalition changed. The last counterpart Kerry got to meet—Paolo Gentiloni—was elevated to prime minister after Matteo Renzi resigned in December 2016.

Despite the compactness of the name, there's a ballet to the bilat. It's rooted in protocol, history, and the task at hand.

Protocol, of course, covers the things like who hosts a meeting and which participant sits where. History can determine how many people are at the table and how long a meeting lasts. And the purpose of the meeting can influence how the discussion begins—and how it ends.

Because of its size and influence in world affairs, the United States is often a target of many countries' bilateral interests.

Most foreign ministers coming to New York City for the United Nations General Assembly ask for a bilat with the United States. Kerry could end up with over sixty meetings—many of them bilats—during that week despite our best efforts to cull the list.

Even if a minister couldn't get on the secretary's schedule, he'd often try to pigeonhole him in a hallway or plead with his aides for a "pull-aside" chat on the margins of a bigger meeting. This would give them a moment to plead their case on a given topic. Many times, a picture with the secretary would suffice, letting the minister convey a sense of gravitas to the folks back home.

Secretary Kerry met Cuban president Raúl Castro in September 2015 in an impromptu manner, bumping into him in a back hallway in the UN Headquarters. They spoke through a Cuban translator, discussing what it would take for President Obama to make a visit to the Communist nation.

Within the State Department, requests for bilats could come from the secretary himself or rise up as requests from the different regional bureaus. Those could be initiated by either the United States or a foreign government.

Whenever the request was formalized, it was treated much like a trip request. It triggered paperwork that covered all the necessary logistics, such as whether either principal needed a translator or podiums to make comments to the media.

The paperwork also included talking points (TPs) for what should be covered in the bilateral conversation, the fount of diplomatic engagement.

SUCH TPs FOLLOWED A formula aimed at making them easier to digest.

There was a summary context paragraph up top, detailing who the meeting was with, how long it would run, and a reminder of when the secretary last met with a counterpart. It would also explain the reason for the conversation.

Next came a list of topics for discussion, each one beginning with a bolded point for the secretary to make. It would be followed by a regular-type summary of background justifying the comment.

The bullet points would usually be listed in order of precedence, so the secretary could ensure he made his most important points before moving on to secondary matters.

The TPs would then include a list of points to be made "if time allows," followed by a series of responses under the heading "Watch out for/If raised."

These were possible points of criticism from the counterpart, along with the secretary's suggested comebacks.

The talking points would be accompanied by a biography of the counterpart, which might include classified intelligence, along with any relevant background on the other meeting participants.

Such material would be placed in a three-ring binder called "The Book" and sent home with the secretary the night before a meeting so he could prepare. Otherwise, he'd get his briefing papers on the plane or in a holding room so he could brush up before the conversation began.

Kerry would routinely pop the TPs out of his binder, fold and neatly crease the pages into quarters, and tuck them in the right front pocket of his suit jacket before he walked into a meeting. He'd pull the papers out again when the conversation began.

Protocol would dictate that the secretary and his counterpart sit across from each other, usually at the center of a long rectangular table. An ambassador or high-ranking deputy would usually sit next to their country's principal, with each side's additional participants sitting farther away from the center, based on their descending rank.

Counterparts from each side would be seated across from each other, so the Department spokesperson would end up looking across the table at the other country's spokesperson, for example.

Just how many seats were at the table could be a matter of protocol or history. The Russians and Chinese always pushed to have lots of people at meetings. Some of the requests could be for subject-matter experts, but others often begged the question of whether an invitee had anything to add or was simply being sent as a minder for the actual negotiators.

On the occasions when the United States couldn't get the number of seats it sought, that denial would be tucked away and recalled when we next hosted the counterpart in our country. If we could get only five seats overseas, our counterpart wouldn't get more than that when they visited the United States. The Chinese were notorious for enforcing this unwritten rule whenever we visited Beijing.

Yes, a diplomatic tête-à-tête can often border on a childish tit for tat.

Protocol and manners often dictated what would be served during a bilat. Coffee was an automatic, but meetings around the lunch or dinner hours might call for snacks or a full meal. Conversations in Islamic countries always included tea served in etched crystal glasses, with two lumps of sugar and a tiny spoon on the accompanying saucer.

Bilats were usually preceded by a guestbook signing, a series of official photographs, and perfunctory welcome comments for the media called a camera spray. A meeting would usually conclude when a host-country Protocol official knocked on the door and poked his or her head inside to announce the allotted meeting time had expired.

We'd often try to spur this along by asking for permission to pass a note to the secretary, telling him how much time remained and how running late could impact other things on our schedule.

Oftentimes, the two principals would then dismiss the rest of the meeting participants and remain behind for a brief "one-on-one," during which they'd talk privately. It allowed them to discuss topics that might be embarrassing in a crowd. It also let each side maintain plausible deniability if the other leaked the contents of this direct conversation.

The principals might also huddle with their respective staffs in separate rooms or different corners of the meeting room before heading out together for a joint news conference. It would be held to recap the conversation and answer reporters' questions about it or anything else in the news that day.

I'd oftentimes use the bilat period to edit and file photographs of the camera sprays. Occasionally, I'd be invited to attend the meeting itself, sitting down the table from the secretary or in a chair behind him as the meat-and-potatoes diplomacy was conducted.

It was like auditing a foreign affairs master class.

Secretary Kerry or his host would begin the conversation, often with summary comments straight out of their talking-point sheets. Then Kerry would start to work his way down his list, sometimes mechanically, usually fluidly, oftentimes not relying on the talking points at all but his own sense of the importance of pending issues.

The conversation could go back and forth, or one side could speak for an extended period before the other interrupted and took control of the mic. That happened literally, as one or the other speaker would press a button to activate a microphone connected to a loudspeaker and, often, the translation booth.

A red light would indicate an active mic, a visual warning to someone who wouldn't want an inadvertent comment heard by their counterpart.

———

ONE TEXTBOOK BILAT I attended occurred July 27, 2016, in the Malacañang Palace in Manila, Philippines. It was between Kerry and Rodrigo

"Digong" Duterte, who'd been sworn in as the country's new president less than a month earlier.

President Duterte had already gained worldwide attention for an election campaign in which he openly supported extrajudicial killings as a way for Filipinos to rid themselves of drug dealers and other criminals. The blunt-spoken politician and former prosecutor said he had personally killed three kidnapping suspects while serving as mayor of Davao City.

President Duterte would go on to call President Obama a "son of a bitch" before a planned meeting in September 2016, and say he could "go to hell" a month later after US criticism of his policies.[98] He also labeled US ambassador to the Philippines Philip Goldberg "the son of a whore," and said he might shift his traditional alliance with the United States to competing ones with China and Russia.[99]

That was a special concern because China had been claiming territorial privileges in the South China Sea. It's close to the Philippines and a place where the United States has historically enjoyed freedom of navigation and access to military ports and airfields.

Knowing what President Duterte had said, and believing him capable of all the things he would go on to say, John Kerry approached him indirectly.

After photographs in a reception hall—where the secretary politely helped the rookie president figure out where to stand, when to shake hands for photographers, and how to introduce his delegation to their counterparts—the two went into an adjacent room for a luncheon with their staffs.

Kerry began not with his talking points but personal anecdotes. The goal was to speak not from a script but from his heart without sounding patronizing. It was a delicate act.

He talked about how an uncle, William Cameron Forbes, had served as governor-general of the Philippines during its period of American colonial rule. He had lived in Malacañang Palace itself and reproduced one of its distinguishing features—its rich mahogany paneling—in the house he later lived at in Milton, Massachusetts. The secretary said the woodwork he saw in Milton gave him an appreciation for Filipino hardwoods that lingered to that day.

Kerry then recalled how he had visited Malacañang numerous times to meet with President Ferdinand Marcos as the United States sought government changes during his twenty-one-year near-dictatorial reign over the nation from the mid-1960s to the mid-1980s.

He noted the first congressional amendment he got passed as a senator made future aid to the Philippines contingent on political reforms, and how he'd returned to prevent fraud after President Marcos responded by calling snap elections to extend his presidency.

"So, there is a real connection here," the secretary said to the new president.[100]

As the conversation continued, we were served a tanigue fish starter, a clam soup, an entree of beef tenderloin, and coconut panna cotta for dessert. Waiters refilled the wineglasses and water glasses as the meal progressed.

President Duterte was solicitous of the United States and committed to the alliance, saying at one point, "We are safe with you; you are safe with us."[101]

At other points, though, he displayed the bravado for which he was famed. He said if an ISIS member wants to die in the name of God, "give it to him. He's not a martyr until he dies." He said there should be no negotiating with terrorists but also no need to behead them, as they'd done to Americans held in the Middle East, or to tourists and Filipinos by rebels in the Philippines.

"One bullet is enough," the president explained.

Only after President Duterte himself brought up the subject of extrajudicial killings did Kerry deliver his message on the topic. It had been atop his talking points, but he reserved it for his parting comment.

Again, though, the secretary tried to do so in a homespun way. He recalled that while he served as a prosecutor in Middlesex County, Massachusetts, he had led an effort to dismantle the notorious Winter Hill Gang in Somerville. Instead of going in with guns blazing, the DA's office used a legal means, charging gang leader Howie Winter with violating a ban on pinball machines. They'd generated huge sums of cash for his gang.

This approach punished the gang in a legal way the public could support, while retaining respect for the law enforcement community.

Looking across the table at President Duterte, Kerry said that "prosecutor to prosecutor," there was great fulfillment in trying a case before a jury.[102]

President Duterte would go on months later to make his disparaging comments about President Obama; but on that day in late July, the secretary of State emerged from his meeting with the new leader having avoided fireworks—but with his message delivered.

I had the chance several times to witness another facet of bilateral engagement: the times when Kerry was not the principal but sitting second chair to President Obama.

It could be disorienting to walk into a meeting room and find the secretary not at the center of the table but sitting one chair to the left or right while the president was the focal point.

On such occasions, principal became staffer and Kerry had to sit quietly while President Obama led the discussion. He waited in case he was called upon to answer a question or reinforce a point.

Otherwise, he sat silently and watched as the president personally conducted the nation's diplomacy.

THE SECRETARY'S VISIT TO the Philippines was part of the Obama administration's Pivot to Asia.

The aim was not to abandon traditional alliances in Europe and the West but to acknowledge our own country's history as a Pacific power. There also was exponential growth and development under way in all corners of the Far East, accelerating its global emergence.

President Obama explained his thinking in November 2011, when he outlined the strategic shift while addressing the Australian Parliament in the capital of Canberra:

> As the world's fastest-growing region—and home to more than half the global economy—the Asia Pacific is critical to achieving my highest priority, and that's creating jobs and opportunity for the American people. . . . The United States will play a larger and long-term role in shaping this region and its future, by upholding core principles and in close partnership with our allies and friends.[103]

This commitment helped shape Kerry's travel itinerary and led to recurring visits to the region.

The first came early in 2013, when the secretary visited Korea, China, and Japan at the end of our first trip around the world. It was important to see leaders in all three during the same trip, or at least not to miss Korea if we stopped in Japan, or vice versa. This was to avoid a slight based on their shared history.

Japan defeated China in the late-nineteenth-century fight for control over the Korean Peninsula. It then invaded China before surrendering control in 1945. Many Koreans harbor disdain for the Japanese to this day over its soldiers' sexual abuse of "comfort women" within the peninsula during World War II.

This dark past created a wariness of the United States favoring one over another, a fear especially acute in Japan and the Republic of Korea, known colloquially as South Korea.

That meant if you had a meeting, news conference, and dinner with the foreign minister in Japan, you'd better schedule the same things when you popped over to the ROK.

Our dealings with China, ironically, often focused on North Korea, not South Korea. No matter how many items there were on the bilateral agenda, a meeting between the United States and China always included a conversation about the hermit kingdom run by the Kim family and deceptively called the "Democratic People's Republic of Korea."

North Korea continued to develop nuclear weapons through successive US administrations, despite attempts at negotiations to stop the program and the imposition of economic sanctions when it failed to do so.

A vow to prevent the DPRK from gaining nuclear weapons proved toothless when the country tested its first atomic bomb in 2006. The United States continued to insist North Korea denuclearize, but it shifted from preventing it from getting a nuclear weapon to stopping it from developing missile technology to deliver a nuclear warhead. When the DPRK subsequently gained that capacity, the line shifted again to preventing North Korea from developing a missile capable of reaching the United States. Once it achieved that ability, the final redline for avoiding US military action was preventing the DPRK from miniaturizing a nuclear warhead to ride on an Intercontinental Ballistic Missile.

President Obama warned President-elect Donald Trump this would be his number one challenge upon assuming office, and it became a flashpoint before the new president had completed six months in office when Kim continued nuclear tests and ballistic missile launches. President Trump responded by threatening "fire and fury" against a rival he labeled "Little Rocket Man." Tensions subsided after the two held a summit in Singapore in June 2018.

President Obama, President Trump, their predecessors, and Secretary Kerry all viewed China as crucial to stopping this chain of events.

"(China) has the greatest amount of commerce with North Korea, the greatest intersection in banking of all of the finances of North Korea, the greatest intersection of trade, of their fuel—all the things they really need go through China," Kerry told CBS News during its September 2016 exit interview.[104]

He'd argue in a variety of venues that China risked what it most feared—an increased US military presence on its doorstep—if it didn't stop North Korea from taking actions that left the United States with no other option.

THAAD antimissile batteries and aircraft carriers didn't need to be around the Korean Peninsula, the secretary explained, if there wasn't a chance the North would take a shot at the United States or a regional ally like Japan.

THE DIFFICULTY IN MAKING this case was that China erected an almost-impenetrable facade when it came to bilateral negotiations.

First, there was the scripted nature of the meetings themselves. Everything was haggled over and then there was no yielding by the Chinese once a plan was set.

The Chinese didn't share the US delegation's respect for its traveling press corps, so they'd become incensed if an American reporter tried to ask unscripted questions of a Chinese official. They'd also herd reporters out of a room at the end of a camera spray by raising a gold-and-red braided rope and pulling those inside the lasso out of the door.

Once each delegation was at the table, President Xi Jinping or Foreign Minister Wang Yi would sound clichéd as they explained issues could best be resolved with "win-win" solutions. Success could be achieved only through "mutual respect," the leaders would add, or with an all-encompassing "respect for our nation's history."[105]

The latter was used to justify everything from China's longtime insistence that the breakaway island of Taiwan remain part of its sovereign territory, to its work during Secretary Kerry's term to convert shoals in the South China Sea into reclaimed islands. Those man-made islands supported Chinese military airfields and ports designed for navy ships, far from the mainland and China's internationally recognized territorial waters.

Such willful ignorance underscored for me the challenge in dealing with Communist or authoritarian leaders, including those in Russia and China.

Unlike the United States, these countries don't have a truly independent media, so their leaders don't often face legitimate reporters or a public that hasn't been subjected to a state-sponsored television view of world events.

This allows them to distort reality with a straight face—and without consequence.

In an effort to keep open the lines of communication, Chinese officials would visit Washington or US officials would travel to Beijing each year for a sweeping Security and Economic Dialogue. These meetings were aimed at addressing both national security and economic issues between the two countries.

During a June 2016 visit to Washington, Chinese officials touted the achievements born from the dialogues during the Obama administration—before lapsing into language typical of these encounters.

"On some issues, perhaps, consensus still eludes us. However, talking to each other could help pave the way to finding a solution, or at least help keep our differences under control," Foreign Minister Wang said. "Talking to each other does not create win-win all the time, but both sides will lose in a case of confrontation. Our dialogue mechanism may not be perfect, but it is an indispensable platform for the two countries to increase mutual trust, deepen cooperation, and manage differences."[106]

After that meeting, Secretary Kerry and Treasury Secretary Jack Lew attended a news conference with US and Chinese reporters.

Their Chinese counterparts skipped it.

During a working lunch in Beijing six months earlier, Secretary Kerry had tried to confront Foreign Minister Wang about North Korea in general and the South China Sea in particular.

He said there was fresh and unimpeachable evidence proving that the Chinese were installing artillery pieces on four islands. That could force the United States to beef up its own military presence in Japan, the Republic of Korea, and the Philippines, and to work out a new military arrangement with Vietnam.

The secretary noted neither side wanted that, so the Chinese needed to stop with the work.

Foreign Minister Wang replied that some of the islands had been militarized by prior occupiers. He said the weapons on them were defensive, not offensive. He branded the landscaping "China's reclamation" in one breath and then in another challenged the secretary's assertion the islands had been nothing more than "rocks under the sea" before the work. That claim, the foreign minister declared, "needs more scientific study."[107]

Nonetheless, he said the construction reflected China's needs in the area, and its size and might as a nation.

The two were scheduled to meet reporters after the lunch, and Chinese officials wanted to issue a joint statement, glossing over much of the maritime conversation—sure to be a focal point for US reporters traveling with Kerry.

The secretary knew he couldn't let that happen, so he and the foreign minister had an elliptical series of conversations about how to make the language more palatable for both sides.

When Kerry offered one sentence, Wang replied, "Mr. Secretary, you're putting words in my mouth." The secretary replied, "I'm not; I'm trying to make you accept words that you said."[108]

Another time, the foreign minister begged off a change, saying any significant alterations had to be approved by his superiors.

The haggling continued until Wang abruptly declared, "Mr. Secretary, we're out of time."[109]

During the ensuing news conference, the Chinese moderator declared: "Each journalist, please limit yourself to one question only. First, an American journalist to Secretary Kerry."[110]

*S*ecretary Kerry and his chief of staff, Jon Finer, were a pair of Ivy Leaguers who could match brainpower over any foreign policy issue.

Once, though, they got in a heated debate in the Beijing Marriott about how to best get the product flowing from a bottle of Heinz Tomato Ketchup.

This was no idle issue for the secretary, because the late husband of his wife, Teresa Heinz Kerry, had been Senator John Heinz—a descendant of company founder H. J. Heinz.

"Tell Heinz to get their shit together," the secretary said to no one in particular while he banged fruitlessly on the bottle as we briefed him over breakfast.

"Hit the 'Heinz 57' on the side," said Finer.

"That's bullshit," replied Kerry, thinking the recommendation was an old wives' tale. But when he did, the ketchup began to pour.

A vindicated Finer said, "See, it works."

"Shut up, Finer," replied our country's leading diplomat.

(Top) Mural of the Forbidden City inside the Great Hall of the People. (Middle) On the Great Wall with Treasury Secretary Lew. (Bottom) The secretary's limousine in Beijing.

The American reporter ignored the statement and asked a three-part question: What did the United States want from China on North Korea? Was China trying to militarize the South China Sea? To Wang, why was China unwilling to more forcefully punish North Korea?

Kerry answered the two questions asked of him, but when it came time for Wang to address the question he was asked, the moderator interrupted and said, "I hope we can all abide by rules. Of course, I respect your intention to raise more than one question. Next question, Xinhua News Agency."[111]

As the US reporters contemplated the dismissal, a reporter from the official press agency of the People's Republic of China stepped into the void and addressed Wang.

"China and the United States are two major countries. What is the significance and effect of an enhanced level of strategic cooperation between China and the United States?" the reporter said.[112]

The softball prompted audible groans from the US side of the audience, apparently noticeable to even the foreign minister.

He replied: "Well, this is a very good question, but I guess many of your colleagues are not interested in this question. They feel this has little to do with them. But let me say this question has a lot to do with the welfare of the Chinese and American peoples. And to satisfy you, I will make a couple of more points on South China Sea and the nuclear issue on the Korean Peninsula as well."[113]

Wang went on to explain that China would abide by all of the commitments related to North Korea that it had made at the United Nations, but it was even more important for both sides to get back to the negotiating table to try to resolve their differences.

Turning to the South China Sea, the foreign minister offered the same debatable argument he'd made privately to Secretary Kerry:

> China has given a commitment of not engaging in so-called militarization, and we will honor that commitment. And we cannot accept the allegation that China's words are not being matched by actions. . . . On the islands and the reefs stationed by China, we have built up quite a few civilian installations and facilities that are able to provide public service. In addition to that, there are some necessary facilities for self-defense, but the international law has given all sovereign countries the right of self-protection and self-defense. And if

one equates such a right to militarization, then the South China Sea has been militarized long ago, and mind you, China was not the first party that started the militarization.[114]

After the news conference, I caught up with a member of our delegation who was experienced in dealing with the Chinese.

I asked how he thought the lunch and news conference went, given the officials' intransigence when Kerry confronted them about their South China Sea policy.

A master of the analogy, our delegation member likened it to the delicate task of recovering a hostage.

"I think we drove a truck through the plate-glass window," he said.

After a pause, he added: "Whether SEAL Team 6 can make it up to the second floor remains to be seen."[115]

———

FOR ALL THE GEAR-GRINDING, the United States and China had a largely cooperative relationship on two big issues: the Iranian nuclear negotiations and a series of efforts that helped produce the Paris climate change agreement.

During Secretary Kerry's first visit to China in April 2013, he met first with Foreign Minister Wang and then was granted the courtesy of a meeting with President Xi in the Great Hall of the People.

The massive building—constructed in just ten months—sits in the center of Beijing, next to Tiananmen Square and across the street from the Forbidden City.[116] The entrance to the City is famously adorned with a giant portrait of Chairman Mao Tse-tung, the founding father of the People's Republic of China.

Following his conversation with President Xi and a walk down the front steps of the GHOP, the secretary drove to a side entrance for the Forbidden City. He pulled up in front of a pagoda and went inside to meet with the country's number two official, Premier Li Kiqiang.

While such high-level meetings were customary for a new US diplomat, Kerry was especially eager for this during his first trip. He wanted to ask Chinese leaders directly if they'd work with the United States to guarantee a successful outcome for the Paris climate meeting two years hence.

A similar UN-sponsored Conference of the Parties in 2009 in Copenhagen had been branded a failure after attendees didn't set binding limits on carbon emissions. The most they could agree on was a nonbinding statement, without target amounts.[117]

Kerry, who'd been an environmental activist since the 1970s, didn't want the same thing to happen in Paris, so he devised a plan before setting off for Beijing. His idea was to have the United States and China announce voluntary caps a year before the Paris meeting, then use the ensuing time to encourage other nations to volunteer their own emissions caps.

The Chinese economy is primarily fueled on high-carbon electricity sources such as coal, and the exhaust from these plants creates dense smog that chokes the local population and greenhouse gases affecting the global environment.

In February 2014, I snapped a photo of our plane on the tarmac at Beijing's Capital International Airport, looking as if it were shrouded in fog.

In reality, it was nearly invisible at high noon because of a blanket of smog. After we took off, the sun shone brilliantly above the haze.

Chinese leaders often had to resort to shutting down factories to the west of Beijing if they wanted visitors downwind to enjoy clear skies. They did so for the 2008 Summer Olympics, as well as our visit to the capital in 2015 for the annual Security and Economic Dialogue meeting.

While the Chinese people are wary of retribution for protesting their leaders, the popular groundswell over pollution prompted government officials to consider ways to clear up the environment.

To push for the secretary's vision, our staff organized an energy and environmental trade fair on April 13, 2013, after the meetings with President Xi and Foreign Minister Wang. The Chinese sent State Councilor Yang Jiechi, whose portfolio included the climate change negotiations, and who the secretary would later host at one of his Hometown Diplomacy events in Boston.

We took his attendance as a sign of respect for the secretary's initiative.

Yang toured the exhibits with Kerry, then sat in the front row as Kerry delivered a speech about the need for US-China leadership on climate change.

"My friends, why is this so important?" the secretary said. "China and the United States represent the world's two biggest economies, we represent the world's two largest consumers of energy, and we represent the two largest emitters of global greenhouse gases. So, if any two nations come to this table with an imperative for action, it is us."[118]

About eighteen months later, in November 2014, Secretary Kerry joined President Obama back in the Great Hall of the People for a meeting with President Xi.

The two sides agreed on new carbon emission reduction targets for the United States, and a first-of-its-kind commitment by China to stop its emissions from growing by 2030.

Both felt it was the necessary prelude for a successful Paris meeting in December 2015.

"A climate deal between China and the United States, the world's No. 1 and No. 2 carbon polluters, is viewed as essential to concluding a new global accord," *The New York Times* would report. "Unless Beijing and Washington can resolve their differences, climate experts say, few other countries will agree to mandatory cuts in emissions, and any meaningful worldwide pact will be likely to founder."[119]

China followed up by working alongside the United States to pass the Paris agreement in 2015. And during a September 2016 visit to China for a G-20 Summit in Hangzhou, President Obama announced the United States and China would both ratify the agreement.

"Where there is a will and there is a vision, and where countries like China and the United States are prepared to show leadership and to lead by example, it is possible for us to create a world that is more secure, more prosperous and more free than the one that was left for us," President Obama said.[120]

President Xi said China would "unwaveringly pursue sustainable development"; and Xi added, "Our response to climate change bears on the future of our people and the well-being of mankind."[121]

Through a series of bilateral engagements, China proved to be an invaluable partner as Secretary Kerry and the United States pushed to make climate change a world priority.

It would prove to be similarly helpful in the multilateral negotiations for Iran to give up its nuclear weapons program.

————

IF THERE'S A BALLET to the bilat, the multilat is more of a line dance.

Numerous parties converge on a single location, where they move in an orchestrated fashion. Almost always, it concludes with a group spectacle.

It's the dreaded "family photo" a picture of all the participants together. The foreign ministers typically assemble in a holding room, then march out in unison and climb on risers for a group photograph by the assembled media.

The particular spot where each minister stands can be based on a number of factors, but the United States is often positioned in the center—usually in the front row, too—and almost always next to the meeting host.

During the years Secretary Kerry took part in family photos, he and his counterparts would usually chat and stand uncomfortably for a few moments before someone inevitably made a wisecrack about the noise from the clicking camera shutters. That would trigger canned laughter and serve as the cue for everyone to disperse and resume their own schedule.

Amid the Pivot to Asia, we spent time twice each year attending meetings of the Association of Southeast Asia Nations, or ASEAN.

The members of this group took these meetings seriously, especially their twist on the family photo: the "ASEAN-Way" handshake.

The organizers would arrange a normal family photo, but before letting everyone go their separate ways, the host would ask the ministers to do one more thing: cross their arms and join hands with the person on either side of them.

Leaders ended up standing in a human chain with their arms crossed. It was as if a kindergartner had cut up a folded piece of construction paper and fanned out a string of interconnected figurines across the stage.

I honestly think the ASEAN-Way handshake photo was the highlight for some of those attending these regional meetings. They cheered when the photographers finished their pictures.

This twist tripped up President Trump when he attended his first ASEAN meeting in November 2017. He grimaced as he struggled to cross his arms and grab hands with his host, Philippines president Rodrigo Duterte, and the person on the other side of him, Vietnamese prime minister Nguyen Xuan Phuc.[122]

Russian prime minister Dmitry Medvedev, standing on the other side of Prime Minister Nguyen, didn't even bother crossing his arms. He simply extended his right hand to the person to his right, his left hand to the person on his left.

He had only so much patience for such theatrics.

In most multilateral situations, the attendees would try to take advantage of the group gathering to hold side meetings of various organizations.

So, while all diplomats might attend a plenary session of an ASEAN meeting, a faction of them might also break off and convene a meeting of the Lower Mekong Initiative. They might even meet as a sub-subgroup of that, convening a session of the Friends of the Lower Mekong Initiative.

This reshuffling might be almost indecipherable if not for another hallmark of ASEAN meetings: enormous backdrops that label the group assembled. In July 2013 in Bandar Seri Begawan, Brunei, I took a photograph of Secretary Kerry standing in front of one such banner. It read, "Press Conference, 46th ASEAN Foreign Ministers' Meeting, Post-Ministerial Conferences, 20th ASEAN Regional Forum, and 3rd East Asia Summit Foreign Ministers' Meeting." It read like a flow chart, running from the full meeting to the regional meeting to the subregional meeting.

The final unique facet of ASEAN meetings was their gala group dinners. They typically were held in a massive convention center, with a long table for the guests of honor and smaller tables around it for other invitees and staff. There'd also be a stage for elaborate song-and-dance shows highlighting the host country's culture and entertainment stars.

The trappings hinted at how important these dinners were for the hosts, making it imperative that John Kerry adhere to another of their traditions: wearing a shirt indigenous to the host country or region.

In China, these could be Mandarin shirts. In Thailand, the shirts would be made of silk. In Southeast Asian nations such as Indonesia, everyone would dress up in a batik shirt.

It was always a production to ensure Kerry had a shirt that both fit the occasion and fit him.

At six-foot-four and with long arms, it wasn't always a sure thing.

We'd send off his measurements in advance, have the shirt delivered upon arrival to ensure it fit, and then carry it in a garment bag to the convention hall so he could slip into a side room to put it on before the dinner.

He'd typically emerge to much fanfare and peals of staff laughter, once sashaying as if walking on a runway, another time doing a little dance-step jig.

I memorialized each occasion by taking a "silly-shirt" photo of the secretary with the succession of Navy admirals who accompanied us on our trips for the Joint Chiefs. They'd sport big grins as Kerry stood in his special shirt and Admirals Harry Harris, Kurt Tidd, or Frank Pandolfe wore their dress uniforms.

―――――

WE DIDN'T JUST ATTEND multilats in Asia.

The most famous series of them occurred across Europe, during the Iran nuclear negotiations.

The secretary usually began a multilateral visit by paying a courtesy call on the people hosting the meeting, whether it be the foreign minister of Switzerland or Austria, the president of the European Union, or the United Nations secretary-general.

When he got to the multilat itself, he might join in a family photo or more informal camera spray with a scrum of photographers from each of the participating countries. Then he'd get down to business with the meeting participants.

Because so many people were in one place, each country was limited in the number of people it could have in the meeting room itself. Typically, a foreign minister and his deputy would be seated at the meeting table, with two or three of the most important or relevant staffers in chairs directly behind them.

Those not making the cut might be ticketed for a listening room, where audio and/or video of the meeting was broadcast for staff who needed to hear the conversation in real time but couldn't be in the actual meeting.

The rest of us would wait in what were known as hold rooms.

As a reporter for nearly three decades, I prided myself on my work ethic. I put in long days, worked nights and weekends routinely, and never went anywhere without my workbag. It was always packed with a laptop, all the cables and hardware I needed to file a story, plus my passport. There was never any impediment to me traveling anytime, anywhere, for whatever story might arise.

For those reasons, it was a huge adjustment when I became a government staffer and had to learn how to waste the prodigious amounts of idle time we spent waiting for the secretary to emerge from his meetings.

One colleague, speechwriter Andrew Imbrie, did the smart thing: he read virtually every minute he wasn't busy drafting the secretary's next set of remarks. Over four years, he could have earned a master's in literature, but he did it one better: he finished off his PhD.

Others had an innate ability to fall asleep no matter the time or place. In truth, sleep often came easy to the jet-lagged.

I'd often spend most of the time editing and filing the photos I just snapped, using my journalism training to speed this chronicle of the secretary's activities back to the State Department. The staff there would post the images on various social media platforms.

Nonetheless, there were still many hours when I'd be left staring at my shoes. I felt I didn't have the solitude or clear conscience to read, since my duties as traveling photographer meant I always had to be ready for a parting photo. Since no one was ever sure when a meeting would end, I was never sure when I'd get the call.

If I didn't look down at my shoes, often I'd look up at what my colleague Steve Krupin and I came to affectionately call "Ridiculous Hold Rooms."

I underwent my State Department indoctrination with Krupin, who'd worked for President Obama's reelection campaign in 2012 before coming over to Foggy Bottom to be John Kerry's original chief speechwriter. We met at the Harry S Truman Building in late January 2013, when we both arrived for our security briefing prior to our swearing-in.

The Diplomatic Security Service had a briefer who was right out of a James Bond movie, referred to by the first initial of his first name, followed by his full last name.

"H. Wallen" spent several hours running over the procedures used at State and the mandatory training we were to receive before he made us sign a series of forms acknowledging our need to keep state secrets and the federal penalties we faced if we broke our agreements.

When Krupin and I walked out of Main State afterward, we looked at each other silently for a moment before simultaneously saying, "Holy shit."

The gravity of what we were about to begin hit us at that moment.

We came up with the term "Ridiculous Hold Rooms" not long after the first day of business during our first trip abroad, when we accompanied Secretary Kerry to No. 10 Downing Street in London so he could meet with British prime minister David Cameron.

We first walked through the iconic glossy black door on the front of No. 10, the home and office of the United Kingdom's leader. Then we were asked to wait in a second-floor library, which we were told was Margaret Thatcher's favorite room while she served as "PM."

That was evident when we looked up and saw the Iron Lady's formal government portrait hanging over the fireplace.

It was February 25, 2013, and we were not even a month into our new jobs. The house staff served us warm pastries and tea in china emblazoned with the crest of Queen Elizabeth II. The caged bookcases ringing the room contained volumes of Burke's Peerage and a collection of books entitled *Parliamentary Debates: Commons*.

When we looked out the window, we saw the prime minister's private backyard, outfitted with his children's swing set. And just outside the hold room's door was No. 10's bright yellow winding staircase, lined with signed black-and-white photos of prime ministers, including Winston Churchill.

Krupin and I looked at each other and could only laugh in disbelief at our good fortune.

During ensuing stops in oil-rich Saudi Arabia, the United Arab Emirates, and Qatar, we looked around—jaws agape—while waiting in rooms with elaborate marble floors, forty-foot ceilings, and gold leaf furniture.

They were, quite simply, ridiculous. Thus, their label.

As we waited in one or another Ridiculous Hold Room, the secretary would be at work in a meeting room. In multilateral gatherings, efficiency was not always the norm.

The host or Kerry would often make opening remarks, and then others at the table would join in the conversation. That meant patiently going from person to person, so everyone could have their say.

While everyone was supposed to adhere to a time limit, it was rarely enforced. And if the topic of conversation was particularly sensitive, everyone might get a second chance to speak.

The challenge for the multilat was to build consensus, so all the talking actually produced a resolution.

The secretary was this consensus builder not only during the Iran nuclear negotiations but also during his multiparty talks in Afghanistan. He also was as he built a sixty-plus nation counter-ISIS coalition, and multinational support for the Paris climate change and Kigali HFC agreements. In addition, he had the vision to tap and work with Special Envoy Bernard Aronson to broker a long-awaited peace settlement between the Colombian government and the country's notoriously fractious FARC rebel group.

John Kerry was often indispensable—a label a prominent foreign minister once attached to him—because he had the patience to let myriad people vent their frustrations and the prestige to coax them, sometimes one by one, into an agreement.

Bilaterally or multilaterally, he was the linchpin to US diplomatic engagement for four years.

5

ISRAEL

ONE OF THE MOST common questions people asked about my four years working for the State Department was "How many frequent-flier miles did you earn?"

Zero.

While I worked for the most-traveled secretary in history and racked up about 1.35 million miles myself flying with him, all were on government aircraft.

The US Air Force doesn't award miles or have a frequent-flier program. If it did, I'd have been a Titanium member.

The rare chance to earn miles came when I flew home from overseas on a commercial airline. That happened a handful of times when my father was sick or when I wanted to attend a family event.

Another time came in March 2013, when we got late word the C-32 we were supposed to fly on to Israel had broken down. The only plane available for Secretary Kerry was a C-37, the Air Force version of Gulfstream V business jet.

Taking the smaller plane forced sharp cuts in the passenger manifest, leaving some of us scrambling for commercial flights.

Jason Meininger, the secretary's senior aide and probably second only to me in terms of staff miles traveled, told me the news in a State Department hallway. We rushed to the luggage-drop area, reclaimed bags that had been headed to Andrews Air Force Base, and caught a cab to Dulles International Airport in suburban Virginia.

When we got to the ticket counter, we learned we'd been assigned business class seats for a Lufthansa flight connecting to Tel Aviv through Frankfurt.

State Department employees have to fly coach unless a trip exceeds fourteen hours and the employee has to report to work upon landing. That's a very high bar to clear, since so few trips around the world are that long. We chuckled later when we learned the European Union allowed its employees to fly business class on flights exceeding four hours.

That's pretty much any place outside continental Europe.

On this particular day, Meininger and I apparently made the cut because of the last-minute booking, the length of our overnight flight to Israel, and the necessity to work when we arrived.

Little did we know having that sleeper seat on a Boeing 747 would be the most comfortable part of what turned out to be a year-plus of dealings with leaders in the Jewish homeland.

John Kerry's engagement in the Middle East peace process was grueling and exasperating, thanks to obstacle after obstacle raised by Israeli leaders, and frustration prompting Palestinian leaders to balk at serious talks about a deal.

It consumed much of our first year at the State Department. It also was the focus of the secretary's last major policy speech before he wrapped up his tenure in 2017.

Middle East peace wasn't the Great White Whale of our diplomatic efforts, because we set our sights on many other achievements after our initial attempts at reaching a settlement, but it remained an elusive target throughout our time in the government.

"In the end, I believe the negotiations did not fail because the gaps were too wide, but because the level of trust was too low," Kerry said in that last policy speech. "Both sides were concerned that any concessions would not be reciprocated and would come at too great a political cost. And the deep public skepticism only made it more difficult for them to be able to take risks."[123]

————

WE SCRAMBLED FOR THAT commercial flight in March 2013 because we had to join Barack Obama on his first visit to Israel as president. He'd been criticized by some Israelis and American Jews for not making the trip during his first four years in office, but the Israeli government was partly to blame for the lingering angst.

Feelings were raw because many in the Obama Administration felt Israeli prime minister Benjamin "Bibi" Netanyahu supported Mitt Romney when the Republican challenged the Democratic president for reelection in 2012. The prime minister's hawkish foreign policy was more attuned to Republican politics.

When I covered Mitt Romney while he served as governor of Massachusetts from 2003 to 2007, he told us several times about how he began his fabulously successful business career working at the Boston Consulting Group alongside another upstart, Bibi Netanyahu.[124]

Despite that personal and political backdrop, Prime Minister Netanyahu was smiling when President Obama stepped off Air Force One in Tel Aviv about noon on March 20, 2013. He conveyed a sense of camaraderie by mimicking his guest after the president took off his suit jacket and draped it over his shoulder.

Prime Minister Netanyahu matched him as the two walked across the tarmac at Ben Gurion Airport to inspect an Iron Dome missile defense system.

Later, during a joint news conference, the prime minister noted the two had met ten times while holding their respective offices. "I want to thank you for the investment you have made in our relationship and in strengthening the friendship and alliance between our two countries," Netanyahu said to the president. "It is deeply, deeply appreciated."[125]

Both the president and prime minister reiterated their shared commitment to resuming peace talks between the Israelis and Palestinians. They'd been the subject of much effort by American presidents almost since Israel's founding in 1948, when the United States became the first nation to recognize Israel— eleven minutes into its existence.[126]

"Israel remains fully committed to peace and to the solution of two states for two peoples. We extend our hand in peace and in friendship to the Palestinian people," the prime minister said.

Looking at the president, he added: "I hope that your visit, along with the visit of Secretary of State Kerry, will help us turn a page in our relations with the Palestinians. Let us sit down at the negotiating table. Let us put aside all preconditions. Let us work together to achieve the historic compromise that will end our conflict once and for all."

President Obama replied, "A central element of a lasting peace must be a strong and secure Jewish state, where Israel's security concerns are met, alongside a sovereign and independent Palestinian state."[127]

He withheld further comment until the following day, when he delivered a speech to the Israeli people before an audience in Jerusalem filled with young people.

"I believe that Israel is rooted not just in history and tradition but also in a simple and profound idea: the idea that people deserve to be free in a land of their own," the president said his speech. "So long as there is a United States of America, 'Ah-tem lo lah-vahd.' You are not alone."[128]

The line prompted cheers and applause from the audience.

The president also tried to make a practical case for seeking peace with the Palestinians:

> Given the frustration in the international community about this conflict, Israel needs to reverse an undertow of isolation. And given the march of technology, the only way to truly protect the Israeli people over the long term is through the absence of war, because no wall is high enough and no Iron Dome is strong enough or perfect enough to stop every enemy that is intent on doing so from inflicting harm.[129]

Wading into more sensitive territory, he added: "The Palestinian people's right to self-determination, their right to justice must also be recognized. And put yourself in their shoes: Just as Israelis built a state in their homeland, Palestinians have a right to be a free people in their own land."[130]

The rest of the president's visit, including his trip to the Palestinian Authority headquarters in Ramallah and the Church of the Nativity in Bethlehem, a basilica built over a cave thought to be where Jesus was born, went off without a problem.

He flew on for meetings in Amman, Jordan, before making a tourist stop to see the pink cliffs and sandstone tombs and temples at the ancient city of Petra.

Secretary Kerry was waiting for President Obama at the airport in Amman when his helicopter returned from Jordan's southwestern desert. Kerry was joined by a jeans-clad Jordanian king Abdullah II. The president spoke with both men, and had an aside with the secretary before climbing the steps to Air Force One to fly back to Washington.

The planeside exchange—coming during just our second trip abroad—represented an informal handoff between the president and his top cabinet officer. Responsibility for the Middle East peace process was being transferred from the White House to the State Department.

With the full backing of President Obama, John Kerry had his shot at a set of issues that had frustrated previous presidents and secretaries of State.

He wasted no time getting down to work. Kerry left the airport even before the president took off and drove across Amman to meet with Palestinian Authority president Mahmoud Abbas.

The pace was emblematic of fourteen months of intense diplomatic efforts that would take us to Israel nine times, the West Bank eight times, and for meetings with Prime Minister Netanyahu and President Abbas in the United States, France, Belgium, Germany, Switzerland, Italy, and—secretly—King Abdullah's walled vacation home overlooking the Red Sea in Aqaba, Jordan.

———

JOHN KERRY WASN'T THE first secretary of State to attempt to negotiate peace between the Israelis and Palestinians. His effort wasn't even the first—or second—during the Obama administration: President Obama made an attempt at the outset of his first term, bringing the two parties together at the White House in September 2010 for direct negotiations, but they imploded three months later.

They couldn't be revived during a second attempt in May 2011.

More famously, Secretary of State James A. Baker III made eight trips to the region from March to October 1991 as he took his own stab at brokering peace on behalf of then president George H. W. Bush.

By 2013, the White House was willing to take another shot because both the president and prime minister had been recently reelected. President Obama had no more election campaigns and could take a second-term political risk. The prime minister, meanwhile, was seen as having the political strength and smarts to win approval for a deal not only within the full Knesset but with the fellow conservatives in his governing coalition.

Two politicians had the cover to make a deal. The question was whether both had the incentive.

The standoff between the Israelis and Palestinians is rooted in history, some of it the most ancient and emotional in the world's own story.

Many Jews trace the beginning of their nation to the kingdoms of David and Solomon, in the biblical times of 950 BC. In the late nineteenth century, Austrian Jewish journalist Theodor Herzl popularized Jewish nationalism and the belief that Jews persecuted in Europe should emigrate southeast to what was then British-controlled Palestine.[131]

Arabs who already lived in the area saw the immigration as a form of colonialism, and they fought with the arriving Jews. When the Brits couldn't stop the fighting, the United Nations voted in 1947 to split the area into Jewish and Arab/Palestinian zones. The two roughly coincided with today's maps showing the West Bank—between Israel and Jordan—and the Gaza Strip—a notch of southwestern land along the Mediterranean Sea extending to the Sinai Peninsula in Egypt.[132]

Egypt, Jordan, Iraq, and Syria—all Arab nations surrounding Israel—opposed the vote, perceiving it as a method for driving Palestinians from their rightful land. They ended up fighting a war that Israel won in 1948, prompting it to declare its independence.

While the UN partition had promised Jews 56 percent of British Palestine, they ended up holding 77 percent. They also gained their own state, while the Palestinians were split between the West Bank, controlled by Jordan, and the Gaza Strip, controlled by Egypt.[133]

The 1948 war also uprooted 700,000 Palestinians, creating a refugee crisis continuing today. Now some 7 million people can claim refugee status, either having been left homeless themselves or by being descendants of the displaced.[134]

The disparity was exacerbated in 1967 when Israel, Egypt, Syria, and Jordan engaged in the Six-Day War. In less than a week, the Israelis beat the Arab nations and took possession of the West Bank and East Jerusalem from Jordan, and the Gaza Strip and Sinai Peninsula from Egypt.[135]

Kerry and his predecessors tried to resolve the dispute arising from Israel's occupation of that added territory, its practice of allowing Jews to build settlements spreading Israeli influence in an area the Palestinians claim, and the Palestinians' sporadic calls for a violent response.

In many ways, this particular secretary had the street credit to play matchmaker. During almost three decades in the US Senate, Kerry compiled a nearly 100 percent pro-Israel voting record. He also had visited Israel many times, and regularly expressed his appreciation for a country wedged into a tight space surrounded by real or potential adversaries.

He often recalled his first trip to Israel in 1986 with Anti-Defamation League New England director Leonard Zakim. The group climbed to the summit of Masada and waited for the echo after yelling out, "Am Yisrael Chai!"—"the people of Israel live!"

He talked about visiting Sderot and seeing the remains of Katousha rockets fired at Israeli children. And he told the story of once skipping out of an official lunch to hop in a jet trainer with an Israeli Air Force flying ace who let the then senator (and pilot) take the controls.

The joy ride turned serious when the Israeli delivered a stern message over the intercom.

"Senator, you are about to go over Egypt. Turn," the secretary remembered in a June 2013 speech to the American Jewish Committee Global Forum.

That prompted him to quip: "I saw the sky below me—above me and the Earth below, and it was really weird. And I thought to myself, 'Wow, finally I am seeing the Middle East clearly: upside down.'"[136]

The story always prompted laughter and knowing nods from his audience.

On a more personal level, the secretary noted his brother, Cam, had married a Jewish woman and converted to the faith three decades earlier. He himself had learned during the 2004 presidential campaign their family had Jewish roots and lost members in the Holocaust.

All that prompted Kerry to repeatedly declare "I take a back seat to no one" when it comes to defending Israel or its right to exist.

From the Palestinian perspective, Kerry could be seen as an honest broker not only because he urged Israel to make peace, but because he did so with empathy for the Palestinian Authority's position.

"We must recognize the Palestinians' fundamental aspirations—to live in peace in their own state with its own clear borders—that has to be our mission as well," the secretary said in that speech to the American Jewish Congress. "Palestinians also deserve to see their daily lives grow and the benefits of economic growth and development."[137]

He added:

> Whenever you think about this challenge and how hard it is, think about what will happen if it doesn't work. We will find ourselves in a negative spiral of responses and counter-responses that could literally slam the door on a two-state solution, having already agreed, I think, that there isn't a one-state one. And the insidious campaign to de-legitimize Israel will only gain steam.
>
> Israel will be left to choose between being a Jewish state or a democratic state, but it will not be able to fulfill the founders' visions of being both at once.[138]

Kerry argued the Israelis risked living in "permanent conflict" with the Palestinians, confronted first with civil disobedience, next with a civil rights movement, and then the possibility of a third Intifada—a Palestinian uprising—and Palestinian factions committed to violence.

The Israelis were especially concerned the Palestinians would go to the United Nations and seek to join more UN organizations. A Palestinian Authority legitimized at the UN could claim territorial rights, sue for them in the International Court of Justice, and accuse Israel within the International Criminal Court of war crimes stemming from its occupation.[139]

To the advantage of both sides, the secretary also was willing to risk his personal and political capital to reach an agreement. Even before beginning his service as secretary of State, he labeled the Israel-Palestinian dispute as one of the "frozen conflicts" worth resolving.

He included the similarly long-running and draining disputes between Greece and Turkey over the disposition of Cyprus—the Mediterranean island-nation off each of their coasts—and the two-decade old disagreement between Armenia and Azerbaijan over the future of Nagorno-Karabakh.

Part of that region lies in Azerbaijan but is controlled by ethnic Armenians, and the two countries fought for control over it until a cease-fire in 1994.[140]

"There are some where I think they're difficult, but you can see how you could get there if people made a certain set of decisions," the secretary said in September 2016 during remarks to The Atlantic and Aspen Institute.[141]

In addition to factors favoring one side or another, both the Palestinians and Israelis stood to benefit because John Kerry had a number of personal traits conducive to the tedium of long and complicated negotiations.

First, he had energy belying his age. He was sixty-nine when he began his term, but he still biked and kite-surfed. He also loved to take brisk walks to reinvigorate himself.

Meanwhile, he had the patience to sit for hours with both Prime Minister Netanyahu and President Abbas and hear each man's complaints. He was willing to fly to the Middle East or drive to the West Bank to hash out problems face-to-face, whether it was day, night, weekend, or holiday. And he was a copious note-taker, carefully chronicling each side's issues and then dutifully relaying them to his staff for action or to the other side for resolution.

Israeli president Shimon Peres lauded him in April 2013 when the secretary visited just before his first one-on-one meeting with Prime Minister Netanyahu after that handoff from President Obama.

"There is a new wind of peace blowing through the Middle East," said President Peres, one of Israel's remaining Founding Fathers and a former prime minister, foreign minister, and defense minister. "President Obama's re-election and his successful visit to the region. Your appointment as secretary of State, total dedication to the cause of peace, and faultless record in tackling complex international affairs. The new government formed here in Israel. All these elements have combined to create a new sense of optimism, a belief that peace is possible. And peace is possible."[142]

There were five major issues that had to be resolved in the peace talks: Israeli security, West Bank borders and Jewish settlements, control over Jerusalem, the so-called right of return for Palestinians wanting to come back to the land they lost in 1947 and 1968, and an end to the conflict and all claims emanating from it.

Given geography, Israel had to feel it could ensure its own security. This was particularly important to the east, where the West Bank and the Jordan River Valley are located. The Israelis were concerned that if they pulled back their defense forces, they'd be subject to ground attack or provide a staging area for fresh rocket attacks.

In terms of West Bank borders, there has been widespread discussion over the years about Israel pulling back to the boundaries existing before the Six-Day War in 1967. The challenge is that since then, about 500,000 Jews have moved into lands that would have been considered part of Palestine.[143] That raises the challenging question of how to remove these settlers or arrange land swaps, letting them remain but providing replacement territory to the Palestinians.

In a similar vein, Jerusalem had been divided before 1967, but Israel seized Jordanian-controlled East Jerusalem during the Six-Day War. That area includes some of the holiest sites in Judaism, Christianity, and Islam, including the Western Wall, the Dome of the Rock, and the al-Aqsa Mosque. The question today is what to do with the large number of Jews who've moved into that area, as well as how to guarantee access for all sides to their respective religious sites.

Finally, "right of return" goes to the heart of Israel's future. An estimated 7 million Palestinians—many living in the West Bank—could move if they were allowed to occupy the homes they or their ancestors formally owned.

The challenge there is that the total population of Israel is only 8 million, including 1.5 million Arabs already living in the country.[144] Allowing a large influx of Palestinians into the State of Israel would leave Jews as a minority within their own country, which the Israelis won't tolerate.

That problem has always propelled talk of a so-called two-state solution: one area for Israelis, another for Palestinians. The Israelis wouldn't want to be subordinate to Palestinians in what they consider their homeland, and the Palestinians wouldn't want to live in an Israel where they didn't have equal rights.

For that reason, Kerry and others said without reaching a deal for two states, Israelis would have to choose between living in a homeland that was Jewish or one that was a democracy. Jews couldn't give equal voting and residency rights to the Palestinians who outnumbered them without surrendering control of their state.

The alternative of a separate Palestinian state prompted talk about compensation for those who wouldn't be allowed to return to their ancestral homes and the Palestinians who'd have to be resettled from Israeli territory.

From virtually his first meetings to his last, Kerry reiterated that the issues were clear. What was needed, he argued, was the will from both sides to resolve them once and for all.

During his speech to the American Jewish Congress, after barely three months of talks, he broached the question many were already asking: "What makes this different from every other time?"

Then the secretary answered himself.

"If we do not succeed now, we may not get another chance," he said.

The secretary believed continued Israeli settlement construction, in particular, could make a contiguous Palestine not just impractical but impossible.

"We can't let the disappointments of the past hold the future prisoner. We can't let the absence of peace become a self-fulfilling prophecy. The absence of peace is perpetual conflict," he said.[145]

Despite the clarity of issues and the simplicity of his argument, Secretary Kerry found himself embarked on an elusive quest.

"Were you ever scared?"

The answer to that question, asked of me by a number of people, is yes, a couple of times.

While we were always well protected, we still felt nervous heading into war zones, such as when John Kerry became the first secretary of State to visit Somalia.

The thing is, we had our guard up there. More surprising were the times we didn't expect trouble.

Once, we were in Addis Ababa, Ethiopia, when I had to head back to our hotel early from the African Union Commission headquarters.

A locally employed staffer from Embassy Addis Ababa drove me and speechwriter Steve Krupin; but since we weren't with Secretary Kerry in the official motorcade, we had to fight through the usual city traffic.

We were fine for a while as the driver took a series of backstreets, but then we turned a corner and came to a dead stop on a road crammed with cars and people.

(Top) Secretary Kerry listens before delivering remarks at Gandhi Memorial Hospital, Addis Ababa, Ethiopia, on May 1, 2014.

Ethiopia is a beautiful, peaceful country, and its people are some of the kindest I met not only in Africa but also back in the United States. But the country and its capital city are also relatively poor, especially those who surrounded us in that traffic jam.

Sitting with valuable camera and computer gear on my lap, I was anxious because we didn't have a clear way out if someone made a grab for it. Police on the streets were carrying AK-47s and large canes. So I asked the driver to take a right, regardless of where it led.

He reluctantly agreed, but soon we hit another road filled with traffic and people. I told him to go right again, just to head in a direction where we wouldn't be surrounded and incapable of moving.

My concerns quickly dissipated after he made a few quick turns and emerged on the road leading to our hotel.

The second time I was fearful also was in Africa, but not because I was concerned about my well-being. I was worried about the people around us.

We were heading into Abuja, Nigeria, to attend the inauguration of newly elected President Muhammadu Buhari when a crowd lining the road began to squeeze in from the shoulders as we came upon a viaduct.

A crowd begins to surround our motorcade en route to the inauguration ceremony for Nigerian president Muhammadu Buhari in Abuja, Nigeria, on May 29, 2015.

I knew our drivers weren't going to stop for anything—that's Security 101—but the stakes ratcheted up exponentially as enthusiastic people surrounded the cars to cheer Secretary Kerry.

A couple splashed the windshield with water from their water bottles, but then one man jumped on the hood of the spare limousine. If he slipped forward, we'd run right over him.

For a few gut-wrenching moments, things hung in suspended animation. Then he was able to roll to the side and off one of the front fenders.

We forged ahead with everyone unscathed.

WE TRAVELED TO ISRAEL so frequently our trips had a familiar routine. As Kerry told his assistant secretaries during a meeting in January 2014, "There's a certain *Groundhog Day* aspect to my visits."[146]

We'd depart from the United States in the evening and refuel in the middle of the night in Shannon, Ireland. We'd then fly on to Tel Aviv. Our plane would make a long taxi across Ben Gurion Airport and pull to a stop under heavy security.

When the secretary stepped off, he'd be greeted by an Israeli Protocol official and US ambassador to Israel Dan Shapiro. The rest of the receiving line usually included members of his negotiating team and other Israeli officials.

There also was the team from the US embassy in Tel Aviv. One, a former Israeli soldier, would take photos for the embassy website. His partner would shoot video. Another staffer would help handle the traveling press corps. And a rotating cast of State Department employees posted to Tel Aviv from the United States would spread throughout the motorcade, making sure everyone got to the right place in time.

While the Israeli nationals were as loyal to the United States cause as the American staffers, in Israel, there is a melding of national and vocational pride. I'd laugh when the US embassy photographer—that former Israeli soldier—would shout instructions to the Israeli prime minister about where to stand for a photo. I also chuckled when the prime minister would invite the photographer to take a photo at what was supposed to be a closed meeting with Secretary Kerry. It also wasn't uncommon to see our press handlers who were Israeli sharing drinks or a meal with the Israeli government Protocol folks after a long day.

Of course such bonding is good professional etiquette, but the Israelis—on either side of the negotiation—shared a communal and nationalistic bond transcending any differences between their own government and the United States.

We'd travel in armored passenger vans from Tel Aviv along Highway 1, through the Ayalon Valley mountain pass, to Jerusalem. Along the way, we'd pass old rusted military vehicles left in place to remind passersby of the armored convoys that tried to bring supplies to Jerusalem during the 1948 War of Independence.[147]

Our first stop usually was the David Citadel Hotel, which became our home away from home. Just down the street from the more famous King David Hotel, the David Citadel offered more modern amenities and an equally commanding view of Jerusalem's Old City.

The secretary stayed each time in a suite named for Yitzhak Rabin, the Israeli prime minister assassinated in 1995 at the end of a rally supporting the Oslo Accords. That 1993 treaty marked the start of peace negotiations between the Israelis and the Palestinians.

Prime Minister Rabin's assassin was an ultranationalist opposed to his efforts in general and the Oslo Accords in particular.[148]

The irony was never lost on anyone, especially as the secretary would meet with Prime Minister Netanyahu in a room filled with portraits and busts of his predecessor.

The secretary's suite had a large balcony with a wide-angle view of the Old City, and he and Netanyahu would often sit one-on-one at a table on the deck so the prime minister could smoke his favored Partagás No. 2 Cuban cigars.

The rest of the US staff stayed in rooms on either side of the hallway leading to the secretary's suite. The Israelis provided heavy security for the remainder of the floor.

Given the conservative nature of Jerusalem, the hotel kept a kosher kitchen, meaning it didn't serve shellfish and didn't mix meat and dairy products. For its American visitors, that meant no cheeseburgers on the room-service menu. Instead, we developed an appreciation for eggs and pasta, plus a variety of salads, chopped raw vegetables, and Mediterranean mezze.

When it was time to leave for a meeting, everyone would head down to the basement to load the vehicles. The van tires squealed as the motorcade circled up the traffic ramp. Once it reached surface level, we'd race through the city, passing traffic and people held at the side of the road by accompanying police officers.

When we got to the prime minister's office, the secretary's limousine would peel off from the rest of the group and pull into a portico immediately sealed off from public view by sliding tarps. He'd exit once the coast was clear, be greeted by Edna Halbani, the director of international visits and longtime handler to a series of prime ministers, and then climb a set of steps to the second floor.

There Bibi Netanyahu would greet him in front of a bank of cameras.

Going to visit the Palestinians in Ramallah was slightly different. Because the Israeli nationals who drove us from the airport or around the city weren't permitted to visit the West Bank, we'd have to take a completely different set of vans—with American security contractors behind the wheel—when we left the David Citadel to meet with Palestinian leaders.

Israeli police would lead our motorcade up Highway 45 to a checkpoint around the corner from the imposing Ofer Prison, before pulling to the side of the road as the motorcade wended its way through a serpentine arrangement of Jersey barriers slowing movement over the border from Israel to the West Bank.

On the other side of the checkpoint, Palestinian police and soldiers would pull into the lead and tail positions, assuming responsibility for the motorcade. They'd escort us through the dusty and pockmarked streets of Ramallah to the compound where the Palestinian National Authority is headquartered.

We knew we had arrived when we drove through the gates and saw a large portrait of the late Yasser Arafat. The Palestinian Liberation Organization chairman and PNA president had been known worldwide for his trademark checked keffiyeh headdress.

Arafat is now entombed in a glass mausoleum in the compound, which a group of us once visited. We'd also pass the hallway to Arafat's former residence when we went to our staff hold room on the compound.

When it came time to sit down and talk with either side, Kerry was primarily assisted by two aides: Martin Indyk, a former US ambassador to Israel who was assigned the new title as "Special Envoy for Israeli–Palestinian Negotiations," and his deputy, Frank Lowenstein, a former Kerry aide in the Senate and son of the late New York civil rights activist Allard Lowenstein.

Indyk was an erudite Australian who helped lead the Brookings Institution, a Washington think tank, but took a leave to return to government service. Lowenstein was less button-down than his boss, but was steeped in the intricacies of the negotiations. He also had Kerry's complete trust, and drew from his lawyer's training as the sides negotiated language or tried to stave off future sticking points.

Prime Minister Netanyahu negotiated for hours face-to-face with Kerry, noteworthy because he was a head of state giving voluminous time not to a peer but a US cabinet official. It was a testament to the stature of the secretary of State and the United States that the prime minister did so.

For the more routine negotiating sessions, the Israeli team was led by former justice minister Tzipi Livni. Always in the background, though, was a nettlesome character: Yitzhak Molcho. As Netanyahu's personal lawyer, he was viewed as a check on Livni.

The prime minister relied on Molcho to flyspeck potential agreements with the Palestinians, often exasperating Kerry and his negotiating team.

"You can't Molcho-us to death," the secretary once screamed into a phone at the prime minister. Molcho was seeking to make just one more tweak to seemingly settled draft language.

President Abbas, meanwhile, was the titular head of the Palestinian team, but Saeb Arakat handled day-to-day negotiations. He was the chief go-between to the US delegation, the principal spokesman to the media, and a trusted aide to President Abbas.

Cagey and wary, Arakat was deeply mistrustful of the Israelis. He wasn't alone in his apprehension. Prime Minister Netanyahu and other Israelis felt the same about him.

The Israeli negotiating perspective was rooted in the state of siege the country felt from enemies on its borders and opponents who'd shoot rockets over them. The Palestinian position had a different premise.

It was rooted in the state of occupation it felt because Israelis controlled the West Bank.

Palestinians were not free to move across the border without permission. Some boundaries were defined by tall concrete blast walls built to prevent suicide bombers from crossing into Israel. Some Palestinian territory was cut in half by walled highways that only the Israelis could use.

Palestinians seeking to work in Israel were instead funneled through checkpoints, where they'd often wait in long lines. And not only did the Israelis control the amount of water, concrete, and other building materials coming into the West Bank, lest it be used for nefarious purposes, but Palestinians complained about other indignities heaped on them.

For example, a trucker seeking to bring product across the border would have to stop at an Israeli checkpoint, dump his load on the ground, and watch as Israelis sifted through it for contraband. Then he'd have to wait as the stone, sand, or other material was reloaded onto his truck.

Finally, the Israelis gave the Palestinian a bill for the inspection.

Against that backdrop, Kerry was realistic about the challenges he confronted following his first meetings with Prime Minister Netanyahu and President Abbas.

"I think all of us have learned in the course of the last years, through many presidents and many secretaries of State, there has been no more intractable problem," he told reporters on March 24, 2013, in Baghdad after his inaugural visits to Israel and the West Bank.

"Expressing optimism when you don't even have negotiations would be foolhardy. What I have is hope. I have hope that the president's words kindled a sense of the possible in the people of Israel and the region and the Palestinians," said Kerry.[149]

Hours earlier, during the flight to Iraq, he telegraphed this feeling to his staff. He said he wanted to low-ball expectations and keep the talks low-key and out of public sight, since a public process would put pressure on both sides.

"I believe we will get a negotiation," the secretary told us. "I can't tell you what the outcome will be. I, personally, believe there is a solution, but that is going to depend on the decisions made by others. I'm not afraid of trying. If we don't make an effort, it would be diplomatic malpractice."[150]

It was a sentiment he'd express every time the talks hit a pothole.

———

SECRETARY KERRY'S FIRST TACK in the negotiations was aggressive. He aimed to get the Israelis and Palestinians to reach a signed agreement on all the core issues dividing them, including guarantees for Israeli security, borders and land swaps for both sides, and the right of return for Palestinians.

The High Dive.

That goal eluded him for about six months, so he shifted his aim. He sought a "framework" agreement under which the two sides committed to general solutions for the core issues.

The Half Gainer.

When the Israelis and Palestinians couldn't agree even to that, Kerry changed once again. He spent his remaining months trying to get both sides to extend the talks through 2014.

President Obama personally intervened with the Israelis and Palestinians in February 2014, but even that modest goal proved unachievable.

The secretary's peace effort ended, for all intents and purposes, on April 29, 2014, when the two sides passed the deadline for reaching an extension without an agreement.

The Belly Flop.

From the outset, Kerry identified the Israelis' biggest issue: security.

"If we can get basic security—not crazy—we can get this done," he told us in April 2013, following a meeting in Jerusalem with Prime Minister Netanyahu. "I got to get a team to get really serious about it."[151]

The secretary and his negotiators settled on an idea to achieve that. They approached John Allen, a newly retired four-star Marine general and former head of US forces in Afghanistan, and asked if he'd head an effort to guarantee Israel's security. In an added bit of service to his country, Allen agreed to rejoin the government and assume the job.

Likewise, the secretary worked to convince the Palestinians they stood to benefit from the talks.

First, he and Vice President Biden convened a meeting on April 29, 2013, at Blair House for members of the Arab League, the principal organizing group for twenty-two Arab members in the Middle East, including the Palestinians.

The two US officials got the Arab leaders to agree to a subtle but substantive shift: while saying they wanted the Israelis to withdraw to their territory before the June 1967 war, they could accept "comparable," mutually agreed, and "minor" land swaps with the Palestinians.[152]

That not only signaled pan-Arabic support for a potential Palestinian concession, but also the breadth of gain the Israelis could achieve should they reach an agreement with the Authority.

"The Arab League delegation expresses its thanks and for the President Obama and for yourself, Mr. Secretary, for your efforts and your commitment for the peace, and also endorses President Mahmoud Abbas' effort for the peace," said Qatari prime minister Sheik Hamad bin Jassim bin Jabr Al Thani, who spoke for the group.[153]

Second, the secretary tried to show the Palestinians the economic benefits they stood to reap from reaching a peace settlement with the Israelis.

He spent time during the first months of the negotiations working with former British prime minister Tony Blair and a personal friend, billionaire investor Tim Collins, arranging a $4 billion proposal for West Bank economic development they said would cut the unemployment rate—then 21 percent—by nearly two-thirds.

The secretary outlined the plan in May 2013 during a speech at a World Economic Forum meeting held at a Dead Sea resort in Jordan. Shimon Peres, the Israeli president, and Mahmoud Abbas, the Palestinian president, sat side by side in the front row as the secretary spoke.

"I just ask you to imagine the benefits from a new, open market next door, a new wave of foreign investment that could flow into both Israel and Palestine—and Jordan, and all of them share it," Kerry said. "The effect that could echo throughout the region, and if we prove that this can work here, that can become a model for what can work in other places that are facing similar confrontations."[154]

He highlighted the benefits from tourism alone if the region were freed from the specter of violence.

"Imagine a welcoming part of the world that boasts the Church of the Nativity in Bethlehem, the site of the Tomb of the Patriarchs and the Ibrahimi Mosque in Hebron, the Western Wall, the Dome of the Rock in Jerusalem, and more of the world's other great sites that have drawn tourists and religious pilgrims for centuries," he said.[155]

Nonetheless, Kerry also gave the first public hints he was encountering difficulties.

"Negotiations can't succeed if you don't negotiate," he said, without calling out either side. "We are reaching a critical point where tough decisions have to be made. And I just ask all of you to keep your eyes focused on what can really be done here."[156]

Before achieving any of that, however, the secretary had to reach an even more fundamental accord. He had to get the two sides to simply agree on a formal negotiation. That meant he spent from April 2013 to July 2013 negotiating just to begin direct negotiations.

That challenge reminded me of his comment about doing acrobatics in that Israeli fighter jet: "I saw the sky below me—above me and the Earth below, and it was really weird. And I thought to myself, 'Wow, finally I am seeing the Middle East clearly: upside down.'"

The secretary hoped to achieve this goal through a controversial confidence-building mechanism. In June 2013, he asked the Israelis to agree to release a group of Palestinians imprisoned before the Oslo Accords. In exchange, he asked the Palestinians to forgo seeking any further membership in UN organizations.

This facet of the negotiations peaked about a month later.

In July 2013, President Abbas called a meeting with senior Palestinian leaders and asked for their approval to resume negotiations with Israel. They initially balked, so Saeb Arakat and another negotiator, Palestinian intelligence chief Majid Faraj, suggested President Abbas shift his demand.

They said that instead of promising to forgo the UN memberships, the Palestinians would directly agree to negotiations with Israel if it agreed to release 104 pre-Oslo Palestinian prisoners.

President Abbas also asked the secretary to give him a letter declaring any talks between the two parties would be based on the prewar 1967 borders between Israel and the Palestinian territories.

The following day, Secretary Kerry relayed the offer to Prime Minister Netanyahu. The prime minister, leading a volatile governing coalition, was nervous about the prospect of releasing prisoners—in some cases convicted murderers—for nothing more from the Palestinians than the promise to return to the negotiating table.

He later called back the secretary and said he'd accept the offer, but with two major conditions. First, he wouldn't release the prisoners all at once, but in four groups of twenty-six. He wanted to space them out to prevent President Abbas from winning the prisoners' release and then quitting the talks once they were home in the West Bank.

Second, the prime minister told Kerry his government would have to approve some new housing settlements—roughly two thousand in total—to preserve his governing coalition. The United States was officially opposed to further settlement activity—a position the secretary reiterated was unchanged. Ever the politician, though, Kerry said he understood the pressures Prime Minister Netanyahu faced.

After hanging up with the prime minister and speaking with President Obama, the secretary delivered a statement to reporters assembled at the airport in Amman. Despite the considerable time he had devoted to the talks, including a helicopter flight just hours earlier between Amman and Ramallah for one final consultation with President Abbas, he was anxious to fly home to Massachusetts to visit his wife. She'd been hospitalized two weeks earlier after suffering a seizure.

"I am pleased to announce that we have reached an agreement that establishes a basis for resuming direct final status negotiations between the Palestinians and the Israelis," the secretary said, declaring it "a significant and welcome step forward."

He added: "The agreement is still in the process of being formalized, so we are absolutely not going to talk about any of the elements now. . . . The parties have agreed that I will be the only one making further comments about this. If everything goes as expected, Saeb Arakat and Tzipi Livni, Minister Livni, and Yitzhak Molcho will be joining me in Washington to begin initial talks within the next week or so, and a further announcement will be made by all of us at that time."[157]

Even with Secretary Kerry's caveats and cautious wording, his announcement surprised many of the Palestinian leaders Abbas had met with the prior evening.

Some said the secretary also misunderstood key details of the prime minister's two conditions, although one negotiator said the two had engaged in a bit of "constructive ambiguity."[158]

First, while Prime Minister Netanyahu outlined the need to announce two thousand more housing units in the West Bank, he never committed that would be it forever.

More important, at least from the perspective of propelling the future talks, the prime minister had committed to releasing only 80 of the 104 prisoners. The final group—which included Israeli Arabs coveted by the Palestinians—would be released only after a separate future vote of the Israeli Cabinet, since those prisoners would have the right to remain in Israel because of their citizenship.

That erected another, higher hurdle for them to clear before their freedom.

———

PRIME MINISTER NETANYAHU SHOWED his political skill and clout by winning the Israeli Cabinet's approval for the initial prisoner releases on July 28, 2013. The twenty-two members voted 13–7, with two abstentions.

The following day, Secretary Kerry sent President Abbas the letter he requested.

"In response to your question regarding our position on the issue of borders, this letter is to confirm that the position set forth by President Obama in his May 2011 speeches, that Palestine's borders with Israel should be based on the 1967 lines with mutually agreed swaps, still represents our position," it said. "As negotiations begin, I reiterate our commitment to this position. As you confirmed, this letter is and will remain private and confidential between you and me."[159]

Kerry also appeared in the State Department Briefing Room to formally announce Martin Indyk as his lead negotiator:

> Ambassador Indyk is realistic. He understands that Israeli-Palestinian peace will not come easily and it will not happen overnight. But he also understands that there is now a path forward and we must follow that path with urgency. He understands that to ensure that lives are not needlessly lost, we have to ensure that opportunities are not needlessly lost. And he shares my belief that if the leaders on both sides continue to show strong leadership and a willingness to make those tough choices and a willingness to reasonably compromise, then peace is possible.[160]

That evening, the negotiators shared an Iftar dinner, the meal eaten by Muslims after sundown during the holy month of Ramadan.

The table, quite literally, was set for the negotiations.

On July 30, 2013, the teams from Israel and the Palestinian Authority gathered in the Monroe Room on the eighth floor of the State Department and sat down across from one another for their first formal negotiating session.

I cracked open a set of sliding mahogany doors, poked in my camera lens, and snapped a photo of Livni and Molcho sitting side by side, with their backs to the Lincoln Memorial and Reflecting Pool. Arakat and his partner, Muhammed Shtayyeh, sat next to each other across from the Israelis. The four spoke alone, for several hours, until Kerry popped in to check on them.

The rawness of the Palestinians' feelings, as telegraphed by Susan Rice's exasperated comment about them "never seeing the big f—ing picture," had been telegraphed by President Abbas the day before. He said in Cairo, "In a final resolution, we would not see the presence of a single Israeli—civilian or soldier—on our lands."[161]

After the first formal negotiating session, Arakat was equally tart as he, Kerry, and Livni delivered what were supposed to be perfunctory opening comments to the media.

Arakat repeated himself and mentioned Palestinian independence three times in a six-sentence statement—the first two sentences of which had been consumed thanking the secretary and Livni for their presence.

"Palestinians have suffered enough, and no one benefits more from the success of this endeavor more than Palestinians," Arakat said. "I am delighted that all final status issues are on the table and will be resolved without any exceptions, and it's time for the Palestinian people to have an independent, sovereign state of their own. It's time for the Palestinian people to have an independent, sovereign state of their own. It's time for the Palestinians to live in peace, freedom, and dignity within their own independent, sovereign state."[162]

Livni, the former Israeli Justice minister, didn't take the bait, showing the comportment Kerry hoped would prevail amid the trials to come. Standing beside Kerry and Arakat under the Great Seal of the United States in the Ben Franklin Room, Livni sought to elevate a political transaction into something transcendent.

"I hope that our meeting today and the negotiations that we have re-launched today will cause, I hope, a spark of hope, even if small, to emerge out of cynicism and pessimism that is so often heard. It is our task to work together so that we can transform that spark of hope into something real and lasting," she said.[163]

Then, in a poetic twist, Livni added, "I believe that history is not made by cynics. It is made by realists who are not afraid to dream. And let us be these people."[164]

Afterward, the talks plodded along weekly in Israel, the West Bank, and Jordan.

Tony Blair, who'd been working on the problem as special envoy for the Quartet—the United Nations, the United States, the European Union, and Russia—once told one of our staffers that both sides "have to know that there is something remorseless and relentless about it, that the process is not going away."[165]

Nonetheless, every seeming bit of momentum was broken by intervening factors.

Before a negotiating session in Jerusalem, the two sides got into an argument when the Israelis brought along a camera crew to film their handshake.

Shtayyeh refused to participate, and then Molcho complained when Arakat suggested the handshakes be limited to just him and Livni.[166]

The first "tranche" of twenty-six prisoners was then released on August 13, 2013. But less than two weeks later, Israeli undercover forces killed three Palestinians following a raid on a Ramallah refugee camp.[167] Then three Israelis were killed in Palestinian attacks, followed by the death of four more Palestinians.

Around the same time, President Bashar al-Assad of Syria was accused of using chemical weapons against his own countrymen to quell antigovernment protests. President Obama tasked Secretary Kerry with building the case for a retaliatory military strike, shifting his attention to a more time-sensitive matter and consuming much of his diplomatic bandwidth for nearly a month.

We ultimately went to Geneva to negotiate an agreement with the Russians under which Syria rid itself of all of its chemical weapons.

Bouncing between the two subjects highlighted the type of high-stakes juggling that became routine for us.

In mid-September, after wrapping up the Syria chemical weapons negotiation in Geneva with Sergey Lavrov, the Russian foreign minister, we traveled directly from Switzerland to Israel so Kerry could reengage directly with Prime Minister Netanyahu.

A week later, the secretary spoke before the Ad Hoc Liaison Committee, a donor group for the Palestinians, during UN week in New York City. He met again with Netanyahu in Washington at the end of the month, and then he invited the Israeli leader to Villa Taverna in Rome for a stocktaking session in October 2013.

The Palestinians had been complaining intermittently about Israeli settlement activity and a lack of overall progress in the talks. They wanted the United States to be more active in the talks, not merely facilitate them.

The Israelis complained about the violence and accused the Palestinians of leaking information about the supposedly secret talks. That prompted the prime minister to tell his cabinet that Jerusalem would not be divided and Palestinians also would not have a right of return in any final settlement.[168]

Those comments left Secretary Kerry frustrated. During our daily senior staff meeting in late October 2013, he expressed his exasperation with Prime Minister Netanyahu, but said he didn't want to blow up the process.

"If he wants to fight, I will lay out what he's refused to do," the secretary told us. "The problem is, it doesn't take us anywhere."[169]

A day later, on October 29, 2013, the process got a boost when the Israelis released the second group of Palestinian prisoners.

Secretary Kerry could come off sounding either endlessly optimistic or hopelessly naive as each permutation of the negotiations went on. And as shown by the ambiguity about the terms surrounding the fourth prisoner release, sometimes he focused more on the endgame than the practical challenges to achieving it.

Nonetheless, the talks wouldn't have even started if he hadn't used his creativity and drive to reach the separate agreements for the prisoner release and the pledge not to seek UN recognition.

Then, as the two sides faltered in reaching a deal on their own, the Palestinians called for him to be more involved. Prime Minister Netanyahu was always much more circumspect, but Kerry kept seeing opportunity on the horizon.

"We're going to get a process today. We're. Going. To. Get. A. Process. Today," he told us in early November 2013, while waiting in his suite before yet another meeting with the prime minister.

Over the next month, though, the Palestinians walked out of the talks, the Israeli negotiators announced there wouldn't be a Palestinian state based on the 1967 borders, and the Israelis unveiled new settlement activity. Some members of the Israeli Knesset also began supporting a bill to annex the Jordan River Valley to block the security plan being developed by General Allen, which the secretary had recently outlined for Israeli officials.

Kerry was so confident in General Allen's security work he'd leveled a challenge to Prime Minister Netanyahu: get a group of your most experienced commandos and have them try to penetrate the system devised by Allen. If they can do it, he said, we will go back to the drawing board.[170]

The prime minister never took him up on his offer.

While the Israelis kept their word and released the third tranche of prisoners on December 30, 2013, it was clear any chance to reach a final-status agreement was over and the next best hope was the framework providing a roadmap for a future deal.

Kerry, ever optimistic, argued that achieving a framework wasn't futile because when it was signed, the Palestinians would know that Israel had agreed to their having a state and the Israelis would know the Palestinians had agreed to measures ensuring their security.

It would be easier to negotiate a final treaty of several hundred pages, he argued, if both sides were clear on the endgame.

The ultimate undoing, though, was tied to the release of that fourth and final group of Palestinian prisoners.

Secretary Kerry cut short his 2013 Christmas break and summoned us all back to Washington so we could head to Israel immediately to start the new year. We took off from Boston on New Year's Day and landed in Tel Aviv on January 2, 2014.

The secretary met in succession with the prime minister and his new foreign minister, Avigdor Liberman, as well as the negotiations skeptic, Defense Minister Moshe Ya'alon. We made several trips to Ramallah to speak with President Abbas and Saeb Arakat, and Kerry had a private dinner with Prime Minister Netanyahu at his residence in Jerusalem.

Before they began eating, I watched as the prime minister showed Kerry his personal office. They looked at his book collection and photos of his family and a picture of Bibi Netanyahu as a young soldier.

Then the prime minister took him across the room to show him a photo of his older brother, Jonathan.

He had the sad distinction of being the only Israeli soldier killed in the July 4, 1976, raid in Entebbe, Uganda, that freed 102 Israeli hostages held by two Palestinian airplane hijackers. The prime minister stood silently looking at Jonathan Netanyahu's picture as the secretary peered over his shoulder.

After getting lost in his thoughts, Prime Minister Netanyahu bit the knuckle on his right index finger, said, "Huh," and turned away, leaving Kerry behind.

It was clear the Israeli leader had not just political but personal history with the Palestinians.

On January 5, 2014, Secretary Kerry updated reporters on the talks before we flew on to Jordan and Saudi Arabia for related discussions with Arab leaders.

"This is deeply steeped in history, and each side has a narrative about their rights and their journey and the conflict itself," he said. "In the end, all of these different core issues actually fit together like a mosaic. It's a puzzle, and you can't separate out one piece or another. Because what a leader might be willing to do with respect to a compromise on one particular piece is dependent on what the other leader might be willing to do with respect to a different particular piece."[171]

The give-and-take elicited "strong responses," the secretary said, including from Moshe Ya'alon, the Israeli defense minister. On January 14, 2014, the Israeli tabloid *Yedioth Ahronoth* quoted his infamous comment that "the only thing that can 'save' us is for John Kerry to win his Nobel Prize and leave us alone."[172]

(Top) Departing from Jordan, a key intermediary. (Bottom) Arriving in Tel Aviv.

(Top) Saeb Arakat addressing Secretary Kerry, media in Ramallah.
(Bottom) Joint news conference in Jerusalem.

(Top) Examining olive wood figurines in Bethlehem.
(Bottom) Landing in West Bank.

(Top) Shabbat dinner with Shimon Peres. (Bottom) Laying a wreath at Yitzhak Rabin memorial in Tel Aviv.

(Top) Secretary Kerry and Prime Minister Netanyahu address media in Rabin Suite.
(Bottom) The secretary and President Abbas in Ramallah, West Bank.

Many Israelis and American Jews leapt to Secretary Kerry's defense, with Liberman, the new, hawkish Israeli foreign minister, labeling him a "true friend of Israel."[173]

New York Times columnist Tom Friedman, a longtime Middle East observer, suggested such barbs stemmed from the secretary forcing Israeli leaders to confront the hard choices embedded in a two-state solution.

"[Secretary Kerry] and President Obama are trying to build Israelis a secure off-ramp from the highway they're hurtling down in the West Bank that only ends in some really bad places for Israel and the Jewish people," Friedman wrote on February 12, 2014.[174]

Uri Dromi, a former Israeli Air Force pilot who was spokesman for the Rabin government during the Oslo talks, wrote in the *Miami Herald*: "Like a good surgeon, [Secretary Kerry] is telling us the truth about the operation necessary to save us from one, binational state, where Israel might either lose its democracy or its Jewish nature. We should thank him, not bad-mouth him."[175]

Among the qualities that emerged over the course of the negotiations was John Kerry's ability to blot out such criticism and remain focused on his goal, in this case the framework language.

While a mantra among the negotiators was that "nothing is agreed until everything is agreed," he moved Prime Minister Netanyahu toward supporting international compensation for both Palestinians and Israelis displaced by the 1947 War. He got the Palestinians to acknowledge there would be no comprehensive right to return, and the Israelis made a commitment to a new border based on the 1967 borders "with mutually agreed swaps."[176]

The prime minister balked at a US proposal under which both sides would have their capital in Jerusalem, and he insisted Israel be proclaimed "the nation-state of the Jewish people," a declaration to which President Abbas objected.[177]

The secretary invited the president and the Palestinian negotiating team to his home in Washington's Georgetown neighborhood in mid-March 2014. During the conversation, he asked whether they would agree to a delay in releasing the fourth group of prisoners.

President Abbas refused and, as *The New Republic* reported in a 2014 reconstruction of the negotiations, concluded the moment was a turning point in the talks.

"If the Americans can't convince Israel to give me twenty-six prisoners, how will they ever get them to give me East Jerusalem?" the magazine reported President Abbas as thinking.[178]

About two weeks later, Kerry asked President Obama to approve a three-way deal he'd crafted to merely keep the talks going.

He proposed having Israel release the final group of prisoners, plus four hundred more of its choosing. He also wanted Netanyahu to halt all new settlement announcements in the West Bank. In return, the Palestinians would agree to continue the talks for another nine months.[179]

The United States, meanwhile, would do something to boost Prime Minister Netanyahu at home: release spy Jonathan Pollard, a Jewish American convicted of stealing Top Secret US intelligence and passing it along to Israel while he worked for the US Navy.[180]

Israeli leaders had tried to free Pollard since he pleaded guilty in 1987, but the US intelligence establishment vehemently objected. Then CIA director George Tenet threatened to resign when President Clinton considered pardoning him.

The fourth group of prisoners was to be released on March 29, 2014, and the day before that, Secretary Kerry joined President Obama aboard Air Force One for a flight from Rome to Riyadh, Saudi Arabia. That evening, he asked the president to approve the three-way Pollard deal to keep the talks alive.

The New Republic revealed the reluctant president's response.

"I'm not doing this because I want to, John," the magazine quoted President Obama as saying. "I'm doing this for you."[181]

EVEN WITH THE PRESIDENT'S endorsement, Secretary Kerry was left at the whim of the Israelis and the Palestinians.

It wasn't for a lack of energy, effort, or creativity—as exemplified by what turned into the most turbulent day of our four years at the State Department.

After accompanying the president on his trip to Saudi Arabia, Kerry was slated to fly home to the United States.

We took off from Riyadh as scheduled on March 29, 2014, but as we flew northwest over Egypt and the Mediterranean Sea, the secretary asked about the feasibility of returning to Israel or Jordan to try to rescue the negotiations through a series of face-to-face meetings.

It's hard for the secretary of State to just pop up in a destination, since his aircraft has to get a diplomatic clearance, his security team has to get in place and secure a motorcade, and The Line has to dispatch Advance officers to organize accommodations and other logistics.

That meant we couldn't just set down in the Middle East; but as the flight bore on, the State Department staff pulled off a near-impossible alternative.

The secretary was told that DS agents who'd been in the Netherlands for the visit he and President Obama had just made to The Hague could jump on a train and get to Paris in time to receive us. Meanwhile, the staff at the US embassy in Paris had good relationships with the local police, vendors, and hotels. They'd be able to get rental cars and rooms at a regular haunt—the InterContinental Paris Le Grande—and lock down travel routes for our visit.

Team Paris was about the most experienced in the State Department in dealing with us, after Kerry had paid more than a dozen visits to their city.

So, somewhere over Europe, the secretary called an audible: we were returning to the Middle East after a pit stop in Europe. The aircraft commander canceled our trip home, made our planned refueling stop in Ireland, and then reprogrammed his flight computer to fly us back to Paris.

When we landed at LeBourget Airport, a place we weren't supposed to have been just six hours before, there was a sight to behold: the DS agents from Holland waiting at the foot of the stairs, a motorcade of freshly rented black minivans lined across the tarmac, and the Gendarmerie sitting on motorcycles with flashing blue lights to help us get downtown. Even Christophe Laure, the general manager of the Le Grand, was standing at the curb when we pulled up to the hotel.

The Building had worked its magic.

During this unexpected visit to Paris, Kerry continued a series of phone calls to Prime Minister Netanyahu and President Abbas to try to salvage the deal.

I captured the frustration of the situation the next morning when I snapped a photo of the then deputy chief of staff, Jon Finer, resting one hand on his forehead while using his other to hold a cellphone to his ear. He was lying on his back in a stairwell at our hotel, the railing for the stairs corkscrewing downward for three stories below him.

When I emailed the photo to Finer, I wrote in the subject line: "Death Spiral."

But as Finer worked the phone in that stairwell, I overheard him relay a sentiment of Secretary Kerry's while he spoke with Lowenstein and Indyk, the leaders of our negotiating team.

"I'd rather get criticized for trying too hard than giving up too easily," Finer told them the Boss said.[182]

The next morning, with our flight crew fully rested, we drove back out to the plane and returned to Israel. We were supposed to meet in both Tel Aviv with Prime Minister Netanyahu and in Ramallah with President Abbas, but the talks with the prime minister dragged on until nearly midnight.

Prime Minister Netanyahu faced a series of challenges within his governing coalition, trying to maintain support from pro-settler forces opposed to a settlement freeze, while also trying to fend off conservatives who opposed the release of the fourth tranche of prisoners—let alone the four hundred more who would be part of the Pollard deal.

When the secretary came back to the David Citadel, he cut a slice from a chocolate cake that had been in the refrigerator and poured himself a frequent drink: half orange juice, half sparkling water.

"Guys, between now and tomorrow, I need a punch list of all outstanding items—and I don't want a long punch list," he said. "I think it's very important to get that vote [of the Israeli Cabinet] tomorrow. We've got to get something cooking."[183]

Little did he know it was too late.

As *The New Republic* later reported, President Abbas was angry the secretary had canceled his trip to Ramallah scheduled for the night of March 31, 2014. To him, it exemplified Kerry's excessive concern for the Israeli position.

There was some truth to that, but the Israelis also had something the Palestinians wanted—the remaining prisoners. If the secretary couldn't deliver them, there wasn't any point talking to the Palestinians about their other demands.[184]

Unbeknownst to Kerry, President Abbas set a deadline of 7 p.m. on April 1, 2014, for winning the prisoners' release. If the Israelis didn't meet it, he'd sign the Palestinian applications for various UN memberships.[185]

The March 29 deadline came and went, as did additional promises for action on two more deadlines, March 30 and March 31, 2014.

We returned to the prime minister's office in Jerusalem at 9 a.m. on April 1, 2014, and Kerry immediately vented as Prime Minister Netanyahu and Molcho, his personal lawyer, quibbled with him and the White House about the details of releasing Pollard.

"Guys, this is what you did with the framework: you're killing it with repetition," the secretary said, pointing to a piece of paper. "It doesn't need to say it eighteen times. It says it once, right there."[186]

The three then spun around and went into the prime minister's personal office.

To underscore the fluidity of the situation, our staff and traveling press corps waited back at the David Citadel, sitting in their idling vans in anticipation of an imminent departure for the airport. We were due to fly back to Europe for a NATO meeting, although no one was quite sure when we'd take off.

We eventually traveled to Brussels, and the secretary was sitting in a bilat with Turkish Foreign Minister Ahmet Davutoglu when we received a bolt of news: President Abbas had made good on his threat. Before an audience at the Palestinian Authority Headquarters in Ramallah, he signed applications for membership in fifteen UN conventions and international treaties.

"I warned them," Kerry said of the Israelis. "I gave them as stark a warning as I could have."[187]

The secretary immediately called Indyk and Lowenstein on his cellphone, before trying to call Prime Minister Netanyahu.

When told Netanyahu was busy, the secretary was remarkably composed.

"Well, let's just keep plugging along," he said. "This could be a good pressure-cooker, steam-valve move: let (the Palestinians) feel good about themselves and then get back to it."[188]

Over the next several weeks, the sides talked in an effort to get an extension, but they largely spoke past one another.

On April 23, 2014, the Palestinians took an even more controversial step that effectively killed the deal: they announced they were forming a unity government with Hamas, the terrorist organization controlling the Gaza Strip, to create a single Palestinian voice.

Hamas refuses to recognize Israel's right to exist, so the Israelis pulled out of the talks with the Palestinian Authority the next day.

Things spiraled from there.

On June 12, 2014, three Israeli teenagers were kidnapped while hitchhiking in the West Bank. The Israelis unleashed a furious response, arresting nearly 350 people and killing five Palestinians during the next eleven days.[189]

Hamas responded by firing rockets into Israel. That prompted the Israeli Defense Force to launch an invasion into Gaza on July 8, 2014. During the next seven weeks, more than 2,100 Palestinians were killed and an estimated 10,000 were wounded. Some sixty-six Israeli soldiers and six civilians also died.[190]

Fearing the third Intifada he'd warned against, Kerry shifted from trying to negotiate a long-term peace to trying to reach an immediate cease-fire. It prompted another of those frenzied resource-burning periods during our tenure.

First, we parked in Cairo, working late into the night across several days as Kerry urged Egyptian, Turkish, and Qatari officials to try to rein in Hamas and restore the Israeli–Palestinian talks.

Prime Minister Netanyahu, however, didn't want to halt the military operation until he dismantled a tunnel network Hamas used to move across Gaza and, on occasion, into Israel.

The talks continued as we traveled on to New Delhi for our annual Strategic Dialogue with Indian leaders. Finally, at 2:19 a.m. local time on August 1, 2014, Kerry exchanged high fives with Finer, his deputy chief of staff, after both sides ostensibly agreed to a seventy-two-hour cease-fire beginning at 8 a.m.

"Pulled it back from the brink-e-rino," the secretary said as they celebrated the moment.[191]

Finer replied: "That was like giving birth to a Dodge Ram."[192]

Later, addressing reporters, Secretary Kerry said: "This is not a time for congratulation and joy, or anything except a serious determination, a focus by everybody to try to figure out the road ahead. This is a respite. It's a moment of opportunity, not an end. It's not a solution. It's the opportunity to find the solution."[193]

The secretary's wariness was well justified. The joy he initially felt was short-lived, as it had been throughout the peace process talks.

Hamas accused the Israelis of destroying nineteen buildings in Gaza as they blew up tunnels at 8:30 a.m.—a half hour after the cease-fire was to begin. The Israelis accused Hamas of attacking a group of Israeli soldiers. Either way, the cease-fire fizzled after little more than six hours after it was announced, and the fighting continued through a second cease-fire.

Finally, a third cease-fire stuck on August 26, 2014, but the long-term damage was done.

What started with the hope of a deal bringing peace between the Israelis and Palestinians fizzled amid new fighting among the parties. Pollard wasn't released until he was granted parole in 2015; and he was kept in the United States, not handed over to the Israelis.

Kerry accepted the futility of the situation and didn't return to Israel for more than a year, until November 24, 2015. In the intervening months, he turned his attention to negotiating a deal with Iran to control its nuclear program.

Prime Minister Netanyahu, meanwhile, focused on scuttling the Iran agreement—most conspicuously by traveling to Washington in March 2015 and addressing a Joint Session of Congress.

The leader of a foreign country was lobbying US legislators—from the podium used for the State of the Union address—against a diplomatic engagement led by a sitting president, Barack Obama.

Kerry labeled the invitation by Republican leaders, who held a majority and controlled Congress, as "treasonous." During one phone call to Harry Reid, the Senate minority leader, he told the Nevada Democrat: "I don't think I've been as upset about anything since I have been secretary of State."[194]

Kerry and Prime Minister Netanyahu met again in Berlin in October 2015, as violence flared between Jews and Muslims over access to the Temple Mount in Jerusalem.

The secretary had a bad cold and was drinking cup after cup of tea loaded with honey as he tried to regain his voice. He asked Lowenstein, who'd since replaced Ambassador Indyk as the special envoy for Israeli–Palestinian negotiations, to make his case to Netanyahu for easing access to the holy site.

Expressing anew frustration he'd felt throughout the broader peace talks, the secretary said to Lowenstein: "It's entirely driven by domestic politics. His entire goal is to stay on Balfour Street."

That's the road in Jerusalem where a prime minister lives.

Kerry took one more stab at revitalizing the peace process in early 2016, when he convened a secret meeting with King Abdullah II, Egyptian president Abdel Fattah al-Sisi, and Prime Minister Netanyahu at the king's winter home in Aqaba, Jordan.

The secretary made the trip without his usual press corps—a rarity—and took only a few members of his staff. I was told not to take any photos, as would have been customary, before receiving different directions in an urgent message from the secretary.

He asked me to join the group on the roof deck so I could snap a picture of him, the prime minister, and their teams talking as the sun set on the horizon.

Later, I returned to the same spot and found the secretary dispirited. The prime minister had rejected a series of proposed parameters for renewing the peace talks.

He did so even though Jordan and Egypt—leaders in the Arab world—had promised that all Arab nations would declare peace with Israel if it could reach a settlement with the Palestinians.

———

THE SECRETARY MET ONCE more face-to-face with the prime minister, the last time on June 26, 2016, at the Parco dei Principi Hotel in Rome.

Kerry was prepared to say he'd devoted three and a half years to trying to revitalize the peace process, but the prime minister hadn't made an equivalent effort.

"This is my break-up meeting with Bibi," he told us.[195]

The truth is, Kerry continued exploring ways to address Israeli concerns or build Arab support for an agreement with the Palestinians.

His interest took on a special poignancy on September 30, 2016, when he made his final trip to Israel as he and President Obama attended the funeral of Shimon Peres. The Israeli president had been such an advocate of Secretary Kerry and his efforts to broker a settlement, and his death was another blow to the effort.

By December 2016, the Obama administration was willing to show it wouldn't blindly support the Israeli leadership. Kerry also followed through on his vow to publicly outline the proposals he'd offered throughout the peace talks, and how both sides had failed to make the moves necessary despite his best efforts to accommodate their needs.

First, just before Christmas, on Friday, December 23, 2016, President Obama had the United States abstain from—rather than vote against—a UN Security Council resolution demanding a halt to all Israeli settlement construction in the territories it occupied.

The resolution said such settlements have "no legal validity," and halting their construction "is essential for salvaging the two-state solution."

Five years earlier, the United States had vetoed a similar resolution—the sole veto cast in the Council by the Obama administration.

While the abstention triggered an outcry from Prime Minister Netanyahu and many Israelis, it wasn't a first for the United States government.

Almost exactly twenty-six years prior, on December 22, 1987, President Reagan—a Republican—had his UN ambassador abstain as the Council adopted a resolution deploring Israel's handling of disturbances in the occupied territories.[196]

That resolution also was approved by the same 14–0 Security Council vote as President Obama's. President Reagan had also approved two prior abstentions on anti-Israel votes in December 1986 and September 1985.[197]

UN ambassador Samantha Power said after the 2016 vote:

> The United States has consistently said we would block any resolution that we thought would undermine Israel's security or seek to impose a resolution to the conflict. We would not have let this resolution pass had it not also addressed counterproductive actions by the Palestinians such as terrorism and incitement to violence, which we've repeatedly condemned and repeatedly raised with the Palestinian leadership, and which, of course, must be stopped.[198]

Less than a week later, on December 28, 2016, the secretary walked into the Dean Acheson Auditorium at the State Department to deliver his own parting thoughts on Middle East peace.

He stood alone at the podium, but he spoke for President Obama, Ambassador Power, and the rest of the administration. The goal wasn't necessarily to put a thumb in the prime minister's eye, but to outline why the chance for peace was on the verge of slipping away.

"The two-state solution is the only way to achieve a just and lasting peace between Israelis and Palestinians," the secretary said. "It is the only way to ensure Israel's future as a Jewish and democratic state, living in peace and security with its neighbors. It is the only way to ensure a future of freedom and dignity for the Palestinian people. And it is an important way of advancing United States interests in the region."[199]

Kerry urged the Palestinians to cease violence against the Israelis. He urged the Israelis to halt settlement activity. And he outlined the six basic parameters to a final-status agreement.

First, a border based on the 1967 lines, with mutually agreed swaps.

Second, two states for two peoples.

Third, resolution for the refugee situation, with international compensation for the Palestinians.

Fourth, Jerusalem as the capital for the two states.

Fifth, security for Israel.

And sixth, an end to all outstanding claims between the parties.

In sum, the same endgame the secretary discussed in March 2013 during his first meetings with both sides.

Kerry recalled his trip to Israel for President Peres's funeral, and a conversation the two had about the disputed land during a Shabbat dinner in Jerusalem in June 2013.

"The original mandate gave the Palestinians 48 percent. Now it's down to 22 percent. I think 78 percent is enough for us," the secretary quoted President Peres as saying.[200]

Secretary Kerry concluded his speech—and his work on the most difficult topic—by telling the world: "As we laid Shimon to rest that day, many of us couldn't help but wonder if peace between Israelis and Palestinians might also be buried along with one of its most eloquent champions. We cannot let that happen. There is simply too much at stake—for future generations of Israelis and Palestinians—to give in to pessimism, especially when peace is, in fact, still possible."[201]

John Kerry was optimistic to the very, very end.

6

THE IRAN DEAL

AFTER AL GORE LOST the 2000 presidential election in a recount contested all the way to the Supreme Court, he grew a beard and gained weight. Then the former vice president headed to the private sector, where he salved his political wounds by making millions as an investor and Apple Inc. board member.

After John Kerry lost another close election four years later, he also indulged his rebel streak. He got on his Harley-Davidson motorcycle and rode west, clearing his head as the miles rolled under his feet.

But he also took advantage of a path not available to Gore, a fellow Vietnam veteran who'd once been elected to the US Senate as part of the same 1985 freshman class. Kerry returned to government and redoubled his efforts in public service.

He rose not just to be chairman of the Senate Foreign Relations Committee; he developed a portfolio as a foreign policy emissary during the first term of the Obama administration.

In 2009, then senator Kerry traveled to Kabul to convince Hamid Karzai to participate in a run-off election following doubts about the voting in Afghanistan's presidential race. Karzai agreed after his visitor described his own bitter experience with a close presidential election.[202]

In 2010, Kerry visited Damascus several times to meet with Syrian president Bashar al-Assad, including once for dinner with their wives. The aim was to see whether Syria and its neighbor Israel could make any agreement as part of the coming Middle East peace negotiation.[203]

In 2011, Kerry went to Pakistan when the Obama administration needed a negotiator. The president wanted to reclaim the stealthy tail rotor of a helicopter that crashed during the Navy SEAL raid that killed Osama bin Laden.[204]

Later that same year, Kerry was dispatched on another, far more secretive mission. It would lead to a diplomatic achievement offsetting his failure in the Israeli–Palestinian peace talks.

————

IN DECEMBER 2011, SENATOR John Kerry boarded a commercial flight headed to Oman, a quiet, peaceful country sitting just across the Persian Gulf from Iran. When he disembarked in Muscat, a port city that is Oman's capital, he carried a gift for its long-serving ruler, Sultan Qaboos bin Said al Said.

It was an antique book about Frederick Law Olmsted, the nineteenth-century Boston landscape designer who crafted the famed Emerald Necklace of parks ringing the city's downtown.[205]

The sultan had overseen Oman's transition from dirt roads to modern highways, and was beloved by his countrymen for his benevolence. He also had a taste for design and the arts, so Kerry thought the gift would resonate.

He made the trip not to deliver presents, though, but a message: the United States would be interested in reopening a quiet dialogue with Iran about its nuclear program, if the sultan could arrange it with his neighbor just across the Strait of Hormuz.

The approach worked. In 2012, State Department diplomats—with the blessing and support of Secretary of State Hillary Rodham Clinton—met in Muscat with their counterparts from Iran. They agreed on the topics that would have to be covered in any negotiation about curbing the weapons program.

By 2013, both the United States and Iran were ready for more serious conversations. The White House dispatched three senior US officials on their own secret missions to Muscat, senior White House Iran adviser Puneet Talwar, Deputy Secretary of State William Burns, and Jake Sullivan, Vice President Joe Biden's national security adviser.

Burns was the No. 2 person in the State Department, a classic and revered diplomat who spoke Arabic, French, and Russian. He'd previously handled sensitive situations in Moscow while serving as the US ambassador to Russia.

Sullivan was a thirtysomething wunderkind who previously served as Clinton's top foreign policy adviser. He'd been State Department deputy chief of staff and director of policy planning before transitioning to the White House shortly after Clinton finished her term at Foggy Bottom in January 2013.

Sometimes joined by up to five technical experts, the group would often fly to the Middle East in an unmarked military Gulfstream jet and use side hotel entrances to get to their meetings.

It was all an effort to maintain the secrecy of their mission.

Kerry, by then secretary of State, was kept abreast of the talks through periodic conversations with Burns and Sullivan. They appeared on his schedule as calls to or from "Embassy Muscat." When staffers started asking about the vague references to an otherwise sleepy outpost, the notation disappeared from his schedule altogether.

The secretiveness was necessary because the United States and Iran had broken off diplomatic relations in 1979. That was when the pro-Western shah of Iran was overthrown and Iranian students—backed by fundamentalists—overran the US embassy in Tehran.

They took fifty-two Americans hostage.

Iranian hard-liners hated the United States for having supported Shah Reza Pahlavi, and the standoff lasted for 444 days—until hostages were released just as Republican Ronald Reagan replaced Democratic incumbent Jimmy Carter as president on January 20, 1981.

US officials themselves were bitter not just because the Iranians had violated the sanctity of an embassy. They also were angry because eight American service members had died in April 1980 in an aircraft crash during an aborted mission to rescue the hostages.[206]

More than thirty years later, President Obama and Secretary Kerry acknowledged that history, but believed it was worth reaching out to Iran. It was progressing with a nuclear program that could conceivably produce a bomb.

If it succeeded, that would further destabilize the Middle East.

Israel, whose existence Tehran refuses to recognize, would likely launch a preemptive strike on Iran's nuclear infrastructure. It did so in 1981, when it blew up an Iraqi reactor being built outside Baghdad. And should Iran obtain a nuclear weapon, far wealthier neighbors such as Saudi Arabia were sure to try to buy their own.

Those two countries follow two different strains of Islam and are bitter opponents. Most Saudis live as Sunni Muslims, and their leaders maintain closer ties to the West. Most Iranians live as Shiites, and their leaders are closer to Russia, China, and Cuba.

Burns, Sullivan, and the rest of the US team met with the Iranians first in March 2013. They held at least five more meetings in Oman and Switzerland during the rest of the year while working to further frame the negotiation.

Kerry maintained his own line of communication with the Iranians through Omani government official Salem ben Nasser al-Ismaily. I unwittingly photographed him giving the secretary a secret letter when the two met on the sidelines of a World Economic Forum conference in Jordan in May 2013.

I didn't know who al-Ismaily was at the time, but I figured something was up when a colleague pulled me aside and told me not to post the picture on the State Department's social media sites.

Fueling the US support for the talks were changes occurring in Iran itself. On June 14, 2013, Iranians elected Hassan Rouhani as their new president. He was considered a moderate, especially in comparison to the hard-liner he replaced, Mahmoud Ahmadinejad.

Ahmadinejad, Iran's sixth president, had drawn worldwide criticism for his anti-Israeli rhetoric, including his 2005 statement that the Holocaust was a "myth."[207] He also suggested the United States was behind the 9/11 attacks on New York City, Pennsylvania, and Washington.[208]

His successor, President Rouhani, was sworn in August 3, 2013. Burns and Sullivan met again with their Iranian counterparts later that month.

On September 26, 2013, Secretary Kerry held his first face-to-face meeting with Iran's foreign minister, Javad Zarif. It was a half-hour conversation in a room at the United Nations Headquarters. The only thing remotely close to dialogue between two leaders at that level came in 2007, when Secretary of State Condoleezza Rice exchanged pleasantries with Iranian foreign minister Manouchehr Mottaki during a luncheon in Egypt.[209]

Later that same day, Kerry and Zarif reconvened for a broader conversation with foreign ministers representing the other permanent members of the UN Security Council: China, Russia, the United Kingdom, and France. Germany also attended, given its outsize role in Europe's economic and defense sectors.

Joining the group was a representative of the twenty-eight-nation European Union.

The following day, President Obama spoke with President Rouhani by phone for fifteen minutes—the first conversation between US and Iranian heads of state in more than thirty-five years. President Obama said afterward he hoped they'd set the conditions for constructive dialogue.

"While there will surely be important obstacles to moving forward and success is by no means guaranteed, I believe we can reach a comprehensive solution," the president said. "The test will be meaningful, transparent, and verifiable actions, which can also bring relief from the comprehensive international sanctions that are currently in place."[210]

And with that, an idea that germinated after a failed presidential campaign blossomed into a full-fledged item on John Kerry's agenda as secretary of State, a job that would conclude his reengagement in public service after he was denied the chance to live in the White House.

IRAN LAUNCHED ITS FIRST nuclear reactor in November 1967, when the five-megawatt Tehran Research Reactor began operation.

Both the reactor itself and the uranium fueling it were supplied by the United States.[211] The United States did so under its "Atoms for Peace" program.[212]

The shah of Iran had ambitious goals for his country at the outset of its own nuclear program. In the mid-1970s, he announced plans to build twenty-three nuclear power plants and generate 23,000 megawatts of energy over twenty years.

His plans foundered when he was deposed, the Islamic Revolution occurred, and the United States and Iran broke off diplomatic ties following the 1979 hostage-taking.

His drive for a peaceful program was replaced by the specter of a nation on the make for a nuclear weapon. Iran did little to dispel that notion with its internal activities or international relations—especially its hostile rhetoric toward Israel and "the Great Satan," the United States.

"Death to America" was a regular Iranian chant reverberating from Tehran back to Washington.

In 1984, the State Department added Iran to its list of state sponsors of terrorism, triggering sweeping economic sanctions. In 2002, suspicions about the country's atomic program were bolstered when an Iranian dissident revealed the existence of two undeclared nuclear facilities at Natanz and Fordow, Iran.[213]

In 2006, the International Atomic Energy Association decided to refer Iran to the UN Security Council, after passing a resolution declaring Iran needed to suspend its enrichment-related activities.[214] The IAEA said Iran wasn't in compliance with its duties as signatory of the Nuclear Non-Proliferation Treaty.[215]

A little more than two months later, Iran announced it had enriched uranium for the first time. That was a potential problem, because it moved Iran from a pure consumer of externally supplied fuel to the producer of a fuel that could be reconfigured to ignite a nuclear weapon.[216]

Two months after that, the "P5+1"—the name for the five permanent Security Council members, plus Germany—proposed the framework of a deal offering incentives for Iran to halt its enrichment activities. Negotiations about how precisely to do that languished for the next decade.

During that span, Iran increased its number of centrifuges from 164 in 2003 to roughly 6,000 in 2009, President Obama's first year in office.[217] The total reached more than 19,000 by the time the Iran nuclear talks began in earnest.[218]

As with the Middle East peace talks, the Iranian negotiations centered on a set of concrete issues. The main one related to Iran's capacity to enrich uranium. A related issue dealt with reprocessing, in which spent atomic fuel could be turned into weapons-grade plutonium.

President Obama's talk about a verifiable agreement highlighted his demand for external monitoring of Iran's program, which would have to be guaranteed by any deal. Iran, meanwhile, wouldn't agree to a deal that didn't provide relief from economic sanctions that had accumulated over the years through United Nations and US congressional votes.

Left unstated wasn't a demand but a belief held by the US side.

Both the president and his secretary of State thought that ridding Iran of its nuclear weapons capability wouldn't just empower moderate elements within Iran but would prompt more work with Rouhani's government on regional matters.

Both also believed—though they were reluctant to say it out loud amid the negotiations—that reaching a deal would spark a yearning for greater freedom and engagement with the West. This would come from Iranians who stood to benefit both from the end of sanctions and their country's reentry into the community of nations.

"When Nixon went to China, Mao was still in power. He had no idea how that was going to play out," President Obama told a group of reporters in August 2015—a month after the Iran deal was completed. "[President Nixon] didn't know that Deng Xiaoping would suddenly come in and decide that it doesn't matter what color the cat is as long as it catches mice, and the next thing you know you've got this state capitalism on the march," he added. "You couldn't anticipate that."[219]

SECRETARY KERRY'S DIRECT INVOLVEMENT in the Iran negotiations began in earnest in October 2013, several weeks after his exploratory meetings with Foreign Minister Zarif at that year's UN General Assembly.

The venue was Geneva, the Swiss city that was home to the League of Nations, the predecessor to the UN. "Genève" had a reputation as the diplomatic hub of proudly neutral Switzerland.

The Iranians preferred to hold the talks in such "UN cities," which explained why we ended up meeting not only in Geneva, Lausanne, and Montreux, Switzerland, but also Rome and Vienna. They also hosted UN operations and had their own diplomatic histories.

Geneva was a familiar venue for us, too, given the time we spent there in September 2013 negotiating the Syria chemical weapons agreement with the Russians. We were used to the InterContinental Hotel, with its hilltop view of Lake Geneva and Mont Blanc when the weather was clear enough to let you see into France.

As with our time in Israel, we also were used to the routine of visiting Switzerland.

We'd fly into Cointrin International Airport and be enveloped by heavy security. The locals were resolute in their commitment to avoid any incidents on their neutral territory and spared no expense to prevent them. We were in a protective cordon wherever we went.

One thing we never got used to, ironically enough, was the prices in Switzerland. Spaghetti Bolognese, a staff staple, cost $35 a plate at Geneva hotels. Cheeseburgers were just as expensive.

We took to buying premade sandwiches at the local Migros and Coop convenience stores, or dashing down the street to Chez Ma Cousine. The restaurant sold roast chicken with potato wedges and a salad for $20 a plate. It was the best deal in town.

All of this elicited little sympathy from my college roommate John Stanton, who happened to live in Geneva. For every price we complained about, he came back with the tale of buying a $17 box of dishwasher soap or spending $120 for a Thanksgiving turkey no bigger than a chicken.

(Top) A return to a Swift Boat dock on Saigon River.
(Bottom) With Bob Kerrey at Rex Hotel.

(Top) A tribute to Anne Smedinghoff in Kabul. (Middle) Hosting British foreign minister in Boston. (Bottom) Exiting French Foreign Ministry in Paris.

(Top) Looking out on Baghdad. (Middle) Visit to mosque in Astana, Kazakhstan.
(Bottom) Bilat lunch with Philippines president Duterte.

(Top) John Kerry locates spot of infamous firefight on Bai Hap River in Vietnam.
(Bottom) A final handshake with former Viet Cong soldier Vo Ban Tam.

(Top) Walking past Churchill and other past British prime ministers while leaving No. 10 Downing Street. (Bottom) Deplaning at Golden Hour at Stansted, UK.

(Top) Posing with young Russian girl before meeting with President Putin in Sochi.
(Middle) Closeup view of tanker transiting Miraflores Locks on Panama Canal.
(Bottom) Greeters waiting in Bishkek, Kyrgyzstan.

(Top) Watching markswoman near Ulaanbaatar, Mongolia. (Middle) Touring shrine in Laos. (Bottom) Checking out antique car in Havana.

*(Top) Touring Lodi Gardens, India. (Middle) Meeting with young people
in Kuala Lumpur, Malaysia. (Bottom) US embassy Bishkek Halloween party.*

(Top) A call from the Leader of the Free World atop a Swiss mountain. (Bottom) A granddaughter looks on as Secretary Kerry signs climate change agreement at UN.

(Top) A man and his moment: John Kerry boards one of the planes he will use to travel 1.4 million miles as secretary of State. (Bottom) Arriving in Saudi Arabia.

(Top) Elephant selfie in Nairobi, Kenya. (Middle/Bottom) A playful exchange with a pair of greeters in traditional dress after Secretary Kerry arrived at Foreign Ministry in Colombo, Sri Lanka.

(Top) Gathering thoughts from Condi Rice, John McCain, James Baker, and others after funeral in Saudi Arabia. (Middle) A meeting with Pope Francis at the Vatican. (Bottom) President Obama visits State.

*(Top) Briefing reporters on Iran deal. (Middle/Bottom) Paying respects after
Charlie Hebdo/Hypercacher terror attack in Paris, at Brussels airport.*

(Top) Touring Hemingway's house in Cuba. (Middle) Hometown Diplomacy stop in Boston by Australian foreign minister. (Bottom) Tarmac soccer break.

(Top/Middle) Hardball/Softie: Meeting with Prime Minister Netanyahu on David Citadel balcony overlooking Old City, and an introduction to his late dog, Kaiya. (Bottom) Familiar view (of Tel Aviv) from my window seat on the world.

(Top) Sailing across onetime frozen bay to receding glacier near Svalbard, Norway.
(Middle) Greeting hosts at second Our Ocean conference in Valparaiso, Chile.
(Bottom) Ridiculous Hold Room in Qatar.

(Top/Middle) A man always in motion: at Orly Airport, Paris; in London City Hall.
(Bottom) Leaving UN Headquarters, New York.

(Top) An impromptu walk in Washington, DC. (Middle) Reviewing notes before UN meeting. (Bottom) Airborne meeting with staff.

*(Top) Mary Rezaian looks on as her son Jason thanks
Secretary Kerry for his freedom. (Middle) Office confab with David Wade
and others. (Bottom) An award from German foreign minister Steinmeier.*

The first round of talks with Iran, aimed at crafting an interim agreement known as the Joint Plan of Action, began with meetings held on two successive days, October 15 and 16, 2013. We flew back to Geneva on November 8, 2013, amid word that Deputy Secretary Bill Burns, Biden national security adviser Jake Sullivan, and Undersecretary of State for Political Affairs Wendy Sherman were close to resolving final sticking points with their Iranian counterparts.

Nonetheless, the talks sputtered and Secretary Kerry and his fellow ministers left two days later. We returned to Geneva on November 23, 2013, for a marathon negotiating session we hoped would seal a deal that would let us get home for Thanksgiving.

Kerry met with Foreign Minister Zarif and a third party instrumental to the talks, Catherine Ashton. A British baroness, Ashton was the de facto European Union foreign minister as the EU high representative for foreign affairs and security policy.

Kerry then met one-on-one with Zarif, had a meeting with Russian foreign minister Sergey Lavrov, and then a series of trilats and various bilats. In between, he killed time shopping for chocolates at Auer, his favorite Swiss candy store, and, at one point, marveling at roses the hotel staff had placed in his room.

"Flowers are a real gift," the secretary told us. "We take them for granted, but when you stop and really think about all the varieties, it's amazing."[220]

About 9:30 p.m., Kerry spoke with President Obama. He told him Zarif had agreed to everything sought by the P5+1, with one exception. The president must have replied, "Congratulations," because Kerry next said, "Well, thanks, but it's a big exception."[221]

It centered on whether the Joint Plan of Action would acknowledge Iran had a "right" to enrich uranium, which could complicate the final negotiations about curbing enrichment.

The discussions continued through several more rounds of bilats and trilats, as well as a midnight pizza delivery to the secretary's suite. Kerry, Burns, and Sherman worked on several rounds of language with the Iranians before the deputy secretary went to meet with his counterpart.

He told him Kerry had the authority from President Obama to reach a final deal on the language he was carrying.

In an artful dodge, the final agreement was ambiguous on Iran's right to enrich, allowing both sides to argue they had won that point.

At 1:45 a.m. on November 24, 2013, Burns returned to the secretary's suite and asked us, "Can you get the secretary, please?"

When Kerry walked out of his bedroom, his deputy told him, "We have an agreed-upon text."

The Joint Plan of Action, the prelude to the final Joint Comprehensive Plan of Action, was complete. The parties assembled at the nearby Palace of Nations and held a news conference at 3:45 a.m. to outline the agreement. The secretary came back to the hotel at 5:30 a.m. for a set of round-robin interviews with our traveling television correspondents.

We left the InterCon and headed to the airport at 9:30 a.m., having slept little more than one hour during the twenty-four hours we were in Geneva.

As expected, Zarif later told reporters the agreement recognized Iran's right to enrich. Kerry replied, "There is no inherent right to enrich." He said in one of a series of interviews the agreement "states that they could only do that by mutual agreement, and nothing is agreed on until everything is agreed on."[222]

En route to London on the way back from Geneva, Kerry told reporters he believed the personal rapport he'd built with Zarif had helped this first round of negotiations.

"Sometimes, you have to talk to people like they're people," the secretary said.[223]

He described his counterpart, an English-speaking, US-educated, former Iranian ambassador to the United Nations, as businesslike and respectful.

"He has a job; I have a job," Kerry told the reporters.[224]

It was the beginning of a relationship that would vacillate between professional and pugilistic as each man tried to get the best deal for his country.

WE BEGAN 2014 WITH a fast start, flying off to Israel on New Year's Day for another round in the flagging Middle East peace talks. We flew back to Geneva the following week to talk with the Iranians about the particulars for implementing the Joint Plan of Action.

It was the bridge to any final agreement curbing Iran's nuclear program.

The negotiations took place January 9–10, 2014, with the aim of implementing the interim agreement on January 20, 2014.

Israeli leaders had been harshly critical of the negotiations even before they began. They said Iran was playing the West for sanctions relief, allowing it to continue sponsoring terrorism and political upheaval in the Middle

East. Prime Minister Benjamin Netanyahu labeled the interim deal "a historic mistake."[225]

The complaints lost some of their sting, though, when the Israelis heard the terms of the JPOA.

It required that all uranium enriched beyond 5 percent be diluted or converted to uranium oxide, making it less likely it could end up in a bomb.[226]

Iran also agreed it wouldn't install any new centrifuges—spun to enrich uranium—and that 50 percent of the centrifuges already installed at Natanz would be left inoperable. At the Fordow enrichment facility, the restriction was even greater. Seventy-five percent of its centrifuges had to be left inoperable.[227]

Meanwhile, the IAEA was granted access to the once-secret Natanz and Fordow plants for the first time. Some sections would be monitored by cameras twenty-four hours a day.[228]

In return, Iran was granted sanctions relief valued at $7 billion, including the release of $4.2 billion in frozen oil revenues. The money was to be paid out in monthly installments of $550 million, a guard against the country grabbing the cash and then violating the terms of the agreement.

The two sides agreed the interim deal would last six months. That was enough time, they hoped, to complete a fuller, follow-on agreement. It would be known as the Joint Comprehensive Plan of Action, indicative of its sweeping scope.

In a twist, though, the success of the JPOA slowed down, undermined, and even threatened progress toward this final, comprehensive agreement.

First, Congress demanded to know what was in the interim deal. It was a reasonable request for transparency, but it proved to be a burden amid the continuing negotiation about the Comprehensive agreement.

President Obama, Secretary Kerry, and members of the negotiating team were forced to trumpet the interim agreement back in Washington and outline its merits in testimony before Congress.

"This is a very delicate diplomatic moment, and we have a chance to address peacefully one of the most pressing national security concerns that the world faces today, with gigantic implications of the potential of conflict," the secretary told members of the House Foreign Affairs Committee on December 10, 2013. "One path could lead to an enduring resolution in international community's concerns about Iran's nuclear program. The other path could lead to continued hostility, and potentially to conflict."[229]

He concluded: "We have an obligation to give these negotiations an opportunity to succeed."[230]

Unfortunately, outlining all the United States won in the interim agreement also highlighted all Iran had given up. That created problems for the Iranian negotiators when they returned to Tehran.

During a May 3, 2014, conference held—pointedly enough—at the former US embassy in Tehran, hard-liners issued a joint statement placing demands on their own negotiating team.

"What we are saying is that this [negotiating] team is entering the talks with a soft position and a diplomacy of smiling, which is not appreciated in a country like Iran that has given martyrs and struggled many years for the victory of its Islamic Revolution," said Mohammad Hossein Karimi-Ghadoosi. The parliamentarian and leading figure of the hard-line Islamic Endurance Front made the comment to LobeLog, a blog focused on US foreign policy in the Middle East.[231]

The second way the interim agreement impeded a permanent one is that opponents of the nuclear deal—primarily Israel—began to latch onto the JPOA. They said it was good enough and didn't have to be superseded by a final, more far-reaching comprehensive agreement.[232]

"He was wrong. And today he is saying, 'Oh, we should extend that interim agreement,'" Kerry said in reference to the opposition initially raised by Prime Minister Netanyahu. The secretary spoke while testifying before the House Foreign Affairs Committee on February 25, 2015.[233]

Iran, however, noted it made the interim deal only as a prelude to a final enduring agreement. That meant US negotiators had to return to the table and sit across an Iranian team determined to win back concessions in the final agreement.

The resulting dynamic: an Obama administration tantalizingly close to an agreement it felt would be a major foreign policy win, facing a delegation from Iran—whose people are famously shrewd negotiators—seeking to exploit that interest by holding out.

One measure of the allies' interest in reaching an agreement? The P5+1 parties repeatedly extended the deadline for moving from the interim agreement to a final deal.

When the interim deal was enacted on January 20, 2014, the parties agreed to a six-month period for negotiating the final deal. That ended July 20, 2014. They then extended it to November 24, 2014—the first anniversary of the interim deal signed in Geneva.

When that deadline also neared, they moved the date again to July 1, 2015. Even that slipped to July 7, 2015, then July 10, 2015, and again to July 13, 2015. The final agreement wasn't sealed by all parties until the early morning hours of July 14, 2015.

That said, Iran's interest in striking a deal was evident in its willingness to continue living by the interim agreement even as the deadline for the final one slipped. Iran was getting some sanction relief, true, but not the full gains it sought.

All that kept continuous pressure not just on the Americans, but also on President Rouhani and Foreign Minister Zarif to wrap up the talks.

Secretary Kerry alluded to some of the criticism he faced on March 9, 2015, while addressing a meeting of his assistant secretaries at the State Department.

"We are not desperate to make a deal," he told the group. "Would I like one? Yes, because the consequences of not getting one are not pretty."[234]

The secretary reiterated he'd "walked away" from the talks—refusing to fly from London to Geneva after one particularly stagnant negotiating session at the deputy level—"and I am prepared to walk away again, if I have to."[235]

On April 2, 2015, following six days of high-level talks at the Beau-Rivage Palace hotel in Lausanne, Iran tentatively agreed to the framework for the final deal. It not only accepted restrictions on its nuclear program lasting varying amounts of time, but also agreed to a heightened regimen of inspections of its nuclear facilities.[236]

While it was an achievement building momentum toward the final deal, Kerry apologized to his assistant secretaries for his long absence during the talks in Switzerland.

He also complained that much of the debate since the interim agreement had been "captivated by a complete lack of information and facts."[237]

Nonetheless, Kerry told the State Department team: "We can't get around that until the final agreement, and some ambiguity is needed to get a final deal."[238]

LESS THAN TWO MONTHS after the outlines of the final deal were agreed to in Lausanne, Secretary Kerry flew back to Switzerland for a one-on-one meeting with Foreign Minister Zarif.

The endgame for the Joint Comprehensive Plan of Action had begun.

The venue was familiar: the hilltop InterContinental Hotel in Geneva. The counterpart also was well known. Additionally, the routine was the same: a posed photo for the media at the top of their 11 a.m. meeting, followed by a closed-door conversation.

A State Department official made anodyne comments to reporters when the meeting ended after six hours.

"Secretary Kerry and Foreign Minister Zarif, along with their teams, had a thorough and comprehensive discussion of all of the issues today," Agence France-Presse quoted the official as saying. "We are committed to working to close the remaining gaps and to staying on the schedule we've set forth to get this done."[239]

In reality, the meeting had grown so contentious, Zarif got up from the table at one point and sat in a chair on the side of the room, his head in his hands. Kerry, meanwhile, slammed his pen down on the table so forcefully it flew across the room and hit one of the Iranian negotiators.

"It stunned everyone, because it was so out of character," one State Department official later told *The New Yorker* for a reconstruction about the negotiations.[240]

The Iranians headed off for the rest of their business abroad. Kerry was set to fly to Madrid the following afternoon, but not before fulfilling a pledge he'd made to himself during his many visits to Switzerland.

The avid cyclist planned to ride his bike through the Col de la Colombière, a mile-high pass in the French Alps just south of Geneva.

It's reached by pedaling up hills that, at points, have a grade of more than 12 percent—a rise of twelve feet in height for every one hundred feet in distance. It's so challenging it served as the 10th Stage of the 2012 Tour de France bicycle race.

Because this wasn't an official event, the press corps and bulk of our staff remained back at the hotel in Geneva. In fact, many members of our usual travel team had stayed at home in Washington to handle other business on what was supposed to be a routine six-day trip to Nigeria, Switzerland, Spain, and Paris.

The secretary set off from the InterContinental around 8 a.m. on May 31, 2015. He traveled in a pared-down motorcade, accompanied in the limousine by his biking companion and senior aide, Jason Meininger. I rode in the spare limo.

We took a beautiful Sunday drive around the end of Lake Geneva before crossing into France and pulling off the highway at the commune of Scionzier. The motorcade stopped in a municipal parking lot so the secretary and Meininger could take off their sweats and get on their bikes.

While Kerry said he wanted a "small footprint" for the ride, that belied the fact that he was our country's chief diplomat and fourth in line to the US presidency. He may have been blasé about taking a bike ride on public roads, but our hosts weren't.

Because we started in Switzerland, we had a Swiss police escort to the border. Because the ride was in France, French police had the security lead, along with the Diplomatic Security Service.

The police didn't want the secretary and Meininger riding alone, so they found experienced cyclists within their ranks who could ride alongside and form a protective peloton, should the need arise.

There were also the requisite helicopters overhead—Swiss to the border, French from there on—and the usual caboose, an ambulance staffed with paramedics.

All in all, it was a sizable group, so much so that the parking lot was filled with cars as the secretary checked his bike and posed for photos with local officials who'd come out to welcome him. Everyone waited as he completed a solemn task: making final edits to a statement we were issuing after the death of Beau Biden, the elder son of Vice President Joe Biden. He'd died of a brain tumor at age forty-six.

When it was finally time to go, Kerry reset the GPS tracker mounted on his handlebars, snapped his cycling shoes into the toe clips on his pedals, and started to move.

I took that as my cue to stop taking pictures and run back to the spare limo, about four cars back. I'd no sooner jumped into the back seat when I looked through the bulletproof windows and saw John Kerry on the ground.

I couldn't believe my eyes.

———

"HE FELL," SAID THE agent sitting in the front seat as he and I bailed out of the passenger-side doors of our Chevy Suburban. When we made it across the parking lot, the secretary was writhing in pain. Meininger, despite being shaken by what he'd just seen, provided an instant and decisive diagnosis: "It's over. He broke his leg."

I tried to process this statement as I looked down at Kerry, sitting on his butt. He was dressed in his helmet, sunglasses, gloves, and a sleek white riding suit. He was trim, muscular, and looked the picture of fitness—except he was now lying next to his bike.

The severity of his injury became evident when he reached down and grabbed his right thigh. The top half moved in one direction, the bottom half in the other. It was as if someone were wiggling a bowl of Jell-O.

In reality, he'd suffered a clean break of his femur, the longest and strongest bone in the human body.[241]

While the security personnel had game-planned for an injury during their preparations, the real thing was a little different from practice.

There was a moment of shock before the full breadth of the team sprang into action. First, agents removed the bike. Then one got behind the secretary and held up his back and head. Then the paramedics ran up from the ambulance.

They opened their medical bags and began treatment immediately.

Kerry was in considerable pain, so the medics checked his vital signs and gave him a dose of morphine. As it started to take effect, he grew woozy and concerned about his heart rate and breathing.

"I'm dying," he said in his haze. The comment startled me and, I'm sure, everyone else within earshot.

We reassured him he wasn't, although none of us could truly be sure the broken bone hadn't pierced his femoral artery, the main carrier of blood in the leg. It wasn't an implausible scenario.

The paramedics looked at him closely, as did a DS agent who happened to be from Massachusetts and was the designated medic on the protective detail that day.

A broken bone was bad, for sure, but this was a potentially dangerous situation.

Meininger started to talk with the security team about the evacuation plan, while I called the senior staff member on the trip—Deputy Chief of Staff Tom Sullivan—to tell him and the others back in Geneva what had happened. Sullivan is one of the calmest and most decisive people I have ever met, but even he was taken aback when he heard the news.

After we hung up, I pulled out a pen and piece of paper and began documenting the times and everything the medics were doing.

The reporter in me did so not just so I could remember, but for the sake of history and the questions sure to come from the rest of the staff, the White House, and Secretary Kerry's younger daughter, Vanessa. She was a doctor at Massachusetts General Hospital.

As the medical team worked to stabilize the secretary, DS agents grabbed umbrellas from their vehicles and opened three to shield him from the brilliant morning sun. A few minutes later, the French Gendarmerie helicopter descended in a buzz of noise and landed in a field next to the parking lot.

The plan was to fly the secretary back to Geneva for treatment at the Hôpitaux Universitaires de Genève, or HUG, the Geneva University Hospitals. It had been designated as the medical facility of choice during the preride planning. That planning included a check to ensure it was stocked with a sufficient quantity of Kerry's blood type.

In addition to the two pilots, there was room for only four passengers in the helicopter: Kerry, the two paramedics, and the DS special agent in charge of the secretary's protective detail. Neither Meininger nor I wanted to lose sight of the Boss, so the flight crew agreed to let one of us also hop on.

Meininger had known the secretary for years and become very close while working with him, driving him, and riding alongside him for hours and miles. Nonetheless, he suggested I take the spot. He deferred to my relative rank in the Department, the note taking I was doing, and my own longtime relationship with our boss.

I shook his hand and jumped aboard.

We were soon airborne and on a flight that would have been enjoyable if not for the circumstances. We climbed to the north and flew past sheer granite cliffs, magnificent in their scale even as the aircraft bounced around in turbulence reflected off them.

Like most helicopter trips, we traveled along a valley and followed the path of a highway, doubling back on the road that had taken us from Switzerland to France little more than an hour earlier. Soon, we were over the outskirts of Geneva. Then, past the window beside the secretary's stretcher, I saw the Jet d'eau, the geyser near the tip of Lake Geneva that's a city landmark.

Once we landed on the HUG rooftop, we were met by local police, hospital officials, and spare DS agents who had scrambled from the hotel after the emergency call.

Kerry was taken downstairs for an evaluation by the hospital staff. Before long, Meininger and the rest of the group from Scionzier materialized in the waiting area. I could only imagine the speed of their motorcade on the thirty-mile trip, because our helicopter hadn't arrived in Geneva much before their cars pulled in downstairs.

Over the next several hours, both the secretary and the situation stabilized. He was no longer in immediate danger, the staff that had stayed behind at the hotel or back in Washington was either on scene or fully in the loop, and Kerry was well enough to make his own decisions about how to proceed.

His first request was to get in touch with Dr. Dennis Burke. He was an orthopedic surgeon at Massachusetts General Hospital who'd previously replaced his two hip joints, including the one atop the femur that was now broken.

———

THE QUESTION KERRY AND his doctors had to resolve was whether he should have surgery to set a femur in Geneva, where he now was, or back in Boston, where he lived and Dr. Burke worked.

The secretary's preference was to get home. Burke consulted by phone with the doctors in Geneva and agreed Boston was preferable, assuming Kerry could be moved in a medically prudent fashion.

Soon, our trip coordinators were examining air ambulance options and even started pulling seats and tables out of our Air Force plane, seeing if they could create enough space to fly a stretcher-borne secretary back to Boston. The stretcher wouldn't be able to turn the corner at the entrance to his usual cabin.

During this period, a subtle but unmistakable tug-of-war broke out between Dr. Burke and the HUG physicians.

The locals were confident they had the expertise and facilities to operate without subjecting Kerry to the risks of a blood clot or pulmonary embolism that might occur on a long pressurized airplane flight home.

Commercial airlines warn passengers about the risk of deep vein thrombosis, a blood clot that can form and travel from the leg to a lung or the brain if someone doesn't get up and walk or stretch during a long flight.

Kerry had to reassure the HUG physicians he could fly, and that anything that might happen in transit wouldn't be their responsibility.

Eventually, the two sides reached an agreement: the secretary would remain overnight at the hospital in Geneva, Burke would fly in from Boston, and if Kerry's vitals were stable in the morning, the visiting physician would assume responsibility for his patient's treatment and accompany him home.

The last remaining logistical challenge was a ride. Reconfiguring our usual plane was proving to be a challenge. There wasn't a commercial air ambulance available with enough space for a medical team and even the bare-bones staff that would have to accompany the secretary of State on a potentially life-threatening flight.

The air ambulances available also were small and would have had to stop both in Ireland and Canada to refuel en route to the United States—even more ups and downs and pressure changes and time aloft.

Fortunately for us, the Air Force had an empty C-17 cargo plane flying from Qatar to its base in Charleston, South Carolina. It was big, by definition, and easily capable of crossing the Atlantic Ocean nonstop.

The plane was rerouted to Ramstein Air Base in southwestern Germany, where it picked up a five-person team of military doctors and nurses from nearby Landstuhl Regional Medical Center. On the morning of June 1, 2015, the bulbous gray plane landed in Geneva and parked not far away from the blue-and-white Air Force C-32 on which Kerry had arrived for his talks with Zarif.

A few hours later, the HUG staff loaded the secretary onto a helicopter. He flew from the roof of the hospital to the airport tarmac, touching down just behind the tail of the cargo plane.

Swiss police had lined up a pair of passenger buses next to the plane to block the view of photographers peering through the airport fence while Kerry was transferred from the helicopter. His stretcher was rolled up the ramp at the tail of the C-17 and secured in the middle of the eighty-eight-foot cargo bay.

The space was large enough to hold 102 fully equipped troops, a fleet of presidential limos, or an Abrams tank.[242]

I joined Meininger, Deputy Chief of Staff Tom Sullivan, and two DS agents on the flight to Boston. The rest of our group got on the C-32 and flew directly back to Washington.

Dr. Burke also rode with us on the cargo plane. He took advantage of the unique circumstance to sit in the cockpit and watch our takeoff. Then he climbed down the ladder from the flight deck and crawled into a medical litter in front of the secretary's stretcher.

He was finally able to sleep after his unexpected overnight flight to Europe.

The rest of us sat in mesh seats along the sides of the cargo bay. We ate box lunches and used a portable latrine lashed down at the front of the cargo bay. A flight surgeon kept tabs on the secretary, who slept, made phone calls, and poked around on a laptop we'd given him.

The ten-hour flight was uneventful, but the nighttime landing was memorable. I watched from the cockpit jump seat. Boston was being pelted by rain, and the runway lights at Logan Airport weren't visible until shortly before the pilots got to the height where they had to decide whether to land or abort their approach.

They were able to see in time and then threw an autobrake switch to ensure they didn't skid when making contact with the ground. They landed on the pavement with an assuring thud that flattened the plane's tires and sent a ripple down its wings.

They parked the airplane near a private aviation terminal such that photographers wouldn't be able to get a picture of Kerry while he was in hospital garments and on a stretcher.

One of the first people aboard was Dr. Vanessa Kerry. We stood back as she greeted her father with a kiss and then gave him her own quick medical assessment. It was a touching blend of loving daughter and cool professional.

Kerry bid farewell to his pilots and doctors, thanking each with a Challenge Coin. A city ambulance backed up to the tail ramp and attendants transferred his stretcher for the trip to Massachusetts General. We arrived fifteen minutes later, pulling into an underground garage connected to the Emergency Room.

The secretary was taken upstairs and surrounded by a waiting team of doctors and nurses. Those of us who had been overseas felt a wave of relief, not just from being back in the United States but also because we were now within range of staff reinforcements. I felt especially good, since I was back in my hometown and unexpectedly close to my wife and sons.

That said, I still couldn't believe what had happened.

A months-old idea and days of intricate planning had all pointed to a single moment: when Secretary Kerry finally pushed his pedal down to begin his ride.

While I took that as my cue to lower my camera and run for my car, a phalanx of French motorcycle officers knew it was their signal to set off at the front of the traveling party. Their job was to make sure the route and each intersection along it were clear.

The sudden roar of their engines prompted the secretary—himself a Harley rider—to look over and watch the bikes pull away.

What he didn't see was a small curb. It was shorter than normal, just tall enough to define a series of parking spaces in front of one of the Scionzier municipal buildings.

While Kerry planned to ride a route that had been a Stage in the Tour de France—a race known for its speed, endurance, and hair-raising moments— he was nowhere near any of that drama.

Instead, he was traveling no more than two or three miles per hour, on maybe his third or fourth pedal stroke, when his front tire ran into the jutting curb. Traveling too slow to go over it, the tire stopped. Looking out instead of down, Kerry was caught off guard. And because his shoes were attached to the pedals by his toe clips, he had no time to snap out and put down his foot to break his fall.

Instead, he tipped over at an angle. His right thigh led the way, coming down hard on the curb, which amounted to a wedge pile-driving into his leg.

The result was a classic paradox: an unstoppable force meeting an immovable object.

The femur was the thing to give.

For all our fears about a rider careening off the road, a tire blowing at high speed, or a nut job trying to attack the passing secretary, the thing that got him was a measly curb. At low speed. In a municipal parking lot.

It sounded like the finale in a perverse game of Clue.

———

DR. BURKE OPERATED THE morning after we returned to Boston. He came out of the OR after four hours looking like he'd been in a knife fight. Nonetheless, he pronounced the surgery a success. He not only replaced the metal ball-and-socket joint in the secretary's hip, but also put in an extra-long post extending through the core of the femur and down past the point of the break.

He drilled screws across the bone before wrapping it with wire for good measure. It was so solid, Secretary Kerry was able to get on his feet the morning after the operation. Within days, he was using a walker to move down his hospital corridor. A week after the surgery, we released the first post-accident shot of him, a picture of the secretary sitting in his room over-looking the Charles River.

He had notes on his lap, a phone to his ear, and a tin of his favorite Boston Chipyard chocolate chip cookies on the table beside him. It wasn't a posed shot. Kerry had a secure phone in his room throughout his hospitalization, and he was on and off with his staff and the administration. The cookies had a nonmedicinal healing power.

One of the first well-wishes he received was an email from Foreign Min-ister Zarif. Perhaps the most gracious came from German foreign minister Frank-Walter Steinmeier, a colleague in the P5+1. Writing on parchment by hand with a blue fountain pen, the foreign minister said Kerry was "indis-pensable" to the nuclear talks and his return was eagerly awaited.

On June 12, 2015, Kerry put on gray slacks, a blue blazer, and a pair of tennis shoes in preparation to leave Massachusetts General Hospital. He stopped on the way out to visit a young man who'd broken his neck in an accident, and then the secretary climbed out of a wheelchair and onto crutches to come outside and address a group of reporters waiting in front of the glistening Charles River.

"It's really wonderful just to get outdoors, see the summertime," he said. "Dr. Dennis Burke is a carpenter-surgeon-genius, and he and his team have been so attentive, unbelievably thoughtful. He's put together a leg that was broken on the femur, and he tells me—and I'm confident—that I'll be as good to go as I was before, if not stronger. So, I look forward to that."

Turning back to business, Kerry argued his time laid up was not wasted.

"The one good thing, I will tell you, about being on your back for few days, it gives you time to think and it gives you clarity," he said. "I've had a lot of time to think about some of the challenges that we face, some things we could perhaps tweak, things we need to do, and also to feel good about the things that I think we're doing very well."[243]

A reporter asked if he felt his injury had hurt the pace of the nuclear negotiations, which were supposed to be concluded by July 1—little more than two weeks away.

"My absence really wasn't an absence in the sense of I had no plans to be personally involved with my foreign minister counterparts until a week or two from now. Our team is in Vienna now working out very complex annexes, details of this agreement," he said.[244]

The secretary rode in a Dodge minivan to his home on Beacon Hill. The next day, he did an interview with the hometown *Boston Globe*, during which he spoke about the irony of his accident.

"I'm just navigating my way at about 2 miles an hour . . . and this curb appears out of nowhere while I'm focused on the motorcycle," he said. "And the bike just freezes."[245]

Nonetheless, he said he planned to ride again.

"Are you kidding?" he told the reporter who asked the question. "I'm just going to make sure I never take my eye—I'm not going to look at the motorcycle instead of what's right in front of me."[246]

He also vowed to adhere to the deadline for completing the talks.

"If you don't get this done on the schedule, then mischief-makers step in everywhere," Kerry said. "You have plenty of folks in Iran who would love to not see the deal, hard-liners. . . . You have people here in the United States who don't want the deal."[247]

Three days later, the secretary got into his van and drove to Logan Airport for the flight back to Andrews Air Force Base. He got on and off his plane with the help of a covered scissors lift. Ten days after that, on June 26, 2015, he felt well enough to climb up the normal red-carpeted steps, even if he was on crutches.

Once the door to our C-32 closed, the plane took off for Vienna, Austria. His broken leg on the mend, John Kerry was headed back to Europe and the Iran nuclear talks.

———

SECRETARY KERRY HAD TWO key partners when he arrived in Vienna. One was US Energy Secretary Ernest Moniz. The other was Jon Umlauf, a US Army Captain who was a physical therapist. Both proved indispensable in their ability to negotiate the final agreement.

Moniz was a fellow Bay Stater and Stanford-trained scientist who once chaired the Physics Department at the Massachusetts Institute of Technology.[248] He was brought into the negotiations five months earlier to serve as a counterpoint to Ali Akbar Salehi, whom the Iranians had named as their top technical expert.

Salehi was head of the Atomic Energy Organization of Iran and, in an amazing coincidence, had earned his doctorate at MIT while Moniz was at the Cambridge, Massachusetts, school.[249]

Not only were the two able to speak the same scientific language, but they also had a personal connection.

Captain Umlauf, meanwhile, was a humble, soft-spoken member of the armed forces tasked with an important mission, albeit not a military one. He had to rehab the secretary of State so he could complete the talks and his recovery from a serious injury.

The Pennsylvanian was the perfect fit for Kerry. Umlauf had no outward opinions on the subject occupying the secretary's mind, but had intense thoughts about how to make his leg better.

Umlauf also broadened his gaze, taking staffers for runs, analyzing their gaits, and making recommendations for improving their strides. He carried a goody bag filled with pamphlets on better eating, sleeping, and exercise habits.

The captain was a godsend halfway through an exhausting term that was rapidly eroding everyone's physical fitness.

The first morning back in Vienna, on June 27, 2015, another of our travel routines took shape, which ended up being a good thing. While the schedule we were handed before landing in Austria called for us to be there only until July 2—the day after the deadline for any final deal—we ended up staying a total of eighteen days.

Once again, each day resembled the plot from the movie *Groundhog Day*.

Kerry huddled first with Undersecretary Wendy Sherman, his top deputy in the negotiations, as well as Moniz, his chief science adviser. Then the secretary would lean into his crutches and make his way down the hall so the group could meet with the Iranians.

When that meeting broke, Moniz and Salehi would often sit down together, seeking to resolve any technical matters factoring into the discussions. Sherman would reconvene with her counterparts and their respective aides, tackling the next items on the staff agenda.

Kerry, meanwhile, would get back in his motorcade and return to his hotel for a PT session with Umlauf.

When the staff and technicians were ready for more senior-level decisions, Secretary Kerry and Foreign Minister Zarif would return and take their seats across from one another to work through the next issue needing high-level negotiation.

They met in the Palais Coburg, a Neoclassical palace turned into a thirty-three-room luxury boutique hotel. With its gilded ceilings and polished marble and parquet floors, it had a five-star rating and prime location next to the Parkring, the innermost of several beltlines around central Vienna. The hotel was run by a gregarious character, general manager Roland Hamberger.[250]

He delighted in welcoming the secretary with a bubbly laugh and energetic handshake each time his motorcade pulled up to the back door. Hamberger also proudly donned a red bib and blue polka-dotted pants for a cookout he threw when the lingering negotiations kept his American guests abroad for their Fourth of July national holiday.

We stayed about six blocks away at the Hotel Imperial, another five-star property built in the Italian neo-Renaissance style. While its guest roster has included many famous names, including Queen Elizabeth II, silent-film star Charlie Chaplin, and rock guitarist Pete Townshend, the Imperial also has a dark past.[251]

Adolf Hitler worked at the hotel while growing up in Vienna, and the German leader returned as an honored guest in 1938.[252] In fact, banners bearing the Nazi swastika once hung from the balcony attached to the suite used by Kerry. We were stunned to hear the story and later find black-and-white photos of that moment.

On a more contemporary note, the hotel also is home to the Imperial Torte, a chocolate cake layered with marzipan. It's tucked into a pinewood box and sold to tourists from around the globe.[253]

Captain Umlauf would lead Secretary Kerry through exercises or massage his muscles to prevent atrophy. He accompanied Kerry when he took walks on his crutches and offered advice when the secretary started to wane physically.

The ebb and flow of the negotiations proved tortuitous, because Kerry had fairly regular opportunities to exercise and rest before having to sit back at a table and plow through difficult disputes.

As *The New Yorker* recounted in its reconstruction of the talks, the parties reached agreement first on the terms to limit Iran's future nuclear program. The more sensitive issues about sanctions relief or other topics usually bogged down because they had a connection to Iran's military, especially the Revolutionary Guard, which was strongly opposed to any softening with the West.[254]

*(Top) Secretary Kerry thanks Jake Sullivan and Bill Burns for their
preliminary work. (Bottom) Negotiations at the Palais Coburg.*

*(Top) One-on-one meeting in New York. (Bottom) A final phone call
to free* Washington Post *reporter Jason Rezaian.*

(Top) P5+1 session in Lausanne. (Middle) Secretary Kerry flying back to Vienna after bike accident. (Bottom) Counsel from expert Jim Timbie.

(Top) Wendy Sherman reviews gives and gets. (Middle) Lobbying French foreign minister for implementation. (Bottom) Signing sanctions relief.

Zarif and President Rouhani, viewed as moderates, tried to minimize antagonizing the hard-liners. That prompted them to broach the possibility of reopening the framework agreement that had been so roundly criticized at home.

Meanwhile, Kerry and the other P5+1 members worried about Iran using money from any sanctions relief to bolster the Revolutionary Guard, or the country's support for terrorist groups such as Hezbollah in Lebanon and Hamas in the Gaza Strip.

"The 30th is tomorrow," Kerry wrote to Zarif in an email he read aloud to us on June 29, 2015. "So, Javad, either we get serious and treat this professionally or it is over."

Referring to the interim agreement, he said, "We are not going to renegotiate Lausanne, plain and simple."[255]

Hours before Hamberger threw the Americans their Fourth of July barbecue dinner, Kerry and Zarif realized the two sides always ate separately.

The Austrian government, keen to host such a historic international negotiation, not only had paid to rent the entire Palais Coburg but also picked up the tab for the lunch and dinner buffets that fed the two negotiating teams. The Iranians would eat in one room, the P5+1 members next door. Both sides would discuss their own strategy while refueling.

Sometimes the Iranians indulged themselves and got takeout from the McDonald's restaurant several blocks away. Fast food was not available in Tehran—home to such knockoff Western restaurants as Pizza Hot and Mash Donald's[256]—so the Iranians had become prodigious consumers of Big Macs and Filet-O-Fish sandwiches during their visits to Vienna.

On July 4, 2015, Zarif asked Kerry if he'd like to come into the Iranian dining room and join his team for lunch. The secretary accepted and the two sides sat down to a buffet of Persian food after the Iranians held their 1 p.m. prayers.

"It was ten times better than the food we ate on our side of the house," a US aide told *The New Yorker*. "It was a moment where it was clear—we knew it, sort of, without remarking on it—that these relationships had really developed over time."[257]

Secretary Kerry himself told Undersecretary Sherman afterward, "Wendy, I think there's a deal there."[258]

She replied, "I agree with you. Yesterday, I wasn't so sure; today, I see the way there."[259]

THE FOLLOWING DAY, UNDERSECRETARY Sherman sat on the floor next to Kerry so the two could review a list of potential "gets" and "gives" written by hand on a piece of oversized paper torn from an easel stand.

The undersecretary for political affairs is one of the most powerful jobs in the State Department. The person holding the title oversees each of the six regional bureaus and all the bilateral policy issues bubbling up in each of them.

Sherman was an experienced and relentless diplomat who previously negotiated with North Korea during the Clinton administration. During the Obama administration, she was perfect for rebutting the Iranian hard-liners. She didn't suffer fools gladly, as any staffer who tried to check a suitcase while traveling with her learned. The undersecretary would tote only a carry-on so she could get to work immediately upon arriving in a foreign capital.

Sherman was deferential to Kerry but didn't feel the same compunction with most others. Once, when the secretary walked into a briefing room, she offered him her chair, saying, "Take mine. I'm sure somebody else will get up and give me theirs."[260]

Her spine was a complement to Kerry's heart.

Sherman managed not only a complex and detailed negotiation with the Iranians but a diverse group of lawyers, technical specialists, and diplomats. She earned the nickname Silver Fox because of her monochromatic hair color, and her staff gave her a T-shirt with a "Team Silver Fox" logo on it during their stay in Vienna.

When Sherman had finished briefing Kerry on July 5, 2015, Zarif came to the secretary's suite for continued discussions.

The parties had already blown through a deadline on July 1, 2015, and there was growing speculation they might miss another on July 7.

Kerry got on his crutches and made his way out the front door of the Palais Coburg so he could address the international press corps, which was now growing impatient by the delays.

"I've said from the moment I became involved in this we want a good agreement, only a good agreement, and we're not going to shave anywhere at the margins in order just to get an agreement," the secretary said on July 5, 2015. "This is something that the world will analyze, experts everywhere will look at. There are plenty of people in the nonproliferation community, nuclear experts, who will look at this. And none of us are going to be content to do something that can't pass scrutiny."[261]

He immediately pivoted on his heels and crutched his way back into the hotel for another formal negotiating session with Zarif. It was quickly clear the two were losing patience themselves.

Sitting in our dining room, which shared a wall with the Blue Salon where Americans and Iranians routinely met, we could hear yelling—mostly the shouts of Zarif.

Jason Meininger, the secretary's senior aide, got up. He opened the door to the negotiating room and told the group that others could hear their noise. The Iranians later spread a story that one of Zarif's bodyguards had to come into the room to restore the peace after his boss's feisty outburst.

The rest of the P5+1 foreign ministers returned to Vienna on July 6, 2015, and worked past midnight, their coats off, their ties loosened.

At one point, Zarif grew angry again when he felt pressure from Federica Mogherini, who had replaced Baroness Ashton as the European Union high representative for foreign affairs. She suggested the talks might end because of Iran's intransigence.

"Never threaten an Iranian!" the foreign minister yelled, according to numerous accounts afterward.[262]

"Or a Russian!" replied Russian foreign minister Sergey Lavrov, seeking to break the tension with a flash of humor.[263]

The group sessions recurred during the next three days—*Groundhog Day*—prompting Secretary Kerry to complain their posturing and speech-making had broken the momentum he created during his one-on-one negotiations with the Iranians.

"We've got to get going," he said to Rob Malley, the White House senior director for Iran, Iraq, and the Gulf States. "We've had too much process. We have to negotiate."[264]

On the afternoon of July 11, 2015, Kerry asked for some time alone in the Palais Coburg courtyard. Sitting on a wicker chair amid well-groomed topiaries, he leafed through documents and used his preferred Uni-ball pen to jot down notes on his favorite paper, a leftover legal pad whose binding was embossed with the words "United States Senate."

The former criminal prosecutor wanted to bring the case to a close—either with a deal or an acknowledgment one couldn't be reached—so he distilled his thoughts into a final argument for his Iranian counterpart.

"At that point, I knew it was up to me," Kerry later told me.[265]

The final forty-eight hours of the negotiations were a frenzy of talks, phone calls from National Security Adviser Susan Rice, and emails with President Obama.

On July 12, 2015, as the momentum continued to build, Kerry had dinner with his fellow foreign ministers at the top of the Hotel Sofitel, a skyscraper overlooking central Vienna.

At 10:35 a.m. the next day, Kerry authorized the US Air Force to release a notice telling the Austrians our plane was departing on July 14, 2015.

"We're leaving tomorrow, folks—one way or another," the secretary told us.[266]

He shuttled between meetings with the Iranians and his fellow foreign ministers the rest of the day.

At 10:03 p.m., Kerry met in his hold room at the Palais Coburg with Mogherini, the EU high representative. At 10:15 p.m., Lavrov—whose Russian Federation held sway with Iran—joined. At 10:48 p.m., Zarif entered.[267]

The three had met for barely two minutes when we heard Zarif shouting again.

After several minutes, Secretary Kerry popped his head out and asked Undersecretary Sherman if there was any small concession they could make to mollify the Iranian.

"It's Middle Eastern pride," Kerry told her.[268]

"No, it's Middle Eastern souk," Sherman replied, referring to the regional bazaars where haggling was expected.[269]

One State Department official was charged with maintaining a list of Iranians who might gain sanction relief under the nuclear deal. He said there were eleven low-level people he'd been holding back who could be added to the agreement without objection from the White House.

Kerry nodded and closed the door.

At 11:05 p.m., I was standing with others from the US delegation in the hall outside when the secretary called my name from behind the door.

When I walked in, he asked me to take a picture of the group.

They'd just reached agreement on the Joint Comprehensive Plan of Action.

———

TRUE TO FORM, THINGS were not done until they were done.

The Russians weren't happy because Lavrov had to leave for another meeting, yet the White House didn't want to announce the deal until 8 a.m. Eastern time the following morning. That was 2 p.m. local time. The Russians wanted to do it at 5 a.m. local time—a nonstarter because that would be 11 p.m. back in the United States.

The EU high representative and Kerry also had to reconvene the rest of the P5+1 to tell them they'd worked out the final sticking points. That meeting started about 1 a.m. on July 14, 2015, and lasted about fifteen minutes. About 1:30 a.m., Zarif joined the group to mark the consensus.

He then held another one-on-one session with Kerry about 2 a.m. to resolve a final language dispute. That session lasted twenty minutes. About ten minutes later, our motorcade pulled up at the Hotel Imperial.

We caught a few hours of sleep before getting up to make final edits to Secretary Kerry's public statement.

About 10:30 a.m., we were rolling to the Vienna International Centre, a complex hosting the United Nations Office at Vienna.

The P5+1 members and the Iranians held a ministerial meeting before standing for a group photo and then reconvening for a final group plenary session to cement the deal.

During the first of those sessions, various ministers made remarks. Secretary Kerry spoke last, and when he did, he recalled his service in Vietnam and the lesson it taught him about exhausting diplomacy before resorting to violence.

"'When I was twenty-two, I went to war,'" Undersecretary Sherman recounted him saying. "And then he choked up, sort of like I did just a few minutes ago. He couldn't get the words out. And everybody was completely spellbound. And he sort of re-got his voice, and said, 'I went to war, and it became clear to me that I never wanted to go to war again.' That's what this was all about. Trying to settle these matters through diplomacy and peaceful means. And it was such a moving moment, that everybody in that small room applauded, including the Iranian delegation."[270]

EU high representative Mogherini and Foreign Minister Zarif left the plenary and went off to address the press assembled at the neighboring Austria Center Vienna. Kerry sat backstage, reviewing his remarks and watching President Obama on an iPad as he spoke to the American people from the White House.

The president had moved up his speech an hour—to 7 a.m. EDT—to accommodate the Russians.

"This deal meets every single one of the bottom lines that we established when we achieved a framework earlier this spring," President Obama said. "Every pathway to a nuclear weapon is cut off. And the inspection and transparency regime necessary to verify that objective will be put in place."[271]

He then turned to the task at hand: winning congressional approval for the agreement.

"Without this deal, there is no scenario where the world joins us in sanctioning Iran until it completely dismantles its nuclear program. Nothing we know about the Iranian government suggests that it would simply capitulate under that kind of pressure," the president said. "We put sanctions in place to get a diplomatic resolution, and that is what we have done."

Kerry picked up the theme during his own remarks.

"Sanctioning Iran until it capitulates makes for a powerful talking point and a pretty good political speech, but it's not achievable outside a world of fantasy," the secretary said. "The true measure of this agreement is not whether it meets all of the desires of one side at the expense of the other; the test is whether or not it will leave the world safer and more secure than it would be without it."[272]

Secretary Kerry finished by taking questions from three journalists. When a fourth begged for one more, our boss offered a bracing reminder about the physical challenge he endured during the long and stressful negotiations.

"You got to bear with me because this is the longest I've stood up for quite a while, guys," he said, standing crutchless at a podium. "I'm going to move out."[273]

We returned to the Hotel Imperial, where the secretary conducted an additional set of round-robin interviews with the US television networks.

About 6:30 p.m., we left the hotel for the final time and drove past sunflower fields en route to Vienna International Airport. After we took off, Energy Secretary Moniz—who has Portuguese roots—pulled out a bottle of Madeira wine given to him by a fellow Massachusetts resident, US ambassador to Portugal Robert Sherman. Moniz told Secretary Kerry he'd been saving it for a special occasion—and this qualified.

I snapped photos as Kerry clinked glasses with Moniz and Sherman.

They finished their drinks while the rest of us went to sleep for the rest of the flight home.

———

SECRETARY KERRY WAS BACK at the State Department the next morning and sitting in his usual seat at the head of the table for his daily senior staff meeting.

"I thought the president did an outstanding job yesterday," he told us, referring to President Obama's televised remarks, "and we're going to win [in Congress] because we have a better argument."[274]

An hour later, the secretary got a taste of the pride his diplomacy had engendered. His assistant secretaries and other Department senior staff members applauded as he came in on his crutches and plopped down for their weekly meeting in the secure conference room on the 7th Floor.

"Never has an act of sitting down received such a response," he said to laughter.[275]

He told the group that both Vienna and the Hotel Imperial were great, "but it could still feel like a prison."[276]

In truth, the historians told us, the time he'd spent in Vienna was the most any secretary had ever spent in one foreign city during peacetime.

Now that he was back in the United States, Kerry couldn't revel in his accomplishment. He and President Obama had to work to ensure the United States held up its end of the deal—something that wasn't guaranteed despite their best efforts.

As we'd been overseas negotiating in Geneva, Lausanne, and Vienna, Congress had been asserting itself back home in several ways.

First, it had called on Kerry to come up to Capitol Hill and testify after the Joint Plan of Action had been reached. This, the secretary had complained, forced him to speak publicly about all he had won in the interim deal before heading back overseas and negotiating with Zarif about the terms of the final deal.

Then, in the midst of the talks to reach the framework for the Joint Comprehensive Plan of Action, House Republican leaders issued that invitation to Israeli prime minister Benjamin Netanyahu to address a Joint Session of Congress.

That decision to invite a foreign head of state to address the US legislative branch, in opposition to a foreign policy pursuit of the president and the executive branch, left Secretary Kerry infuriated.

"I, personally, as an ex-Member of Congress, take umbrage that they will be manipulated this way," he told us during our February 25, 2015, senior staff meeting.[277]

On March 9, 2015, US Senator Tom Cotton, a Republican from Arkansas, enlisted forty-six other Republican senators to endorse an open letter he wrote to the leaders of Iran.

In it, Cotton explained that under the Constitution, any deal not approved by Congress was considered nothing more than an executive agreement with the sitting president. He also noted that President Obama's term would end in January 2017, while many members of Congress would remain in office "perhaps decades" beyond that date.

"What these two constitutional provisions mean is that we will consider any agreement regarding your nuclear-weapons program that is not approved by Congress as nothing more than an executive agreement between President Obama and Ayatollah Khomeini. The next president could revoke such an executive agreement with the stroke of a pen and future Congresses could modify the terms of the agreement at any time," Cotton and his colleagues wrote.[278]

A month later, US senator John McCain, a Republican from Arizona, publicly called Secretary Kerry "delusional" for thinking he could negotiate phased sanctions relief with the Iranians. He also said, "I don't know who's more believable"—Secretary Kerry or Ayatollah Khameini—amid the competing narratives about the terms of the framework agreement that had just been negotiated in Lausanne.

That prompted a rebuke from President Obama, who said such acts by Cotton, McCain, and others were "an indication of the degree to which partisanship has crossed all boundaries."[279]

In May 2015, US senator Bob Corker, the Tennessee Republican chairing the Senate Foreign Relations Committee, succeeded in passing the Iran Nuclear Agreement Review Act. It required congressional review of any final nuclear agreement with Iran before the president could waive any sanctions.

The timing of the bill not only left the secretary urging the Iranians to commit to a deal Congress might ultimately reject, but it included a trigger affecting the pace of the final negotiations. If an agreement wasn't reached by July 9, 2015, the law said a thirty-day period for Congress to review it would double to sixty days.

While that ostensibly was to allow Congress time to take its annual August recess, it also gave critics even more time to mount their opposition to the deal.

One of the early complaints about the final Joint Comprehensive Plan of Action was that it contained sunset clauses. For example, Iran had to place two-thirds of its uranium-enriching centrifuges in storage, but only for ten years. It also was required to limit its enrichment of uranium to 3.67 percent and cap its stockpile at 660 pounds, both below levels needed to build a bomb, but only for fifteen years.

All in all, the "breakout time"—the interval required for Iran to produce enough fissile material for one bomb—was increasing from two months before the negotiations began to at least a year for a period of more than ten years.

The secretary expressed his exasperation about concern over the sunset clauses on July 20, 2015, not even a week after the final deal was reached.

"If they're worried about what happens in Year 15, they're going to move it up to tomorrow" by killing the deal and leaving Iran's nuclear program unrestrained, he told his senior staff.[280]

He noted Iran had agreed to live in perpetuity with an enhanced protocol with the International Atomic Energy Association for ensuring it had a peaceful nuclear program.

The secretary also argued congressional rejection of the deal not only would destabilize the Middle East and leave the United States isolated from its P5+1 partners, but would undermine the United States in seeking any nonproliferation agreement with a country that already had nuclear weapons: North Korea.

While that sentiment may have been overzealous, his concerns about US credibility were rooted in fact.

The agreement also had to be viewed beyond the chasm of the country's partisan political divide.

While Kerry and the United States were the lead negotiators for the Iran deal, the early meetings and final agreement were facilitated by the twenty-eight-member European Union—an organizing body for the disparate nations of Europe.

The final deal, meanwhile, also was accepted by the P5+1 nations—the Permanent Members of the United Nations Security Council, namely the United States, United Kingdom, France, Russia, and China, plus Germany. All of whom are nuclear powers.

When, some asked, had the UN Security Council agreed to anything? Its lack of consensus, and the irksome practice of Russia vetoing many US-led initiatives, made its unity about the Iran agreement noteworthy.

The whole of the Security Council voted 15–0 to endorse the deal.

In a volatile area of the world, with nuclear proliferation a concern for the region, the United States had brokered a deal receiving support from the EU and the full UN Security Council. That was an achievement in and of itself.

Were the United States to walk away from it, whether because it didn't like the terms or because it felt continued or additional sanctions would earn a better bargain, the rest of the world seemed to disagree.

In that case, the United States faced the specter of being abandoned in the broad sanctions regime that had ultimately brought Iran to the negotiating table, during which it accepted diplomacy over military confrontation. Other nations, meanwhile, stood on the cusp of doing business with Iran, to the detriment of the US economy.

"Rejecting this agreement would not be sending a signal of resolve to Iran; it would be broadcasting a message so puzzling most people across the globe would find it impossible to comprehend," Secretary Kerry said in September 2015 at the National Constitution Center in Philadelphia. "They've listened as we warned over and over again about the dangers of Iran's nuclear program. They've watched as we spent two years forging a broadly accepted agreement to rein that program in. They've nodded their heads in support as we have explained how the plan that we have developed will make the world safer."

He said: "Who could fairly blame them for not understanding if we suddenly switch course and reject the very outcome we had worked so hard to obtain?"[281]

Less than a week later, the administration won relief. US Senator Barbara Mikulski, a Maryland Democrat set to retire in 2016, announced she supported the deal. She was the thirty-fourth senator to do so, ensuring President Obama had the votes to support a veto of any Republican resolution disapproving the deal.

"No deal is perfect, especially one negotiated with the Iranian regime," Mikulski said in a statement, but the Joint Comprehensive Plan of Action is "the best option available to block Iran from having a nuclear bomb."[282]

On September 9, 2015, all hopes for defeating the deal ended when, by a Senate vote of 58–42, opponents failed to win a procedural vote against the agreement. The forty-two senators now in opposition were enough to ensure a filibuster could block any vote against the deal under the Corker law.

The congressional review period lapsed on September 17, 2015.

All that was left was one last hurdle: implementing the terms of the final agreement.

SECRETARY KERRY AND DEFENSE Secretary Ashton Carter were meeting with their Filipino counterparts in the Ben Franklin Room on January 12, 2016, when aides approached each one and passed them identical notes.

Ten US sailors had been detained by Iranian naval forces after their boats had strayed into Iranian waters off Farsi Island. Not only was it in the middle of the Persian Gulf, but it had been used as a base for Iranian Revolutionary Guard speedboats since the 1980s.

The timing couldn't have been more explosive, given Kerry was due to return to Vienna in four days for Implementation Day of the Iran nuclear deal.

The secretary excused himself and came down to his office to call Foreign Minister Zarif on his cell phone.

"Do you know what this could do to the deal if it's not resolved promptly?" he said to his Iranian counterpart.

After at least four more calls with the foreign minister and several rounds with National Security Adviser Susan Rice and General Joseph Dunford, the chairman of the Joint Chiefs of Staff, Zarif pledged the sailors would be released at sunrise the following day.

"Well, we handled a hot potato today," the secretary later said to me as he sat calmly at his desk.[283]

In fact, he argued, the incident underscored the value of his diplomacy with Iran in several ways.

First, because of his personal engagement with the foreign minister, Kerry had a cell phone number and Gmail address that immediately put him in direct contact with his peer. Second, because the two had worked out other differences previously, they trusted each other and could speak without hyperbole.

Finally, because both sides stood to gain from implementing the deal, each also had something to lose if they repeated the 1979 hostage crisis.

"We can all imagine how a similar situation might have played out three or four years ago," Kerry said the following day at the National Defense University in Washington. "These are situations which, as everybody here knows, have the ability, if not properly guided, to get out of control."[284]

We left later that day for London, where the secretary met with Saudi Arabian foreign minister Adel Al-Jubeir to talk about Syria, Iran, and Middle East peace. The bulk of his agenda, though, was to work from his United Kingdom staging area on the final terms of implementation with Iran.

The lever was controls on Iran's nuclear program in exchange for sanctions relief. While Iran took steps through the summer, fall, and early winter of 2015–2016 to ship out uranium stockpiles, shutter centrifuges, and deactivate plants, the details of the sanctions relief rested on some technicalities.

The two sides were also trying to resolve two other separate but related issues.

First, Iran wanted to close a case at an international tribunal in The Hague under which it sought to regain $400 million, plus interest. It had paid the money to the United States for fighter jets that went undelivered after the two sides broke off diplomatic relations in the late 1970s.

Meanwhile, the United States wanted to win the release of a group of Americans, including *Washington Post* reporter Jason Rezaian, an Iranian American who'd been held hostage in Tehran on espionage charges since 2014. US officials said they were trumped up to give Iran leverage in its dealings with the United States.

Resolution of The Hague case involved an ugly transaction in which Iran demanded the United States refund its $400 million payment—in cash. Iran also wanted the money sitting on a plane destined for Tehran before Rezaian was allowed to leave the country through the other negotiation.

That led to the headline-grabbing story a month later in which *The Wall Street Journal* reported that "wooden pallets stacked with Euros, Swiss francs, and other currencies" were flown to Iran on an unmarked cargo plane.[285]

This transfer was followed by two more cash payments in which the additional $1.3 billion in interest was sent to Iran, a sum that sent critics of the deal howling.[286]

Senator Cotton, who served in Iraq and Afghanistan as a member of the Army, accused President Obama of paying "a $1.7 billion ransom to the ayatollahs for US hostages."[287]

Others accused the administration of trying to conceal the settlement.

In fact, this wasn't true.

President Obama mentioned it in nationally televised remarks he delivered on January 17, 2016, his first on the agreement's implementation.

"For the United States, this settlement could save us billions of dollars that could have been pursued by Iran," the president said. "So there was no benefit to the United States in dragging this out. With the nuclear deal done, prisoners released, the time was right to resolve this dispute as well."

Secretary Kerry also issued a statement that day detailing payment of the claim and the accompanying interest.

"Iran's recovery was fixed at a reasonable rate of interest, and therefore, Iran is unable to pursue a bigger Tribunal award against us, preventing US taxpayers from being obligated to a larger amount of money," the statement said.

By some estimates, Iran could have received $10 billion through a judgment in its favor.[288]

The Hague settlement coincided with an even bigger deal, at least in media circles. Journalists throughout the United States and the world had taken up Rezaian's cause, thanks to an intense lobbying effort by his family. Relatives also reported that Rezaian had fallen ill in Tehran's infamous Evin Prison and could die in captivity.

Secretary Kerry brought up the case repeatedly in his negotiations with Foreign Minister Zarif, not directly linked to the nuclear deal but taking advantage of any face-to-face meeting to pursue this second track of conversation.

In fact, I snapped a photo of Kerry buttonholing the foreign minister and Hossein Feridon, the brother of Iranian president Rouhani, urging them to win Rezaian's release. I took that photo backstage in Vienna after the nuclear deal was announced on July 14, 2015.

Now his diplomacy continued six months later with a phone call to his Iranian counterpart as implementation of the agreement hung in the balance.

"Javad, how are you?" the secretary asked from London at midday on January 15, 2015. When the foreign minister apparently repeated the question back to him, Kerry laughed and said, "I'm fine; wrestling with alligators—as you are."[289]

Kerry worked on details of implementation, the Hague settlement, and the Rezaian release throughout the day. He also took a walk through London, even stopping at a gun shop to look at hunting rifles. Throughout dinner at a Chinese restaurant, his iPhone screen illuminated his face as he typed an email to the foreign minister.

At 12:55 a.m. on January 16, 2015, the day the Iran deal was supposed to be implemented, now chief of staff Jon Finer and I walked into Kerry's suite at the Grosvenor House Hotel. We found the Boss on his iPad.

"What are you doing?" we asked.

"Playing Internet Scrabble," he answered.

Incredulous, Finer asked, "Does the person you're playing realize he's playing against the secretary of State?"

Kerry smiled and said, "Nope."

We laughed as he asked us for a four-letter word ending in "nt."

When we suggested "tint," he replied, "That's good, but it only gets you five [points]. You need to get at least twenty, or you're dead. Right now, I'm ahead."[290]

———

SIX HOURS LATER, WE were just about to leave the Grosvenor House when Finer got a message from the team in Vienna.

"Holy shit," he said. "Jason Rezaian is leaving the prison in forty-five minutes. This is happening."[291]

Yet like everything else in each phase of the Middle East peace talks or the Iran nuclear negotiations, things were not that simple.

We flew from London to Vienna because EU high representative Mogherini refused to allow the implementation to occur in Geneva, where the P5+1 ministers had planned to meet.

Soon we found ourselves in a familiar place: in the Palais Coburg, and facing a familiar opponent: the French.

Throughout numerous negotiations during Secretary Kerry's tenure, we found French foreign minister Laurent Fabius and his team to be particularly frustrating as counterparts.

The foreign minister, who viewed himself as French presidential timber, would routinely announce that France was "a great country" or "a proud country" needing to be respected. His political director for Iran, Nicolas de Riviere, wasn't above playing one side against the other, or leaking details of the negotiations to make France look good and other parties look bad.

In that context, both of them also weren't beyond stalling progress in the P5+1 talks while they lined up potential business deals in Iran for Airbus, the French airplane maker, Citroën and Peugeot, both French automakers, or any number of other French businesses.

Both Kerry and Undersecretary Sherman took the unusual step of publicly admonishing France after a business delegation representing more than one hundred French firms traveled to Tehran in early 2014. That happened just as the rest of the P5+1 was trying to reinforce with Iran that it needed to come to terms on a final nuclear deal. They warned it risked losing the temporary sanctions relief it received in the November 2013 interim agreement.

"This is not helpful," Sherman testified to the Senate Foreign Relations Committee on February 4, 2014. "Tehran is not open for business because our sanctions relief is quite temporary, quite limited, and quite targeted."[292]

Now, nearly two years later, France's Fabius was the lone holdout as the P5+1 ministers sought to implement the nuclear deal. It, in fact, would provide permanent sanctions relief.

Fabius complained about wording in a section of the agreement relating to inspections that would have to be performed by the International Atomic Energy Association.

Zarif, who'd flown to Vienna for an Implementation Day announcement, came to Kerry's room at the Palais Coburg to complain about the delay.

He said it "humiliated" President Rouhani after all the work on the nuclear agreement, the Hague dispute, and the Rezaian affair. Kerry and Zarif then walked together to High Representative Mogherini's suite, surprising an aide who casually answered their door knock.

Soon, all three of them were in the secretary's suite as Kerry unloaded a depth charge to break the stalemate.

Speaking on his cellphone, he called Fabius and told him, "We're really feeling quite vital to reach a resolution."

Then Zarif spoke up on the speaker phone, saying, "Hello, Laurent. We are all on the same side! . . . Let's get this done, before this gets out of hand."

He added, "I am worried, my good friend, that this will be misunderstood back in Tehran."

With that, Kerry read aloud the wording for the upcoming statement being delivered by Zarif and Mogherini.

Zarif asked, "Is that good to Laurent?"

The French foreign minister, who'd later complain he was both taken by surprise and outnumbered by the three-way call to his personal phone, replied, "Yes."[293]

Several minutes later, we called in some of our traveling photographers to capture the scene as Kerry formally signed paperwork lifting the US sanctions against Iran. When the secretary was done writing his name on each page, he pulled the papers together, banged them down on the table to straighten the stack, and prepared to leave for the Vienna International Centre, the UN compound where the deal had been announced the previous July.

Less than five minutes later, though, he found out there was a problem. Rezaian had arrived at a military plane set to fly him to freedom in Switzerland, but he was refusing to climb aboard because neither his wife, an Iranian reporter named Yeganeh Salehi, nor his mother had not been allowed to join him. Although American-born, Mary Rezaian had come to Iran to advocate for her son's release.

Feeling exposed after having just provided Iran with its sanctions relief, Kerry once again called Zarif on his cellphone.

"The document is clear," he said. "I need your immediate intervention here."[294]

Chief of Staff Finer soon told the secretary that while the two sides had agreed Rezaian's wife and mother would join him, the text did not specifically guarantee it. This omission frustrated Kerry, so he raced over to the VIC to press the point with Zarif before delivering his own remarks commemorating Implementation Day.

Adding to the tension was an unyielding deadline. Under the Air Force crew-rest rules, if we didn't take off by 11:20 p.m., we wouldn't make it back to Washington before the flight crew's duty day expired. That would force us to spend another night in Vienna.

Groundhog Day.

Kerry cited those "very tight constraints" as he began his speech, then raced through the text without taking questions from the media afterward.

"Today, more than four years after I first traveled to Oman at the request of President Obama to discreetly explore whether the kind of nuclear talks that we ultimately entered into with Iran were even possible, after more than two and a half years of intense multilateral negotiations, the International Atomic Energy Agency has now verified that Iran has honored its commitments to alter—and in fact, dismantle—much of its nuclear program in compliance with the agreement that we reached last July," he said.

Kerry added: "I think we have also proven once again why diplomacy has to always be our first choice, and war our last resort. And that is a very important lesson to reinforce."[295]

We raced from the Vienna Convention Centre back to the airport, skipping our customary courtesy photos on the tarmac with embassy staffers and our police escort.

When the door closed and the wheels started to roll, I looked down at my watch. It read, 11:20:35 p.m.

The US Air Force had given us a thirty-five-second grace period. We took off several minutes later, as Kerry continued to work the phones in his cabin.

Five minutes afterward, he called the White House.

"Crisis resolved," the secretary declared.

Authorities in Tehran had awakened a judge and got his consent for "Yeghi" Salehi and Mary Rezaian's departure from Iran.

As our plane and the one carrying the Rezaian family flew west through the night sky, a cargo plane took off from Switzerland and began to fly east toward Iran.

Secretary Kerry and the P5+1 had consummated the Iran nuclear deal. Jason, Yeghi, and Mary Rezaian, as well as two other Americans on a separate commercial flight, had won their freedom.

And the Iranians were about to reclaim money they paid for fighter jets back in 1979, shortly before those students climbed over the walls of the US embassy in Tehran.

*S*ecretary Kerry asked for company during an outing in Oslo, Norway, that took us to another unexpected place.

It was the home where he and his family lived while his father was stationed in Scandinavia for the State Department.

The homeowner, Hedda Ulvness, greeted us and invited us inside, where her two boys excitedly showed the secretary of State what they knew only as their house.

Kerry looked around, in part with a face of familiarity, in part puzzlement while trying to recall exactly how things looked when it was his own family's home.

The boys raced him up the stairs to the second floor, where they showed him their rooms. One excitedly jumped on his bed as the Boss asked them about school and their lives in Norway.

Afterward, we went into the backyard, where the secretary posed with the family against a backdrop of their shared residence.

Secretary Kerry's brother, Cam, had the best memory of where they lived, and he was able to pinpoint the location from a Google Maps satellite image.

Diplomatic Security Service agent Seth Emers had the task of walking up to the front door, knocking, and asking Ulvness if she'd be willing to have a visitor.

She smiled, agreed, and opened her door to a familiar stranger.

7

RUSSIA

JOHN KERRY WAS AT the end of a quick trip to Europe when he and British foreign secretary William Hague stepped up to a pair of podiums at the Foreign and Commonwealth Office in London on September 9, 2013.

They were there for a routine news conference following a typical meeting between two established allies.

Both men told reporters their working breakfast covered the Middle East peace talks, counterterrorism efforts, and the civil war in Syria.

The latter topic was timely, since Syrian president Bashar al-Assad was accused of using chemical weapons to kill more than 1,200 of his own people in an attack three weeks earlier.

"Our government supports the objective of ensuring there can be no impunity for the first use of chemical warfare in the 21st century," said Hague. "As an international community, we must deter further attacks and hold those responsible for them accountable."[296]

The United States, with Secretary Kerry taking the lead, had initially built the case for an immediate military response, but then President Obama decided to seek congressional approval for a strike. He switched just days after members of the British Parliament voted against Prime Minister David Cameron's request to join any US-led attack.

"The United States of America, President Obama, myself, others are in full agreement that the end of the conflict in Syria requires a political solution. There is no military solution," Kerry told reporters. "If one party believes that it can rub out countless numbers of his own citizens with impunity using chemicals that have been banned for nearly 100 years because of what Europe learned in World War I, if he can do that with impunity, he will never come to a negotiating table."[297]

When it came time for questions, Margaret Brennan, the State Department correspondent for CBS News, stood up and directed one to Kerry.

Referring to Assad, she asked, "Is there anything at this point that his government could do or offer that would stop an attack?"[298]

The secretary scoffed and delivered a tongue-in-cheek reply.

"Sure. He could turn over every single bit of his chemical weapons to the international community in the next week. Turn it over, all of it, without delay, and allow a full and total accounting for that," he said.

"But he isn't about to do it, and it can't be done, obviously."[299]

How prescient the question and how bated the response.

We left the media center and briefly returned to our hold room before heading to the airport. State Department spokesperson Jen Psaki told Kerry she was concerned about his remark. Reporters, she said, were likely to seize upon it just as the administration was trying to strengthen its diplomatic hand by winning support for a military option against President Assad.

What neither she nor her boss anticipated was that someone else also was ready to latch onto the comment.

As Psaki answered questions from the traveling press corps during our flight back to Washington, the phone rang in Kerry's cabin.

The caller was Sergey Lavrov, the Russian foreign minister. He had an intriguing proposal: If Russia were able the get the Syrian regime to comply with the secretary's off-the-cuff demand, would the United States be willing to go along?

Kerry was intrigued but noncommittal. Yet by the time we landed, the idea had circulated within the White House and State Department.

The consensus was that Russia should be put to the test.[300]

It was the beginning of a long and complicated relationship with our former Cold War opponent throughout Secretary Kerry's tenure. It would tack from unity over Syrian chemical weapons to division over the bifurcation of Ukraine, back to unity during the Iranian nuclear negotiations, before a final split after accusations of Russian meddling in the 2016 US presidential election.

Less than nine months after we left office, Lavrov delivered a tart assessment of US–Russia relations emblematic of the power plays, strategic leveraging, harsh language, and selective memory permeating our dealings. The Russian minister even included a potshot at a former president of the United States.

"US-Russia relations are suffering not from the fact that there are conflicts but rather because the previous US administration was small-hearted and they were revengeful," Lavrov told reporters attending the 2017 UN General Assembly. "They put this time bomb in US Russia relations. I didn't expect that from a Nobel Peace Prize winner."[301]

The United States may have an economy dwarfing that of Russia, and it may be the country where people from around the world—including Russians—want to visit and live, but the two nations had crept into being adversaries in a second Cold War.

———

SECRETARY KERRY FLEW AWAY from the UK after that news conference because he had to get back to Washington to brief Congress that evening before a potential vote on using force in Syria.

He was back on Capitol Hill the next day and addressed the Russian proposal during testimony to the House Armed Services Committee.

"We have made it clear to them—I have in several conversations with Foreign Minister Lavrov—that this cannot be a process of delay, this cannot be a process of avoidance," he said. "It has to be real, has to be measurable, tangible. And it is exceedingly difficult—I want everybody here to know—to fulfill those conditions. But we're waiting for that proposal, but we're not waiting for long."[302]

He didn't have to. The two sides agreed to meet in two days in Geneva to see if they could reach an agreement.

Our bags barely unpacked after returning from London, we got back on our plane on the evening of September 11, 2015, for another flight to Europe. When we arrived the next morning, the secretary met first with Lakhdar Brahimi, the UN special envoy for Syria, before holding an evening meeting and working dinner with Lavrov.

Fortunately, the groundwork had been laid.

As flippant as Kerry's comment seemed, it had been preceded by several months of private conversations between United States and Russian leaders about securing Syria's chemical weapons arsenal.

President Obama and President Putin broached the idea in June 2012 during the G-20 meeting in Los Cabos, Mexico. The two leaders renewed their discussion when they spoke face-to-face on the sidelines of the G-20 meeting in St. Petersburg, Russia, just the week before Kerry made his comment in London.

There was good reason for President Obama to deal with President Putin.

Russia is a vast and proud country, as well as a nuclear power. It spans eleven time zones and sacrificed over twenty million of its citizens—more than eight million of them soldiers—fighting against the Nazis in World War II.

By one estimate, over twenty Soviet troops died for each service member from what the United States would label its "Greatest Generation."[303]

In a 2005 speech, Putin called the collapse of the Soviet Union, which he served as a KGB officer, "the greatest geopolitical catastrophe" of the twentieth century.[304] Despite a dismal economy overly reliant on energy resources, the country had a technical prowess especially evident in its aviation and space industries, the latter shown when the Soviet Union beat the United States and launched the first man into space in 1961. Today, the United States relies on Russia to launch its astronauts to the International Space Station after retiring its space shuttle fleet.

In another measure of national rivalry, the United States labeled its 1980 Olympic hockey victory over the Russians the "Miracle on Ice."

Analysts said Putin believed the United States got cocky after the fall of the Soviet Union in 1991 and didn't show due respect to the new Russian Federation. It supported an expansion of NATO on Russia's border, particularly by seeking to add the former Soviet republic of Georgia, and rebuffed Russia's post-9/11 efforts to cooperate on counterterrorism. President Putin, after all, had been the first foreign leader to telephone President George W. Bush following the attack.

The trend continued, in Putin's eyes, with what he perceived to be meddling in 2011 parliamentary elections, his 2012 reelection campaign, and encouragement for a 2014 revolution in another former Soviet republic, Ukraine.

Nonetheless, he and President Obama discussed ridding Syria of its chemical weapons in 2012 and 2013, and Secretary Kerry and Foreign Minister Lavrov had parallel conversations in April 2013 and during the ensuing months.

That didn't stop outsiders from noting the nontraditional path that ultimately led the two diplomats to the negotiating table.

"While making a case for military strikes in Syria, Secretary of State John F. Kerry became an inadvertent peacemaker this week, and highlighted the risks and rewards of a chief diplomat who loves to talk but does not love the talking point," *Washington Post* diplomatic correspondent Anne Gearan wrote about the situation.

The headline above her article read, "Candid Remark from Kerry Leads to Syria Disarmament Proposal."[305]

Whoever the instigator and however circuitous the route, Kerry and Lavrov now stood before reporters at the outset of their talks in Geneva.

Lavrov deployed a favorite tactic during his opening: trying to hem in an interlocutor with his own words.

"We proceed from the fact that the solution on this problem will make unnecessary any strike on the Syrian Arab Republic, and I am convinced that our American colleagues, as President Obama stated, are firmly convinced that we should follow the peaceful way of resolution of the conflict in Syria," he said.[306]

The foreign minister spoke for fewer than 350 words.

In his own opening, Kerry also tried to pigeonhole his fellow diplomat.

"Expectations are high," the secretary said. "They are high for the United States, perhaps even more so for Russia to deliver on the promise of this moment. This is not a game, and I said that to my friend Sergey when we talked about it initially. It has to be real. It has to be comprehensive. It has to be verifiable. It has to be credible. It has to be timely and implemented in a timely fashion. And finally, there ought to be consequences if it doesn't take place."[307]

But Kerry's remarks ran nearly 1,300 words—almost four times as long as Lavrov's—and his counterpart disagreed with some of what the secretary tried to ascribe to him.

Asking for "just two words" of rebuttal, Lavrov called attention to an op-ed column by President Putin in the previous day's *New York Times*. President Putin wrote:

> From the outset, Russia has advocated peaceful dialogue enabling Syrians to develop a compromise plan for their own future. We are not protecting the Syrian government, but international law. We need to use the United Nations Security Council and believe that preserving law and order in today's complex and turbulent world is one of the few ways to keep international relations from sliding into chaos. The law is still the law, and we must follow it whether we like it or not. Under current international law, force is permitted only in self-defense or by the decision of the Security Council. Anything else is unacceptable under the United Nations Charter and would constitute an act of aggression.[308]

President Putin went on to say—despite all physical and anecdotal evidence to the contrary—that while no one disputed chemical weapons had been used in Syria, there was "every reason to believe" it was by opposition forces to instigate a US response.[309]

His foreign minister told the press corps in Geneva, "I'm convinced that all of you read this article, and I decided not to lay out here our diplomatic position. The diplomacy likes silence."[310]

When Kerry complained he didn't hear the translation of that last part, Lavrov quipped, "It was OK, John. Don't worry."[311]

Kerry replied: "You want me to take your word for it? It's a little early for that."[312]

The laughter that followed was only partly in jest.

———————

THE TWO SIDES MET into the night at Geneva's InterContinental Hotel before resuming the next morning at the nearby Palace of Nations and then moving back to the hotel. They ran through a working lunch and a set of staff dinners before ending around midnight.

By 10 a.m. the following day, Secretary Kerry was dressed in a blue pin-striped suit as he strode across the deck around the hotel's outdoor pool.

It was time to end the negotiation, he felt. He wanted to meet with the foreign minister alone at a teak table and umbrella where the usual conversation centered on whether to order a club sandwich or Caesar salad.

The two were soon joined by their deputies—Undersecretary of State Wendy Sherman and Deputy Foreign Minister Sergei Ryabkov, respectively—as well as technical experts.

Within an hour, the parties reached an agreement. Kerry stood up and shook hands with Lavrov and his team. The two took a brief walk alone along the pool deck before reconvening after an hour for a news conference outlining their deal.

Under the terms of the agreement, Syria acknowledged for the first time it possessed chemical weapons. It also agreed to provide a comprehensive list of them within a week to the Organization for the Prohibition of Chemical Weapons, the UN-based implementing body for the Chemical Weapons Convention. In addition, Syria said it would allow an initial OPCW inspection of its declared sites by November 2013.[313]

All weapons had to be removed from Syria and destroyed by June 30, 2014.

"This situation has no precedent," Amy E. Smithson, an expert on chemical weapons at the James Martin Center for Nonproliferation Studies, said in the next day's *New York Times*. "They are cramming what would probably be five or six years' worth of work into a period of several months, and they are undertaking this in an extremely difficult security environment due to the ongoing civil war."[314]

Kerry noted that in addition to creating benchmarks, the agreement called for proving their achievement through verification. He said:

> If we can join together and make this framework a success and eliminate Syria's chemical weapons, we would not only save lives, but we would reduce the threat to the region, and reinforce an international standard, an international norm. We could also lay the groundwork for further cooperation that is essential to end the bloodshed that has consumed Syria for more than two years. . . . The United States and Russia have long agreed that there is no military solution to the conflict in Syria. It has to be political. It has to happen at the negotiating table. And we, together, remain deeply committed to getting there.[315]

Lavrov skipped rehashing the agreement, saying everyone could read it for themselves.

One point he chose to highlight, though, was that punishment for any violation of the deal would have to be approved by the UN Security Council—where Russia joins the United States and other Permanent Members in holding veto power.

When a reporter asked a follow-up question about that apparent wiggle room, the foreign minister said: "When we are sure, 100 percent, then we in the Russian Federation will be ready to adopt new resolution of the Security Council to embed the measures to punish the perpetrators of this violation, and it's nonsense to continue the speculations on the matter today."[316]

Kerry noted the agreement called for accountability of violations under Chapter 7 of the UN Charter—which allows for military action to enforce its decisions. When he tried, though, to say that means it "*will* impose measures commensurate with whatever is needed," Foreign Minister Lavrov interrupted him.

"*Should, should,*" he said.

"*Should,*" Secretary Kerry acknowledged. "And as Sergey knows, under any circumstances, there would be a debate in the Security Council, even now. So there's no diminishment, there's no diminution of option."[317]

The exchange highlighted one of the Kerry–Lavrov dynamics that would cement itself over the remaining three and a half years of their work together.

Kerry would typically assume the roles of both lead negotiator and chief salesman for agreements, while Lavrov would stay on the sidelines and speak up only when there were opportunities to enshrine the Russian position. Afterward, he'd say only the bare minimum about things to which he had agreed.

And if someone ever tried to put words in his mouth or oversell a Russian commitment, he was quick to stop them.

Kerry's aspirational wishes for his diplomacy were always grounded by Lavrov's stark realities.

As much as Kerry sought to foster or maintain personal relationships, and aspire to the better angels of diplomacy for current and future causes, Lavrov stuck to national interests, cold hard facts, and the matter immediately at hand.

A deal was what was written within the four corners of an agreement— nothing more.

The two soon said their goodbyes and Kerry set off to thank the State Department team for an extraordinary week of diplomacy and technical support. His deft work with Undersecretary Sherman was a prelude to their teamwork on the Iran nuclear negotiations.

Afterward, Kerry asked senior aide Jason Meininger and me if we wanted to grab lunch with him. A Swiss member of our protective detail recommended the hilltop Kempinski Hotel in nearby Montreux. It offered a spectacular view of Lake Geneva and the Dents du Midi.

That string of seven mountain summits held sentimental value to the secretary, because he used to look at them through the window of his bedroom while attending boarding school in Switzerland.

We ate and then were on a walk through lesser hills a few miles away when the Boss's cell phone rang. It was President Obama, calling with his congratulations for the agreement.

As Kerry spoke, I positioned myself behind him, snapping photos. A man stood on a mountaintop, looking out at the horizon, accepting thanks from the Leader of the Free World for the fruits of his diplomacy.

It was heady stuff. Yet both the president and his secretary of State would soon come back to earth, with plenty of thanks to Russia.

SEVERAL MONTHS AFTER THE United States and Russia worked jointly on the Syria chemical weapons agreement, Assistant Secretary of State for European and Eurasian Affairs Toria Nuland made an appearance in Kiev, generating headlines far beyond Ukraine.

Clad in a blue down parka, she held open a plastic grocery bag and offered packets of biscuits to activists camped out in Independence Square, also known as the Maidan.

Several thousand people had congregated there in early December 2013 to call for the resignation of Ukranian president Viktor Yanukovych. They were mad he reneged on a promise to sign an agreement aligning Ukraine with the European Union.[318]

It would have established a free-trade zone and deepened political and other ties between Ukraine and the European bloc. President Putin strongly opposed the move, and President Yanukovych agreed in mid-December to strengthen ties with Russia after Putin offered $15 billion in loan assistance and the delivery of cheaper natural gas.[319]

The Euromaidan protestors cheered when the police initially abandoned their efforts to dismantle their camp in the public square, but things turned violent in January 2014 when President Yanukovych's supporters in Parliament passed laws aimed at repressing the protests.

Rioting broke out in mid-February when police cracked down on the protestors just hours after Russia delivered the first $2 billion of its promised $15 billion in aid.[320]

At one point, Russian prime minister Dmitry Medvedev mocked President Yanukovych by saying he needed to stop behaving like a "doormat."[321]

He also said further loan installments would be withheld because of concessions President Yanukovych was making to the protestors, including promising amnesty in exchange for their surrendering occupied government buildings.

Yanukovych's government responded by initiating a brutal crackdown on February 18, 2014. Security forces opened fire with rubber and live ammunition on protestors; they responded with Molotov cocktails and cobblestone pavers pulled from the street.

By the following day, the government conceded eighteen protestors and ten police had been killed; but on February 20, 2014, the death toll skyrocketed after at least thirty-four more protestors were shot and killed by the police. In some cases, the police were perched on surrounding rooftops, like snipers.[322] The protestors set fires to try to obscure their view and stop further killing. In all, more than one hundred died in the protests.[323]

The violence subsided on February 21, 2014, when three visiting foreign ministers—Frank-Walter Steinmeier of Germany, Laurent Fabius of France, and Radosław Sikorski of Poland—negotiated a settlement between President Yanukovych and the main opposition leaders.[324]

The president called for two days of national mourning, but the protestors continued to demand his ouster and introduced an article of impeachment in Parliament.

President Yanukovych dropped out of public view on February 22, 2014, and protestors stormed his gilded Presidential Palace when security forces abandoned their posts.[325] The president eventually resurfaced in Russia, reportedly after flying there on a Russian military jet.

As the events unfolded, I remember watching the excitement in Assistant Secretary Nuland. As former US ambassador to NATO, she had a long experience with Russia and was under no illusions about dealing with President Putin.

She felt the former KGB agent was a strongman and untrustworthy, and she was concerned that Foreign Minister Lavrov took advantage of Secretary Kerry's good nature and eagerness to engage with him.

She was openly enthusiastic to see Ukraine—a former Soviet republic—move toward the West. And she was thrilled opposition figure Yulia Tymoshenko had been released from prison on February 22, 2014, and another favored opposition leader, Arseniy Yatsenyuk, was on the cusp of transitioning to the new national leadership.

Nuland was no stranger to the spotlight she garnered with her handout of foodstuffs. In addition to having formerly served as NATO ambassador, she was finishing up a stint as State Department spokesperson when Kerry took over from Secretary of State Hillary Clinton.

Nuland presided over the Daily Press Briefing, earning her a following in the international media and near-celebrity status when we landed overseas. She was, in many quarters, the face of the State Department.

She also was highly regarded within the Department itself, especially by younger women. They reveled in her rise from Ivy League student to member of a Russian fishing boat crew before she used her diplomatic skill and Russian language command to rise to the rank of ambassador. Now she was one of six regional assistant secretaries of State. And she did all that as a working mother.

Many of her supporters saw her as a potential replacement for Wendy Sherman as undersecretary of state for political affairs should Clinton be elected president in 2016.

But Nuland also tended to bend rules and protocol, especially when she was trying to achieve a political end. She publicly called John Kerry the more chummy "Boss," not the honorific "Mr. Secretary" virtually everyone else in the Department used in his presence. She also liked to jump uninvited into his limousine or buttonhole him while he was walking into a meeting, giving her the final say over other advisers.

While Kerry respected Nuland's energy, smarts, and unyielding advocacy, and promoted her from spokesperson to assistant secretary, the Russians didn't share his feelings for her. What came off as misogyny factored into our diplomacy with them.

President Putin and Foreign Minister Lavrov disliked Nuland. Each had monitored her press briefings and routinely complained about her remarks. Lavrov, in particular, was known to make sexist jokes in the presence of her or other women in our delegation.

Both Russians harbored similar feelings toward Secretary Clinton, who famously began her term at the State Department attempting a fresh start with the Russians. Relations had plummeted following the Russian invasion of independent Georgia in August 2008, at the tail end of the Bush administration.

Clinton made a good-natured attempt to reach out when she held her first meeting with Lavrov on March 6, 2009, in Geneva.

With cameras rolling, she presented her dinner companion with a mock Staples "Easy" button labeled with Cyrillic Russian lettering that ostensibly read, "Reset." The foreign minister publicly corrected her by explaining the letters actually translated to "Overcharged."[326]

An embarrassed Clinton recovered by saying, "We won't let you do that to us, I promise."[327]

Lavrov never let her live it down, continuing to bring it up during our later meetings with the Russians.

President Putin also disliked Secretary Clinton because he believed she'd meddled in Russian affairs by labeling the 2011 parliamentary elections in his country "neither fair nor free."[328]

He continued to stoke anti-American sentiment for his own benefit while seeking reelection in 2012, and relations took a nosedive at the end of that year when Congress passed and President Obama signed the Magnitsky Act.

It was written to sanction Russian human rights abusers by punishing those responsible for the death of tax accountant Sergei Magnitsky. He was fatally beaten in 2009 while being held in a Moscow prison after investigating fraud by Russian tax officials.[329] The law named in his honor requires that the State Department annually update the list of those being sanctioned under the Act.

The Russian Duma responded by voting 400–4 in December 2012 to ban US adoptions of Russian children.[330]

Against that backdrop, Kerry tried his own reset with the Russians after becoming secretary of State in February 2013. He met in Berlin with Lavrov during his first trip abroad. He then traveled to Moscow in May 2013 to solicit President Putin's views on world events, especially ending the civil war in Syria.

The secretary showed due deference to our World War II ally by placing a wreath at the Tomb of the Unknown Soldier on the edge of Red Square. Then he waited patiently at his hotel for their appointed meeting hour. It passed with no call from the Kremlin. Even after being summoned to the gilded seat of the Russian Federation, Kerry was forced to sit again in a waiting room until President Putin was ready to receive him.

In all, the Russian president kept the US secretary of State on hold for three hours. This was one of his common moves to put his opponents off balance.[331]

Kerry regained fresh hope for the relationship after his work with Lavrov on the Syria chemical weapons agreement. He presented his counterpart with a box of oversized potatoes from Idaho—where the secretary has a ski home—when the two met in Paris just four months later.

The foreign minister's spokesperson, Maria Zakharova, had her own gift for her State Department counterpart, spokesperson Jen Psaki: a pink "Ushanka." The fur hat with ear flaps sported a red Russian star on its brow. Kerry and Lavrov smiled during a group photo with their two aides.

The showdown in Ukraine overtook those goodwill gestures, however.

The Russians felt throughout 2013 that the Americans were interfering with Ukraine's affairs by encouraging President Yanukovych and, later, his opponents in their westward tilt.

Those accusations gained currency in early February 2014, just before the crackdown in Independence Square, when an audio recording was posted on YouTube. It appeared to reveal Assistant Secretary Nuland and the US ambassador to Ukraine, Geoffrey Pyatt, talking about plans for a replacement government in Kiev.

"I don't think Klitsch [Vitaly Klitschko, one of three main opposition leaders] should go into the government," said a voice sounding like Nuland's. "I don't think it's necessary, I don't think it's a good idea."[332]

A voice sounding like Pyatt's replied, "Just let him stay out and do his political homework and stuff."

The voice purported to be Nuland's says, "I think Yats [opposition leader Arseniy Yatsenyuk] is the guy who's got the economic experience, the governing experience."[333]

That voice later expresses exasperation with the European Union, which had been more reluctant than the United States to provoke Russia over Ukraine.

"You know, fuck the EU," says the voice attributed to Nuland.[334]

The blunt talk went off like a bomb within the refined salons of diplomacy.

And there was little doubt what leader stood to benefit from its disclosure, or which country possessed the means to bug a cellphone conversation between top US diplomats.

While Nuland made amends to her European counterparts, President Obama spoke out against the crackdown on Ukrainian protestors.

Secretary Kerry monitored developments in Ukraine and even visited Kiev and the Maidan in March 2014 at Nuland's urging. Nonetheless, his primary focus at the time was fostering a Middle East peace process.

For one brief shining moment, roughly the third week of February 2014, Assistant Secretary Nuland and Ambassador Pyatt reveled in the ouster of President Yanukovych and the installation of a caretaker government headed by Arseniy Yatsenyuk.

Soon, though, they were rendered powerless when President Putin unleashed a vigorous response to what he had branded a "coup d'etat."[335]

CRIMEA HAS RUSSIAN ROOTS stretching back to 1783, when the Black Sea peninsula became part of the Russian Empire.[336]

The province of Crimea was transferred from the Russian Soviet Federative Socialist Republic to the Ukrainian Soviet Socialist Republic in 1954, and it remained part of Ukraine when it gained its independence in 1991 during the breakup of the Soviet Union.[337]

Nonetheless, Crimea maintained strong ties to Russia. It has an ethnic Russian majority and many of its residents continue to speak Russian. Russia itself has a major interest in Crimea because its city of Sevastopol is headquarters for the Russian Navy's Black Sea fleet.

The warm water port lets Russia project power not only around the Black Sea but also into the Mediterranean and surrounding countries such as Syria. Russia used its base in Sevastopol to ferry troops and conduct a naval blockade against Georgia during its 2008 invasion.[338]

Russia also has combat aircraft stationed at Crimea's Kacha and Gvardeisk air bases, which help defend its southern flank.[339]

While Russia had a lease in Sevastopol extending to 2042, President Putin didn't want to risk losing access to the Crimean peninsula after President Yanukovych was ousted. He later acknowledged convening an all-night meeting with his security forces to discuss extricating the deposed president after he had disappeared from public view.

When the meeting finished on the morning of February 24, 2014, according to a subsequent documentary that included an interview with President Putin, "I said to my colleagues: 'We must start working on returning Crimea to Russia.'"[340]

The comment affirmed a criticism leveled by former Secretary Clinton, who had traveled to perhaps Crimea's most famous city—Yalta—after leaving office, to support Ukraine. She said President Putin was trying to "re-Sovietize" parts of the former Soviet Union, a complaint that angered him despite its subsequent validity.[341]

Pro-Russian demonstrations had already broken out in Sevastopol, and they continued on February 24, 2014. The next day, Sevastopol illegally elected a Russian citizen as its mayor.

Two days later, an estimated 4,000 to 5,000 Crimean Tatars—Turkish ethnic residents—and other supporters of the Euromaidan movement faced off against 600 to 700 supporters of pro-Russian organizations and the Russian Unity Party near the Supreme Council of Crimea building.[342] Thousands also clashed during opposing rallies in Simferopol, a city that would emerge as the de facto capital of Crimea.[343]

The battling effectively came to an end the following day when Russian Special Forces invaded sovereign Ukrainian territory and seized control of the buildings housing the Supreme Council of Crimea and the Council of Ministers in Simferopol.

They raised a Russian flag over each.[344]

Additional Russian forces, aided by Ukrainian special forces formerly loyal to President Yanukovych, established checkpoints on the Isthmus of Perekop and the Chonhar Peninsula, which separate the Crimea peninsula from the Ukrainian mainland.[345]

The actions collectively isolated Crimea from Ukraine and put Russia in control of the province for the first time since 1954.

Not only had Russia invaded a sovereign country and laid claim to non-contiguous territory, but it had violated the 1994 Budapest Memorandum on Security Assurances.

Under that agreement, Ukraine had surrendered control of its nuclear weapons—at the time the third largest arsenal in the world—in exchange for assurance from the Russian Federation, the United States, and the United Kingdom that the three nuclear powers would "respect the independence and sovereignty and existing borders of Ukraine."[346]

The three also affirmed their obligation "to refrain from the threat or use of force against the territorial integrity or political independence of Ukraine."[347]

Not that President Putin immediately conceded his involvement in Crimea or violation of the Memorandum.

In a shameless bit of denial, the Russians not only refused to admit their forces had seized Crimea but they spun stories about how Crimea was being defended by pro-Russian nationalists. They said average citizens had spontaneously sprung to arms to protect themselves against "terrorists."

They said so even though troops at key strategic points across Crimea all spoke Russian and wore green Russian military uniforms, minus the insignia of the Russian Federation.

The so-called little green men also used helmets and other equipment only issued to Russian Special Forces, including the new 7.62 mm PKP machine gun.[348]

Addressing that, President Putin suggested Crimeans had seized the uniforms from Ukrainian military depots they looted. He also told reporters in early March 2014 that "local forces of self-defense" had seized the buildings.[349]

He said residents in Crimea had the right of self-determination against terrorists and extremists, and any aid to them amounted to humanitarian assistance.

Secretary Kerry expressed disbelief at President Putin's denials when he arrived in Kiev that same day.

"He really denied there were troops in Crimea?" Kerry said.[350]

President Obama also didn't buy the explanation.

"There have been reports that Putin is pausing and reflecting on what's happened," he said on March 4, 2014. "There is a strong belief that Russian action is violating international law. Putin seems to have a different set of lawyers, but I don't think that is fooling anyone."[351]

The remark harked back to that *New York Times* op-ed, written by President Putin, that Lavrov had so eagerly thrown in Kerry's face during their news conference after the chemical weapons agreement.

That deal in Geneva had been struck to head off US military intervention in Syria, which Putin said would violate international law. President Putin went on to intervene militarily in Ukraine, even invading Crimea, but he ignored his prior admonition to the United States:

> We need to use the United Nations Security Council and believe that preserving law and order in today's complex and turbulent world is one of the few ways to keep international relations from sliding into chaos. The law is still the law, and we must follow it whether we like it or not. Under current international law, force is permitted only in self-defense or by the decision of the Security Council. Anything else is unacceptable under the United Nations Charter and would constitute an act of aggression.[352]

When President Putin was called out for violating the Budapest Memorandum, he told reporters it wasn't operative because Ukraine had gone through a change of leadership.[353] He also took it a step further, accusing the United States itself of violating the Memorandum by fomenting the Euromaidan movement.[354]

His foreign minister was even more strident in February 2016. Sergey Lavrov said the Memorandum only contained one obligation: "Not to attack Ukraine with nukes."[355] He simply ignored the first of the six obligations spelled out by the document, as well as the four that followed the one he referenced.

That prompted Steven Pifer, a former Foreign Service officer who helped negotiate the Budapest Memorandum, to write in Canada's *National Post*: "What does it say about the mendacity of Russian diplomacy and its contempt for international opinion when the foreign minister says something that can be proven wrong with less than 30 seconds of Google fact-checking?"[356]

The Russians never flinched in the face of such duplicity. As Pifer hinted, this practice was something that would wilt in a country with a free press like the United States. That underscored a major challenge for the Obama administration in dealing with the Russian government.

While the United States spent time in February and March 2014 offering $1 billion in loan guarantees to the new government in Ukraine and joining with the European Union in levying sanctions against Russia and its elite, the actions did little to deter it.

Russia supported a March 16 referendum in Crimea the rest of the world deemed illegal. When a reported 96 percent voted in favor of leaving Ukraine and joining Russia, the pretext for President Putin's annexation of Crimea was complete.

And not only did Russia seize control of Crimea, but it massed forty thousand troops along Ukraine's eastern border under the guise of holding military exercises in Russian territory. When fighting broke out in Ukraine's Donetsk and Luhansk provinces in April 2014, the Russians denied their troops were involved despite the presence of little green men on a new front.

Russian military leaders would go on to tell families back home that soldiers who died in the fighting had been killed in military exercises—if they offered any explanation at all when their coffins returned to Russia.[357]

Such acts, while being criticized by some families in Russia, would never be tolerated in the United States, especially in the post Vietnam era. It was another measure of the difficulty in dealing with the Russian government.

It was not the last one, though.

President Putin and Russian officials similarly stonewalled after a Malaysia Airlines civilian jet was shot down on July 17, 2014, by an antiaircraft missile fired over eastern Ukraine.

All 283 passengers and 15 crew members aboard the Boeing 777, which was flying from Amsterdam to Kuala Lumpur, were killed.

Dutch investigators later determined the plane was downed by an advanced Russian Buk surface-to-air missile launched from a pro-Russian area of eastern Ukraine.[358] Meanwhile, the new government in Kiev released video the day after the crash showing a mobile Buk launcher—with two of its four missiles gone—as it was being driven from eastern Ukraine toward the Russian border immediately after the crash.[359]

Radio transmissions also appeared to show separatist forces saying they had accidentally downed a civilian airliner.[360]

The Russians follow a well-worn playbook in such circumstances.

First, they stonewall by saying they can't comment until they receive "information" about an event. Then, when confronted with evidence, they demand to examine it and know how it was gathered. US officials don't see this as a means to ensure due process but a way to glean insight into intelligence methods so they can avoid the same mistake twice.

In the case of the Malaysia Airlines jet, the Russian government dismissed the voluminous and detailed Dutch evidence. The Russians suggested the plane had been shot down by a Ukrainian military jet; by a Ukrainian missile battery; or by pro-Russian separatists who'd seized control of a Ukrainian missile battery—not one of their own.[361]

Ultimately, the Russians refused to accept responsibility for any facet of the crash despite proof the aircraft had been downed by a missile fired by one of its systems temporarily staged in a rebel-held area of eastern Ukraine.

In the best-case scenario based on the facts, not rhetoric, it had been as if they gave a drunk a loaded gun and then disavowed any responsibility when he fired it.

This shirking of responsibility contrasted with the public accounting and humiliation the United States faced in 1988 after the USS *Vincennes*, one of the Navy's most advanced guided missile cruisers, accidentally shot down an Iranian commercial jet over the Persian Gulf.

The United States publicly acknowledged its mistake and paid a $132 million settlement, something the Russian government never felt any responsibility to do after the Malaysia Airlines crash.[362]

The challenge that repeatedly cropped up for President Obama and Secretary Kerry was being publicly accountable for decisions and their consequences while dealing with a country and leaders who faced no such accountability.

(Top) A bread-and-salt greeting at hotel. (Middle) Honoring Russians at their Kremlin Tomb. (Bottom) A photo with the press secretaries.

(Top) A potato gift amid efforts to build bridges.
(Bottom) The two counterparts in Geneva.

(Top) Addressing reporters in the Kremlin. (Middle) A walk in Moscow.
(Bottom) Assistant Secretary Nuland at a meeting with President Putin.

(Top) President Putin and Foreign Minister Lavrov betray no reaction as Secretary Kerry addresses them. (Bottom) Red Square and the Kremlin under a full moon.

This point was underscored during one visit to Moscow when we drove past the Bolshoy Moskvoretsky Bridge, which crosses the Moscow River just outside the Kremlin Wall. It was on that bridge in February 2015 that one of President Putin's most prominent critics, former deputy prime minister Boris Nemtsov, was shot four times in the back and killed. He was assassinated just two days before participating in a rally against Russia's financial crisis and its involvement in the eastern Ukraine fighting.[363]

President Putin denied any involvement and pledged to Nemtsov's mother—who previously said she feared he would kill her son—that he would ensure "the organizers and perpetrators of a vile and cynical murder get the punishment they deserve."[364]

Five Chechen contract killers were later convicted in the murder and sentenced to jail, but their alleged leader was not captured.[365]

One thing President Putin later did admit in regard to Ukraine was that those little green men in Crimea had been Russian soldiers, after all. During his annual televised meeting with the nation on April 17, 2014, he said the soldiers' presence was necessary so Crimeans could vote freely in the referendum about their future.

"We didn't want any tanks, any nationalist combat units, or people with extreme views armed with automatic weapons," President Putin said. "Of course, Russian servicemen backed the Crimean self-defense forces."[366]

There was no wave of criticism after admitting his lie. Rather, there was a surge of nationalist pride in Russia and Crimea.

President Putin was hailed in both Moscow and Sevastopol on May 9, 2014, when he presided over annual Victory Day parades paying tribute to Russia's victory over Nazi Germany in World War II.

"There is a lot of work ahead," he said while making his first visit to Crimea since its annexation, "but we will overcome all the difficulties because we are together, and that means we have become even stronger."[367]

———

ALL TOLD, WE MADE five trips to Russia. The first, to Moscow, was especially eye-opening because everything was new to me.

We departed from Andrews Air Force Base at mid-afternoon on May 6, 2013, and stopped in Shannon, Ireland, to refuel our plane and grab a customary pint of Guinness. We flew on to Vnukovo International Airport, about seventeen miles southwest of Moscow, and landed the morning of May 7, 2013.

While the airport is now a civilian one, we taxied over to a private terminal used by military planes, including Air Force One when it brought President Reagan to Russia in 1988.

The red lettering on the building reads "MOCKBA."

We traveled down clean streets, crossed the Moscow River, and passed the redbrick walls of the Kremlin before pulling up to the Ritz Carlton Hotel. As luxurious as that may sound, it's a standard destination for business travelers because it's next to Red Square and the Kremlin and offers the usual Western amenities. There's also a rooftop bar—the O2 Lounge—that has a sweeping nighttime view of Red Square and the Kremlin.

Inside the lobby, a woman dressed in a traditional Russian sarafan jumper dress gave Secretary Kerry a traditional bread-and-salt greeting: a loaf of bread placed on a rushnik—an embroidered towel—with a pinch-bowl of salt on top.

He dipped a piece of bread into the salt before eating it.

We had several hours of free time before the secretary set out for his wreath-laying ceremony at the Tomb of the Unknown Soldier. We then received word of the delay in our meeting with President Putin, so one of our hosts offered to give him a tour of neighboring Red Square and the Kremlin walls.

We walked through the entrance and across heavy black cobblestones into Red Square. To me, it felt like a movie set after I had seen it on TV so many times while Soviet soldiers, tanks, and missiles streamed through during the annual May Day Parade.

There directly across the Square was St. Basil's Cathedral, a cluster of eight churches whose brightly colored domes look like the flames of a bonfire. It's perhaps the most recognizable building in the city.

There to the right was Lenin's Tomb, a squat granite mausoleum where the embalmed body of Soviet leader Vladimir Lenin remains on public display.

I was surprised by the sight on the left, though. It was the GUM department store, a Harrods-like shopping mall whose shape and windows are illuminated with strings of white lights. I didn't expect such a capitalist presence in what was once the heart of a Communist country.

We'd been in Russia only a short time, but I'd already realized that was no longer the case.

Despite its recent Soviet history, Russia—or at least, Moscow—is brimming with examples of Western influence. There are the luxury hotels on the edge of Red Square, a McDonald's on Tverskaya Street, a main drag in the city, and a swirl of Mercedes, Lexus, and Toyota automobiles driving around the Kremlin.

Photographers asked the secretary to pose with St. Basil's in the background, a request he grudgingly granted. Our host then led him over to the Kremlin Wall Necropolis behind Lenin's Tomb, where the ashes of various Russian heroes are interred.

We saw the plaque marking the spot for the remains of Yuri Gagarin, the first human in space, and we walked by a granite bust of Joseph Stalin. It marks his grave in a plot of land at the foot of the Wall.

We all then returned to our hotel and awaited the call for Secretary Kerry's meeting with President Putin.

Traveling to countries like Russia or China is no simple feat for US government officials. Both are deemed "high-threat" locations because the host government is known to aggressively conduct electronic and personal surveillance.

Whenever we visited locations like these, we left all our regular electronics behind. That meant cellphones, laptops, and anything that might be compromised for future use, or monitored while on site.

Instead, we were issued burner cell phones and other single-use equipment. We carried them while in the country and then discarded them even before we got back to our plane. And despite using such disposable technology, we were reminded we still couldn't speak freely because the airwaves were vulnerable.

The briefing papers we got in every hotel room we used around the world, known as the "Notes to Party," contained bleak warnings in high-threat destinations.

"All non-USG facilities, including hotels, are considered compromised and classified material should not be discussed or processed in any of them," read that first notice we got in Moscow.

"Visitors to Russia have NO expectation of privacy. Visitors should assume that their movements and conversations may be monitored by host government personnel. Exercise a high degree of caution and remain alert when patronizing in restaurants, bars, theaters, etc., especially during peak hours of business," said another section of the notice.

The point was underscored when I got into the shower. As the steam built under the flow of hot water, it got more difficult to see through the glass door and into the rest of the bathroom. But on the shower wall itself, a solitary square of glass remained fog-free.

I wondered if I was being watched over while I washed up.

The experience prompted me to look warily at the mirror in my bedroom and the blinking red light in the smoke detector on the ceiling. It's one reason our security personnel erected a tent within the secretary's suite: so he had an isolated space in which to read any sensitive documents.

We were told former Secretary of State Condoleezza Rice used to change clothes in her tent to escape prying eyes.

While I have no doubt the US government treats its Russian visitors similarly, this first exposure to the world of espionage and tradecraft was bracing for someone little more than four months into diplomatic service.

All of our other visits to Russia brought us back to Moscow, except for one where Secretary Kerry met with President Putin and Foreign Minister Lavrov in the Black Sea resort of Sochi.

More often than not, though, we met with the Russians outside either of our countries. We attended many of the same multilateral gatherings as the United States and Russia sought to exert their influence in Europe or Africa or Asia, and our two teams got to know each other well.

Both sides tried to be professional in their interactions with each other; but from a communications perspective, it was often a challenge dealing with our Russian counterparts.

First of all, we traveled with a large and independent press corps. Since it paid its expenses to follow the secretary of State around, it expected access and the chance to ask him about what he was doing.

The Russians had some of their own traveling reporters, but their independence was questionable and their questions often were directed at Secretary Kerry rather than at Foreign Minister Lavrov.

In mid-March 2014, the two met in London at Winfield House, the spacious residence of the US ambassador to the Court of St. James, with that huge backyard rivaling the one at Buckingham Palace.

Kerry and Lavrov talked for six hours before deciding to take a walk across the grass as they continued their discussion about Ukraine and Syria and other affairs.

When they finished, they stopped next to a soccer ball and net belonging to the children of US ambassador Matthew Barzun. Without warning, Lavrov wound up and gave the ball a giant kick across the yard. He later explained he'd been a soccer player.

Despite that brief moment of levity, the two sides clashed over a joint statement about Ukraine, the type of communication called a "Joint Understanding."

Maria Zakharova, the foreign minister's spokesperson, said only partly in jest, "We should label it 'Joint Mis-Understanding.'"[368]

Another irritant was more a fault of our system of government and process of administration.

When the meetings broke and it was time to address reporters, Lavrov often
grew impatient because Kerry routinely asked for time to review his notes.

Not only did the secretary need to check if there was any breaking news
he might be asked about, but as a diplomat whose words were closely monitored around the world, he had to make sure anything he said had gone
through the normal administration clearance process.

That meant White House officials and State Department subject-matter
experts had seen and approved most remarks, and the Pentagon and intelligence community had been given insight through the interagency process.

Lavrov had only one person to worry about when he spoke—President
Putin—and little visible clearance process. He often walked up to the podium
with nothing more than an index card or a stray piece of paper scribbled with
notes he'd just made with a pen kept in his breast pocket.

Kerry would arrive at his podium toting a large crimson binder filled with
his statement, printed in thirty-two-point type and placed in plastic sleeves.
The vetted responses to potential questions were on tabbed pages underneath.

Our cumbersome process also contrasted with the nimbleness of Russia's
when both sides issued press releases on one world development or another.
Spokesperson Zakharova would often distribute Russia's the moment something happened or a meeting ended; on the US side, that was usually just the
start of a clearance process that might not end for several hours.

The disparity was especially evident in the aftermath of the Crimea invasion. *The Washington Post* reported in December 2017 that an intercepted
Russian military intelligence report dated February 2014 "documented how
Moscow created fake personas to spread disinformation on social media to
buttress its broader military campaign" in Crimea.[369]

Meanwhile, RT, an international television network funded by the Russian government, was aggressively promoting the Russian view within the
United States.

The US government had no similar counterweight abroad.

President Clinton and Congress had shut down the US Information Agency,
charged with influencing foreign populations, in 1999, eight years after the
Soviet Union had collapsed. Russia, however, sought ways to compensate for
its diminished military power and stood up RT in 2005. It also staged cyber-
attacks in Estonia in 2007 and against Georgia before its 2008 invasion.[370]

I remember being struck while walking to the State Department from my apartment in Washington's West End and passing several bus stops festooned with RT ads on their sides. Former CNN host Larry King had a talk show on RT's American network.

I didn't see anything similar for a US government network during our visits to Moscow.

I also never saw op-eds by President Obama in the Russian version of *The New York Times*—because there wasn't a publication of similar national impact or international stature.

"We are not competitive with the Russian PR machine," Undersecretary of State for Public Affairs Rick Stengel told us when our communications team gathered in Washington on March 12, 2014.

Stengel, the former editor of *Time* magazine, would spend the rest of the term seeking to close that gap with Russia. He also focused on recruiting Muslim social media forces to stand up to another threat: the Islamic State messaging machine.

While disagreements within the Obama administration prevented a more broad-based counter-propaganda response, top officials also felt the Russian efforts would fall on deaf ears in the United States.

"I thought our ground was not as fertile," former Deputy Secretary of State Tony Blinken told *The Washington Post* for its December 2017 report about the failed response to Russia's propaganda. "We believed that the truth shall set you free, that the truth would prevail. That proved a bit naive."[371]

In a piece for *Politico* published about the same time, Stengel wrote: "I wish I could say we figured out what to do about Russian disinformation and that we had seen what Russia would do in the 2016 [US presidential] election. We didn't and I didn't."[372]

Despite these and other challenges, Secretary Kerry forged ahead in his dealings with Russia. To him, it was a necessary evil. The country was a nuclear power in its own right, and it held sway not only in Iran and North Korea but Syria. In addition, its UN veto power forced the United States and others to always account for Russia diplomatically.

Those factors forced him to, in his words, "compartmentalize" his interactions.

Beyond the goodwill gift exchanges with Foreign Minister Lavrov or his solicitations of President Putin, the secretary genuinely tried to focus on the big picture and areas of common interest. "We have a disagreement about the facts and how we got there, but the art of diplomacy is how to thread the needle," he told one journalist during an interview in March 2014.[373]

And even amid the Russians' insults, feigned ignorance, or duplicity, he persevered.

I remember during a phone call hearing him ask Lavrov about a report he'd read on the Internet regarding Russian activity in Ukraine.

"I don't comment on websites," his counterpart replied in a comment that would grow rich with irony over time. "The Internet is your invention."[374]

Kerry ignored this and similar statements, and a year later, I heard him succinctly explain why.

"If we respond to all their jerkisms, we'll never get anything done," he told his assistant secretaries during a meeting in February 2015.[375]

He made that comment just as the final stage of the Iran nuclear talks was beginning.

True to form, after Kerry spent more than a year painstakingly negotiating that deal, Russia and its foreign minister were there at the very end to coax a settlement from an ally—in this case, Iran.

And then Lavrov complained when the news conference celebrating the achievement was delayed to the waking hours back in the United States.

He wanted to do it on Moscow's timetable.

————

ONE REASON THE RUSSIANS may have felt free to exert themselves in Ukraine and Crimea was because President Obama publicly stated he didn't believe the American people would support going to war for their freedom.

At the very least, that was an imposing military and political challenge, with Russia and its army sitting on Ukraine's border. But the president also felt the United States had no appetite for a new battle as it continued to debate the wisdom of its war in Iraq, as well as its ongoing presence in Afghanistan.

"We are not going to be getting into a military excursion in Ukraine," Obama told San Diego's NBC-TV affiliate during an interview in March 2014. "What we are going to do is mobilize all of our diplomatic resources to make sure that we've got a strong international coalition that sends a clear message."[376]

President Putin exploited this reality in eastern Europe, as he did several months later in Syria. Syria met the terms of the 2013 chemical weapons agreement negotiated between Russia and the United States, as observed by those who destroyed its declared stockpile and as subsequently verified by the OPCW.

Nonetheless, Syrian opposition forces and some in the US government criticized the deal. They believed President Obama had blinked on his threat of force, both by seeking congressional approval for a strike and then by making the agreement with the Russians.

Their argument was that President Assad had avoided any punishment for a war crime—using chemical weapons in Ghouta, Syria—despite crossing a red line drawn by President Obama in 2012. They also said Russia's intervention through its negotiations with the United States had effectively propped up its Middle Eastern client by sparing it a strike from a superpower.

Secretary Kerry would rebut that criticism by noting members of Congress themselves had said they wanted to approve any military action.

"When we take what is a very difficult decision, you have to have buy-in by members and buy-in by the public," Representative Mike Rogers, a Michigan Republican and chairman of the House Intelligence Committee, said on MSNBC on August 29, 2013. "I think both of those are critically important and, right now, none of that has happened."[377]

The secretary also argued the chemical weapons agreement had achieved a far larger disarmament than the United States would have gained through a cruise-missile strike.

"Here we were going to have one or two days to degrade and send a message," he said on April 8, 2014, during testimony to the Senate Foreign Relations Committee. "We came up with a better solution."[378]

Kerry made that argument even though he had been a staunch advocate of using force to respond to the attack. He made the case passionately in the two speeches he delivered within a week of the gas attack on Ghouta.

"We know that after a decade of conflict, the American people are tired of war," he said in the latter speech, delivered August 30, 2013. "Believe me, I am, too. But fatigue does not absolve us of our responsibility. Just longing for peace does not necessarily bring it about. And history would judge us all extraordinarily harshly if we turned a blind eye to a dictator's wanton use of weapons of mass destruction against all warnings, against all common understanding of decency. These things we do know."[379]

While he'd continue to appeal to the White House for a more forceful response the remainder of his term, the former Navy man also said he accepted the chain of command. "Look, the final say on these things is in his hands," he said of the president during an interview with journalist Jeffrey Goldberg, who wrote an April 2016 article in *The Atlantic* titled "The Obama Doctrine."[380]

President Putin stepped in a vacuum left by the Americans. In September 2014, Russian forces started an air campaign in Syria that effectively propped up President Assad just as opposition forces were making gains on the battlefield.

Similar to his actions in Crimea, President Putin denied he was involving himself in the country's political debate but said instead he was helping to create the proper climate amid terrorist incursions.

There was legitimate concern in Russia, the United States, and other countries around the world about the rise of the Islamic State terrorist group in eastern Syria, especially as it aired videos of grisly beheadings and destroyed cultural artifacts during its rampage across the Middle East.

But Syria was a longtime client state of Russia, and much like it felt in regards to Sevastopol, the Russian military didn't want to lose access to an eavesdropping base in Latakia, Syria—its largest outside the homeland—or a small Navy base at Tartus, Syria.[381]

Russia, Syria, Iran, and Iraq proposed setting up a joint information center in Baghdad to coordinate their anti-ISIS campaign. Russia invited the United States to join, and Lavrov met with Kerry several times as the two sides sought to work out the parameters for cooperating, but the Pentagon repeatedly balked.

Not only did Defense Secretary Ash Carter oppose getting tactical coordination with the Russians, but the intelligence community didn't trust Russia with information about the location of moderate opposition troops fighting ISIS and the Assad regime.

"I didn't want the United States to be associated, either politically or morally, with what the Russians were doing," Carter said in February 2018 during an interview with *Politico*'s Susan Glasser. "They were intent upon trapping us, or beguiling us into what they called cooperating with them, and I was against cooperation."[382]

The two sides continued with their respective air campaigns, the United States eventually eliminating ISIS strongholds and Russia helping Assad effectively beat his opposition.

On December 11, 2017, President Putin made a surprise visit to Syria's Khmeimim Air Base and ordered a "significant part" of Russia's military force to begin withdrawing the following week.

"In just over two years, Russia's armed forces and the Syrian army have defeated the most battle-hardened group of international terrorists," the president told his troops. "The conditions for a political solution under the auspices of the United Nations have been created."[383]

He added: "The Motherland awaits you."[384]

Despite that flourish, most of the forces remained, apparently for years to come.

————

SECRETARY KERRY WAS ADDRESSING the State Department's annual Chiefs of Mission Conference on March 15, 2016, when he touched on the dynamic he faced in dealing with Foreign Minister Lavrov.

He noted his counterpart had graduated from the Moscow State Institute of International Relations, an elite school where, he said, aspiring Russian diplomats are taught to argue "that red wine is white."[385]

He also pointed out the foreign minister lived in the United States from 1994 to 2004 while serving as Russia's ambassador to the United Nations. That allowed him to not only become fluent in English but skilled in the mechanics of drafting—and defeating—UN resolutions.

The secretary highlighted their work on the Syria chemical weapons agreement as well as the Iran nuclear deal, despite their concurrent disagreement on other topics, such as Ukraine and the Syrian civil war.

Kerry said part of good diplomacy "is seeing the aspirations of the country you are dealing with not through your lens, but theirs."[386]

He said in the case of Russians in particular, the facts of a situation may not matter as much as their perception of it.

"Perceptions are what leaders react to when they are making policy," the secretary told the assembly of ambassadors and chiefs of mission.[387]

I couldn't help but remember Secretary Clinton complaining in 2011 about the parliamentary elections being "neither fair nor free," and President Obama—in the aftermath of the Crimea annexation—labeling Russia a "regional power" that doesn't "pose the No. 1 national security threat to the United States."[388]

By any electoral or economic index, both statements were 100 percent true. But President Putin and his government didn't take kindly to either perception, especially in light of their perceived disrespect following the collapse of the Soviet Union, and the Russians had the reputation for responding disproportionately.

All of this fueled their predicate for interfering in the 2016 US presidential election, pitting Hillary Clinton against Donald Trump—however shaky the logic. President Putin may not have thought Trump could win, but there's no doubt he would relish a Clinton loss.

We arrived on our final trip to Russia and Moscow about four months before the general election, on July 14, 2016.

Secretary Kerry's first meeting was with President Putin and ended up being delayed two hours. Originally set to begin at 8 p.m., it didn't start until 10 p.m. and then stretched until 1 a.m. as the two talked about ways to boost military and intelligence cooperation against the Islamic State.[389]

By 10 a.m. that same day, we were back across town at the Osobnyak Guesthouse, a villa used by the Foreign Ministry. The secretary participated in a bilateral meeting, working lunch, and joint news conference.

State Department Chief of Staff Jon Finer, who attended numerous sessions with the Russians, described the dynamic of these bilateral meetings during an April 2017 interview with National Public Radio:

> The challenge with these conversations is always how much time you will spend on your own agenda, on the ideas and plans that you come in to the meeting with to try to get the Russians to buy into, versus how much time you will spend more on your back foot, responding to Russian classical counter-accusations. They have a way of trying to start these meetings with a long litany of grievances, going back sometimes decades in their view of kind of American transgressions in foreign policy. . . . There's a greatest hits tape that they can run just from memory that includes the Iraq War, the Libya intervention, you know, episodes from the Cold War and many others. . . .
>
> The advice that we tended to give to Secretary Kerry was to not take the bait and rebut every single one of these charges because they often are all rebuttable. But to focus, absorb, and then try to pivot and focus on your own agenda so you can actually try to get something out of these meetings.[390]

During the lunch that followed, Foreign Minister Lavrov picked at sunflower seeds that were a stand-in for the Parliament cigarettes he usually smoked on the sidelines of his meetings. Our servers poured not one, not two, but three shots of Tzarskaya Gold vodka between courses that included a green pepper stuffed with elk meat and a dessert of strawberry biscuit.

During the conversation, Lavrov welcomed the appointment of the colorful Boris Johnson as the new foreign secretary in the United Kingdom.

"We need some fun in foreign policy," he said.[391]

Kerry threw out the idea of Lavrov visiting Cape Cod and Nantucket for an installment of his Hometown Diplomacy series. The foreign minister said he had a scheduling conflict and had already been to the Cape, as well as Kennebunkport, Maine.

The secretary turned serious for a moment, saying the world was looking to the two countries for leadership, especially amid the raging civil war in Syria.

"The local impact of Russia and the United States coming to terms on this could open up new things" he said.[392]

Kerry noted he'd recently been to Silicon Valley and talked with tech industry representatives about impending changes in commerce.

When the foreign minister noted many of the key players in the Valley were Russians, the secretary said, "Yes, but the world is changing and that is where we should be directing our energy."

Lavrov replied: "I agree."[393]

Alas, it was not to be.

The stalemate over Syria continued through the remainder of the year—the final of President Obama and Secretary Kerry's terms—and soon the US government was convulsing with evidence of Russian interference in the 2016 presidential election.

The Democratic National Committee was hacked sometime before May 2016, and emails from its top officials were published by DCLeaks and Wikileaks in June 2016 and July 2016. Some included embarrassing evidence the party was working against the candidacy of Senator Bernie Sanders of Vermont, an insurgent who threatened Hillary Clinton, the eventual nominee and President Putin's onetime foil.

In mid-August 2016, federal officials began hearing about "scanning and probing" of voter databases in some states.[394]

Wary of being perceived as interfering in an election that Donald Trump was also suggesting would be rigged, the Obama administration withheld public disclosure until October 7, 2016.

On that date, Secretary of Homeland Security Jeh Johnson and Director of National Intelligence James Clapper issued a joint statement.

"These thefts and disclosures are intended to interfere with the US election process," it read. "Such activity is not new to Moscow—the Russians have used similar tactics and techniques across Europe and Eurasia, for example, to influence public opinion there. We believe, based on the scope and sensitivity of these efforts, that only Russia's senior-most officials could have authorized these activities."[395]

That same day, however, Wikileaks began publishing another trove of emails, this time from John Podesta, chairman of Hillary Clinton's presidential campaign.

The emails included criticism of the former first lady for using a private email server while secretary of State, as well as a twelve-page memo from an aide to her husband, President Clinton. It described how he could use his consulting company to aid the Clinton Global Initiative and direct personal income to the former president.[396]

It's unclear what effect the disclosures had on the presidential vote the following month, but the Democrats were stunned when a veteran politician like Clinton lost to a political upstart like Trump.

One could only imagine the reaction in Moscow.

A little over a month later, President Obama responded to the interference by announcing he was ejecting thirty-five suspected Russian intelligence operatives from the United States and sanctioning two of Russia's leading intelligence services, the GRU and the FSB.

Separately, Secretary Kerry and the State Department said they were closing two waterfront estates—one on the Eastern Shore of Maryland, the other on Long Island in New York—the Russians claimed were diplomatic retreats.

The United States contended they were intelligence outposts.[397]

"These actions follow repeated private and public warnings that we have issued to the Russian government, and are a necessary and appropriate response to efforts to harm US interests in violation of established international norms of behavior," President Obama said in a statement.[398]

President Putin withheld any immediate reaction to the sanctions, a development that came amid allegations that President-elect Trump's incoming national security adviser, Michael Flynn, had urged the Russians to defer to the new administration.

Putin unleashed a disproportionate response on July 30, 2017, though.

Three days earlier, Congress had voted near unanimously to pass new sanctions against Russia for the election interference, and a day later, now president Trump said he would sign them into law.[399]

President Putin replied by announcing the US embassy in Moscow would have to cut its staff by 755 employees, far more than the 35 expelled by President Obama. President Putin said the cut would leave 455 American diplomats in Russia, the same as his country had at its missions in the United States, despite the United States issuing more than twice as many nonimmigrant visas to Russians than the other way around.[400]

He also said he was seizing two diplomatic compounds used by US embassy employees, a veritable eye-for-an-eye retaliation.

"We waited for quite a long time that, perhaps, something will change for the better, we held out hope that the situation would somehow change," President Putin told state-run Rossiya 1 television. "But, judging by everything, if it changes, it will not be soon."[401]

It was a moment typifying the hair-pulling challenges we'd confronted during our dealings with Russia under Vladimir Putin.

Its leader blamed the United States for punishing a Russian act against the United States.

8

PARIS

AS ELECTION DAY DAWNED over the United States in November 2016, Secretary Kerry was at the outskirts of the country and heading about as far away as possible.

We took off from Joint Base Pearl Harbor-Hickam in Honolulu about 8:30 a.m. and set off for Christchurch, New Zealand. Our visit to Hawaii had been a refueling stop before we were to board a military transport Down Under and fly to our final destination: Antarctica.

The secretary of State wasn't fleeing the country out of political exasperation. Instead, he was heading to the South Pole to see the effects of climate change and global warming.

Antarctica would end up being the seventh and final continent we visited during our four years at the State Department.

That's not to say there wasn't an interest in the election outcome as we set off from Andrews Air Force Base while the campaigning finished a day earlier. We also moved up our departure from Hawaii by six hours so we'd cross through a communications dead zone in the South Pacific before the polls closed, which would also get us to our hotel before the winner was announced.

As a longtime US senator and former presidential candidate himself, Kerry was able to get a line on the early exit-poll results shortly after leaving Hawaii. They showed Hillary Clinton leading Donald Trump.

But then, as predicted, we flew into an electronic black hole over the South Pacific and were cut off from the outside world for several hours.

I remember the instant our satellite link came back up and the first bits of Internet service began pulsing through our airplane. There wasn't enough bandwidth to let us load web pages or stream video, but there was enough data to make everyone's Twitter feed chirp.

As the polls began to close across the country and the vote-counting started, tweet after tweet began telling us Trump was picking off the first of the states Clinton was supposed to win. By the time we got to our hotel in New Zealand, the dominoes were falling more decisively through the must-wins.

Florida. Pennsylvania. Michigan. Wisconsin.

The firewall had crumbled.

One staffer was glued to a *New York Times* web graphic showing the statistical likelihood of either Hillary Clinton or Donald Trump winning the race.

Like a gas gauge heading toward empty, the loss of each state shifted the needle from solidly Clinton to assuredly Trump.

While American television commentators were still wary of calling the race for Trump, Kerry offered his own verdict: "It's over. I've seen this before."[402]

Moments later, I read aloud an all-but-official verdict from the Associated Press. The wire service moved a Flash, its highest level of bulletin, declaring Donald Trump had won and was president-elect of the United States of America.

The news hit President Obama's political appointees on the staff—many of them active Democrats before taking their State Department Hatch Act vows of political celibacy—like a bowling ball leveling a set of pins.

Senior Aide Matt Summers sat on a couch in the secretary's room, holding his head in his hands. Kerry himself couldn't believe the outcome and tried to get a handle by calling old political hands back in Washington and Boston.

Yet as stunned and disillusioned as he was, the secretary almost immediately realized the potential impact of the election results on everything he'd worked for—not only in his current job but also as a senator and political activist before that.

One of his biggest concerns was the environment, something he'd made a focus during the culmination of his career in public service. Donald Trump was on the record saying, "I don't believe in climate change." He also had labeled it a "hoax."[403]

During his victory speech, President-elect Trump tried to gloss over his differences with his rivals, saying, "To all Republicans and Democrats and independents across this nation, I say it is time for us to come together as one united people."[404]

The secretary scoffed at the remark, responding to the television in his room, "Come together? Why should we? And do away with climate change?"[405]

His spine stiffened, and before heading to bed, he vowed to create a political movement to support what he believed.

"I'm ready to continue to fight," Kerry would later tell a *New York Times* science reporter who accompanied us on the trip. "We've made too much progress."[406]

EVEN BEFORE PRESIDENT OBAMA tapped John Kerry to replace Hillary Clinton as secretary of State, two of the Massachusetts Democrat's most loyal and trusted aides drafted an outline of the possible pillars for a tenure at the State Department.

Senate chief of staff David Wade and Heather Higginbottom, a former congressional staffer then working for the Obama administration at the Office of Management and Budget, scribbled a list of major themes. Wade would go on to be State Department chief of staff for the first two years of the secretary's term, while Higginbottom would have the No. 3 job as deputy secretary of State for management and resources.

They envisioned a focus on traditional diplomacy through both bilateral and multilateral engagement and some management reforms at Foggy Bottom. They also suggested a riskier willingness to tackle "frozen conflicts," such as the Middle East peace process and lingering territorial disputes in Cyprus and Nagorno-Karabakh.

In addition, a would-be Secretary Kerry would focus on economic development, using the State Department staff and the instruments of diplomacy to advance US business development both domestically and abroad.

But also making the short list was the environment, particularly the perils of global warming and the climate change it had triggered. They felt the secretary of State, with his global portfolio and focus on issues transcending national borders, was uniquely positioned to take up the cause around the world.

While those issues weren't a major focus of his sixty-seven predecessors as secretary of State, John Kerry had a lifelong interest in the environment and had made its preservation a focus of his public life.

He helped organize the first Earth Day in Massachusetts in 1970, and led the first hearings on acid rain after being elected lieutenant governor of Massachusetts in 1982.

He came to the US Senate in 1985 with Al Gore, who would go on to write *Earth in the Balance* and gain worldwide fame for his own devotion to preserving the environment. The two worked alongside Senators Tim Wirth of Colorado and Frank Lautenberg of New Jersey to focus the country on the issue.

John Kerry also regularly attended the Conference of Parties environmental summits organized by the United Nations. He was reintroduced to Teresa Heinz in 1992 at the "Earth Summit" in Rio de Janeiro that laid the foundation for the COP meetings. The couple married two years later.

When Senator Kerry was nominated at the end of 2012 to become Secretary Kerry, he staked out his ground during his confirmation hearing.

"Climate change is already prompting substantial changes in many parts of the world, and if not effectively addressed, presents a range of security and economic risks, many of them quite serious," he testified. "Understanding the behavior of polar ice sheets in a warming planet, for example, is essential to understanding the rate and magnitude of sea-level rise, which could have far-reaching economic and humanitarian impacts."[407]

Once sworn in, the secretary began not only to execute on his plan to elevate climate change in the context of diplomacy, but also to pass a meaningful climate change agreement at the 2015 Conference of Parties meeting in Paris.

The first piece of the puzzle, as he saw it, was getting China on board with announcing voluntary limits before the COP meeting. He launched this effort during his first visit to Beijing in April 2013 and kept at it through Chinese state councilor Yang Jiechi's trip to Boston in October 2014.

During President Obama's own trip to Beijing in November 2014, he and President Xi Jinping cemented their deal.

The New York Times labeled that a "landmark agreement" that was "the signature achievement of an unexpectedly productive two days of meetings between the leaders."[408]

It was just the first outcome from Kerry's multipronged approach.

In May 2013, we flew to Stockholm not only for a brief bilateral visit with Swedish leaders but also, more significantly, as the jumping-off point for a trip above the Arctic Circle.

We made the trek to Kiruna, Sweden, for a meeting of the Arctic Council, a forum for addressing issues faced by countries within the Arctic and their residents. Those nations are Canada; Denmark, representing Greenland and the Faroe Islands; Finland; Iceland; Norway; Sweden; Russia; and the United States, through its purchase of Alaska in 1867.[409]

Sweden held the chairmanship in 2013 and, by tradition, the annual council meetings are held above the Arctic Circle. That brought us to the northernmost town in Sweden, home to 17,000 people and a massive iron ore mine fueling the community's economy.[410]

The sun doesn't rise for most of December, nor does it set from late May to mid-July.

In remarks to the Council, Secretary Kerry recalled his work with the late senator Ted Stevens of Alaska to end driftnet fishing in the high seas, and his efforts to protect fisheries by helping write the Magnuson-Stevens Act.

He said the Arctic, a peaceful place despite territorial claims by eight countries encircling the North Pole, needed to be carefully managed amid increased energy exploration and a loss of ice that opened new global shipping lanes. He said:

> Last September, the extent of sea ice covering the Arctic reached a record low, threatening marine mammal life and the indigenous and local communities that depend on them. . . . Warming also erodes the natural barrier of ice that shields Alaska's coast from hostile waters, and that causes homes to fall into the sea, it causes pollution. And the thawing of the permafrost, which is increasingly releasing methane— which is 20 times more damaging than CO_2—that has led to the first Arctic wildfires in thousands of years.
>
> So, the scientific research in each of our countries is more imperative than ever in order to protect the atmosphere, the global economy, the food chain, and the air we breathe.[411]

We'd attend a similar meeting the following year in Iqaluit, Canada, where organizers erected an igloo outside the conference center. In September 2016, the United States played host to an Arctic Council meeting in Barrow, Alaska.

———————

KERRY GOT A MORE definitive look at climate change in the northern hemisphere during another trip in June 2016, during his stint as the council's chairman. On a hopscotch itinerary not atypical for his tenure, we headed to Norway, Denmark, and Greenland—via the Caribbean.

The secretary had a standing commitment in Santo Domingo, Dominican Republic, for the Organization of American States' 46th General Assembly. But then he flew nine and a half hours north to the Nordic states to speak at the Oslo Forum, an annual retreat for conflict mediators. He also attended bilateral meetings with Norwegian and Danish leaders in each country's capital.

The highlight of his trip, though, was the opportunity to learn about climate change in some of the most remote yet accessible places in the Arctic region.

His first such stop was Svalbard, Norway, a cluster of islands about 650 miles from the North Pole. The archipelago is home to the northernmost year-round settlement on Earth.[412]

He was accompanied by Norwegian foreign minister Børge Brende, who shared the secretary's concern about climate change and had been a steadfast ally in many of his diplomatic endeavors. The two had also developed a friendship by dint of the foreign minister's cheerful demeanor. It was hard to find anyone in the diplomatic community who didn't like Brende.

We flew our big C-32 from Oslo to Svalbard Airport in Longyearbyen, Norway, a trip taking us up the Scandinavian Peninsula shared by Norway and Sweden, and then across the confluence of the Norwegian, Barents, and Greenland seas. We switched to a twin-engine propeller plane for an additional flight a half hour north.

We landed on a hilltop runway at Ny-Ålesund, a town that is home to the Ny-Ålesund Arctic Research Station. Its brightly colored huts house about 120 people in the summer, and some 35 year-round. Reindeer walk through the village and the locals often tote rifles as protection against the polar bears that also wander downtown.

The remoteness was underscored when we stepped off the plane and one of our hosts pointed up into the hills of nearby Spitsbergen. There, poking out the side of a sandstone mountain, was the concrete portal to the Svalbard Global Seed Vault.

It is, in essence, a doomsday storehouse for plant seeds held in other gene banks around the world. It's considered the ultimate fallback because its vault is about 400 feet inside the mountain, located in a place without tectonic activity, and 430 feet above sea level.[413]

The seeds, stored in triple-sealed packets, would remain dry even if both polar ice caps melted and rising seas pushed ocean water up the mountain.

That was a fitting fact, because scientists who briefed Secretary Kerry at the Research Station told him how global warming was leading to changes in plant life and animal migration and causing glaciers to recede. He also got a firsthand look when he boarded a research boat and motored across the Kongsforden inlet to see the Kronebreen and Kongsvegen glaciers.

We in the staff chased along in a flotilla of Zodiac-style rubber boats. We wore boots and dry suits to guard against hypothermia in the event we fell overboard.

Our mode of transport was telling in and of itself: the scientists said the only way to formerly reach the glaciers was to snowmobile across the fjord's frozen surface. Now everyone was bobbing in boats floating on sparkling water.

Climate change had turned solid to liquid.

We all marveled at the deep blue color of the glacial ice several hundred yards away, and the soil that had become embedded in it as the glaciers plowed their way from land to sea.

Jan Gunnar Winther, a glaciologist and head of the Norwegian Polar Institute, told Kerry the glaciers were melting away not only on top because of rising atmospheric temperatures, but also from below by warmer seawater undermining them.[414]

The visit left an impression on the secretary as he walked back into the village for our flight to Denmark.

"This is the center of the biggest transition taking place, the greatest evidence of change, and I thought it was really important to come here and listen to scientists and learn what they're seeing and get a firsthand view of this transition," he told a TV interviewer. "What is at stake is, literally, the survivability of people on the planet if we don't reduce greenhouse gas emissions and limit the rise of temperature."[415]

The following day, Kerry and Danish foreign minister Kristian Jensen boarded our plane for a nearly five-hour flight from Copenhagen to Kangerlussuaq, Greenland. The Dane hosted the secretary because Greenland, while an independent country, is part of the Kingdom of Denmark.

Kangerlussuaq is a small town at the eastern end of a fjord on the south-western coast of Greenland. The airport was a US airbase during World War II, and it seemed like we stepped back in time when we got off the plane.[416] There was virtually nothing around us except for the high walls of the fjord and a ribbon of water separating them and running off into the horizon.

We transferred to a chartered Air Greenland propeller plane for a forty-five-minute flight—complete with drink service—further north to Ilulissat, Greenland. The trip was eye-opening.

We flew over rocky hills and water in varying shades of blue. Bright white ice bobbed in spots and the pilots pointed out places where glaciers formerly stretched to the sea. Then, taking advantage of the good weather, they turned east and flew all the way up the Jakobshavn Glacier, which was breaking up after having formerly reached the ocean intact.

When we got to the calving front—the point where the splits in the glacier end and the solid ice resumes—they slowed and circled to let us see deep crevices in the ice and brilliant pools of turquoise water on the glacier's surface.

While Jakobshavn is thought to have produced the iceberg that sunk the RMS *Titanic*, the speed with which the glacier has moved toward the ocean recently, coupled with the retreat of the calving front, indicate the ice is thinning and the entire ice sheet over Greenland is draining into the ocean more rapidly.[417]

The phenomenon was captured in the 2012 film *Chasing Ice,* when photographers who'd camped in a tent overlooking the glacier filmed a nearly two-cubic-mile piece breaking off the glacier and falling into the nearby ocean.[418]

An estimated 86 million metric tons breaks off the Jakobshavn Glacier each day. If melted, that daily deposit would provide enough water to serve New York City for a year. Similar activity in ice sheets around the world contributes to sea-level rise, a threat to low-lying development globally.

It also portends even greater problems in Antarctica, because the loss of ice has the potential to be one hundred times worse than that in the Arctic, according to David Holland, an American scientist from New York University who briefed the secretary.[419]

We drove from the airport to Ilulissat Harbor, where Kerry boarded the HMS *Thetis*, a Danish Navy vessel, for a firsthand look at the ice floes that had separated from the glacier. Sunglasses perched atop his head, he looked out across Disko Bay at icebergs hundreds of yards across—and that was only the 10 percent visible on the surface.

The scenery was prone to hyperbole, but for all those who saw it first-hand, the secretary's remarks to reporters afterward were not.

"This has been a significant eye-opener for me, and I've spent twenty-five years or more engaged in this issue," Kerry said. "There's no mistaking that we are contributing to climate change—we human beings—and we have choices that can undo the damage that is being done or reduce, at least miti-gate, the worst effects, so that we can preserve life as we know it and want it to be on this planet."[420]

THE SECRETARY'S TRAVELS ACROSS the northern hemisphere, particularly in June 2016, were buttressed by similar exploratory trips and related environmental diplomacy around the belly of the Earth throughout his term.

In June 2013, just months after broaching the idea of voluntary carbon caps during his first trip to China, Kerry chose his first trip to another impor-tant country—India—to deliver a tough message on the topic of climate change.

More than half of the massive nation's power comes from burning coal. At the same time, 300 million people—roughly the population of the United States—lack electricity.

The secretary argued that switching to clean, renewable power would not only help the environment but also provide energy to people currently off the grid. One idea was creating community solar arrays: installing a cluster of solar panels to power a village, instead of waiting for it to be connected via wires strung across hundreds of miles of countryside.

Leaders in developing nations often take offense at such arguments, regardless of their practicality. They point out the United States and other developed countries fueled their economic rises with an Industrial Revolu-tion powered by cheap fossil fuels such as coal and oil. They say it's their inherent right to do what they need to do to catch up economically and developmentally.

But the secretary also highlighted the rising concentration of carbon diox-ide in the atmosphere— reported the month prior at four hundred parts per million, an unprecedented level in record keeping—as part of another cost to India and other nations around the globe.

The secretary said:

> When the desert is creeping into East Africa, and ever more scarce resources push farmers and herders into deadly conflict, where people are already, in parts of the world, fighting over water, then this is a matter of shared security for all of us. When we face major threats from extreme weather events of the kind that were predicted by climate science, including in my country, we all have to act. When the Himalayan glaciers are receding, threatening the very supply of water to almost a billion people, we all need to do better.[421]

Part of "doing better," to the secretary's way of thinking, was investing in clean energy. It could not only provide renewable power but also create economic opportunity by letting entrepreneurs tap into a market that could serve up to 4 billion people and be worth up to $6 trillion.

"I emphasize the dynamic, forward-looking India of today is not going to find its energy mix in the 19th century or the 20th century solutions," Kerry said. "It won't find it in the coal mines. India's destiny requires finding a formula in the 21st century that will power it into the 22nd."[422]

A little more than a month later, the secretary visited the Zero Point Power Plant in Islamabad, Pakistan. He wanted to learn about how a similar dearth of electricity in India's neighbor was impeding its economic development. Pakistani minister of power and water Khawaja Asif pronounced it "a bigger menace to our economy, to our existence, than the war on terror."[423]

The US Agency for International Development, which works in conjunction with the State Department to disburse foreign assistance, had provided funding for better metering of Pakistan's existing supply. That helped to manage service outages.

"One of the greatest single restraints, one of the greatest pullbacks against growth, is the lack of energy," Kerry said after touring the power plant. "If a company is going to situate itself somewhere and open its manufacturing doors, it needs to have energy. If a school is going to open, it needs to have energy. To build homes, people need to have energy."[424]

In October 2013, we visited Bali to join President Obama in Indonesia for the annual Asia-Pacific Economic Cooperation forum. The president ended up canceling his attendance because of a government shutdown back in Washington. Secretary Kerry represented him at the APEC meeting in Bali, which assembled leaders of twenty one Pacific Rim economies.

We took time on that trip to visit fishermen at nearby Benoa Port to learn about their efforts to create a sustainable fishery. Allowing fish stocks to replenish is vital to maintaining the primary source of protein for 60 million Indonesians, as well as the fish supply for more distant consumers frequenting Outback Steakhouse restaurants and Whole Foods grocery stores in the United States.

Several fishermen and government and industry leaders briefed Kerry as he climbed across fishing boats and poked at freshly caught tuna being held on ice.

"We face the same challenge in our fisheries in America," the secretary told them. "Just as in New England or in the Pacific—in the state of Washington or California, where we have fishermen—we need scientific information to be able to make the best fishing decisions."[425]

During our final trip in 2013, we detoured from Manila to Tacloban City on the island of Leyte in the Philippines to see the damage caused by Typhoon Haiyan. It had roared through the region a month earlier and proved to be the deadliest hurricane to hit the Philippines in history.

It killed 6,300 people just in that country alone, and had peak winds tying the record for a typhoon making landfall.[426]

Kerry focused on that point after flying over homes covered with blue tarps, driving past flattened trees and crops, and touring a center distributing grain from the USAID.

"We . . . know that while no single storm can be attributed to climate change, we do know to a certainty that rising temperatures will lead to longer and more unpredictable monsoon seasons and will lead to more extreme weather events," the secretary said. "So, looking around here, you see an unmistakable example of what an extreme weather event looks like, and a reminder of our responsibility to act to protect the future."[427]

In February 2014, Kerry delivered his second truth-to-power environmental speech, this time during a visit to Jakarta, Indonesia. A developing nation like India, Indonesia is the world's fifth-largest emitter of greenhouse gases, attributed not to increased technology use but to its development of forests and peatlands. Both activities release carbon dioxide into the atmosphere.[428]

At the same time, Indonesia is considered one of the countries most vulnerable to climate change, because it's another archipelago prone to droughts and heavy rainfall. Kerry noted some scientists were predicting a one-meter rise in the sea level by the end of the twenty-first century. That would put half of Jakarta—a city of nearly 10 million people—underwater.

While the United States and China were willing to do their part heading into the 2015 COP meeting, it also was incumbent on nations such as Indonesia to do their share, Secretary Kerry said during his speech.

"There is still time for us to significantly cut greenhouse emissions and prevent the very worst consequences of climate change from ever happening at all," he said. "But we need to move on this, and we need to move together now."[429]

Kerry took special aim at climate-change deniers, those who doubt humans are contributing to climate change despite 97 percent of peer-reviewed climate studies showing the phenomenon is occurring, and human activity is responsible for it.

"President Obama and I believe very deeply that we do not have time for a meeting anywhere of the Flat Earth Society," the secretary said.[430]

He put climate change in the same category as terrorism or nuclear proliferation, two problems that can't be solved individually but only collectively. He said:

> In a sense, climate change can now be considered another weapon of mass destruction, perhaps the world's most fearsome weapon of mass destruction. . . . The fact is that climate change, if left unchecked, will wipe out many more communities from the face of the Earth. And that is unacceptable under any circumstances—but is even more unacceptable because we know what we can do and need to do in order to deal with this challenge.[431]

That comment was criticized by those who said there was no equivalency between the threat posed by climate change and the wave of Islamic terrorism then sweeping the world.

Kerry reiterated his belief in July 2016 as he lobbied to amend the 1987 Montreal Protocol and phase out hydrofluorocarbons from appliances like air conditioners and refrigerators.

"Yesterday, I met in Washington with 45 nations—defense ministers and foreign ministers—as we were working together on the challenge of Daesh, ISIL, and terrorism," the secretary said on July 22, 2016, in Vienna. "It's hard for some people to grasp it, but what we—you—are doing here right now is of equal importance, because it has the ability to literally save life on the planet itself."[432]

That prompted derisive headlines in conservative media of the sort seen on the Fox News website: "Kerry: Air conditioners as big a threat as ISIS."[433]

Kerry closed out 2014 much like he had 2013, warning about the consequences of ignoring climate change. This time his venue wasn't the Philippines but Peru, and the occasion was the twentieth UN-sponsored Conference of Parties—the last before COP 21 in Paris.

A key focus of his remarks was rebutting those who argued it was too costly to address such a massive problem. The secretary turned that analysis on its head. He noted extreme weather events in the United States cost $110 billion just in 2012, while coping with Typhoon Haiyan cost $10 billion.[434]

"You start adding up these 100 billions and 10 billions here in country after country, and think if that money had been put to helping to subsidize the transition to a better fuel, to an alternative or renewable, to cleaner, to emissions-free, to clean emissions capacity," the secretary said.[435]

Collectively, these trips around Middle Earth encapsulated Kerry's concerns about climate change.

To address it, big emitters like China, the United States, and India needed to set ambitious targets. And developing countries like Indonesia couldn't just take a pass, because their populations were at risk from bad air, rising seas, and other climate change effects.

Each type of country, meanwhile, stood to gain from investing in renewable energy. They could tap a market that could fuel their economy or gain technology allowing them to expand their electrical grid.

Arguing that digging up or pumping fossil fuels was less expensive than installing high-tech alternatives like solar panels was really a false argument, he said, when you added up the public health costs from breathing dirty air. That figure was compounded with the death toll and damages caused by superstorms lashing the planet.

Finally, promoting a clean environment would help prevent conflict from water shortages or forced migration triggered by drought, while also preserving fishing stocks needed to feed an expanding global population.

It was this final point that also inspired another of Secretary Kerry's major environmental initiatives.

———

THE BOSS WAS NEVER short of inspiration. Nor was he ever one not to think big.

That meant some on his staff were a bit dismissive when, during just our second day on the job, he announced he wanted to do something to call attention to the plight of the world's oceans.

John Kerry already had a few stock phrases he used in Senate speeches about the topic, complaining about massive trawlers "strip-mining" the ocean as "too much money chased too few fish." We would come to hear him say the popular film series *Planet Earth* should really be called *Planet Ocean*, because there was more water than land around the globe.

Now, the secretary wanted to go beyond the rhetoric. He felt oceans were under siege from overfishing and acidification caused by, among other things, fertilizer runoff. Fish were not only being swallowed up by factory ships sweeping through huge swaths of water but being choked by man-made plastic ending up in the sea.

Oceans covered more than two-thirds of the earth, yet few were sounding the alarm over their protection despite evidence of climate change on land.

Kerry envisioned compiling empirical data from sources around the world to create an unimpeachable repository of scientific evidence that spelled out the threat. He also proposed working with National Geographic and some of the world's great filmmakers, like James Cameron, to produce a movie about the challenge. And the secretary was so sure of what he wanted to say, he said he was willing to write and direct it himself.

Since he had just assumed a busy day job, we convinced him to settle for something else—but it ended up being only slightly less ambitious.

Secretary Kerry gave birth to the State Department's first Our Ocean conference. It brought together foreign ministers, environmentalists, and ocean experts from around the world for two days of meetings aimed at producing tangible results toward addressing such problems.

And not only did Kerry host the inaugural gathering in June 2014, but he traveled to Valparaiso, Chile, a year later for the second meeting. He then reprised the event in Washington in 2016 for one final push before leaving office.

All told, those three conferences generated over $9.2 billion to protect the ocean and commitments from countries around the world to safeguard 3.8 million square miles of water.

That area is roughly the size of the United States.

In a tribute to vision, though, the conference has lived on even after he finished his term.

The 2017 meeting was held on the Mediterranean island-state of Malta. The 2018 in Indonesia. And Norway asked to host the 2019 meeting.

Undersecretary of State for Economic Growth, Energy, and the Environment Cathy Novelli was tasked with organizing the first and third conferences. She used her contacts in the environmental community and from her prior job at Apple to transform a State Department auditorium into a virtual aquarium.

Fish and waves moved across video screens lining three of the room's four sides, while one of the courtyards in the middle of the Harry S Truman Building became a showcase for new technology, a breakout space for lectures, and a gathering spot for conference attendees.

Novelli deliberately chose the name Our Ocean—rather than Oceans—to communicate that scientists consider the seven seas a single waterway interconnected around the planet.

Kerry was thunderstruck when he walked into the meeting hall on June 16, 2014, and saw his vision achieved before an audience from more than eighty countries. Among the visitors was Prince Albert II of Monaco, an environmentalist who paid special attention to ocean acidification.

"When anybody looks out at the ocean—we're all sort of guilty of it one time or another—when you stand on a beach and you look out at the tide rolling in, you feel somehow that the ocean is larger than life, that it's an endless resource impossible to destroy," the secretary said in his opening remarks. "Most people underestimate the enormous damage that we as human beings are inflicting on our ocean every single day."[436]

The attendees set off to learn about how to prevent such damage at panels focused on marine protected areas, sustainable fisheries, marine pollution, and climate-related impacts on the ocean.

President Obama greeted them via video the second day before keynote speaker Leonardo DiCaprio took the stage for remarks. The actor/environmentalist announced a $7 million pledge from his foundation to support ocean preservation during the ensuing two years.

"These last remaining underwater bio-gems are being destroyed because there isn't proper enforcement or sufficient cooperation among governments to protect them," DiCaprio said. "If we don't do something to save our oceans now, it won't be just the sharks and the dolphins that will suffer; it will be all of us including our children and our grandchildren."[437]

Attendees ended up pledging $1.8 billion—$800 million focused on the ocean, $1 billion focused more generally on climate change.[438] President Obama also designated the largest marine protected area in the world, expanding the Pacific Remote Islands Marine National Monument by almost six times.[439]

The second conference, in Chile, was held October 5–6, 2015. Secretary Kerry was especially happy the branding had carried over, giving continuity to the conferences. It was temporarily renamed "Nuestro Oceanos" to reflect the language of our Spanish-speaking hosts.

Chilean president Michelle Bachelet attended and spoke at the conference, as did businessman and environmentalist Richard Branson.

In his remarks, Kerry recalled the fundamental problems confronting the audience:

> We're not just fishing unsustainably, my friends; we are living unsustainably. Our ocean is taking in a massive amount of pollution—8 million tons of plastic alone every single day. To put that into context, scientists say that the ocean may soon contain one ton of plastic for every three tons of fish. Not only that, but the chemistry of our ocean is changing rapidly. Why? Because nearly a third of greenhouse gases that are coming out of tailpipes of cars and smokestacks of power plants end up getting absorbed by the ocean.

Among other solutions, he called for establishing Sea Scout, a network aimed at integrating all existing and emerging technologies—and linking responsible entities and agencies around the world—to cut down on illegal fishing or pollution via a unified network.

"Today, various nations are working hard to track and address illegal fishing, but the fact is no nation is currently capable of policing the entire range of the oceans," Secretary Kerry said. "On the other hand, we have an obligation to make certain that no square kilometer of ocean is beyond the law."[440]

The final conference of Secretary Kerry's term was held September 15–16, 2016, in Washington. Participants announced over 136 new initiatives on marine conservation and protection that were valued at more than $5.24 billion—far more than the $1.8 billion from the first year. They also made new pledges to protect over 1.5 million square miles of the ocean.

President Obama gave special endorsement to the meeting, addressing the attendees in person this time.

In his remarks, Kerry sought to maintain the momentum established since his first brainstorming about the conference.

"With every positive step that we take, with the marine protected areas that we create, with the networks that we create and the safeguards that we enforce to protect against illegal fishing, with the cooperation we pursue to combat climate change and to deepen scientific research—with each of these steps, we drop a pebble on the side of restoring and preserving the health of the ocean," he said.[441]

Through 2018, the conferences had generated commitments of $28 billion in pledges and vows to protect 10.2 million square miles of ocean—a sweeping legacy emanating from a simple idea expressed on the secretary's second day at work.[442]

*P*erhaps my favorite two-day stretch at the State Department was
    June 6–7, 2014.

My wife came to Paris to join us for a visit to Normandy, France,
which President Obama and Secretary Kerry were visiting to commemorate the seventieth anniversary of the D-Day invasion. The family junket
was especially fitting because my wife, Cathy, was born on June 6.

We watched the president address survivors of the Allied invasion and
pay tribute to those who died just below us on Omaha Beach. Some are
buried under bleached-white crosses in the American Cemetery.

Then he and Secretary Kerry headed off for another commemorative event, so we piled into vans for a drive up the Brittany coast. Our
destination was Saint-Briac-sur-Mer, the seaside town where Rosemary
Forbes Kerry had the family home that had been occupied by the Nazis
during World War II.

Secretary Kerry wanted to go back in his official position to pay tribute to three Americans who had died liberating the area. He also had a
very personal reason. He wanted to thank the townspeople who went to
his family homestead and recovered heirlooms after the fleeing Germans
turned their guns on the house and nearly leveled it.

Memorial wreaths for three Americans.

John Kerry says one of his earliest childhood memories is walking up the pockmarked driveway of Les Essarts and hearing his mother weep at the sight.

We spent the night of June 6 in nearby Dinard before setting off early the next morning for a wreath-laying ceremony at a memorial pillar outside Saint-Briac. It was erected in honor of the three fallen GIs.

In a Forrest Gump twist typical of Secretary Kerry, his father, Richard, apprenticed for the sculptor who built the memorial. The summer he was there, he met Rosemary Forbes while she visited her family home.

Joining the secretary for the ceremony was his cousin, Brice Lalonde, who'd been mayor of Saint-Briac, as well as a renowned World War II combat photographer, Tony Vaccaro. He snapped an iconic photo on August 14, 1944, of an American soldier kissing a little girl while women danced around them to celebrate Saint-Briac's freedom.

After the wreath laying, the secretary was scheduled to drive to the town square where Vaccaro took the picture, so he could deliver his thank-you speech. Instead, he opted to walk, prompting the several hundred who'd come out to the memorial to join in an impromptu march back to town.

Joined by his cousin, the then-mayor of Saint-Briac, and other officials, Secretary Kerry played Pied Piper while leading the group along the seaside streets and into the town square, which itself was already jammed.

He then stood on a balcony at town hall to deliver his thanks. Joining him was Vaccaro and a ninety-two-year-old woman who'd been one of the dancers in the backdrop of the photo now known as The Kiss of Liberation.

It was an emotional moment for everyone involved.

Afterward, we staffers were set to drive back to Paris while the secretary spent the night at his family home.

But before we left, he invited us to join him for drinks on the patio. As the sun set on the Brittany coast, Secretary Kerry led us around the grounds where several generations of the Forbes family had summered.

Among the stops was a bunker still remaining from World War II.

It was a landmark in which Secretary Kerry played as a child.

(Top) Secretary Kerry and Saint-Briac Mayor Vincent Denby-Wilkes lead
a procession back into town after laying a wreath at a World War II memorial
on June 7, 2014. (Bottom) Speech to Saint-Briac residents.

*(Top) Tony Vaccaro and his photo. (Bottom) Woman hands
Secretary Kerry scrapbooks of him she kept.*

SECRETARY KERRY HAD AN unexpected ally in sounding the alarm about climate change. And *ally* is an appropriate term.

Just as few may have expected a diplomat to focus on a topic usually reserved for the National Oceanic and Atmospheric Administration or the US Environmental Protection Agency, some were surprised to learn the US Department of Defense shared the State Department's concern about climate change.

The military is charged with addressing all credible threats to the nation's security, and it has concluded that climate change can cause direct threats in the form of rising sea levels, or indirect threats such as political instability triggered by water shortages.

They are considered a "threat multiplier" to more commonly perceived challenges, such as an opposing army or rogue nuclear actor.

The Pentagon outlined these concerns during the Obama administration in its 2014 Quadrennial Defense Review, as well as a 2015 report titled "National Security Implications of Climate-Related Risks and a Changing Climate."

The latter report quoted the former in saying, "Climate change is an urgent and growing threat to our national security, contributing to increased natural disasters, refugee flows, and conflicts over basic resources such as food and water. These impacts are already occurring, and the scope, scale, and intensity of these impacts are projected to increase over time."[443]

The Center for Climate & Security, a nonpartisan policy institute advised by an array of retired military leaders, detailed the concern on its website:

> Climate change effects such as sea-level rise have the ability to compromise coastal military installations that are critical for such operations. . . . Extreme drought or flooding in areas where militaries are engaged in warfighting, for example, can compromise water supply lines, and thus threaten military personnel directly. . . . In the Arctic, a melting ice cap, coupled with increasing tensions between Russia and other Arctic nations, could increase the likelihood of conflict. . . . Migrating fish stocks in the South China Sea may create pressures on the fishing industry to move into contested water, leading to increased tensions between China, its neighbors, and the United States.[444]

For anyone believing the Defense Department or think tanks were doing the bidding of liberals during a Democratic administration, similar alarms were sounded by the national security establishment during the final year of the Republican administration led by President George W. Bush.

Secretary Kerry saw and heard about all these threats in November 2015 when he visited Naval Station Norfolk on Virginia's coast.

The installation is the largest naval station in the world—home to seventy-five ships utilizing fourteen piers. The adjacent Chambers Field hosts about 130 aircraft in eleven hangars.[445]

The scale was evident when the secretary walked up the gangplank and climbed to the bridge of the USS *San Antonio* for a briefing.

He was told that all he could see from atop the stealthy Marine landing vessel—a view of some $5 billion in taxpayer investment—was at risk because of rising sea levels. That included the piers where six aircraft carriers tie up, as well as the roads and railways transporting all the supplies and people needed to operate them.

When the secretary asked the ship's captain, J. Pat Rios, about the life expectancy of the base, he replied, "Twenty to fifty years."[446]

A *Rolling Stone* reporter who was with us later wrote, "There was a slight but perceptible pause among the naval officers and State Department officials on the bridge."[447]

Kerry outlined his concerns later during a speech nearby at Old Dominion University:

> The bottom line is that the impacts of climate change can exacerbate resource competition, threaten livelihoods, and increase the risk of instability and conflict, especially in places already undergoing economic, political, and social stress. And because the world is so extraordinarily interconnected today—economically, technologically, militarily, in every way imaginable—instability anywhere can be a threat to stability everywhere.

He said USAID was working to develop flags highlighting areas of risk. The Pentagon was also developing strategies to shore up Norfolk and similar bases. But a month out from the COP 21 meeting in Paris, John Kerry continued to argue that nations around the world had to agree to cut greenhouse gas emissions and shift to renewable sources of energy.

He harped on the economic opportunities that would accompany the health benefits:

> I'm not going to tell you that a global climate agreement is going to be the silver bullet that eliminates the threat posed by climate change. But the truth is, we won't eliminate it without an agreement in Paris. And the kind of agreement that we're working toward is one that will prove that the world's leaders finally understand the scope of the challenge that we are up against.[448]

————

I'D NEVER SET FOOT in Paris before we went there in February 2013 during our first trip abroad. By the time we paid our last visit in January 2017, it was a familiar place.

I had a favorite bistro—Bar Romain on Rue de Caumartin—and a favorite running route—up the Champs-Élysées to the Arc de Triomphe, over to the Trocadéro plaza, down to the Seine River and Eiffel Tower, through the 7th Arrondissement, and across the Place de la Concorde. I also had a favorite memory—a visit from my wife to coincide with our trip to Normandy, France, for a ceremony marking the seventieth anniversary of D-Day. That was her birthday.

In fact, Paris was the city we visited most during Secretary Kerry's four years leading the State Department.

We went there thirty-six times, primarily because it was a diplomatic crossroads and natural venue for diplomats from Eastern and Western Europe. It also offered a welcome climatic and scenic change for their counterparts from the Middle East and Africa.

We returned for a Bastille Day and the World War II commemorations, and twice in 2015 to represent the United States after the *Charlie Hebdo* and Bataclan terrorist attacks.

But we also couldn't deny a couple of overseas meetings were held in Paris simply because the secretary loved the city and seized the opportunity to visit if he could justify it.

Of course, he had another of those Forrest Gump connections to the French capital.

In July 1940, his mother, Rosemary Forbes, fled a family home on the Brittany coast just before an invasion of German forces. She went to Paris, where things were equally grim ahead of the Nazi onslaught.

She described the scene in the Place de la Concorde in a letter to her future husband, Richard Kerry, which was included in a biography of John Kerry written by *The Boston Globe* during his 2004 presidential campaign.

The Place de la Concorde, the city's central square, was filled with cars "laden with every kind of house belongings, in hay carts drawn by weary, perspiring horses, on foot with perambulators, handcarts, wheelbarrows, tricycles carrying invalids and babies dragging dogs, cats, or birdcages. It was a terribly grim and unforgettable sight," she wrote on July 14, 1940.[449]

A nurse by training, Rosemary Forbes wanted to stay and help the Red Cross, but she had fled Paris a month earlier as the Germans marched in and set off explosions to announce their arrival.

She eventually boarded a boat to the United States after ducking to avoid strafing runs by German fighters while making her way to Portugal.

I heard Secretary Kerry choke up several times recounting the story of her bravery.

Our visit to Paris in December 2015 was part of a marathon month of travel around the world.

But when we returned on December 7, 2015, after an overnight flight from Washington, the secretary said he wasn't going to leave before the COP 21 approved a transparent, verifiable agreement to cut greenhouse gas emissions. He didn't let up for five straight days that included his seventy-second birthday.

The Conference of Parties was held at LeBourget Airport in pavilions used annually for the Paris Air Show. Organizers did their best to walk their talk, serving water not in disposable bottles but glass carafes, putting recycling bins everywhere you looked, holding meetings in rooms built of unfinished particle board, and having speakers stand at a plain wooden podium.

Striding through the conference center late on December 8, 2015, the secretary delivered a now-familiar refrain for those of us who had been with him during the Middle East peace process or Iran nuclear talks: "Long day. I spent longer here that I expected. But we're getting things done. That's what we came here to do."[450]

While negotiators haggled over each country's respective emissions pledge or other overall tolerable limit for increasing the Earth's temperature, Kerry focused on the bigger picture.

He felt that if countries from around the world reached consensus in Paris, it would not only chart a path to improve the environment but send a signal to business leaders globally that governments are finally serious about climate change.

That in turn should prompt them to invest in solutions addressing it.

"I don't believe that governments are going to wind up making the fundamental decision that in fact changes the world to this low-carbon economy. We're going to set our stage, we can create frameworks, we can lower costs, we can make decisions; but in the end, it's you," he said during the Caring for Climate Business Forum on December 8, 2015, in what amounted to his keynote address. "It's businesses and the choices that you make and the kinds of buildings that you build, the investments that you make, the products you create, the sustainability of your products from start to finish that will make the difference."[451]

Four days later, representatives from 195 nations attending the convention reached agreement. They committed to submitting plans of varying scope and ambition that, nonetheless, represented their vow to curb greenhouse gas emissions.

While scientists said these commitments were unlikely to prevent the Earth's temperature from rising beyond the targeted 2 degrees Celsius, or 3.6 degrees Fahrenheit, "the Paris deal could represent the moment at which, because of a shift in global economic policy, the inexorable rise in planet-warming carbon emissions that started during the Industrial Revolution began to level out and eventually decline," *The New York Times* reported.[452]

Bolstering the agreement was a legally binding requirement for each nation to reconvene every five years, starting in 2020, to offer updated plans with tightened emissions targets. While those targets wouldn't be mandated, the requirement for updated plans was viewed as a catalyst for curbing the overall climate change trajectory.

In return, developing countries celebrated a commitment from wealthier countries to provide at least $100 billion a year to help poorer countries respond to climate change.

The *Times* story highlighted the dynamic set in motion by Secretary Kerry during his first trip to Asia:

> Negotiators from many countries have said that a crucial moment
> in the path to the Paris accord came last year in the United States,
> when [President] Obama enacted the nation's first climate change

policy—a set of stringent new Environmental Protection Agency regulations designed to slash greenhouse gas pollution from the nation's coal-fired power plants. Meanwhile, in China, the growing internal criticism over air pollution from coal-fired power plants led President Xi Jinping to pursue domestic policies to cut coal use.[453]

The sentiment was echoed in a story in *Huffington Post* written by *Global-Post*'s Charlie Sennott. He formerly worked for *The Boston Globe* and wrote a lengthy profile of then senator Kerry during his 1996 reelection campaign against William Weld. In the *Huffington Post* article, Sennott wrote:

> Kerry's hair has gone from a candidate's salt-and-pepper to a statesman's silver gray. . . . It struck me as I watched Kerry speaking that in a month swirling with breaking news on terrorism and climate change, there are few public officials in the world who have as measured a grasp of how climate change fits within the matrix of threats the world is presenting these days. Increasingly, we are waking up to a globe where climate change in a resource-constrained world is fueling civil instability that stands to shape conflict in the 21st century.[454]

JUST BEFORE SECRETARY KERRY flew to Antarctica in November 2016, Russia made another reversal in its willingness to cooperate with the Obama administration.

After five prior votes against it, the Russian Federation agreed to join the United States, twenty-two other nations, and the European Union in transforming the Ross Sea in Antarctica's Southern Ocean into the world's largest MPA, or marine protected area.

The Ross Sea is considered pristine, and the krill flourishing in its chilly water feed killer whales and Adélie and Emperor penguins.

Britain's *Guardian* newspaper underscored the importance of the agreement: "The Ross Sea is a deep bay in the Southern Ocean that many scientists consider to be the last intact marine ecosystem on Earth—a living laboratory ideally suited for investigating life in the Antarctic and how climate change is affecting the planet."[455]

Secretary Kerry gave a nod to the Russians in a statement that said, "The creation of the Ross Sea MPA is an extraordinary step forward for marine protection, and the United States is grateful for the cooperation with our New Zealand co-sponsors of the proposal, and of all [Commission for the Conservation of Antarctic Marine Living Resources] members, including Russia, to make this achievement possible."[456]

Our visit to Antarctica was a logistical feat given the remoteness of the continent and its unique governance.

The mass encircling the bottom of the Earth exists under a 1959 treaty in which twelve original signatories—including the United States—agreed that Antarctica would be reserved for peaceful purposes. The signatories also committed to protecting the environment and conducting scientific research.

Seven countries—Australia, New Zealand, Chile, Argentina, the United Kingdom, France, and Norway—claim slices of the continental "pie" making up Antarctica. Some of their pieces in fact overlap. The United States and the Russian Federation never made any similar claim, but they also don't recognize the claims of any other country.

Nonetheless, the United States works closely with New Zealand, and McMurdo Station is located near the Kiwis' Scott Base in the area claimed by their country.

All told, there are about eighty stations on the continent, thirty of them year-round.

The United States program, the largest in Antarctica, is run by the National Science Foundation under a presidential directive. Day-to-day responsibility is held by the United States Antarctic Program, which runs three year-round stations.

Palmer Station is on the Antarctic Peninsula, which extends about eight hundred miles due north toward Argentina. About fifty people live there, and it is primarily used for bird research.

McMurdo Station, located across the continent closer to New Zealand, is the US logistical hub and a research center. About 1,200 people live there in the summer, but only about 250 people are "winter-overs" who stay there through the blackness of winter, when there are no cargo flights or ship traffic in or out.

The third site is the Amundsen Scott South Pole Station, where the summer population of about two hundred dwindles to about fifty people during the winter. It's been continuously occupied since 1956.

The newly renovated station sits at 9,000 feet in elevation, several hundred yards from the geographical South Pole. That spot is denoted with a geographic marker reset each year as the ice underneath it shifts. There's also a ceremonial barber pole nearby for picture taking.

The stations are reached by a logistical bridge extending more than ten thousand miles. The so-called Peninsula System leapfrogs from the United States to Santiago and Punta Arenas, Chile, before ending at Palmer Station. The Continental System runs through New Zealand and connects to McMurdo Station, the interim stop for any visitor to Amundsen Scott Station at the South Pole.[457]

The only period for outsiders to visit Antarctica is during the local summer, coming during the winter months in the northern hemisphere. The US Air Force provides the most frequent flights between New Zealand and McMurdo Station, and a New York Air National Guard Airlift Wing runs Operation Deep Freeze to the South Pole, flying that last leg between McMurdo and Amundsen stations.

Each takeoff and landing at those bases is dependent on the weather, and visitors frequently get trapped at one end or the other due to quickly changing conditions. Other times, planes are forced to turn back when weather deteriorates en route, sometimes even after they've flown up to five hours to reach their destination.

Amid concerns about stranding the secretary of State for an inordinate amount of time, planners paid special attention to ensuring John Kerry would be able to get in and out on the days he visited.

———

OUR TRIP STARTED ON November 7, 2016, with a nonstop flight from Washington to Hawaii. We boarded the same plane for our Election Day flight from Hawaii to New Zealand.

After we arrived, we held a bilateral meeting with Foreign Minister Murray McCully and then waited out the weather on November 9, 2016. The secretary took a walk through Hagley Park before grabbing lunch at a tapas place called the Curators House.

Christchurch, the largest city on New Zealand's South Island, has an English feel, but was still rebuilding at that time after damage caused by two earthquakes in 2010 and 2011.

We also visited a US Antarctic Program depot so we could be fitted for our "ECW": extreme cold weather gear that included polar jackets, pants, boots, and thick leather gloves.

Very early on November 10, 2016, we got the all clear to fly from New Zealand to Antarctica. Secretary Kerry carried an orange duffel bag filled with his loaner gear as he climbed into a C-17 cargo plane for the flight to McMurdo Station.

The four-engine transport—the same kind Kerry flew on after breaking his leg—is the most modern in the Air Force fleet. It was operated by a crew from McChord Air Force Base near Seattle. They fly the plane south for about six weeks, make several continuous round trips a week between New Zealand and Antarctica, and then take their plane back home while another McChord crew flies in a fresh C-17.

The cost and infrequency of the flights between Christchurch and McMurdo Station make each one prized, so our group wasn't alone on the plane. There were several scientists also traveling, and the rest of the cargo hold was filled with supplies—including a big four-bladed replacement propeller for one of the C-130s flying between McMurdo and the South Pole.

Riding in a cargo plane is disorienting compared to a normal commercial airliner. You may sit sideways on the mesh seats running the length of the fuselage, or in the middle of the cargo hold in a section of airline seating that slides on or off via tracks in the floor. The only windows are coaster-sized holes on the doors and a pair of portals overlooking each wing that let crew members look at the engines and perform safety checks.

Since there's no other outside view, you have to rely on your hearing and sense of balance to tell you if you're climbing, descending, or turning left or right. Landing is heart-stopping because you hear the engines winding down and can feel the airplane flare into the proper approach position, but you hang in suspense until the unseen moment when the wheels slam into the ground.

The one big exception is in the cockpit, where wraparound windows offer a full view out, up, and down. Secretary Kerry took the extra seat up on the flight deck so he could see outside as we flew to a place not seen by many people.

The beginning of our five-hour flight south was boring, the plane passing over water extending in every direction. But about an hour before landing, we began to see Antarctica, invigorating those lucky enough to find a place to peek outside.

The biggest landmark amid the endless snow and ice was Mount Erebus, the second-highest volcano on the continent and the southernmost active volcano on Earth. It rises about 12,500 feet above Ross Island, the ice-covered land-mass that's also home to McMurdo Station.[458]

Ross Island would be surrounded by the Ross Sea if not for the cold and geology of Antarctica. Instead of being encircled by water, it's bordered by the Ross Ice Shelf, a thick floating platform of ice that flows from a glacier to a coastline and then floats on top of the water.

The Ross Ice Shelf is the largest in Antarctica—about 200,000 square miles and 500 miles across, roughly the size of France—and is nearly 2,500 feet thick in some places.[459] The vertical wall at the end can rise 50 to 150 feet above the ocean surface.

The Ross Sea adjacent to McMurdo is passable in the summer months, allowing ships to reach the station to deliver supplies and take away garbage.

We flew past Mount Erebus before the pilots made a final turn to line up with the Pegasus Field, a "white-ice" runway on the Ross Ice Shelf. The ice beneath it is about 110 feet thick and covered with three to four inches of compacted snow.[460] Our arrival was announced with a solid thud followed by an unexpectedly smooth rollout on the snowy surface. We taxied for several seemingly interminable minutes before coming to a halt.

When the loadmaster opened the door, we entered another world.

First of all, you felt like you were stepping onto the moon because you were wearing a spacesuit of sorts. I had on long underwear, thin and thick socks, pants, a shirt and undershirt, a sweat jacket—and then all my ECW.

It consisted of white snow boots, black snow pants held up by braces over my shoulders, and a fur-trimmed orange snorkel parka covering from the middle of my thighs to the top of my head.

I also wore a hat and inner and outer gloves, as well as sunglasses to fend off the blinding light.

Second, you felt like you were in no place you'd ever been before because of the absolute lack of sound. There was a bit of a breeze, of course, but there were no buildings to catch it, no passing cars or rustling trees or planes flying overhead.

The sound of silence is like a pure vacuum.

While it was about zero degrees outside, our gear protected us from the elements. The bigger challenge was moving in the clothes while also toting your ECW duffle bag and, in my case, protecting camera gear against the freezing cold.

Moving with the grace of sumo wrestlers, we made our way to a caravan of red Ford Econoline vans. They were just like the ones used back home but outfitted for Antarctica with monster truck-sized snow tires. We clambered in and set off for Williams Field. It was another airport built atop 25 feet of snow covering more than 8 feet of ice—floating on 1,800 feet of water.

We were meeting another plane for the flight to "Pole," the singular term locals use for the South Pole.

Our half-hour trip between airports was akin to taking a drive across a frozen lake. There was no pavement or painted lines, but the right side of the route was marked with orange flags stuck in the snow. There were a couple of intersections, but no other traffic and no traffic lights.

When we reached "Willy," the propellers on an old gray C-130 named the *City of Albany* were already spinning so we could take off immediately on our three-hour flight. The plane was specially outfitted with skis protruding around each set of its tires.

Everyone quickly sat down for takeoff, but almost as soon as we buckled our seat belts, we got disappointing news: the weather at the South Pole had deteriorated just since we landed at Pegasus Field. The trip was being canceled.

We'd been onboard barely enough time to use the tarp-shrouded latrine. Despite the disappointment, we adjusted by falling back to Plan B.

We left Williams Field and drove to McMurdo Station, where we boarded a pair of helicopters for a six-hour tour of the area. I ended up riding knee to knee with Secretary Kerry aboard a Huey chopper similar to those flown during the Vietnam War.

Our tour guides were Dr. Kelly Falkner, director of the National Science Foundation's Office of Polar Programs, and Dr. Scott Borg, leader of the Office's Antarctic Sciences Section.

We flew north over McMurdo Sound for about twenty-five miles before setting down at Cape Royds, a promontory west of Mount Erebus where there is an Adélie penguin rookery and the preserved hut of explorer Sir Ernest Shackleton.

Shackleton was an Irishman who led three British expeditions to Antarctica. The second of them, the Nimrod Expedition that got within 115 miles of the South Pole, lasted from 1907 to 1909. Its members spent the winter of 1908 in a hut built of wooden planks and tarpaper.[461] The wood-burning stove still works, and the walls have shelves stocked with canned goods the group never used. A seat remains on the snow-filled commode outside.

The secretary marveled at the thought of fifteen people living in the space, sharing bunks covered with furs.

We walked across a volcanic surface up a rocky hill several hundred yards away so we could look at the rookery, a breeding ground for Adélie penguins. The wind was over 60 miles per hour, numbing our exposed skin and forcing us to lean into the breeze. The air reeked with the smell of penguin poop.

Looking down on clusters of penguins, we realized they too were fighting the elements. Most were squatting down, their heads pointed into the wind and the slipstream moving over their well-oiled backs.

We posed for pictures outside Shackleton's hut before flying on past snowy cliffs and the occasional Weddell seal napping in the sunshine.

We crossed McMurdo Sound and landed at the Marble Point Air Facility, It's a US Antarctic Program way station with six above ground tanks to refuel helicopters and an orange corrugated metal hut where the ground crew and their cook live.

Our visit underscored the uniqueness of the work in Antarctica and the people who undertake it.

As in other spots we visited, the people who greeted us were cheerful and welcoming. They lead remote lives, many of them centered around scientific research, and they exude the kind of heartiness needed to endure the elements.

Our cook made a lunch of sauerbraten and spaetzle, a vinegary beef dish that only my Germanic mother and aunt had ever made for me. The cook also generously used her monthly allotment of fresh greens to compose a salad for us.

There was nobody around for miles, but there was a real sense of community among the fifteen or so people who shared a meal inside that metal hut. I felt bad leaving the cook behind.

We took off and flew south to Taylor Valley, one of the McMurdo Dry Valleys with extremely low humidity and surrounding mountains that block the flow of ice from nearby glaciers.[462] We turned west and flew up the valley to the tip of the Taylor Glacier, a massive flow of ice and snow whose end is marked by Blood Falls.

In that spot, a plume of saltwater colored orange by iron oxide bubbles over onto the icy surface of West Bonney Lake.[463]

We continued on to our final stop at New Harbor. The research station was nothing more than a pair of Quonset huts sitting side by side on a lake bed against a backdrop of Mount Erebus. About a half-dozen people were living there, including a sketch artist working under a federal art grant and a pair of scientists who wedged through holes cut in the nearby ice to study the marine life living underneath.

When we emerged, we were greeted by a lone stray Adélie penguin. It was as curious about us as we were about it, so it waddled over, its wings swept back at forty-five-degree angles to maintain its balance.

"Come on, walk up here, buddy!" the secretary said. The penguin obliged, stopping about ten yards away.

The rule in Antarctica is that visitors can't approach wildlife, but wildlife is free to approach visitors, so everyone stood still and preserved the moment with cellphone pictures and video.

Some footage caught by Chief of Staff Jon Finer ended up appearing on *The New York Times* website.[464]

Our return to civilization was heralded by a lone snowmobile track across the frozen Ross Sea. It led to the hillside cluster of about one hundred buildings looking like a mining town but denoting McMurdo Station.

We landed and made our way to Hut 10, where the secretary, the DS special agent in charge, and I would spend the night. We all had a chance to shower and eat dinner.

I took a moment to contemplate what I'd seen during not just our trip to Antarctica but also the trips to the Arctic Circle preceding it.

Up north, the damage caused by climate change is readily apparent. It's evident in the fjord that's no longer frozen, the glacier receding farther and farther inland, the larger and larger icebergs breaking off the ice shelf.

Down south, the current damage is less perceptible—but only because of the vastness of scale. Ice thousands of feet deep. Snow hundreds of feet high. Stretches untouched by man for as far as you can see. The absolute absence of life—or sound—for miles.

Antarctica is the world's ice chest, and if it's broken, there's no man-made tool big enough to fix it.

I kept thinking back to that Arctic researcher aboard the HMS *Thetis*, as we floated off the coast of Greenland and took stock of what, ironically enough, amounted to a canary in a coal mine.

He said that as bad as things already were up north, they could end up being one hundred times worse down south.

Secretary Kerry touched on this reality a couple weeks later during a speech at the Women's Foreign Policy Group Conference in Washington.

"Climate change is growing as a threat in so many ways that are very hard to convey to people. It's very hard to talk about the nature of the threat, which is existential, and get people to relate to it because it is so enormous and so big. People look at the oceans and say, 'My God, how could I affect what's going on in the oceans?'" he said.

"We can't afford public people who ignore science. We can't afford to simply turn our backs on these realities."[465]

*(Top) Arrival at Pegasus Field. (Bottom) Six-hour
helicopter survey of vast Antarctica.*

(Top) Inside Shackleton's hut. (Bottom) Braving high winds and penguin poop at Adélie rookery.

(Top) Snow ripples and striated mountains. (Middle) Letting an Adélie penguin come to us at New Harbor. (Bottom) Addressing McMurdo residents.

*(Top) Seeing core sample at Scott Base. (Middle) Secretary Kerry crosses
an ice field near Scott Base en route to a Weddell seal resting spot.
(Bottom) After over 100,000 photos of him, one with the Boss.*

LIFE AT MCMURDO STATION is not for the timid, especially for those who winter over and have to endure total darkness for months on end.

In addition to the bitter weather, there are limited places to go. And not just anyone is allowed to work in Antarctica.

While there are medical facilities at the station, all visitors have to undergo a rigorous physical before making the trip to ensure they have the proper fitness. The State Department doctors likened America's exams for those going to Antarctica to the examinations faced by astronauts, with a full medical history and blood workups, as well as an EKG, and, in some cases, a stress test.

Everyone also has to be tested for HIV, since McMurdo residents participate in a living blood bank. If someone needs a pint, volunteers pull up their sleeve and provide it.

Most of the people living at McMurdo Station aren't scientists but logisticians who support them and their work. Besides those stationed at the South Pole or remote stations like those at Marble Point or New Harbor, there are dozens of scientists working at the Crary Labs within McMurdo itself.

The secretary toured the labs our second day on site and was overwhelmed by the biology, earth sciences, atmospheric sciences, and aquatic research under way.

Residents at McMurdo Station work a twenty-four-hour schedule. They live in assigned lodging and are served up to four meals per day in light of the round-the-clock schedule. They have Internet service, albeit slow, and get mail. Visitors to the South Pole can get their letters and postcards stamped at a post office offering the unique "South Pole" postmark.

Residents also can attend spiritual services at the Chapel of the Snows and receive mental health counseling if the way of life gets to them.

In addition, they may blow off steam at Gallagher's Pub and Southern Exposure, two clubs that serve alcohol.

I had to work late to transmit pictures from our helicopter tour back to the United States, but a couple of colleagues visited the clubs and came back with a report on the local way of life.

They were told that, given the limited number of people on base and everyone's assured good health, McMurdo has a tradition of relationships running from holiday to holiday. Couples will form, say, on Memorial Day and then break up on the Fourth of July, only to have each individual find a newly single mate for another relationship lasting until Labor Day.

This circle of life continues around the Gregorian and federal holiday calendars, the State Department visitors were told.

Secretary Kerry missed out on that insight, but he lauded everyone who lived and worked at McMurdo Station while addressing a staff assembly in the dining hall after his helicopter tour.

He explained the scientists he met up north in the Arctic Circle urged him to make the trip because it would further highlight the planetary risk from climate change. He said he understood after what he saw and heard while flying across Antarctica.

The secretary also implored them to forge ahead with their research, even if the incoming administration questioned the science behind climate change or followed up on its threat to abandon the prior year's Paris climate change agreement.

"I don't know if that's going to happen. I'm not predicting anything. I'm not getting into any political fight here or anything like that," Kerry said. "But I'm just saying to you that I've seen the curves, I've seen the ups and downs of this process for over thirty years, and we've made gains and we've had setbacks. And we've never made the gains without fighting for them, and we've always had a difficulty in being able to make the gains because we haven't necessarily had the quality of the science that we need to be able to prove to people what's happening."[466]

He echoed the thought two days later, after returning to Christchurch and flying on to Wellington, New Zealand, for a meeting in the capital with Prime Minister John Key.

When a reporter asked Secretary Kerry whether he was concerned President-elect Trump would abandon the Paris accord, the veteran politician said "there is sometimes a divide between a campaign and the governing."[467]

While Kerry wasn't sure a President Trump would do the things a Candidate Trump promised, the secretary said the places he'd visited during his four years at the State Department, and the things he'd seen firsthand, deepened his resolve to fight on.

"I believe the evidence is clear, and the question now that we, this administration, are going to continue to address is how we will implement the Paris agreement," he said. "And until January 20th, when this administration is over, we intend to do everything possible to meet our responsibility to future generations to be able to address this threat to life itself on the planet."[468]

Six months later, President Trump announced he was withdrawing the United States from the Paris climate change agreement. The decision would take effect November 4, 2020—the day after the next presidential election.

A call to political arms had been sounded. As another Vietnam veteran, former senator, national leader, and environmentalist had put it, the fate of Earth was in the balance.

9

THE TRUMP ERA,
AND BEYOND

WHAT I JUST DESCRIBED is the motif of traditional diplomacy. What followed Secretary Kerry's time at the State Department was anything but.

Both President Trump and the person he nominated to succeed Kerry, Exxon Chairman Rex Tillerson, dismissed diplomatic conventions as they began their jobs during the winter of 2017.

Trump, a businessman-turned-politician, picked a nominee for secretary of State with worldwide business connections and company operations on six continents—but no experience in government or the policymaking it entails.

Tillerson, like Trump himself, was new to both Washington and the dynamics of its power games. Instead of reaching out, the new secretary turned inward and made overhauling the State Department bureaucracy his first priority.

What followed was Draconian. There were cuts to and the loss of the top echelon of the diplomatic corps, paralysis among those who remained because of Tillerson's languishing organizational analysis, and questions from US allies about who was handling the nation's foreign policy: President Trump; his son-in-law, Jared Kushner, who was given a diplomatic portfolio; or Tillerson.

It ended in just fourteen months in the most undiplomatic of manners, with the president tweeting he'd hired a new secretary of State. White House Chief of Staff John Kelly later told reporters Tillerson had been on the toilet, ill and overseas, when he was told he was being fired.

That crass treatment drew sympathy even within the Harry S Truman Building, evidenced by the applause the outgoing secretary received after delivering his farewell remarks.

He spoke from the same spot in the C Street Lobby where Kerry had said his own goodbye to the Department little more than a year earlier.

"I hope you will continue to treat each other with respect," a deflated Tillerson said. "Regardless of the job title, the station in life, or your role, everyone is important to the State Department. We're all just human beings trying to do our part."[469]

———

AS DISAPPOINTED AS SECRETARY Kerry was while in New Zealand when he realized Donald Trump had been elected president, and as concerned as he was about perpetuating the Iran nuclear deal, Paris climate change accord, and other areas of focus during his time in office, he also was clear to the entire State Department team when Rex Tillerson's nomination was announced.

We were to assist with an orderly transition in every manner possible, "so that the incoming administration can pursue the important work of US foreign policy around the world." That was how he termed it in a statement issued the day the president-elect named his nominee.[470]

Our efforts were rebuffed.

Not only did Tillerson spur three attempted meetings offered by Kerry, but virtually his entire incoming team did the same.

A whole wing of transition offices set up on the first floor of Main State went largely unused, except for a few coordinators dispatched from Trump transition headquarters near the White House.

The incoming chief of staff and other senior aides didn't meet with their existing counterparts, whether they be policy experts, the Department spokesperson, or the staffers who helped organize a secretary's trips.

I was alarmed as I walked down the 7th Floor hallway for the final time—at 11:40 a.m. on January 20, 2017, just twenty minutes before my presidential appointment expired—and prepared to turn in my BlackBerry.

I was doing so without having made any kind of hand-off to the person who would replace me after Trump was sworn in as president at the stroke of noon.

I certainly didn't have the most vital role in the Department, but I'd been by the outgoing secretary's side for his entire four-year term. I was willing to offer the benefits of my experience to any of the newcomers. And I felt this way despite them coming from a different political party than the administration I served.

Most of my colleagues felt exactly the same. I think the reason we did was the gravity of what we'd learned during the prior four years.

I had little appreciation for it as I entered the federal government, but national security jobs have a unique pressure and responsibility.

Momentous news could come at any time, day or night, and from any time zone in the world, and equally momentous decisions might have to be made in response. You learn to live with a low-grade sense of concern at all times—even as you sleep. You might turn off the ringer on your phone, but not the vibrator. Mine would shimmy across the nightstand as emails arrived while I intermittently dozed and awakened.

Meanwhile, the work is so intertwined with the safety of our country you never want to be off the clock without knowing for sure who's standing watch for you. Even then, you're never beyond the reach of the Ops Center, the State Department version of the White House Situation Room. It's staffed with workers who had every possible phone number for Department employees and government outsiders alike.

Vacations are short and infrequent and subject to world events.

When I handed over my smartphone at the IT office and took the elevator down to an empty C Street Lobby that final day, I was relieved to no longer have the responsibility that had followed me everywhere I went.

It had been a long, stressful, and tiring four years.

But I also was alarmed as my taxi drove away from Main State. I knew there was a gap in The Building's leadership, and it would take time for our replacements to get up to speed on the demands of their new jobs.

Our country was vulnerable, at the very least.

I found this especially churlish, because even if the Trump administration wanted to do everything the opposite of the Obama administration, it was a stretch to believe there wasn't anything the incoming State Department team could learn from their predecessors.

There was nothing insightful John Kerry could tell Rex Tillerson about dealing with the Russian foreign minister? There was no low-hanging diplomatic fruit anywhere in the world that could help the new team establish itself? There was no issue best discussed face-to-face rather than written on a piece of paper that might never be routed to the right eyes or read?

My personal lament only foreshadowed the feelings that would permeate the State Department and its workforce in the coming weeks.

———————

THE NEWS THAT PRESIDENT-ELECT Trump had tapped Tillerson to be secretary of State was, initially, a relief for many at Foggy Bottom and posts around the world.

In the preceding weeks, there'd been speculation the job would go to former New York mayor Rudy Giuliani, former Massachusetts governor Mitt Romney, or former UN ambassador John Bolton.

While Giuliani openly pined to be secretary of State, he had a series of business connections that would have jeopardized his Senate confirmation. Bolton reportedly suffered from a different problem amid talk he was under consideration for secretary or national security adviser: his mustache was too bushy for the president-elect's tastes.[471]

"Trump doesn't think he looks the part," Michael Wolff quoted former White House Chief Strategist Steve Bannon saying in his book *Fire and Fury*.[472] Ultimately, the president warmed to Bolton enough to make him his third national security adviser.

Romney, meanwhile, had called Donald Trump a "phony" and "fraud" during the election campaign, even delivering a speech warning against his election.[473] The two met after Election Day to settle their differences, but the president-elect later decided against picking a man who'd been the Republican Party's presidential nominee just four years earlier.

Tillerson was endorsed by former secretaries of State James A. Baker III and Condoleezza Rice, both still extremely popular within the Department. He also kept a low profile throughout an application process resembling a casting call. He had his initial meeting with the president-elect after slipping into Trump Tower through a back door; he didn't parade through the main lobby—and past the waiting media pool—like so many other candidates.

In fact, there wasn't a single photograph or public sighting of Tillerson until after the president-elect formally nominated him on December 13, 2016. He later said he hadn't been looking for work but planning to retire the coming March to spend more time with his grandchildren.

He said his wife convinced him he should serve the nation.[474]

"His tenacity, broad experience and deep understanding of geopolitics make him an excellent choice for secretary of State," President-elect Trump said in a statement announcing Tillerson's appointment.[475]

In his opening remarks to the staff, Tillerson strummed all the right chords. He told everyone in the State Department lobby they were "among the finest public servants in the world."[476] He was careful to praise not just the Foreign Service officers but the civil servants as well. He said the safety of everyone in every job would be his top priority, every single day.

He also showed deference to the entire seventy-thousand-plus person workforce, which had an average tenure of eleven years.

"I have 25 minutes," he said, prompting laughter. "Hi, I'm the new guy."[477]

But Tillerson equally acknowledged the "hotly contested" campaign that resulted in Donald Trump's beating Hillary Clinton, who'd formerly led the very same people as secretary of State.

Many in the Department had expected to serve her again as president of the United States, and that isn't a subjective statement.

Clinton arrived and departed from the State Department as a political celebrity, having already been first lady, lived in the White House, and elected a US senator. She'd run for president immediately before serving as secretary, and she left the Department with the clear expectation she'd mount a second campaign for the presidency.

When we got the news in New Zealand that Hillary Clinton had lost and Donald Trump had been elected president, I saw a career diplomat at our hotel begin to cry. The Department grew demoralized in the coming weeks as a cold reality set in.

They were all professionals trained to soldier on no matter which political party held the White House; but what many lamented was losing the prospect of serving a president who respected the State Department for the reality of working for one who didn't.

———

WARFARE BETWEEN THE ADMINISTRATION and the Department broke out even before Tillerson was confirmed in the Senate by a 56–42 vote—the most votes in US history against a nominee to be secretary of State.[478]

First, the incoming administration made clear it wasn't going to carry over any of the Obama-era political appointees as ambassadors. This was normal, as each president has the right to tap whoever he wants to represent him abroad. But within the Department, some political appointees resented having to leave their jobs immediately.

Many had expected a grace period. Without one, some had to pull their kids out of schools midyear instead of being given the option to continue serving until summer vacation. Despite the personal inconvenience, the decision shouldn't have surprised them. Elections have consequences.

Second, Team Trump riled up the career employees by firing or driving out a wave of top-level Foreign Service officers who provided broad Department leadership.

In any presidential transition, political appointees on the State Department staff are expected to submit a resignation letter so the incoming president can fill any and all slots desired. Then White House chief of staff Denis McDonough sent all of us a memo immediately after Trump was elected, stating we had to submit our resignations to him by the first week of December 2016.

Within the federal bureaucracy, however, there also is an understanding certain people offer continuity within a department. They are a bridge of knowledge and experience that can serve an incoming administration—or at least help it launch smoothly. Incumbents are usually retained until their successors can be appointed, or nominated and confirmed by the Senate.

The Trump administration didn't share that sentiment or follow that practice.

In a single afternoon, Undersecretary of State for Management Patrick Kennedy, Assistant Secretary of State for Administration Joyce Anne Barr, Assistant Secretary of State for Consular Affairs Michele Bond, and Director of the Office of Foreign Missions Gentry O. Smith simultaneously submitted their resignations.[479]

Kennedy reportedly had been told he would be reassigned, and the other three considered themselves doomed even though they were career Foreign Service officers who would have been eligible for other postings.

Those resignations followed a pair on Inauguration Day by Greg Starr, the assistant secretary of Diplomatic Security, and Lydia Muniz, the director of the Bureau of Overseas Building Operations.[480]

"It's the single biggest simultaneous departure of institutional memory that anyone can remember, and that's incredibly difficult to replicate," David

Wade, who'd served as Secretary Kerry's first chief of staff, was quoted as saying in *The Washington Post*.[481]

The American Foreign Service Association issued a statement saying such changes were "nothing unusual. It added, "Given the talent available in our diplomatic corps, we expect that the new secretary will have no trouble finding the right people at State to fill out his senior leadership team."[482]

The comment proved optimistic, especially after the president instituted a federal hiring freeze on January 23. He'd later go on to propose a 31 percent cut in the State Department and USAID budgets, and Tillerson would suspend two incoming A-100 classes supposed to include minority students already promised spots in the Foreign Service.[483]

The perception was that the Department was being cut off and hollowed out.

AT THE SAME TIME, President Trump issued a ban on Muslims entering the United States from select Middle East and African nations. It triggered not only international concern and domestic political debate but also a "dissent cable" from State Department employees.

Over nine hundred of them declared they didn't support the administration's policy.

Such cables were created in the 1970s to provide an outlet for employee grievances, but the scale of the one about the Muslim ban made clear the Trump administration wasn't just facing a small disagreement but a large-scale revolt against its policies.

The public airing prompted White House press secretary Sean Spicer to say, just two days before Tillerson was sworn in, that "career bureaucrats" at the Department could "get with the program or they can go."[484]

Tillerson himself acknowledged the election dispute and its outgrowths during his arrival remarks.

"We do not all feel the same way about the outcome," the new secretary said. "Each of us is entitled to the expression of our political beliefs, but we cannot let our personal convictions overwhelm our ability to work as one team."[485]

He said his goal would be to focus the Department in the most efficient way possible.

"That may entail making some changes to how things are traditionally done in this department," said Tillerson. "But we cannot sustain ineffective traditions over optimal outcomes."[486]

He'd go on to launch a pair of management reviews aimed at generating the data he needed to reorganize the Department, but his own transition got off to an inauspicious start. President Trump rejected Tillerson's choice for his top deputy, Elliott Abrams, after learning Abrams criticized him during the 2016 campaign.[487]

The White House rejection of Abrams, coupled with the slow rollout of more junior staffers and new ambassadors, forced Tillerson to rely on existing State Department staffers to fill vital roles on an acting basis. It also left numerous US embassies under the control of veteran Foreign Service officers who otherwise would have been the No. 2 official below one of the new president's political appointees.

In a sense, the efforts to sideline or eliminate some diplomats ended up empowering those left behind.

Tillerson also proved to be press-shy, which took his diplomatic efforts out of the public spotlight.

The Department didn't hold its usual Daily Press Briefing for almost two months after the new secretary took office. It was sporadic in giving readouts of his calls with foreign leaders. When Tillerson traveled, he did so on a smaller government plane than his predecessors. That sharply reduced or even eliminated the traveling press corps typically accompanying a secretary of State.

"I'm not a big media press access person. I personally don't need it," he told the lone reporter he took with him on his first trip to Asia.[488]

Just three weeks after Tillerson was sworn in, *The Washington Post* published a story headlined "In first month of Trump presidency, State Department has been sidelined."[489]

"The biggest factor is the confusing lines of communication and authority to the White House, and Trump's inclination to farm out elements of foreign policy to a kitchen cabinet of close advisers," wrote veteran *Post* diplomatic correspondents Carol Morello and Anne Gearan.[490]

A month later, another *Post* headline read, "Secretary of State Rex Tillerson spends his first weeks isolated from an anxious bureaucracy."[491] A complaint both within the Department and at the White House was that Tillerson's chief of staff, Navy veteran and former US Patent official Margaret

Peterlin, was distrustful of the bureaucracy and kept a chokehold on the information flow to her boss.

Gearan and Morello wrote:

> Eight weeks into his tenure as President Trump's top diplomat, the former ExxonMobil chief executive is isolated, walled off from the State Department's corps of bureaucrats in Washington and around the world. His distant management style has created growing bewilderment among foreign officials who are struggling to understand where the United States stands on key issues. It has sown mistrust among career employees at State, who swap paranoid stories about Tillerson that often turn out to be untrue. And it threatens to undermine the power and reach of the State Department, which has been targeted for a 30-percent funding cut in Trump's budget.[492]

Fueling concern was a management survey sent out by Insigniam, one of the two private consulting firms hired by the secretary. It asked questions like, "To optimally support the future mission of the Department, what one or two things should your work unit totally stop doing or providing?"[493]

Employees considered the process a Trojan horse for slashing their ranks.

SECRETARY TILLERSON SOUGHT TO counter that narrative by holding an employee town hall meeting the first week of May. Rather than the give-and-take typical of such sessions, he took no questions. Instead, the secretary recapped the administration's policies by outlining how President Trump's "America First" policy was being implemented around the world.

Near the end of his forty-minute remarks, he touched on his reorganization efforts. He reiterated they were necessary to pull the Department into the twenty-first century, but he conceded the angst he was creating in the process:

> There's nothing easy about it, and I don't want to diminish in any way the challenges I know this presents for individuals, it presents to families, it presents to organizations. I'm very well aware of all of that. All I can offer you on the other side of that equation is an opportunity to shape the future way in which we will deliver on mission, and I can almost promise you—because I have never been through one of these

exercises where it wasn't true—that I can promise you that when this is all done, you're going to have a much more satisfying, fulfilling career, because you're going to feel better about what you're doing.[494]

The outreach didn't help much, either with employees or the media.

In June 2017, *The New York Times* published a story headlined, "Where Trump Zigs, Tillerson Zags, Putting Him at Odds with White House."[495]

It noted how Tillerson had engaged in seven days of shuttle diplomacy to try to resolve a dispute between Saudi Arabia and its Persian Gulf neighbor, Qatar, only to have President Trump undo it with a single tweet siding with the Saudis.

"I'm not involved in how the president constructs his tweets, when he tweets, why he tweets, what he tweets," the secretary later told reporters.[496] The *Times* story went on to say, "Foreign governments do not know whether to believe Mr. Tillerson's reassuring words or Mr. Trump's incendiary statements."[497]

By the end of July, *Foreign Policy* published a feature story headlined "How the Trump Administration Broke the State Department." It opened with an anecdote about cubicles being added to the Department's Policy Planning staff, which the widely read diplomatic magazine said was part of an effort to create a parallel staff of loyalists that wouldn't have to interact with the rank and file.

By August, about six months into Tillerson's tenure, seventy-one ambassadorships remained unfilled, including those for close allies like Australia and key regional players such as South Korea. The same was true for the assistant secretary job overseeing the East Asian and Pacific region—despite the concerns about North Korea and its saber-rattling in the region.[498]

When the dispute about who murdered Saudi dissident and journalist Jamal Khashoggi erupted in October 2018, the United States still didn't have ambassadors to either Turkey or Saudi Arabia—two Middle East powers and the principals in the diplomatic crisis.

The vacancies existed even though the Republican Party controlled not only the White House but also Congress. The GOP could confirm virtually anyone nominated, but names were not forwarded.

"By failing to fill numerous senior positions across the State Department, promulgating often incoherent policies, and systematically shutting out career Foreign Service officers from decision-making, the Trump administration is undercutting US diplomacy and jeopardizing America's leadership role in the world," said the *Foreign Policy* story, based on interviews with more than three dozen current or former diplomats.[499]

The concern was underscored on October 1, 2017, when the president released another tweet criticizing his secretary of State's efforts to negotiate an arms control agreement with the North Koreans. Trump had already threatened to rain "fire and fury" on the nation if it continued to threaten the United States with ballistic missiles.

"I told Rex Tillerson, our wonderful secretary of State, that he is wasting his time trying to negotiate with Little Rocket Man," the president wrote, using his nickname for Kim Jong Un, president of the Democratic People's Republic of Korea. In a follow-up tweet, President Trump added: ". . . Save your energy Rex, we'll do what has to be done!"

The situation headed toward the untenable, though, three days later.

––––––––––

NBC NEWS, QUOTING A dozen current and former senior administration officials, reported Tillerson had been on the verge of resigning during the summer and was talked out of it only after Vice President Mike Pence urged him to stay at least until the end of 2017.[500]

Both President Trump and his secretary of State had already been dogged by questions of a "Rexit" due to dissatisfaction on both sides.

The true bombshell in the report, however, was that Tillerson supposedly called the president a "moron" after a July 20 national security meeting at the Pentagon. Another version said the secretary had used the words "fucking moron."

The report prompted a media feeding frenzy, heightened when Tillerson delivered hastily drafted remarks to reporters at the State Department. The secretary looked rattled as he walked up to the podium, carrying a stack of papers with his comments.

"The vice president has never had to persuade me to remain the secretary of State because I have never considered leaving this post," Tillerson said.[501]

He added: "While I'm new to Washington, I have learned that there are some who try to sow dissension to advance their own agenda by tearing others apart in an effort to undermine President Trump's own agenda. I do not and I will not operate that way, and the same applies to everyone on my team here at the State Department."[502]

The secretary refused to answer whether he, in fact, had called the president a moron. He told CNN in one interview, "I'm not playing. These are the games of Washington. These are the destructive games of this town. They're not helpful to anyone. And so my position on it is I'm not playing."[503]

During the same interview, CNN host Jake Tapper asked about a comment made by Bob Corker, the Tennessee Republican who chaired the Senate Foreign Relations Committee. He complained President Trump had "castrated" Tillerson with repeated comments undercutting his diplomacy.

"I checked," Tillerson replied lightheartedly. "I'm fully intact."[504]

By Thanksgiving 2017, lawmakers from both parties were complaining about the secretary's refusal to fill senior diplomatic posts.

Tillerson had already offered $25,000 buyouts in an effort to cut two thousand career diplomats and civil servants, and he'd filled only ten of the top forty-four political positions in the State Department.

The number of career ambassadors and career ministers—veteran Foreign Service officers who are the Department's version of four- and three-star generals—was set to drop from thirty-nine to nineteen as of December 1.

The secretary's spokesman disputed the cuts had diminished State's effectiveness.

"There are qualified people who are delivering on America's diplomatic mission," R. C Hammond told *The New York Times*. "It's insulting to them every time someone comes up to them and says that the State Department is being gutted."[505]

About a week later, there were widespread reports the White House chief of staff, John Kelly, had drafted a plan to replace Secretary Tillerson with CIA Director Mike Pompeo. He in turn would be replaced by Senator Tom Cotton, the Arkansas Republican and Kerry diplomatic critic who also was an Army combat veteran.

The secretary labeled the reports "laughable," but they hung in the air until President Trump sent a tweet saying, "He's not leaving and while we disagree on certain subjects, (I call the final shots) we work well together and America is highly respected again!"[506]

Tillerson convened another employee town hall, this time taking questions while trying to allay concerns about his job security. He also granted a lengthy interview to *60 Minutes* in which he fleshed out his personality. The Eagle Boy Scout said he lived by a "Code of the West" where his word was his bond.[507]

He also said he subscribed to the cowboy maxim you "ride for the brand," meaning a person remains steadfast to his employer.

"I'm here to serve my country. I committed to this president. My word is my bond. I ride for this brand," Tillerson said.[508]

But a month later, during a trip to Africa, he got his call from Chief of Staff Kelly, telling him he'd been fired.

The message was delivered on March 13, 2018, as Tillerson wrapped up what had been devised as a goodwill tour. The secretary was making the rounds after President Trump was said to have disparaged the continent less than three months earlier.

He reportedly asked why the United States should accept immigrants from Haiti and some "shithole countries" in Africa.[509]

TILLERSON HANDED OVER HIS duties to Deputy Secretary of State John Sullivan at midnight on March 13, the end of the day he learned he'd been sacked. He didn't formally leave the State Department until March 31, and it was nearly another month before Pompeo replaced him.

Pompeo's arrival at the Department was delayed by a trip he took immediately after being confirmed and sworn in on April 26. The new secretary headed directly for Andrews Air Force Base and flew overnight to Brussels for NATO meetings. He then traveled to Saudi Arabia, Israel, and Jordan before entering the Harry S Truman Building on May 1 for his first day in the office.

"I think I have the record for the longest trip to the first day of work," he joked to the hundreds of employees who greeted him in the C Street Lobby.[510]

He went on to say he hoped to help the Department reclaim its "swagger," a public acknowledgment of the demoralization that had occurred during Tillerson's tenure.

Pompeo expanded on the theme two weeks later, both in an email announcing he was lifting the Department's hiring freeze and during an interview on Fox News Sunday.

"We've got to go put the diplomatic team on the playing field," he told host Chris Wallace. "We're going to get our swagger back, and the State Department will be out in front in every corner of the world leading America's diplomatic policy, achieving great outcomes on behalf of President Trump and America."[511]

In September, he launched his Instagram account with a Photoshopped State Department seal reading "Department of Swagger."

The declarations improved the mood at the State Department, because they hinted at a return to the relevance it enjoyed under Secretary Kerry and most of his predecessors. But they also masked a shift between the diplomatic approaches held by Pompeo and Tillerson.

Secretary Tillerson often found himself out of sync with President Trump's tweets because he pursued policies largely maintaining the approach used by the Obama administration and Secretary Kerry.

For example, when it came to North Korea, President Trump threatened "fire and fury," but Tillerson took a diplomatic tack by enlisting China to bring its client state to heel—as Secretary Kerry did during each of our trips to Beijing. The same was true with the Iranian nuclear deal; President Trump railed against it, but Tillerson succeeded four times in getting his boss to maintain the sanctions relief signed in Vienna by Secretary Kerry.

Tillerson also didn't exhibit the same hostility for the Paris climate agreement expressed by President Trump.

The president announced on June 1, 2017, he planned to withdraw from the accord. In September 2017, though, Tillerson said the United States could remain "under the right conditions."[512]

The president had previously said much the same himself, but such comments from Tillerson bolstered repeated news stories portraying him, Defense Secretary James Mattis, and then National Security Adviser H. R. McMaster as the "adults in the room" with Trump.

The three sober business and military men were described as a counterbalance to the more volatile president.

The day he fired Tillerson, the president abandoned his prior support and branded the secretary "totally establishment in his thinking," *The Wall Street Journal* reported.[513]

By contrast, *Rolling Stone* tartly described Pompeo as "a blustering hawk in sync with Trump's worst instincts for confrontation and go-it-alone risk-taking in global affairs."[514]

President Trump had announced a week before the firing he'd meet with North Korean leader Kim Jong Un without preconditions. It was a move Pompeo—not Tillerson—had helped negotiate while CIA director. The incoming secretary also strongly opposed the Paris accord and the Iran deal, which the president ultimately abandoned two months after firing Tillerson.

Similarly, Pompeo sided with President Trump when he supported Saudi Arabia in the dispute with Qatar that Tillerson had tried so fervently to resolve. As a former congressman, Pompeo also had the political skills the outgoing secretary lacked.

Unlike Tillerson, Pompeo called up all the living secretaries of State—including John Kerry and Hillary Clinton, whom he'd slammed in Congress over the Benghazi attack—asking for their insights and advice before his confirmation hearing.[515]

Speaking with reporters after firing Tillerson, the president acknowledged the contrast between the two secretaries he had picked.

"We were not really thinking the same," Trump said of Tillerson. "With Mike Pompeo, we have a very similar thought process. I think it's going to go very well."[516]

NUMEROUS PEOPLE HAVE ASKED if I'm despondent the Trump administration undid many of the diplomatic achievements from Secretary Kerry's tenure.

It's frustrating, of course, but I don't view my service in that context. I know I worked as hard as I could, every day and night for four years, to help my boss, the president, and his administration in their diplomatic endeavors.

I'm proud of the successes, understand the failures, and feel any reversal isn't a reflection on the quality of our work but on the different views held by our successors.

My former employer, *The Boston Globe*, asked me to write an op-ed following President Trump's May 2018 decision to pull out of the Iran nuclear deal. The editor wondered whether I was personally deflated, especially after all that time we spent holed up in Vienna and traveling before and after the final agreement.

I felt no one cared how the decision affected me personally, but I could write about my concerns for its effect on our country.

"In vowing to go alone, Trump is turning our country against an agreement it negotiated. The others will remain parties to the deal, selling the Iranians their cars, airplanes, and weapons systems," I wrote. "He will also buttress Iranian hard-liners," and "do so just before sitting down with Kim Jong Un of North Korea, a country that already has nuclear weapons, and asking him to dispose of them in exchange for promises of military and economic relief."[517]

None of that added up to a smart decision, in my mind.

Likewise, for all the criticism of the Obama administration's efforts to negotiate Middle East peace, the Trump administration showed no immediate success in its own efforts, despite them being spearheaded by one of the president's own family members, Jared Kushner.

In fact, it widened the gulf between the Israelis and Palestinians by moving the US embassy in Israel from Tel Aviv to Jerusalem, allowing additional Israeli settlement construction, and cutting US aid to the Palestinians.

The most bothersome of President Trump's reversals was his administration's willful ignorance about global warming and climate change.

The greatest gift from my work with Secretary Kerry was the first hand insight I gained about our planet's changing environment.

As I've written, the effects near the North Pole are already evident. Glaciers are receding and calving, once-frozen bays now brim with whitecaps, and the temperature is steadily increasing.

Those aren't political statements but documentable facts.

And while such changes aren't yet as apparent near the South Pole, the scale of Antarctica is so vast I can't conceive how mankind recovers once it crosses its tipping point.

That's why I have no patience for anyone questioning the science or evidence, especially someone with the ability to see the same things we all saw. And the president of the United States has the time and resources, if he or she is so inclined.

As Secretary Kerry said repeatedly, if you're wrong about climate change but act to address it, the worst that can happen is you improve the environment and advance renewable energy. But if you're right and do nothing, the consequences are disastrous.

On November 21, 2018, the eve of Thanksgiving, President Trump confused weather with climate when he tweeted, "Brutal and Extended Cold Blast could shatter ALL RECORDS—Whatever happened to Global Warming?"

When I saw that tweet, I lost the self-control I'd embraced since leaving Washington. I responded to my first presidential tweet.

"You're a fucking idiot," I wrote, before urging him to use his privileged position to see the world and learn for himself. Climate change isn't a political issue, I added, but a fact of life that will affect his children and grandchildren.

I later deleted the tweet, faulting myself for my use of profanity toward a president of the United States. But I have absolutely zero patience or respect for climate-change deniers after what I saw from 2013 to 2017.

AT THE SAME TIME, my beliefs about the new administration weren't absolute.

For example, while I joined many in feeling mortified when President Trump threatened "fire and fury" against a leader he childishly labeled "Little Rocket Man," if that approach ultimately brought the North Korean leader to the negotiating table—as happened in Singapore—I give the president credit for his achievement.

The negotiation halted missile tests that bedeviled the Obama administration, and it gained freedom for two American hostages. President Trump engaged diplomatically rather than militarily in what President Obama had warned him would be his No. 1 foreign policy challenge. It also broke the precedent of prior administrations that continually issued empty threats as the DPRK crossed each threshold for advancing its nuclear weapons capability.

If an unconventional approach yielded an agreement to denuclearize the Korean peninsula, President Trump would deserve all the credit he could get.

Many friends have also asked me what I learned about leadership, and what I might recommend for achieving our country's foreign policy objectives given my experience at the State Department.

In terms of leadership, I was surprised by a common denominator between President Obama, Secretary Kerry, and the military brass accompanying us on our trips.

All of them were readers.

Of course, plenty of what they read was required for their jobs, from voluminous briefing papers to news clippings keeping them abreast of current events. But each of them also found time to read, usually history and other nonfiction books.

I sat across the aisle from Senator John McCain in January 2015 as we flew to Saudi Arabia for the funeral of King Abdullah. After we chitchatted, he reached into his seatback and pulled out Robert Caro's *Master of the Senate*. The Navy veteran, former prisoner of war, congressman, and two-time presidential candidate still felt there was something he could learn about President Johnson and the institution he had been serving for nearly thirty years.

I also listened and watched as Frank Pandolfe studied French on his computer—a year before he would retire as a three-star Navy admiral.

This focus reminded me of a comment by James Mattis, the Marine Corps general who'd go on to be Defense secretary. He was asked in 2003 about the importance of reading, particularly in the context of leading members of the armed forces.

"The problem with being too busy to read is that you learn by experience (or by your men's experience), i.e. the hard way," Mattis replied. "By reading, you learn through others' experiences, generally a better way to do business, especially in our line of work where the consequences of incompetence are so final for young men."[518]

I hope this book contributes to such important enlightenment, for reasons both personal and professional.

As for my foreign policy recommendations, the major one is our country shouldn't be shy about asserting itself diplomatically in ways that previously might have been seen as undiplomatic.

I can understand President Trump's obsession with border control not for the xenophobia seeming to underpin it, but because it's a fact of life around the world.

The Saudis have long been free to visit the United States, for example, but until 2018, US citizens could not get a tourist visa to visit Saudi Arabia.[519] They could go only for educational, religious, or business reasons, which in many cases meant advising the Saudis about ways to improve their government, economy, or educational systems.

Small countries such as Switzerland strictly enforce their own border, as do mammoth ones like China. Diplomats, including the president of the United States, need a visa and must have their passport checked before entering almost any country in the world.

It only makes sense for the United States to use similar controls, if only for equity's sake. But I believe there's a special reason in the aftermath of 9/11 and the lingering threat of other terrorist attacks.

People should be coming into our country only in a controlled, verifiable manner. And how another country treats our citizens when they try to visit abroad should be given greater weight when we decide how to treat citizens from that country who want to visit the United States.

I also believe the United States should recognize several assets making our country so attractive to visitors, and better leverage them to its benefit.

The US banking system, real estate market, and assembly of colleges and universities are coveted by people around the world. Access to them should be considered in a foreign policy context.

Why should US companies be forced to enter into technology-sharing agreements with Chinese counterparts in order to sell goods or services to Chinese citizens? The United States vets foreign deals for national security reasons but doesn't have the same requirement.

The same is true with real estate. Americans must live in China for at least a year before they're allowed to buy a single residence, which they then must occupy themselves. A Chinese citizen, by contrast, can buy as many US residential or commercial properties as they want on the drive in from the airport, as one real estate expert put it.[520]

Properties across New York are being gobbled up by Russian oligarchs and Middle Eastern sheikhs, and the tallest condominium building in Boston has dozens of absentee owners from China.

There's either no reciprocity for US citizens in the home countries of such buyers, or a US citizen faces disincentives like red tape, eavesdropping, or government minders where they're allowed to move in.

Likewise, many wealthy and influential foreigners send their children to boarding school, college, or graduate school in the United States. The daughters of two of our country's most vexing foreign policy opponents both went to college in the United States. Those enrollments highlight the draw of the US higher education system for even the most oppositionist foreigners.

To my mind, access to US banks, real estate, and colleges should be a tool for advancing our country's interests—even if they're reserved as the ultimate fallback devices. They can be assets to prevent things like intellectual property theft or the murder and dismemberment of a government critic.

Google the word *diplomacy* and one of the resulting definitions is "the art of dealing with people in a sensitive and effective way." Most often, our country's benevolence, altruism, and ideals have caused it to act sensitively—and rightly so.

But in a world and century where the United States faces increasing challenges to its stature and national interests, it must also consider additional tools allowing it to act effectively.

MY BIGGEST TAKEAWAY FROM this experience? We who are fortunate to live in the United States and much of the Western world are incredibly lucky.

It's not an overstatement to say that many, many others on Earth are in a daily struggle just to survive. I remember seeing a man lying on the side of the road during one of our drives through Africa. He was barely alive. What was it that was going to compel him to stand up and carry on? Or how sad was it going to be if that dusty patch was where he took his final breath, all alone?

When I hear people lament clothing or technology they lack, or food not cooked the way they like, I shake my head mentally.

I didn't know how lucky I was to have my health, a home, and an intact family until I traveled the world and saw so many who lacked it all.

I urge you to see for yourself. Until then, know you should count your blessings.

In late August 2016, Secretary Kerry made good on a promise to himself. He got back on his bike and set off to conquer his nemesis: the Col de la Colombière.

As I looked around the parking lot in Scionzier, I realized many of the people gathered had been there the prior May—including the paramedics who'd rendered first aid after he fractured his femur.

The secretary's riding partners were different, though.

One was a friend, businessman Tim Collins. The other was a fellow government official, United Arab Emirates national security adviser Sheikh Tahnoon bin Zayed. He was an avid cyclist, and he enthusiastically embraced the challenge of conquering a onetime Tour de France stage.

The trek was grueling, prompting Collins to drop out about halfway up. But Secretary Kerry pedaled on. Near the peak, I hopped out of my car and ran backward to get a perfect picture of him against the surrounding mountains.

John Kerry nears the summit of a onetime section in the Tour de France bike race.

When he crossed a pavement marker indicating they'd reached the summit at 1,613 meters (5,291 feet), the secretary embraced bin Zayed.

The relaxation was short-lived, however. The two took off, speeding down the backside of the mountain. All I could think about was someone blowing a tire or sliding off the gravel shoulder. One grueling rehab had been enough for the Boss.

Luckily, they made it down safely and then had lunch overlooking Lake Annecy.

"I wanted to go back," the secretary later told The Boston Globe. "I said, 'I've got to go pick up where I left off.'"[521]

As I'd seen firsthand for four years, John Kerry played just like he worked.

EPILOGUE

US SENATOR PAUL TSONGAS walked into the Massachusetts State-house on January 13, 1984, with a surprising announcement: He wasn't going to seek a second term the coming fall because he'd been diagnosed with cancer.

The decision was a shock to voters but an unexpected opportunity for a group of politicians eager to succeed him. The scramble for a coveted Senate seat alongside Edward M. Kennedy, the famed Democrat also representing Massachusetts, was eventually won by John Kerry, the state's lieutenant governor.

When Tsongas was finally ready to leave office, he had another surprise. He resigned January 2, 1985, the day before the incoming congressional class was to be sworn in, so Lieutenant Governor Kerry could take office twenty-four hours before his fellow freshmen.

That minor boost in seniority launched John Kerry on a congressional career that would continue through four reelection campaigns. During a span of nearly thirty years, he'd emerge not only as the Democrats' 2004 presidential nominee, but, toward the end of his time in elective office, as an unofficial foreign affairs emissary for Barack Obama, his former Senate colleague and the newly elected president of the United States.

Kerry also rose to the role of chairman of the Senate Foreign Relations Committee, the same panel the Navy veteran addressed in 1971 as a Vietnam War opponent.

The blend of experience on the national and international stages, plus a measure of gratitude for Kerry selecting him to deliver the keynote address at the 2004 Democratic National Convention, prompted President Obama to nominate him to be the country's sixty-eighth secretary of State.

"In a sense, John's entire life has prepared him for this role," the president said on December 21, 2012. Kerry and his wife, Teresa Heinz Kerry, were standing next to him and Vice President Joe Biden at the White House.

"I think it's fair to say that few individuals know as many presidents and prime ministers, or grasp our foreign policies as firmly as John Kerry," the president added. "And this makes him a perfect choice to guide American diplomacy in the years ahead."[522]

————

ON JUNE 12, 1985, six months after John Kerry began his Senate career, I strode across an outdoor stage at Lawrence University in Appleton, Wisconsin, ready to receive my bachelor of arts degree. In a last attempt for a laugh, I'd used athletic tape to spell out the words "Hi Mom" on my mortarboard.

While the school prided itself on its liberal arts tradition, not teaching for jobs but how to "learn to learn," I'd majored in government and focused on English with the specific purpose of preparing myself for a career in journalism.

The aspiration had come circuitously. As a middle schooler growing up north of Boston, I won a free-throw-shooting contest during a practice for my youth basketball team. My coach, Rick Harrison, was a sportswriter for *The Sun* of Lowell, Massachusetts, and he promised to take the two top finishers to a Boston Bruins game he had to report about the following week.

When that night arrived, I sat in the rollicking Boston Garden, practically hanging out over the ice in a press box bolted to the face of a balcony. Afterward, I waited outside the steamy Bruins locker room as my coach was inside, interviewing Bobby Orr and other players about the night's game.

The experience was transformative. Imagine, I thought: a job where you get a literal front-row seat to history and the chance to meet with and speak to famous people, before telling everyone else all about it.

From that day on, my career was charted.

Over the years Kerry worked his way up the ranks of seniority in the US Senate, I did the same on the ladder of journalism.

First it was the City News Bureau of Chicago, which spawned famed city columnist Mike Royko and novelist Kurt Vonnegut. Then *The Salem Evening News* in Salem, Massachusetts, which has a broom-riding witch in its logo evoking its historical past. Then the *Lowell Sun* itself, where I became one of Rick Harrison's coworkers. Finally, the major leagues: the Associated Press and *The Boston Globe*—twice each—working for both in Boston and Washington.

On January 15, 2013, I was a fifty-year-old reporter sitting at my desk in the *Globe*'s main newsroom when my cellphone rang. On the other end was Kerry, asking if we could have a private conversation. The senator promised the exchange would be lost to posterity if I didn't like what he said. Intrigued, I stepped into a nearby conference room and closed the door as the senator began to speak.

———

ALMOST FIFTEEN YEARS EARLIER, on April 28, 1998, I'd arrived at the Museum of Flight in Seattle for a reception kicking off a two-day aviation safety conference put on by the Boeing Company. I was the AP's national transportation writer at the time.

Entitled "Airplanes 101," the conference was aimed at aviation correspondents and devised to teach us about the safety enhancements engineered into Boeing airplanes. It was a none-too-subtle effort to influence our writing, should one of the company's planes ever crash.

One of the most convincing demonstrations was a film showing a plane undergoing its static wing test. In the test, a crane lifts a cable attached to a wingtip, arcing it higher and higher until the moment—precisely calculated in advance by Boeing engineers—when the wing breaks in half amid a concussion of sound and a spray of metal parts.

"If you look out the window and can still see the wingtip bouncing between the top and bottom of the pane, you don't have anything to worry about," an engineer said.[523]

It was his rule of thumb for anyone who worried a Boeing plane could be knocked out of the sky by turbulence.

After the course ended, I returned to Boeing Field with some company staffers. Just down the runway from the Museum of Flight, we looked at the shop used to paint 737s after they'd been flown over from their assembly plant a few miles away in Renton, Washington.

Lining the tarmac were a couple of dozen planes flying the flags of a United Nations' worth of airlines, with logos in a palette of colors and names of airlines from Europe, Africa, and Asia emblazoned across their fuselage.

Also on the tarmac sat two more conspicuous planes, a pair of Boeing 757s—also built in Renton—that had been painted in a blue-and-white livery.

Across the middle of their fuselages, just above the windows, read the words *United States of America*. On each tail was an American flag.

I asked about the planes and was told they were just about to be delivered to the US Air Force for worldwide travels by senior government officials.

When I asked about the amenities in the customized commercial airliners, a Boeing representative laughed and said only, "I think the passengers will be quite comfortable on them."

———

AS SENATOR KERRY BEGAN to speak while I pressed into my cellphone, he said up front, "Listen, I know this is sensitive for you as a reporter, because it is for me as a politician. So if you don't like what you're about to hear, we can both forget we ever talked and keep the relationship we've always had."

We'd met in 1993, when I was covering City Hall for the *Lowell Sun*, which happened to be Senator Paul Tsongas's hometown newspaper. *The Sun* is a gritty paper, deeply invested in its hometown, unafraid to hold elected officials accountable. Though rooted in a heavily Democratic city, it had a strongly conservative editorial page, perilous to politicians of all stripes.

It also was not shy about covering the big stories.

That's why a local paper had a sportswriter like Rick Harrison covering the big-city Bruins. It's also why it sent its own reporter across the country to trail Tsongas when he decided, after his cancer treatment, to return to politics by running for president in 1992. I was tapped for that assignment, my first presidential campaign.

John Kerry came to *The Sun*'s Kearney Square offices a year later for an editorial board meeting—the kind of affair where editors get to grill an elected official about whatever they wanted, and the official hopes to earn credit for being willing to face anything thrown at him.

As I looked across the table, Kerry leafed through a packet of *Sun* news clippings given to him by his staff, so he'd know what had been written about him by some of the people now waiting to probe him.

When the senator began speaking, I began writing in my notebook.

We went on to cross paths numerous times during the next decade, as I covered the Massachusetts statehouse for the AP. It was from my desk in Room 456, a pressroom pasted with the bumper stickers of campaigns long past, that I chronicled Kerry's epic 1996 reelection campaign against the Republican governor of Massachusetts, William F. Weld.

We were later rejoined in Washington. I was assigned to cover the Massachusetts congressional delegation for *The Globe* immediately after covering the 2000 presidential campaign in which Republican George W. Bush beat Kerry's Senate freshman colleague, Democrat Al Gore.

Six months after President Bush was sworn in, Kerry took a trip to Seattle for a hearing of the Senate Small Business Committee, which he chaired, and an intriguing meeting with Democratic donors.

The fact the senator was holding court with political financiers, and then planned to travel immediately from the West Coast to Iowa for an annual picnic hosted by Democratic governor Tom Vilsack, prompted speculation Kerry himself was planning to run for president in 2004.

"You cover the congressional delegation; he's your guy. You go," *Globe* Washington bureau chief David Shribman said in assigning me to tag along.[524]

From 2001 through 2004, I covered the arc of Kerry's campaign, from the team building and fundraising that established it; to the convention where Obama spoke that codified Kerry's nomination; to the night in Copley Square in Boston when his running mate, John Edwards, announced the pair wouldn't immediately concede the election because of lingering questions about the vote total in Ohio.

After Kerry bowed out, I'd see him occasionally over the next eight years, when he held events back in Massachusetts or I returned to Washington and swung by his office to trade political gossip.

Our contact grew more frequent, though, as President Obama sought to follow up his historic 2008 victory with another win in the 2012 campaign.

Hillary Rodham Clinton had already announced she wouldn't continue as secretary of State in a second Obama term. Kerry had been a close runner-up for the job four years earlier, and another possibility for succeeding Clinton— United Nations ambassador Susan Rice—had been accused of misleading the public in September 2012 after the Benghazi attack.

If President Obama was to win in November and Clinton was stepping down but Rice was unable to replace her, there was a good chance the president could tap Kerry to be the new secretary of State. And if Kerry was to resign as senator, it could touch off a crazy race to replace him.

That head-spinning Hot Stove League of speculation had put Kerry and me in frequent touch as President Obama campaigned against Republican John McCain, went on to win the 2012 election, and then made the decision to nominate him as the nation's chief diplomat.

––––––––

ON THE PHONE WITH me that mid-January morning in 2013, Kerry outlined his proposal.

Inauguration Day was nearing and it looked as if his nomination as secretary of State was not only progressing through the Senate but that his colleagues would soon confirm him.

Kerry and his staff were looking to add fresh faces to the team heading to the State Department, and Chief of Staff David Wade had spoken very highly of me as the group discussed filling a communications role.

So, Senator Kerry wanted to know, would I be interested in "leaving the dark side and coming over to the light?"[525] It was a clever reversal of the way reporters thought of politicians and their respective professions, but it meant would I consider surrendering the neutrality of reporting in favor of working for a partisan administration, in this case a Democratic one.

The idea would be to travel with the secretary of State, be in the room when big decisions were made, help explain them to the press corps, keep the Boss in touch with the folks back in Boston, and handle special projects as they cropped up over the next four years.

"Do you think I can handle it?" I asked. I'd just written a story about how being secretary of State wasn't *a* cabinet job, but *the* cabinet job. It was the oldest and first in seniority; it came with a worldwide portfolio and recognition; its holder was fourth in the line of presidential succession and flew on his own plane; and he and his team were protected by a twenty-four-hour phalanx of security guards, akin to the president.

Kerry chuckled at the question and replied, "Do *you* think you can handle it? If you're not comfortable with it, don't do it."

I asked for twenty-four hours to consider it, knowing I didn't want to make a rash decision. At the same time, I was aware I couldn't linger in this contemplation of the "dark side" if I hoped to maintain any credibility as a neutral political observer should I decide to turn down the offer.

"Take the time you need, but there's not a lot of time here," the senator replied.[526]

During a family dinner, my wife and sons quickly dismissed any concerns. This is the opportunity of a lifetime, they said. You have to do it, each argued I thought all those things to myself, because the odds were long I'd ever again know someone who might be tapped to be secretary of State.

Say no, I felt, and you will live with a lifetime of regret.

Late that night, I emailed Brian McGrory, who'd recently been promoted from columnist to *The Globe*'s editor, and asked if we could meet for breakfast the following day. I wanted to relay my decision face-to-face. McGrory agreed, and we settled on Mul's Diner in South Boston.

Heavy snow was falling when the sun rose, though, trapping McGrory in traffic. "What's up?" he asked when he called my cellphone to apologize. When I explained I had accepted a job offer from the incoming secretary of State, McGrory didn't offer the condemnation I feared but support I didn't expect.

"Listen, if you were going to work for the Massachusetts Democratic Party, I'd tell you, you were making a big mistake. But this is a once-in-a-lifetime opportunity. In good conscience, I can't talk you out of it," McGrory said.[527]

Saddened but relieved, I then called Kerry.

"If the offer is still good," I said, "I accept."

It was, the secretary-designate replied, adding he was happy with the decision.

ON FEBRUARY 24, 2013, I wore jeans and a trench coat as I rolled my carry-on bag through the rain at Andrews Air Force Base. I was all set for my first trip abroad with the secretary of State.

Some of my former journalism colleagues were clambering up their usual entrance to the secretary of State's plane—the back steps. As a staffer, I had access to a set of red-carpeted stairs leading to the front door.

When I reached the top step, I looked down the blue-and-white fuselage and the words now at eye level: *United States of America.* I then boarded the aircraft with tail number 80002—one of those 757s I'd seen parked on Boeing's tarmac fifteen years earlier.

Kerry himself arrived in his motorcade a short time later, and soon all of us aboard were speeding north along the runway, lifting off on a flight to London.

It was the first of 109 international missions over four years for Secretary Kerry. Along the way, we spent over 120 days aloft—more than four months ensconced in one of those planes that made Boeing officials so proud. I took well over 100,000 photos during our travels in an added role I never anticipated: official State Department travel photographer.

The beginning of that first trip closed a circle for the secretary and me.

Two people who'd set down different paths in 1985 came together in 2013 as they left jobs each had held for nearly thirty years in favor of a new career opportunity together.

Now, riding on the same plane to the same destinations, we'd promised to support one another while confronting some of the world's most intractable problems.

Along the way, there was turbulence on land and in the air; but as I looked out my window seat on the world, I took confidence.

The wingtips never bounced beyond the edges of my windowpane, and the scene outside was mesmerizing until our final landing.

Glen Johnson
North Andover, Massachusetts
December 5, 2018

ACKNOWLEDGMENTS

FIRST AND FOREMOST, I want to thank John Kerry for the opportunity of a lifetime.

From the moment I started working for him, he fully embraced and welcomed me into the fold. Despite my past as a reporter, there was never any qualifier that something this politician said or did was "off the record." He put complete trust in me the second I accepted his job offer, and working so closely with him gave me an in-depth appreciation of his smarts, energy, creativity, and patience.

It also gave me an experience I never expected. I'd covered government for nearly thirty years, but hadn't seen it from the inside. And while I'd traveled across the country, my international exposure had largely been to the typical stops on a beer-sodden Eurail pass: London, Munich, Amsterdam, and Vienna among them.

All that changed as we spent virtually every day together across four years and all seven continents.

At home, I was the person to greet him most mornings when he stepped off the elevator at the State Department. On the road, we were companions for all I've described in the preceding pages. We saw each other good, bad, and ugly, and when each of us was hurting—me when I flew alongside him in that helicopter after he broke his leg biking, him checking on me in my hotel room in Paris as I stood doubled over, wheezing, after breaking three ribs when I fell on an icy street.

That, of course, happened while I was trying to catch up to him during our last trip abroad—which had been a perpetual challenge of our time together.

I still marvel at a November 2016 photo of the two of us on the Pegasus ice runway in Antarctica, him with a thumbs-up while we were cloaked in down parkas and the remnants of our ECW gear. For the guy who took tens of thousands of pictures of Secretary Kerry, it was a rare one with me in the frame with him.

Working together was no automatic, though.

When I was a reporter, I wrote my share of tough pieces about him. We also had our run-ins. The most memorable came in 2003, when I noticed the prospective 2004 Democratic presidential candidate didn't seem to be himself. I asked—as he got into his car—whether he was sick. Then Senator Kerry told me no; but only ten days later, he called a news conference in the US Capitol to announce he had prostate cancer.

When the time came for questions, I asked why he'd lied to me—using that word. Needless to say, the exchange was pointed and especially insulting to his wife, Teresa Heinz Kerry, and daughters, Alex and Vanessa. They felt he had the right to make his announcement at the time and place of his own choosing. I'd been more simplistic in my analysis, a hometown reporter simply comparing a prior question with a current answer.[528] I think I would have been more tactful with age.

The passage of time and my continuing professional engagement with the senator patched up those differences, and we all were struck in later moments by the unlikeliness of me ending up as a member of his staff.

I never would have gotten that opportunity, either, had it not been for David Wade.

David was a smart and aspiring Brown University student who fleshed out his own political ideals early in his life as a Truman Scholar and president of the College Democrats of America.

He landed a job on Senator Kerry's staff as a twenty-two-year-old and quickly rose from speechwriter to communications director. He ultimately was named chief of staff.

We got to know each other particularly well from 2001 to 2003, that period when I was pretty much the only reporter covering the run-up to John Kerry's 2004 presidential campaign. Often, I ended up traveling with or chasing after three others: the senator, David, and personal aide Marvin Nicholson. "The Marv" is a special person who can make you laugh while teaching you life lessons about how to treat others.

By the time Senator Kerry won the 2004 Democratic nomination, Wade was traveling press secretary.

Titles, however, don't explain the essential part he remains today in Team Kerry. I heard the secretary himself once label him "brilliant," and to be blunt, John Kerry's policies, speeches, memoir, and public image would not be what they are if not for Wade's strategic thinking and inexhaustible work ethic.

Pete Rouse, who'd been Barack Obama's Senate chief of staff, asked Kerry if Wade could work on the 2008 Obama presidential campaign. The senator gave his blessing to David and Marvin, who eventually would become one of the president's closest aides. David himself ended up on the staff of Obama and Kerry's Senate colleague, vice presidential nominee Joe Biden. After the election—despite working alongside the man who ended up only a heartbeat from the presidency—David turned down a sure job in the White House.

Instead, he returned to Kerry's staff and remained at his boss's side as he moved from the Senate to the State Department in 2013.[529]

Such loyalty must have its own chromosome in Wade's DNA, because when it came time to put together the State staff, David took it upon himself to raise my name and make the case for my hiring.

When the secretary called to offer me a job, he made a point of saying that Wade had provided his stamp of approval. I later learned he had done much more than that.

I take it all as the ultimate compliment, because David knew me well as a reporter, and better than anyone about the ups and downs of my relationship with John Kerry.

I wouldn't have gotten the opportunity I was offered without David's initiative and support. For those reasons and many more, I was sad to see him leave State in 2015 but not surprised at his decision. His Lone Star wife, Elizabeth Alexander, was about to have their first child, and Wade felt he couldn't be a good father if he continued to devote all of his attention 24/7/365 to the Department.

His departure didn't stop the secretary from calling him whenever he needed a gut check on any important decision, or then how to prepare for and execute his transition out of public service and back into private life.

Wade also led me to Disruption Books, the publisher of this book, just as I had about concluded my only option was self-publishing.

Next, I want to thank my wife, Cathy, and my two sons, Patrick and Kelley.

Cathy deservedly got her own place of recognition at the start of this book, but I couldn't finish it without singling out the boys for praise, too.

When John Kerry called, everyone came home for a family dinner where I outlined the job offer. All three were effusive in their encouragement, which surprised me.

For Cathy, the price was a lot of Friday and Saturday nights alone, and no one to talk through the trials and tribulations of every other day of the week.

Emblematic of her support was how she filled in over the July Fourth holiday in 2015, when we had family friends coming to Washington for the State Department fireworks—and I ended up marooned in Vienna, Austria, as the Iran nuclear talks dragged on.

Cathy ably showed everyone the usual tourist sights and even joined them in the Oval Office—a place even I had never been.

She also supported our household for two years while I worked on this book and plotted the next steps in my career. As our savings balance got lower and lower, she only sold more and more real estate.

I couldn't have taken the job at the State Department or anywhere else during my career without her unflinching support.

As for Patrick and Kelley, the truth is they've enjoyed a lot of benefits from my jobs. They've attended events like political conventions, sat next to or in the laps of network anchors, and shaken hands with the president of the United States.

They also got to go to the White House after the New England Patriots won their first Super Bowl and stand in the Rose Garden chatting alone with MVP-winning quarterback Tom Brady. He even let them try on his Rose Bowl ring, which preceded all of his NFL jewelry. A class act and great role model. Patrick came to the White House the Friday before 9/11, and when President Bush was walking to Marine One, he veered over to me and asked, "Glen, is this your boy?" Kelley, dressed in his new military uniform, had Al Pacino seek him out for conversation when we all were at a State Department dinner preceding the 2016 Kennedy Center Honors.

But it's equally true the two boys had to endure my absences when I traveled during presidential campaign years or when I became a commuter for the four years I worked at State.

They were older by then, but kids still need their parents. They never complained when I missed a birthday, had to renege on plans to go to a pro sports event, or couldn't answer the phone at the moment they called.

They both blossomed into wonderful young men, Pat with smarts and a personality that prompts constant compliments to his mother and me, Kelley with an athleticism and street sense that makes both of us jealous.

Just before I left the State Department, Kelley gutted his way through Officer Candidates School and was commissioned as a 2nd lieutenant in the US Marine Corps.

He alone carried the family mantle of service when I completed my own government appointment on January 20, 2017.

Days later, Kelley drove up from Quantico, Virginia, to my apartment in Washington so he could help me pack a moving truck for the ride home. When I arrived in Massachusetts, Pat was in the driveway, waiting to help me unload.

My pride swelled on both ends.

I'd also be remiss if I didn't thank President Obama for the honor of his political appointment, or the trust of Ben Rhodes when I interviewed with him after being nominated by the State Department. I felt immediately comforted when I walked into his office at the White House and found my old campaign friend Tommy Vietor sitting in the reception area.

When I got to State, I made a host of new friends, most especially Jason Meininger, Matt Summers, and Julie Wirkkala. We were all part of the original Team Kerry and they supported my transition from outsider to insider.

Jason and I became very close, since we spent almost all day, every day together as he served Secretary Kerry and I took pictures of the Boss while we crisscrossed the world. We shared a lot of early morning jogs and late-night beers. I also saw his entire courtship and marriage to his wife, Georgiana Cavendish. Matt Summers, meanwhile, provided ceaseless dark comedic relief back in our shared office space at State—as well as an epic road tale when he subbed for Jason in Bahrain.

David and Rose Thorne were the most amazing hosts in Rome and companions for a memorable car ride and lunch in Brittany, France, alongside Andre Heinz and María Marteinsdóttir. Drew O'Brien, Leigh Garland, Julia Frifield, Nancy Stetson, Chris Flanagan, Maura Hogan, Alex Costello, Mary deBree, Josh Rubin, and Nick Christiansen also were great Kerry teammates, and Doug Frantz was the first to encourage me to jot down color for a possible book.

I have the same reverence for my fellow road warriors: Jen Psaki, Tom Sullivan, John Kirby, Marie Harf, Mark Toner, Steve Krupin, Andrew Imbrie, Stephanie Epner, Patrick Granfield, Reem Nuseibeh, Dr. Will Walters, Dr. Kathleen McCray, Lee Smith, and the epitome of toughness, Lisa Kenna.

The team that greeted us at State, including Bill Burns, Tom Shannon, John Bass, Jen Davis, Kathleen Hill, Claire Coleman, Linda Landers, and George Rowland, was extremely helpful in our transition, as were innumerable S Specials and members of The Line. The Dep Execs—among them Paco Palmieri, Julietta Valls Noyes, Ted Allegra, Kent Logsdon, Elisabeth Millard,

Kelly Degnan, Harry Kamian, Baxter Hunt, and MaryKay Carlson—were great, as were Deputy Secretary Tony Blinken, Assistant Secretary Evan Ryan, Executive Secretary Joe Macmanus, Deputy Chief of Staff Jen Stout, Sujata Sharma, and Joe Semrad. There is only one John Natter, too, and the same is true of Cindy Chang.

I also can't express enough thanks to the members of the Public Affairs team: Rick Stengel, Mike Hammer, Dean Lieberman, Brenda Smith, Hattie Jones, Ashley Yehl, Melissa Turley Toufanian, John Echard, Courtni Wyatt, Ryan Jones, Lauren Hickey, Alec Gerlach, Stephanie Beechem, and the BlackBerry goddess, Elizabeth Kennedy Trudeau.

The same can be said for the Office of Digital Engagement, which embraced my request to mount a twenty-four-hour operation so we could get my photographs on the State Department's social media sites in real-time fashion. Richard Buangan, Vinay Chawla, Cynthia Brown, Luke Forgerson, Sarah Thomas, Hannah Lyons, Alison Bauerlein, Aaron Bruce, Yvonne Gamble, Tara Maria, Jaclyn Cole, and Danielle Hawkins were tireless in their support. They also gave me the nicest going-away present I could have imagined.

I also appreciate State Department photographers Michael Gross, James Pan, and Mark Stewart for showing me the ropes and letting me fake it on the road.

The DS folks are too numerous to mention in full, but I have to give a shout-out to Scott Moretti, C. J. Jones, Bill Inman, Ron Roof, Matt Childs, Jerry Aylward, Wade Boston, Maureen McGeough, Steve Antoine, Kevin Maloy, Nic Masonis, Seth Emers, Mark Woods-Hawkins, Brian Wells, Kathryn Huffman, Liz Marmesh, April Germanos, Tom "Candle Wax" Carey, Jessica Pierce, Russell Adams, Julie Yapp, and Jose Mercado. Julie was a constant throughout our four years, and Jose stayed by my side all night at a hospital in Paris after I broke my ribs.

Otis Pearson also provided me countless thrills and several rides home while serving as the secretary's unparalleled driver. And there's no way to quantify how many ways George Rowland and his team—including Danny, Coop, Mac, and all the others—helped me around The Building, or to and from my 109 trips.

In addition, I'm indebted to the State Department staffers who assisted with the mandatory national security review of this text: Eric Stein, Alden Fahy, and Behar Godani.

One of the best aspects of my time at State was meeting and working closely with the men and women of our military.

It was a high honor to travel alongside Admirals Harry Harris, Kurt Tidd, and Frank Pandolfe, and their aides who also answered my endless questions about ships and planes: Curt Renshaw, Scott Thompson, John Richardson, Brian McCarthy, Megan Gumpf, Nicole Chambers, and John Esposito. It was an honor, too, to speak with General Joe Dunford, Admiral Bill McRaven, and former Navy SEAL Jeff Eggers through this job.

Oorah, also, to Marine Captain John Pratson for inviting me to address TBS Bravo Company 2-17 in April 2017.

I also want to pay tribute to Navy Captain Spencer Abbot, an aide to Admiral Pandolfe, who provided advice as Kelley made his application to the Corps. Spencer committed suicide in November 2017, a shock to all who knew and loved him, and part of an epidemic within the military and among veterans. It was a stark reminder to not only care for those who appear low but also people who seem to be soaring high.

The same sentiment applies to Jack Manahan, an Army veteran and one of our early DS agents. His business card was tacked to the bulletin board behind me as I wrote this book.

The Protocol team got their own chapter, but individual thanks to Natalie Jones, Mark Walsh, Jeannie Rangel, Lauren Bernstein, Jessica Zielke, Sheila Dyson, Sam Tubman, David Solomon, Shawn Lanchantin, Jennifer Wham, Jen Nicholson, Nick Schmit, Asel Roberts, Araz Pourmorad, and Izumi Cintron.

And everyone knows the Diplomatic Reception Rooms don't run without Essandra Collins and Sixto "Manny" Mercado, and no secretary eats without chefs Chris James and Jason Larkin.

Randy Bumgardner also was a great host and tour guide at Blair House, as were Declan Cregan and Angela McAteer no matter the time—day or night—we passed through Shannon Airport.

Thanks, as well, to my friends in DC. First among them were Franco Nuschese and Manuela Cavalieri at Cafe Milano, who embraced me like family for meals and events, including once in Abu Dhabi. Franco is an internationalist beyond being a world-class restaurateur and host, and Manuela embraces the social consciousness of an icon, Dr. Martin Luther King Jr. They provided Secretary Kerry with a quiet venue for numerous official meetings over an array of fresh pastas. Grazie a tutti e due.

Among my many other supporters in Washington were my neighbor Larry La at Meiwah, another person deeply interested in foreign affairs, and my former *Lowell Sun* colleague Mary Boyle. She pushed me to write this book, was always willing to grab a last-minute drink, and gave this text a final line edit. Any remaining typos are her fault.

Bastien LeClerc was a great host to me and Cathy at Bar Romain in Paris, as was Lorenzo Lisi, who serves wonderful seafood at Pierluigi in Rome. And no hotel general manager made us feel more at home than Alvaro Rey at the InterContinental Park Lane in London.

My time at the State Department and in Geneva in particular gave me an unexpected chance to reconnect with my expat college roommate, John Stanton, as well as his wife, Monique Deul, and their three boys, Oliver, Noah, and Sebastian. They all were interested in my work for the government, and they provided me and members of the traveling team with a home away from home during our many visits to Switzerland.

Thanks, too, to the small group of friends who followed me on Facebook while I worked at State. I didn't want to share what I was doing too widely, because my former journalism colleagues would be compelled to report on any real insights I shared.

But the people I befriended expressed enthusiasm for my reports and photos from the road, and their questions helped me flesh out this book.

There also was a collection of supporters who kept my wife sane and occupied while I was away for the better part of four years. Chief among them is our yellow Lab, Willow, who filled the void with her constant companionship and by claiming my spot in bed for herself.

I also appreciate the physical and mental support of the staff and members at the Institute of Performance and Fitness in North Reading, Massachusetts. It's one of the best gyms in the United States, and Walter Norton Jr., Jamie Damon, Liz Keady, and their colleagues kept Cathy in shape and with a 5 a.m. family. The same is true for her closest workout partners, Carol Martini, Pam Roche, Diane Barrett, Allie Navarro, and Laurie Fraser.

Mrs. Fraser, an IPF Hall of Famer, claimed the first signed copy of this book.

Our "Hometown Diplomacy" series also got a boost from some hometown supporters, including Roger Berkowitz and Shion Hara at Legal Sea Foods; three of my North Andover homies, Boston Marathon race director Dave McGillivray and Merrimack Strider icons Tom and Lyn Licciardello; and four-time race winner "Boston" Bill Rodgers.

Dick Friedman also hosted a night to remember in Paris.

I especially appreciate the three people I asked to review my manuscript: Jon Finer, Jim Loftus, and my former *Boston Globe* colleague Scott Helman.

Finer is a Rhodes scholar and former journalist, and he had the perspective not only as a State Department chief of staff but also as director of its Policy Planning operation. Any policy errors remaining in the text are his.

Loftus, meanwhile, is a former campaign press wrangler and event organizer who came to State to help with those tasks. He read the manuscript with his perspective as a former screenwriter and staffer at the US embassy in Tel Aviv.

As for Helman, I wanted the insight of an outsider who would also understand my perspective as a former journalist as well as John Kerry's stature in Massachusetts. Scott came through with a detailed letter of suggestions for improving this book that provided a road map to its completion.

I also benefited from the solitude of several special writing places. I built an office for myself at home in my former master bedroom and then proceeded to disregard the advice of novelist Stephen King and his book, *On Writing*, by putting a big table in the middle from which to work. I read his recommendation to put a small desk in the corner only after I plunked down my credit card at Walker Creek furniture in Essex, Massachusetts. Nonetheless, my setup worked for me because I could organize my accumulated papers in subject-matter piles and then proceed from one to the next as I worked from chapter to chapter.

I wrote as well in the Boston Public Library's magnificent Bates Hall reading room; the Soho dining room of John Stanton's business partner Jim Carney; Kramerbooks in Washington; the Market Cafe at the Market Basket in Salem, New Hampshire (during a November 2017 power outage); the Westin Hotel in Princeville, Hawaii; P. J. Carney's pub in New York City, and aboard several Greyhound buses and American Airlines jets.

Thanks, too, to Kris Pauls and Disruption Books for helping me publish this work. Kris is an amazingly thoughtful and responsive executive, and she patiently guided me through each step of the publishing process. Disruption itself has a thoughtful business model giving a lot of freedom to authors, especially first-timers. I especially appreciate Kim Lance for her cover design, and Mary Hardegree for her painstakingly thorough copy edit.

I also want to thank Don Naylor of 16thirty in Boston for patiently designing a cover when I considered self-publishing this book, my former AP colleague Lisa Pane of L. M. Pane Photography in Boise, Idaho, for the book jacket photo, and Shawn Gross of shawngross.com for helping me design and launch my personal website to help market this. Thanks, also, to attorney Christine Bernardini of North Andover for her excellent handling of my Author's Contract.

Danny Marte and Warren Osterman at the FedEx Office Print & Ship Center in Salem, N.H., also were invaluable when I needed proof copies for reviewers and others.

I waited until I felt worthy to write my first book, and it felt amazing to finally hold it in my hand. I must give part of the credit to the many editors, colleagues, and bosses who developed me as a journalist. They helped me realize the story unfolding before my eyes, and gave me the skills to capture it in words and photos and then tell it to a broader audience.

I also want to thank my college professor and mentor Minoo Adenwalla. I went out to Lawrence University site unseen, and among the many friends I made in Appleton, Wisconsin, was a government professor who had studied journalism. He taught me about critical thinking, proper writing, and the Constitution. He also was good company over pints in London and single malts at his home on North Union Street.

Praise, too, to Lin-Manuel Miranda, not only for writing *Hamilton*, but his daily Twitter Gmorning and Gnight messages encouraging everyone to forge ahead with their dreams and ideas. They propelled me from being a consumer to part of the group of people who are creators.

I especially appreciate the patience of my mother, Joan, who constantly wondered what was up with this mythical book and when I was going to get another job after leaving State—but said so out loud only a handful of times. She's immersed herself in books her entire life and gave my manuscript the most thorough proofreading it received. She also provided immeasurable support to Cathy while I was away. Not bad for eighty-five.

Special tribute, too, goes to my older brother, Gary, who has gutted it through two rounds of leukemia treatment, including one after a relapse I learned about when I was on the other side of the world in Tokyo.

My younger brother, Steve, also supported this work, as did my aunt, Marilyn Johnson, who once took me and my cousin Linda Goetz out for a great family dinner while our plane made a refueling stop in San Francisco. My college classmate Margie LaVelle Gater bought me a drink there, too. Cousin Doug and his wife, the "other" Linda Goetz, met me during another stop in Los Angeles, as did my childhood friend Mark Easton. My cousin Mary Goetz and her husband, Dave Shockley, prolifically "Liked" my photo essays and steered me to *On Writing*.

I also have special appreciation for John Diamond, a fellow New Englander and AP alum who has provided friendship and hospitality throughout my two stints living in Washington. John's background as a journalist and author, as well as his book-filled townhouse, attest to his love for reading—and telling—a good story.

He gave me the cherished gift of a first edition of Dean Acheson's seminal work about the State Department, *Present at the Creation*. When I needed an epigraph for my lesser attempt at recounting the work performed at Foggy Bottom, I reached onto my shelf, pulled down the book, and leafed through it until I found the perfect quote.

Last, I wanted to save my final thanks for my late father, Jack, and his wife, Louise.

Until I returned home in July 2016 to celebrate with Kelley after he had been accepted at OCS, virtually the only travel with Secretary Kerry I'd missed was because of my dad's deteriorating health. He actively fought prostate cancer and then a pituitary issue before succumbing to cancerous brain lesions. My stepmother, Louise, remained his companion throughout it all.

The fact is, my dad was less than thrilled by me taking this job.

He was a Republican and cast not just his but my late grandfather's vote in 2000 for George W. Bush. I'm sure he voted the same way when President Bush and John Kerry faced off in 2004. And I could tell he wasn't elated when I wrote him an email in 2013 to explain I was leaving the only career he had known for me—journalism—to join the federal government, a Democratic administration, and the staff of someone who challenged a president he supported.

Strike one. Strike two. Strike three.

But father never stopped loving son, or asking about his work and travels. My dad also appreciated the secretary letting me bolt from London, Paris, and New York when I wanted to return to North Carolina for his medical treatments.

He eventually died on September 29, 2015, which, ironically, was my mom's birthday. I felt fortunate to be there with him. We bid him farewell at a memorial service on October 3, 2015, and I immediately flew back to Washington so I could join Secretary Kerry the following morning for a trip to Chile.

When our last day in office came and I walked out of the State Department for the final time, I felt understandable relief but also some angst—and not just because of my concerns about national security.

The last business card I'd given my father, the last phone number he knew to call me at, the last email address he had for me—all were now obsolete.

I wouldn't be able to tell him about the next chapters of my life—the ones in this book, or everything else to come personally and professionally.

I trust he knows, though, because he's now looking down from his own window seat on the world.

-30-

NOTES

1. Author's notes, June 6, 2013.

2. John Kerry, Remarks, "Meeting with Consulate Ho Chi Minh Staff and Families," Ho Chi Minh City, December 14, 2013, https://2009-2017.state.gov/secretary/remarks/2013/12/218722.htm.

3. Ibid.

4. John Kerry, Remarks, "Remarks on Climate Change and the Environment," Mekong Delta, December 15, 2013, https://2009-2017.state.gov/secretary/remarks/2013/12/218726.htm.

5. John Kerry, Remarks, "Remarks on U.S.–Vietnam: Looking to the Future," Hanoi, August 7, 2015, https://2009-2017.state.gov/secretary/remarks/2015/08/245789.htm.

6. Ibid.

7. CBS News, interview with John Kerry, *CBS Sunday Morning*, May 23, 2016.

8. Katherine Seelye, "The 2004 Campaign: Military Service; Cheney's Five Draft Deferments During the Vietnam Era Emerge as a Campaign Issue," *The New York Times*, May 1, 2004, https://www.nytimes.com/2004/05/01/us/2004-campaign-military-service-cheney-s-five-draft-deferments-during-vietnam-era.html.

9. CBS News, interview with John Kerry, May 23, 2016.

10. Noel Brinkerhoff, "Ambassador to Italy and San Marino: Who is David Thorne?" *AllGov*, December 28, 2009, http://www.allgov.com/news/appointments-and-resignations/ambassador-to-italy-and-san-marino-who-is-david-thorne?news=840094.

11. Author's notes, May 24, 2016.

12. Office of the Press Secretary, "Press Briefing with Secretary Kerry, Deputy NSC Advisor Ben Rhodes, and Principal Deputy Press Secretary Eric Schultz," Ho Chi Minh City, May 24, 2016, https://obamawhitehouse.archives.gov/the-press-office/2016/05/24/press-briefing-secretary-kerry-deputy-nsc-advisor-ben-rhodes-and.

13. Ibid.

14. John Kerry, Remarks, "Remarks at the Fulbright University Vietnam Establishment Ceremony," Ho Chi Minh City, May 25, 2016, https://2009-2017.state.gov/secretary/remarks/2016/05/257701.htm.

15. Ibid.

16. Ibid.

17. Carol Morello, "Back on the Mekong Delta, John Kerry meets a man who once tried to kill him and finds exoneration," *The Washington Post*, January 14, 2017, https://www.washingtonpost.com/world/back-on-the-mekong-delta-john-kerry-finds-a-man-who-once-tried-to-kill-him-and-exoneration/2017/01/14/89ae82a0-d9ce-11e6-a0e6-d502d6751bc8_story.html?utm_term=.e6c708b14573.

18. Ibid.

Chapter 1

19. Author's recollection.

20. John Kerry, Remarks, "Meeting with Staff and Families of Consulate General Istanbul," Istanbul, April 7, 2013, https://2009-2017.state.gov/secretary/remarks/2013/04/207155.htm.

21. Author's recollection.

22. John Kerry, Remarks, "Remarks with Turkish Foreign Minister Ahmet Davutoglu," Istanbul, April 7, 2013, https://2009-2017.state.gov/secretary/remarks/2013/04/207162.htm.

23. John Kerry, Remarks, "Welcome Remarks to Employees," District of Columbia, February 4, 2013, https://2009-2017.state.gov/secretary/remarks/2013/02/203717.htm.

24. Ibid.

25. Ibid.

26. John Kerry, Remarks, "Remarks with Turkish Foreign Minister Ahmet Davutoglu," Istanbul, April 7, 2013, https://2009-2017.state.gov/secretary/remarks/2013/04/207162.htm.

27. John Kerry, Remarks, "Memorial Ceremony in Honor of Embassy Guard Mustafa Akarsu," Ankara, March 1, 2013, https://2009-2017.state.gov/secretary/remarks/2013/03/205515.htm.

28. Ibid.

29. John Kerry, Remarks, "Meeting with Staff and Families of Embassy Moscow," May 8, 2013, https://2009-2017.state.gov/secretary/remarks/2013/05/209120.htm.

30. Andrea Strano, "Foreign Service Women Today: The Palmer Case and Beyond," *Foreign Service Journal*, March 2016, http://www.afsa.org/foreign-service-women-today-palmer-case-and-beyond.

31. "Does the Department of State Reflect America's Diversity?" Discover Diplomacy, https://diplomacy.state.gov/discoverdiplomacy/diplomacy101/people/207755.htm.

32. Ibid.

33. John Kerry, Remarks, "Welcome Remarks to Employees," District of Columbia, February 4, 2013, https://2009-2017.state.gov/secretary/remarks/2013/02/203717.htm.

34. Ibid.

35. "Agency for International Development (USAID)," U.S. Diplomacy, http://www.usdiplomacy.org/state/abroad/usaid.php.

36. Author's journal, November 26, 2013.

37. Ibid.

38. Author's notes, March 4, 2014.

39. Domani Spero, "Tillerson Delivers Performance Management Tip, and EER Drafters Everywhere Cheer," DiploPundit, December 8, 2017, https://diplopundit.net/tag/employee-evaluation-reports/.

40. Paulo Acoba, "A Russian Military Helicopter Reportedly Buzzed An American Diplomatic Car in Alleged Election Payback," Foxtrot Alpha, June 25, 2017, https://foxtrotalpha.jalopnik.com/a-russian-military-helicopter-reportedly-buzzed-an-amer-1796402488.

41. Reuters, "Inside the historic Havana mansion that will host America's first family when Obama becomes the first US president to visit Cuba in 88 years," *DailyMail*, March 19, 2016, http://www.dailymail.co.uk/news/article-3499356/U-S-mansion-Obama-stay-Havana-built-impress.html.

42. "Edward R. Murrow," Public Diplomacy Wikia,http://publicdiplomacy.wikia.com/wiki/Edward_R._Murrow.

43. Jennifer Delgado, "After death, young diplomat's 'go-to bag' carries memories," *Chicago Tribune*, May 27, 2013, https://www.chicagotribune.com/suburbs/oak-park/ct-xpm-2013-05-27-ct-met-anne-smedinghoff-bookbag-20130527-story.html.

44. Stephenie Foster, email message to author, March 7, 2018.

45. John Kerry, Remarks, "Meeting with Staff and Families of Consulate General Istanbul," Istanbul, April 7, 2013, https://2009-2017.state.gov/secretary/remarks/2013/04/207155.htm.

46. Ibid.

47. Author's journal, April 16, 2013.

Chapter 2

48. Foreign Service Institute, "Protocol for the Modern Diplomat," July 2013, https://www.state.gov/documents/organization/176174.pdf.

49. "President's Guest House (includes Lee House and Blair House), Washington, DC," Overview, General Services Administration, https://www.gsa.gov/historic-buildings/presidents-guest-house-includes-lee-house-and-blair-house-washington-dc.

50. Ibid.

51. Ibid.

52. "Diplomatic Reception Rooms," About, U.S. Department of State, https://diplomaticrooms.state .gov/About/.

53. U.S. Department of State Bureau of Public Affairs, "The Great Seal of the United States," 2004, https://www.state.gov/documents/organization/27807.pdf.

54. John Kerry, Remarks, "Secretary of State John Kerry at the U.S. Chairmanship of the Arctic," District of Columbia, May 21, 2015, https://ge.usembassy.gov/remarks-secretary-state-john-kerry-u-s -chairmanship-arctic council-reception-may-21/.

55. "Kennedy Center Honors," Wikipedia, https://en.wikipedia.org/wiki/Kennedy_Center _Honors#2010s.

56. U.S. Department of State, "Vice President Biden Swears In Secretary Kerry," YouTube, February 6, 2013, https://www.youtube.com/watch?v=xOonFCZHcGM.

57. *The New Yorker*, April 19, 2004.

58. CBS News, interview, September 12, 2016.

59. Ibid.

60. John Kerry, "Interview with Adam Boulton of Sky News," interview by Adam Boulton, Marshall and John Jay Rooms, September 15, 2016, https://2009-2017.state.gov/secretary/remarks /2016/09/261979.htm.

61. Author's notes, April 27, 2016.

62. ABC News, "'This Week' Transcript: U.S. Ambassador to the United Nations Susan Rice," September 16, 2012, https://abcnews.go.com/Politics/week-transcript-us-ambassador-united-nations -susan-rice/story?id=17240933.

63. Ben Birnbaum and Amir Tibon, "The Explosive, Inside Story of How John Kerry Built an Israel-Palestine Peace Plan—and Watched It Crumble," *The New Republic*, July 20, 2014, https://newrepublic.com/article/118751/how-israel-palestine-peace-deal-died.

64. Barack Obama, Remarks, "Remarks by the President at Nomination of Senator John Kerry as Secretary of State," District of Columbia, December 21, 2012, https://obamawhitehouse.archives.gov /the-press-office/2012/12/21remarks-president-nomination-senator-john-kerry-secretary-state.

65. U.S. Department of State, "Vice President Biden Swears In Secretary Kerry," YouTube, February 6, 2013, https://www.youtube.com/watch?v=xOonFCZHcGM.

Chapter 3

66. Author's journal, February 13, 2013.

67. Author's journal, December 9, 2014.

68. Lesley Wroughton, "U.S. top diplomat Kerry's personal diplomacy piles up the miles," Reuters, October 15, 2013, http://www.reuters.com/article/usa-kerry-travel-idINDEE99E0AK20131015.

69. "Kerry Comes Full Circle," CBS News, http://www.cbsnews.com/videos/kerry-comes-full-circle/.

70. Alex Pappas, "Carly Fiorina Takes on Hillary: 'flying is an activity, not an accomplishment,'" *Daily Caller*, January 24, 2015, http://dailycaller.com/2015/01/24/carly-fiorina-takes-on-hillary-flying-is-an -activity-not-an-accomplishment/.

71. John Kerry, Remarks, "Remarks at India Institute of Technology Delhi," New Delhi, August 31, 2016, https://2009-2017.state.gov/secretary/remarks/2016/08/261424.htm.

72. CNN, interview, September 18, 2016.

73. John Kerry, Remarks, "Remarks at India Institute of Technology Delhi," New Delhi, August 31, 2016, https://2009-2017.state.gov/secretary/remarks/2016/08/261424.htm.

74. Author's journal, November 12, 2013.

75. John Kerry, Remarks, "Remarks at The Atlantic and Aspen Institute," District of Columbia, September 29, 2016, https://2009-2017.state.gov/secretary/remarks/2016/09/262581.htm.

76. John Kerry, Remarks, "Remarks at the Diplomatic Culinary Partnership - Milan Expo Reception," District of Columbia, April 21, 2015, https://2009-2017.state.gov/secretary/remarks/2015 /04/240965.htm.

77. Bryan Bender, "John Kerry's brand of Boston diplomacy pays off," *Boston Globe*, November 14, 2014, https://www.bostonglobe.com/news/nation/2014/11/14/secretary-state-john-kerry-brand -boston-diplomacy-pays-off/MMTJZKyos77wBcQWXgdxEL/story.html.

78. CNN, interview, September 18, 2016.

79. John Kerry, Remarks, "Conversation with Harvard's John F. Kennedy School of Government Director of the Belfer Center for Science and International Affairs Professor Graham Allison," Cambridge, October 13, 2015, https://2009-2017.state.gov/secretary/remarks/2015/10/248187.htm.

80. Ibid.

81. John Kerry, Remarks, "Remarks with Luxembourg Foreign Minister Jean Asselborn Before Their Meeting," Luxembourg City, July 16, 2016, https://2009-2017.state.gov/secretary/remarks/2016/07/260139.htm.

82. Gil Stern Hoffman, "Ya'alon Criticized for Reportedly Calling Kerry 'obsessive, Messianic,'" *Jerusalem Post*, January 14, 2014, http://www.jpost.com/Diplomacy-and-Politics/Yaalon-criticized-for-reportedly-calling-Kerry-obsessive-messianic-338109.

83. Ibid.

84. CNN, interview, September 18, 2016.

85. Ibid.

86. Michael Crowley, "Inside John Kerry's Diplomatic Save in Afghanistan," *Time*, July 18, 2014, http://time.com/3001703/kerry-afghanistan-civil-war/.

87. Karen DeYoung and Tim Craig, "Finessing a power-sharing agreement in Afghanistan," *The Washington Post*, September 22, 2014, https://www.washingtonpost.com/world/national-security/finessing-a-power-sharing-agreement-in-afghanistan/2014/09/22/769e99ba-427d-11e4-b437-1a7368204804_story.html?utm_term=.7072cd97d816.

88. Isiaka Wakili, "2015 election: Kerry told Jonathan and I to behave and we did—Buhari," *Daily Trust*, March 12, 2018, https://www.dailytrust.com.ng/2015-election-kerry-told-jonathan-and-i-to-behave-and-we-did--buhari.html.

89. Coral Davenport, "Nations, Fighting Powerful Refrigerant That Warms Planet, Reach Landmark Deal," *The New York Times*, October 15, 2016, https://www.nytimes.com/2016/10/15/world/africa/kigali-deal-hfc-air-conditioners.html?_r=0.

90. Author's recollection, March 6, 2013.

91. John Kerry, Remarks, "Press Availability in Dhaka, Bangladesh," Dhaka, August 29, 2016, https://2009-2017.state.gov/secretary/remarks/2016/08/261339.htm.

92. CBS News, interview, September 9, 2016.

93. Author's notes, March 29, 2014.

94. Marcus Weisgerber, "Pentagon Wants to Get Started on New Air Force Two and Doomsday Planes," *Defense One*, May 30, 2017, http://www.defenseone.com/business/2017/05/pentagon-wants-get-started-new-air-force-two-and-doomsday-planes/138269/.

95. Author's recollection.

96. Associated Press, "UN ambassador Samantha Power's motorcade kills child in Cameroon," *The Guardian*, April 16, 2016, https://www.theguardian.com/world/2016/apr/18/un-samantha-powers-motorcade-kills-child-cameroon.

97. Author's journal, September 16, 2016.

Chapter 4

98. Marina Koren, "The Philippine President's Vulgar Warning to Obama," *The Atlantic*, September 5, 2016, https://www.theatlantic.com/news/archive/2016/09/duterte-obama-extrajudicial-killings/498710/.

99. Jackie Northam, "He Did It Again: Philippine President Keeps Insulting the U.S. (And Obama)," National Public Radio, October 5, 2016, http://www.npr.org/sections/parallels/2016/10/05/496721265/he-did-it-again-philippine-president-keeps-insulting-the-u-s-and-obama.

100. Author's notes, July 27, 2016.

101. Ibid.

102. Ibid.

103. Barack Obama, Remarks, "Remarks by President Obama to the Australian Parliament," Canberra, November 17, 2011, https://obamawhitehouse.archives.gov/the-press-office/2011/11/17/remarks-president-obama-australian-parliament.

104. CBS News, interview with John Kerry, September 12, 2016.

105. Author's notes, January 27, 2016.

106. John Kerry, Remarks, "The U.S.-China Strategic & Economic Dialogue / Consultation on People-to-People Exchange," District of Columbia, June 23, 2015, https://2009-2017.state.gov/secretary/remarks/2015/06/244120.htm.

107. Author's notes, January 27, 2016.

108. Ibid.

109. Ibid.

110. John Kerry, Remarks, "Press Availability with Chinese Foreign Minister Wang Yi," Beijing, January 27, 2016, https://2009-2017.state.gov/secretary/remarks/2016/01/251708.htm.

111. Ibid.

112. Ibid.

113. Ibid.

114. Ibid.

115. Author's notes, January 27, 2016.

116. "Great Hall of the People," Wikipedia, https://en.wikipedia.org/wiki/Great_Hall_of_the_People.

117. Helene Cooper, "Leaders Will Delay Deal on Climate Change," *The New York Times*, November 14, 2009, http://www.nytimes.com/2009/11/15/world/asia/15prexy.html?_r=1.

118. John Kerry, Remarks, "Remarks at Energy Cooperation Event," Beijing, April 13, 2013, https://2009-2017.state.gov/secretary/remarks/2013/04/207474.htm.

119. Mark Landler, "U.S. and China Reach Climate Accord After Months of Talks," *The New York Times*, November 11, 2014, https://www.nytimes.com/2014/11/12/world/asia/china-us-xi-obama-apec.html?mcubz=1.

120. Tom Phillips, Fiona Harvey, Alan Yuhas, "Breakthrough as US and China agree to ratify Paris climate deal," *The Guardian*, September 3, 2016, https://www.theguardian.com/environment/2016/sep/03/breakthrough-us-china-agree-ratify-paris-climate-change-deal.

121. Ibid.

122. Scott Neuman, "President Trump Caught Off-Guard by 'ASEAN-Way Handshake,'" National Public Radio, November 13, 2017, https://www.npr.org/sections/thetwo-way/2017/11/13/563697970/president-trump-caught-off-guard-by-asean-way-handshake.

Chapter 5

123. John Kerry, Remarks, "Remarks on Middle East Peace," District of Columbia, December 28, 2016, https://2009-2017.state.gov/secretary/remarks/2016/12/266119.htm.

124. Michael Barbaro, "A Friendship Dating to 1976 Resonates in 2012," *The New York Times*, April 7, 2012, http://www.nytimes.com/2012/04/08/us/politics/mitt-romney-and-benjamin-netanyahu-are-old-friends.html.

125. Benjamin Netanyahu and Barack Obama, Remarks, "Remarks by President Obama and Prime Minister Netanyahu of Israel in Joint Press Conference," Jerusalem, March 20, 2013, https://obamawhitehouse.archives.gov/photos-and-video/video/2013/03/20/president-obama-holds-press-conference-prime-minister-netanyahu-is#transcript.

126. National Archives, "National Archives Celebrates 60th Anniversary of the State of Israel," July 9, 2018, Press Release, https://www.archives.gov/press/press-releases/2008/nr08-89.html.

127. Benjamin Netanyahu and Barack Obama, Remarks, "Remarks by President Obama and Prime Minister Netanyahu of Israel in Joint Press Conference," Jerusalem, March 20, 2013, https://obamawhitehouse.archives.gov/photos-and-video/video/2013/03/20/president-obama-holds-press-conference-prime-minister-netanyahu-is#transcript.

128. Barack Obama, Remarks, "Transcript of Obama's Speech in Israel," Jerusalem, March 21, 2013, http://www.nytimes.com/2013/03/22/world/middleeast/transcript-of-obamas-speech-in-israel.html.

129. Ibid.

130. Ibid.

131. Zack Beauchamp, "What is the Israeli-Palestinian peace process?," *Vox*, May 14, 2018, https://www.vox.com/cards/israel-palestine/peace-process.

132. Ibid.

133. Ibid.

134. Ibid.

135. Ibid.

136. John Kerry, Remarks, "Remarks at the American Jewish Committee Global Forum," District of Columbia, June 3, 2013, https://2009-2017.state.gov/secretary/remarks/2013/06/210236.htm.

137. Ibid.

138. Ibid.

139. "Q&A: Palestinians' upgraded UN status," BBC, November 30, 2012, https://www.bbc.com/news/world-middle-east-13701636.

140. Lesley Wroughton, "Kerry calls for 'ultimate resolution' of Nagorno-Karabakh conflict," Reuters, March 30, 2016 http://www.reuters.com/article/us-usa-azerbaijan-conflict/kerry-calls-for-ultimate-resolution-of-nagorno-karabakh-conflict-idUSKCN0WW2QB.

141. John Kerry, Remarks, "Remarks at The Atlantic and Aspen Institute," District of Columbia, September 29, 2016, https://2009-2017.state.gov/secretary/remarks/2016/09/262581.htm.

142. Israel Ministry of Foreign Affairs, "President Peres meets with US Secretary of State John Kerry," April 8, 2013, http://mfa.gov.il/MFA/PressRoom/2013/Pages/Peres-meets-with-Kerry.aspx.

143. Zack Beauchamp, "What is the Israeli-Palestinian peace process?," *Vox*, May 14, 2018, https://www.vox.com/cards/israel-palestine/peace-process.

144. Ibid.

145. John Kerry, Remarks, "Remarks at the American Jewish Committee Global Forum," District of Columbia, June 3, 2013, https://2009-2017.state.gov/secretary/remarks/2013/06/210236.htm.

146. Author's notes, January 1, 2014.

147. "Highway 1 (Israel)," Wikipedia, https://en.m.wikipedia.org/wiki/Highway_1_(Israel).

148. Serge Schmemann, "Assasination in Israel: The Overview; Rabin Slain after Peace Rally in Tel Aviv; Israeli Gunman Held; Says He Acted Alone," *The New York Times*, November 5, 1995, https://www.nytimes.com/1995/11/05/world/assassination-israel-overview-rabin-slain-after-peace-rally-tel-aviv-israeli.html?pagewanted=all.

149. John Kerry, "Solo Press Availability in Baghdad, Iraq," Baghdad, March 24, 2013, https://2009-2017.state.gov/secretary/remarks/2013/03/206591.htm.

150. Author's notes, March 3, 2013.

151. Author's notes, April 9, 2013.

152. Associated Press, "Arabs loosen stance on Israel's 1967 border," CBS News, April 23, 2013, https://www.cbsnews.com/news/arabs-loosen-stance-on-israels-1967-border/.

153. John Kerry, Remarks, "Remarks with Qatari Prime Minister Sheikh Hamad bin Jassim bin Jabr Al Thani After Meeting With Arab League Officials," District of Columbia, April 29, 2013, https://2009-2017.state.gov/secretary/remarks/2013/04/208544.htm.

154. John Kerry, Remarks, "Remarks to Special Program on Breaking the Impasse World Economic Forum," Dead Sea, May 26, 2013, https://2009-2017.state.gov/secretary/remarks/2013/05/209969.htm.

155. Ibid.

156. Ibid.

157. John Kerry, Remarks, "Press Availability in Amman, Jordan," Amman, July 19, 2013, https://2009-2017.state.gov/secretary/remarks/2013/07/212213.htm.

158. Author's notes, March 31, 2018.

159. Ben Birnbaum and Amir Tibon, "The Explosive, Inside Story of How John Kerry Built an Israel-Palestine Peace Plan—and Watched It Crumble," *The New Republic*, July 20, 2014, https://newrepublic.com/article/118751/how-israel-palestine-peace-deal-died.

160. John Kerry, Remarks, "Remarks with Ambassador Martin Indyk," District of Columbia, July 29, 2013, https://2009-2017.state.gov/secretary/remarks/2013/07/212516.htm.

161. Sharona Schwartz, "As Obama Admin Pushes Peace Process, Abbas Vows No Israelis In Palestine: 'Racist and Hateful Vision,'" Yahoo, July 30, 2013, https://www.yahoo.com/news/obama -admin-pushes-peace-process-abbas-vows-no-113622595.html.

162. John Kerry, Remarks, "Remarks on the Middle East Peace Process Talks," District of Columbia, July 30, 2013, https://2009-2017.state.gov/secretary/remarks/2013/07/212553.htm.

163. Ibid.

164. Ibid.

165. Author's notes, June 28, 2013.

166. Ben Birnbaum and Amir Tibon, "The Explosive, Inside Story of How John Kerry Built an Israel-Palestine Peace Plan—and Watched It Crumble," The New Republic, July 20, 2014, https://newrepublic.com/article/118751/how-israel-palestine-peace-deal-died.

167. Associated Press, "Israeli soldiers kill 3 Palestinians in West Bank raid," The National, August, 26, 2013, https://www.thenational.ae/world/mena/israeli-soldiers-kill-3-palestinians-in -west-bank-raid-1.307502.

168. Tovah Lazaroff, "Netanyahu Rejects Palestinian Right of Return to Israel," Jerusalem Post, October 28, 2013, http://www.jpost.com/Diplomacy-and-Politics/Netanyahu-rejects-Palestinian-right -of-return-to-Israel-329895.

169. Author's journal, October 10, 2014.

170. Author's recollection.

171. John Kerry, Remarks, "Remarks at Solo Press Availability," Jerusalem, January 5, 2014, https://2009-2017.state.gov/secretary/remarks/2014/01/219298.htm.

172. Gil Stern Hoffman/jpost.com Staff/ Yaakov Lappin, "Ya'alon Criticized for Reportedly Calling Kerry 'obsessive, Messianic,'" Jerusalem Post, January 14, 2014, http://www.jpost.com /Diplomacy-and-Politics/Yaalon-criticized-for-reportedly-calling-Kerry-obsessive-messianic-338109.

173. Lazar Berman and Rebecca Shimoni Stoil, "Liberman: Kerry is 'a true friend' of Israel," The Times of Israel, February 7, 2014, https://www.timesofisrael.com/liberman-kerry-is-a-true-friend -of-israel/.

174. The New York Times, February 12, 2014.

175. Miami Herald, February 12, 2014.

176. Ben Birnbaum and Amir Tibon, "The Explosive, Inside Story of How John Kerry Built an Israel-Palestine Peace Plan—and Watched It Crumble," The New Republic, July 20, 2014, https://newrepublic.com/article/118751/how-israel-palestine-peace-deal-died.

177. Ibid.

178. Ibid.

179. Ibid.

180. Ibid.

181. Ibid.

182. Author's notes, March 31, 2014.

183. Ibid.

184. Ben Birnbaum and Amir Tibon, "The Explosive, Inside Story of How John Kerry Built an Israel-Palestine Peace Plan—and Watched It Crumble," The New Republic, July 20, 2014, https://newrepublic.com/article/118751/how-israel-palestine-peace-deal-died.

185. Ibid.

186. Author's notes, April 1, 2014.

187. Ibid.

188. Author's notes, April 4, 2014.

189. "2014 kidnapping and murder of Israeli teenagers," Wikipedia, https://en.wikipedia.org/wiki /2014_kidnapping_and_murder_of_Israeli_teenagers.

190. "2014 Israel–Gaza conflict," Wikipedia, https://en.wikipedia.org/wiki/2014_Israel–Gaza_conflict.

191. Author's notes, August 1, 2014.

192. Ibid.

193. John Kerry, Remarks, "Remarks on the Humanitarian Cease-fire Announcement in Gaza," New Delhi, https://2009-2017.state.gov/secretary/remarks/2014/08/230072.htm.

194. Author's notes, March 9, 2015.

195. Author's notes, June 6, 2016.

196. Paul Lewis, "U.N. Council 'Deplores' Israeli Actions in Unrest," *The New York Times*, December 23, 1987, http://www.nytimes.com/1987/12/23/world/un-council-deplores-israeli-actions-in-unrest.html.

197. Ibid.

198. Samantha Power, Remarks, "Full text of US envoy Samantha Power's speech after abstention on anti-settlement vote," New York City, December 23, 2016, https://www.timesofisrael.com/full-text -of-us-envoy-samantha-powers-speech-after-abstention-on-anti-settlement-vote/.

199. John Kerry, Remarks, "Remarks on Middle East Peace," District of Columbia, December 28, 2016, https://2009-2017.state.gov/secretary/remarks/2016/12/266119.htm.

200. Ibid.

201. Ibid.

Chapter 6

202. Karen DeYoung and Joshua Partlow, "Afghanistan's Karzai accepted runoff election only after hours of tense talks," *The Washington Post*, October 21, 2009, http://www.washingtonpost.com /wp-dyn/content/article/2009/10/20/AR2009102001071_2.html?sid=ST2009102001049.

203. David Remnick, "Negotiating the Whirlwind," *The New Yorker*, December 14, 2015, https://www.newyorker.com/magazine/2015/12/21/negotiating-the-whirlwind.

204. CNN Wire Staff, "Kerry: Pakistan to return tail of chopper used in bin Laden raid," CNN, May 17, 2011, http://www.cnn.com/2011/WORLD/asiapcf/05/17/pakistan.raid.helicopter/index.html.

205. Bryan Bender, "How John Kerry opened a secret channel to Iran," *The Boston Globe*, November 26, 2013, https://www.bostonglobe.com/news/nation/2013/11/26/john-kerry-developed-secret-dialogue -with-iran-through-oman/rRBZZ8aeDrsP2Q2HdoWJEJ/story.html.

206. "Operation Eagle Claw," Wikipedia, https://en.wikipedia.org/wiki/Operation_Eagle_Claw.

207. "Holocaust comments spark outrage," BBC, December 14, 2005, http://news.bbc.co.uk/2/hi /middle_east/4529198.stm.

208. Michael O'Brien, "Iranian leader wants 'fact-finding mission' into causes of 9/11 attacks," *The Hill*, September 24, 2010, http://thehill.com/blogs/blog-briefing-room/news/120845-iranian-leader -wants-fact-finding-mission-into-causes-of-911-attacks.

209. Mariam Karouny and Sue Pleming, "Rice meets Syrian minister, greets Iranian," *Reuters*, May 3, 2007, https://www.reuters.com/article/us-iraq-syria-usa/rice-meets-syrian-minister-greets-iranian -idUSL036981720070503.

210. Jeff Mason and Louis Charbonneau, "Obama, Iran's Rouhani hold historic phone call," Reuters, September 27, 2013, https://www.reuters.com/article/us-un-assembly-iran/obama-irans -rouhani-hold-historic-phone-call-idUSBRE98Q16S20130928.

211. "Timeline of Nuclear Diplomacy with Iran," Fact Sheets & Briefs, Arms Control Association, https://www.armscontrol.org/factsheet/Timeline-of-Nuclear-Diplomacy-With-Iran.

212. "Atoms for Peace," Wikipedia, https://en.wikipedia.org/wiki/Atoms_for_Peace.

213. "Joint Plan of Action," Wikipedia, https://en.wikipedia.org/wiki/Joint_Plan_of_Action#cite _note-5.

214. "Timeline of Nuclear Diplomacy with Iran," Fact Sheets & Briefs, Arms Control Association, https://www.armscontrol.org/factsheet/Timeline-of-Nuclear-Diplomacy-With-Iran.

215. "Joint Plan of Action," Wikipedia, https://en.wikipedia.org/wiki/Joint_Plan_of_Action#cite _note-5_.

216. "Timeline of Nuclear Diplomacy with Iran," Fact Sheets & Briefs, Arms Control Association, https://www.armscontrol.org/factsheet/Timeline-of-Nuclear-Diplomacy-With-Iran.

217. David Albright and Christina Walrond, "Iran's Gas Centrifuge Program: Taking Stock," Institute for Science and International Security, February 11, 2010, http://isis-online.org/isis-reports /detail/irans-gas-centrifuge-program-taking-stock/8.

218. Patrick Goodenough, "'19,000 Centrifuges Already Spinning': Kerry Implies Iran's Enrichment Capacity Grew Mostly Under Bush," CNS News, July 20, 2015, https://www.cnsnews.com/news /article/patrick-goodenough/19000-centrifuges-already-spinning-kerry-implies-irans-enrichment.

219. Max Fisher, "Obama opens up on Iran," Vox, August 7, 2015, https://www.vox.com/2015/8/7 /9115653/obama-interview-iran.

220. Author's notes, November 23, 2013.

221. Ibid.

222. Aaron Blake, "Kerry on Iran: 'We do not recognize a right to enrich,'" The Washington Post, November 24, 2013, https://www.washingtonpost.com/news/post-politics/wp/2013/11/24/kerry-on-iran -we-do-not-recognize-a-right-to-enrich/?utm_term=.05c16b3d92e6.

223. Author's notes, November 25, 2013.

224. Ibid.

225. William Booth, "Israel's Netanyahu calls Iran deal 'historic mistake,'" The Washington Post, November 24, 2013, https://www.washingtonpost.com/world-israel-says-iran-deal-makes-world-more -dangerous/2013/11/24/e0e347de-54f9-11e3-bdbf-097ab2a3dc2b_story.html?utm_term=.fbb490b975af.

226. "Joint Plan of Action," Wikipedia, https://en.wikipedia.org/wiki/Joint_Plan_of_Action#cite _note-5.

227. Ibid.

228. Ibid.

229. "The Iran Nuclear Deal: Does It Further U.S. National Security?" Hearing, Committee on Foreign Affairs House of Representatives, http://docs.house.gov/meetings/FA/FA00/20131210/101577 /HHRG-113-FA00-Transcript-20131210.pdf.

230. Ibid.

231. Adnan Tabatabai, "Iran Nuclear Talks: What Do Rouhani's Hard-Line Critics Want?," LobeLog, May 11, 2014, https://lobelog.com/iran-nuclear-talks-what-do-hard-liners-rouhanis-critics-want/.

232. Barak Ravid, "Netanyahu Was Wrong: There Was Never Going to Be a Good Deal with Iran," Haaretz, July 15, 2015, https://www.haaretz.com/.premium-the-perils-and-the-promise-of-the-iran -deal-1.5305064.

233. "Advancing U.S. Interests in a Troubled World: The FY 2016 Foreign Affairs Budget," Hearing, Committee on Foreign Affairs House of Representatives, http://docs.house.gov/meetings/FA /FA00/20150225/103066/HHRG-114-FA00-Transcript-20150225.pdf.

234. Author's journal, March 9, 2015.

235. Ibid.

236. "Iran nuclear deal framework," Wikipedia, https://en.wikipedia.org/wiki/Iran_nuclear_deal _framework.

237. Author's journal, April 21, 2015.

238. Ibid.

239. Nicolas Revise, "Kerry, Zarif fail to make breakthrough in nuclear talks," Yahoo, May 30, 2015, https://www.yahoo.com/news/kerry-zarif-launch-key-nuclear-talks-geneva-ahead-093556106.html.

240. Robin Wright, "Tehran's Promise," The New Yorker, July 20, 2015, https://www.newyorker .com/magazine/2015/07/27/tehrans-promise.

241. "Femur," Wikipedia, https://en.wikipedia.org/wiki/Femur.

242. John Pike, "C-17 Globemaster III," Military Analysis Network, April 25, 2000, https://fas.org /man/dod-101/sys/ac/c-17.htm.

243. John Kerry, Remarks, "Remarks Upon Leaving Massachusetts General Hospital," Boston, June 12, 2015, https://2009-2017.state.gov/secretary/remarks/2015/06/243787.htm.

244. Ibid.

245. Matt Viser, "John Kerry back at home, but not for very long," *The Boston Globe*, June 14, 2015, https://www.bostonglobe.com/news/politics/2015/06/13/john-kerry-reflects-his-bicycle-accident-exclusive-globe-interview/nRK32wk1YCJ15Mmd4tcoJJ/story.html.

246. Ibid.

247. Ibid.

248. "Ernest Moniz," Wikipedia, https://en.wikipedia.org/wiki/Ernest_Moniz.

249. "Ali Akbar Salehi," Wikipedia, https://en.wikipedia.org/wiki/Ali_Akbar_Salehi.

250. "Palais Coburg," Wikipedia, https://en.wikipedia.org/wiki/Palais_Coburg.

251. "Hotel Imperial," Wikipedia, https://en.wikipedia.org/wiki/Hotel_Imperial.

252. Ibid.

253. Ibid.

254. Robin Wright, "Tehran's Promise," *The New Yorker*, July 20, 2015, https://www.newyorker.com/magazine/2015/07/27/tehrans-promise.

255. Author's notes, June 29, 2015.

256. Robin Wright, "Tehran's Promise," *The New Yorker*, July 20, 2015, https://www.newyorker.com/magazine/2015/07/27/tehrans-promise.

257. Ibid.

258. Author's notes, July 4, 2015.

259. Ibid.

260. Author's notes, November 22, 2014.

261. John Kerry, Remarks, "Remarks on the Iran Negotiations in Vienna," Vienna, July 5, 2015, https://2009-2017.state.gov/secretary/remarks/2015/07/244603.htm.

262. *AFP*, "Zarif warns West: 'Never threaten an Iranian,'" *Times of Israel*, July 9, 2015, https://www.timesofisrael.com/zarif-warns-west-never-threaten-an-iranian/.

263. John Allen Gay, "Why Is Iran's Foreign Minister So Angry?" National Interest, July 9, 2015, http://nationalinterest.org/blog/the-buzz/why-irans-foreign-minister-so-angry-13303.

264. Author's notes, July 7, 2015.

265. Author's notes, July 12, 2015.

266. Author's notes, July 13, 2015.

267. Ibid.

268. Ibid.

269. Ibid.

270. Shoshana Weissmann, "Kerry Invokes Vietnam at Iran Talks: 'I Never Wanted to Go to War Again,'" *The Weekly Standard*, July 16, 2015, http://www.weeklystandard.com/kerry-invokes-vietnam-at-iran-talks-i-never-wanted-to-go-to-war-again/article/991543.

271. Barack Obama, Remarks, "Read President Obama's Remarks on Iran Nuclear Deal," District of Columbia, July 14, 2015, http://time.com/3957036/obama-iran-nuclear-deal-transcript/.

272. John Kerry, Remarks, "Press Availability on Nuclear Deal with Iran," Vienna, July 14, 2015, https://2009-2017.state.gov/secretary/remarks/2015/07/244885.htm.

273. Ibid.

274. Author's journal, July 16, 2016.

275. Ibid.

276. Ibid.

277. Author's journal, February 25, 2015.

278. Sean Sullivan, "With Iran letter, Tom Cotton emerges as leading GOP national security hawk," *The Washington Post*, March 11, 2015, https://www.washingtonpost.com/politics/with-iran-letter-tom-cotton-emerges-as-leading-gop-national-security-hawk/2015/03/11/4ce05a4e-c74f-11e4-a199-6cb5e63819d2_story.html?utm_term=.72e2ad20c674.

279. Steve Benen, "McCain's dilemma: trust Ayatollah or trust U.S. officials?" MSNBC, April 15, 2015, http://www.msnbc.com/rachel-maddow-show/mccains-dilemma-trust-ayatollah-or-trust-us-officials.

280. Author's journal, July 20, 2015.

281. John Kerry, Remarks, "Remarks on Nuclear Agreement with Iran," Philadelphia, September 2, 2015, https://2009-2017.state.gov/secretary/remarks/2015/09/246574.htm.

282. Tribune wire reports, "Obama seals Iran deal win as Senate Democrats find 34 votes," *Chicago Tribune*, September 2, 2015, http://www.chicagotribune.com/news/nationworld/ct-iran-nuclear-deal -20150902-story.html.

283. Author's notes, January 12, 2016.

284. John Kerry, Remarks, "Remarks on the United States Foreign Policy Agenda for 2016," District of Columbia, January 13, 2016, https://2009-2017.state.gov/secretary/remarks/2016/01/251177.htm.

285. Jay Solomon and Carol E. Lee, "U.S. Sent Cash to Iran as Americans Were Freed," *The Wall Street Journal*, August 3, 2016, https://www.wsj.com/articles/u-s-sent-cash-to-iran-as-americans-were-freed -1470181874.

286. Associated Press, "$1.7-billion payment to Iran was all in cash due to effectiveness of sanctions, White House says," *Los Angeles Times*, September 7, 2016, http://www.latimes.com/nation/nationnow /la-na-iran-payment-cash-20160907-snap-story.html.

287. Jay Solomon and Carol E. Lee, "U.S. Sent Cash to Iran as Americans Were Freed," *The Wall Street Journal*, August 3, 2016, https://www.wsj.com/articles/u-s-sent-cash-to-iran-as-americans-were-freed -1470181874.

288. John Kerry, Remarks, "Hague Claims Tribunal Settlement," District of Columbia, January 17, 2016, https://2009-2017.state.gov/secretary/remarks/2016/01/251338.htm.

289. Author's notes, January 15, 2015.

290. Ibid.

291. Author's notes, January 1, 2015.

292. "Senate Foreign Relations Committee Holds Hearing on the Iran Nuclear Negotiations, Panel 1," Hearing, Senate Foreign Relations Committee, https://www.shearman.com/~/media/Files/Services/Iran -Sanctions/US-Resources/Joint-Plan-of-Action/4-Feb-2014--Transcript-of-Senate-Foreign-Relations -Committee-Hearing-on-the-Iran-Nuclear-Negotiations-Panel-1.pdf.

293. Author's notes, January 16, 2015.

294. Ibid.

295. John Kerry, "Remarks on Implementation Day," Vienna, January 16, 2016, https://2009-2017 .state.gov/secretary/remarks/2016/01/251336.htm.

Chapter 7

296. John Kerry, "Remarks with United Kingdom Foreign Secretary Hague," London, September 9, 2013, https://2009-2017.state.gov/secretary/remarks/2013/09/213956.htm.

297. John Kerry, Remarks, "Proposed Authorization to Use Military Force in Syria," District of Columbia, September 10, 2013,https://2009-2017.state.gov/secretary/remarks/2013/09/214028.htm.

298. Ibid.

299. Ibid.

300. Michael R. Gordon and Steven Lee Myers, "Obama Calls Russia Offer on Syria Possible 'Breakthrough,'" *The New York Times*, September 9, 2013, http://www.nytimes.com/2013/09/10 /world/middleeast/kerry-says-syria-should-hand-over-all-chemical-arms.html?pagewanted=all.

301. Somini Sengupta, "Russia Says 'Small-Hearted' Obama Administration Spoiled Ties," *The New York Times*, September 22, 2017, https://www.nytimes.com/2017/09/22/world/europe/russia-obama -lavrov.html.

302. John Kerry, Remarks, "Proposed Authorization to Use Military Force in Syria," District of Columbia, September 10, 2013,https://2009-2017.state.gov/secretary/remarks/2013/09/214028.htm.

303. "Worldwide Deaths in World War II," Research Starters, The National WWII Museum New Orleans, https://www.nationalww2museum.org/students-teachers/student-resources /research-starters/research-starters-worldwide-deaths-world-war.

304. Associated Press, "Putin: 'Soviet collapse a genuine tragedy,'" NBC News, April 25, 2005, http://www.nbcnews.com/id/7632057/ns/world_news/t/putin-soviet-collapse-genuine-tragedy /#.XLeGN-hKjD5.

305. Anne Gearan, "Candid remark from Kerry leads to Syria disarmament proposal," *The Washington Post*, September 10, 2013, https://www.washingtonpost.com/world/national-security /candid-remark-from-kerry-leads-to-syria-disarmament-proposal/2013/09/10/d4e37474-1a2d-11e3 -8685-5021e0c41964_story.html?utm_term=.9c24583536ad.

306. John Kerry, Remarks, "Remarks with Russian Foreign Minister Sergey Lavrov," Geneva, September 12, 2013, https://2009-2017.state.gov/secretary/remarks/2013/09/214156.htm.

307. Ibid.

308. Vladimir V. Putin, "A Plea for Caution from Russia," *The New York Times*, September 11, 2013, http://www.nytimes.com/2013/09/12/opinion/putin-plea-for-caution-from-russia-on-syria.html.

309. Ibid.

310. John Kerry, Remarks, "Remarks with Russian Foreign Minister Sergey Lavrov," Geneva, September 12, 2013, https://2009-2017.state.gov/secretary/remarks/2013/09/214156.htm.

311. Ibid.

312. Ibid.

313. "Destruction of Syria's chemical weapons," Wikipedia, https://en.wikipedia.org/wiki /Destruction_of_Syria%27s_chemical_weapons.

314. Michael R. Gordon, "U.S. and Russia Reach Deal to Destroy Syria's Chemical Arms," *The New York Times*, September 14, 2013, http://www.nytimes.com/2013/09/15/world/middleeast/syria-talks.html.

315. John Kerry, Remarks, "Remarks with Russian Foreign Minister Sergey Lavrov After Their Meeting," Geneva, September 14, 2013, https://2009-2017.state.gov/secretary/remarks/2013/09/214250.htm.

316. Ibid.

317. Ibid.

318. "2014 Ukrainian revolution" Wikipedia, https://en.wikipedia.org/wiki/2014_Ukrainian _revolution#cite_note-93.

319. Ibid.

320. Ibid.

321. Ibid.

322. Ibid.

323. Ibid.

324. Ibid.

325. Sam Frizell, "Ukraine Protestors Seize Kiev As President Flees," *Time*, February 22, 2014, http://world.time.com/2014/02/22/ukraines-president-flees-protestors-capture-kiev/.

326. Jill Dougherty, "Clinton 'reset button' gift to Russian FM gets lost in translation," CNN, March 6, 2009, http://politicalticker.blogs.cnn.com/2009/03/06/clinton-reset-button-gift-to-russian -fm-gets-lost-in-translation/.

327. Ibid.

328. Will Englund, "The roots of the hostility between Putin and Clinton," *The Washington Post*, July 28, 2016, https://www.washingtonpost.com/world/europe/the-roots-of-the-hostility-between-putin -and-clinton/2016/07/28/85ca74ca-5402-11e6-b652-315ae5d4d4dd_story.html?utm_term =.b20d765226da.

329. "Magnitsky Act," Wikipedia, https://en.wikipedia.org/wiki/Magnitsky_Act.

330. Ibid.

331. "Putin keeps John Kerry waiting for THREE HOURS during his visit to Russia for meetings over Syria as relationship between the U.S. and Russia remains frosty," *Daily Mail*, Mary 7, 2013, http://www.dailymail.co.uk/news/article-2321001/Vladimir-Putin-keeps-John-Kerry-waiting-THREE -HOURS-visit-Russia-Syria-talks.html.

332. "Ukraine crisis: Transcript of leaked Nuland-Pyatt call," BBC, February 7, 2014, http://www .bbc.com/news/world-europe-26079957.

333. Ibid.

334. Ibid.

335. "Annexation of Crimea by the Russian Federation," Wikipedia, https://en.wikipedia.org/wiki
/Annexation_of_Crimea_by_the_Russian_Federation.

336. Ibid.

337. Ibid.

338. Paul N. Schwartz, "Crimea's Strategic Value to Russia," Center for Strategic and International
Studies, March 18, 2014, https://www.csis.org/blogs/post-soviet-post/crimeas-strategic-value-russia.

339. Ibid.

340. AFP, "Putin describes secret operation to seize Crimea," Yahoo, March 8, 2015, https://www
.yahoo.com/news/putin-describes-secret-operation-seize-crimea-212858356.html.

341. Will Englund, "The roots of the hostility between Putin and Clinton," *The Washington Post*, July
28, 2016, https://www.washingtonpost.com/world/europe/the-roots-of-the-hostility-between-putin-and
-clinton/2016/07/28/85ca74ca-5402-11e6-b652-315ae5d4d4dd_story.html?utm_term-.b20d765226da.

342. "Annexation of Crimea by the Russian Federation," Wikipedia, https://en.wikipedia.org/wiki
/Annexation_of_Crimea_by_the_Russian_Federation#cite_note-Yahoo News-34.

343. "Simferopol ," Wikipedia, https://en.wikipedia.org/wiki/Simferopol.

344. "Annexation of Crimea by the Russian Federation," Wikipedia, https://en.wikipedia.org/wiki
/Annexation_of_Crimea_by_the_Russian_Federation#cite_note-Yahoo_News-34.

345. Ibid.

346. "Conference on Disarmament," United Nations, December 21, 1994, https://undocs.org
/CD/1285.

347. Ibid.

348. "Little green men (Ukrainian crisis)," Wikipedia, https://en.wikipedia.org/wiki/Little_green_men
_(Ukrainian_crisis)#cite_note-5.

349. Bill Chappell and Mark Memmott, "Putin Says Those Aren't Russian Forces in Crimea,"
National Public Radio, March 4, 2014, https://www.npr.org/sections/thetwo-way/2014/03/04
/285653335/putin-says-those-arent-russian-forces-in-crimea.

350. Ian Traynor, "Vladimir Putin and Barack Obama engage in war of words over Ukraine," *The
Guardian*, March 4, 2014, https://www.theguardian.com/world/2014/mar/04/ukraine-crisis-putin-obama
-war-of-words.

351. Ibid.

352. Vladimir V. Putin, "A Plea for Caution from Russia," *The New York Times*, September 11, 2013,
http://www.nytimes.com/2013/09/12/opinion/putin-plea-for-caution-from russia-on-syria.html.

353. ※РОДИМИЧЪ※, "Пресс-конференция Владимира Путина по Украине
[4.03.2014]," YouTube, March 4, 2014, https://www.youtube.com/watch?v=ZwspcvY5kvg.

354. "Медведев: Россия не гарантирует целостность Украины," BBC, March 20, 2014,
http://www.bbc.com/russian/rolling_news/2014/05/140520_rn_medvedev_ukraine.shtml.

355. @RussianEmbassy, "Lavrov: Russia never violated Budapest memorandum. It contained only 1
obligation, not to attack Ukraine with nukes," Twitter, January 27, 2016, 4:22 A.M., https://twitter
.com/RussianEmbassy/status/692321689254830080.

356. Michael Colborne, "Russia's bald-faced lies," *National Post*, February 4, 2016, http://national-
post.com/opinion/michael-colborne-russias-bald-faced-lies.

357. Terrence McCoy, "What does Russia tell the mothers of soldiers killed in Ukraine? Not much,"
Washington Post, August 29, 2014, https://www.washingtonpost.com/news/morning-mix
/wp/2014/08/29/what-does-russia-tell-the-mothers-of-soldiers-killed-in-ukraine-not-much/?utm
_term=.37da7141a583.

358. "Malaysia Airlines Flight 17," Wikipedia, https://en.wikipedia.org/wiki/Malaysia_Airlines
_Flight_17.

359. "Malaysia Airlines crash: video claims to show missile launcher being smuggled into Russia,"
Telegraph, July 18, 2014, http://www.telegraph.co.uk/news/worldnews/europe/ukraine/10976191/
Malaysia-Airlines-crash-video-claims-to-show-missile-launcher-being-smuggled-into-Russia.html.

360. "Malaysia Airlines Flight 17," Wikipedia, https://en.wikipedia.org/wiki/Malaysia_Airlines _Flight_17.

361. Ibid.

362. "Iran Air Flight 655," Wikipedia, https://en.wikipedia.org/wiki/Iran_Air_Flight_655.

363. "Boris Nemtsov," Wikipedia, https://en.wikipedia.org/wiki/Boris_Nemtsov#cite_note-76.

364. Ibid.

365. "Nemtsov killer sentenced to 20yrs behind bars, accomplices to 11-19yrs," RT, https://www.rt .com/news/396191-nemtsov-killers-sentence-jail/.

366. Kathy Lally, "Putin's remarks raise fears of future moves against Ukraine," *The Washington Post*, April 17, 2014, https://www.washingtonpost.com/world/putin-changes-course-admits-russian -troops-were-in-crimea-before-vote/2014/04/17/b3300a54-c617-11e3-bf7a-be01a9b69cf1_story.html?utm _term=.fdd52bb344a9.

367. "Ukraine crisis: Russian victory parade buoyed by Crimea," BBC, May 9, 2014, http://www .bbc.com/news/world-europe-27336461.

368. Author's notes, March 14, 2014.

369. Adam Entous, Ellen Nakashima and Greg Jaffe, "Kremlin trolls burned across the Internet as Washington debated options," *The Washington Post*, December 25, 2017, https://www.washingtonpost .com/world/national-security/kremlin-trolls-burned-across-the-internet-as-washington-debated-options /2017/12/23/e7b9dc92-e403-11e7-ab50-621fe0588340_story.html?utm_term=.2ed30fba4190.

370. Ibid.

371. Adam Entous, Ellen Nakashima, and Greg Jaffe, "Kremlin trolls burned across the Internet as Washington debated options," *The Washington Post*, December 25, 2017, https://www.washingtonpost .com/world/national-security/kremlin-trolls-burned-across-the-internet-as-washington-debated-options /2017/12/23/e7b9dc92-e403-11e7-ab50-621fe0588340_story.html?utm_term=.2ed30fba4190.

372. Rick Stengel, "What Hillary Knew About Putin's Propaganda Machine," *Politico*, November 15, 2017, https://www.politico.com/magazine/story/2017/11/15/hillary-clinton-putin-russia-propaganda -election-215826.

373. Author's notes, March 11, 2014.

374. Ibid.

375. Author's journal, February 18, 2015.

376. Mark Mullen, Christina London and R. Stickney, "President Obama: No U.S. Military Action in Ukraine," NBC San Diego, March 19, 2014, https://www.nbcsandiego.com/news/local /Obama-Military-Action-Russia-Ukraine-Crimea-Tensions-Troops-251067481.html.

377. Andrea Mitchell, "Rep. Rogers 'concerned' about declassified briefing," MSNBC, August 29, 2013, https://www.msnbc.com/andrea-mitchell-reports/watch/rep-rogers-concerned-about -declassified-briefing-45739587713.

378. United States Committee on Foreign Relations, 113th Congress, Second Session, "National Security and Foreign Policy Priorities in the Fiscal Year 2015 International Affairs Budget," United States Committee on Foreign Relations, April 8, 2014, https://www.foreign.senate.gov/imo/media /doc/04%2008%202014,%20International%20Affairs%20Budget1.pdf.

379. John Kerry, Remarks, "Statement on Syria," District of Columbia, August 30, 2013, https://2009-2017.state.gov/secretary/remarks/2013/08/213668.htm.

380. Jeffrey Goldberg, "The Obama Doctrine," *The Atlantic*, April 2016, https://www.theatlantic .com/magazine/archive/2016/04/the-obama-doctrine/471525/.

381. Julian Borger, "Russian military presence in Syria poses challenge to US-led intervention," *The Guardian*, December 23, 2012, https://www.theguardian.com/world/2012/dec/23/syria-crisis-russian -military-presence.

382. Susan B. Glasser, "The War America Isn't Fighting," *Politico*, February 19, 2018, https://www.politico.com/magazine/story/2018/02/19/ash-carter-russia-pentagon-plan-obama -trump-217027.

383. Andrew Osborn, "Putin, in Syria, says mission accomplished, orders partial Russian pull-out," Reuters, December 11, 2017, https://www.reuters.com/article/us-mideast-crisis-syria-russia-putin /putin-in-syria-says-mission accomplished-orders-partial-russian-pull-out-idUSKDN1E50X1.

384. Ibid.

385. Author's notes, March 15, 2016.

386. Ibid.

387. Ibid.

388. Scott Wilson, "Obama dismisses Russia as 'regional power' acting out of weakness," *The Washington Post*, March 25, 2014, https://www.washingtonpost.com/world/national-security /obama-dismisses-russia-as-regional-power-acting-out-of-weakness/2014/03/25/1e5a678e-b439-11e3 -b899-20667de76985_story.html?utm_term=.7378bb6b929d.

389. David Brunnstrom and Denis Dyomkin, "Kerry meets with Putin about cooperating against Islamic State in Syria," Reuters, July 14, 2016, https://www.reuters.com/article/us-mideast-crisis -syria-usa/kerry-meets-with-putin-about-cooperating-against-islamic-state-in-syria-idUSKCN0ZU25O.

390. David Greene and Jonathan Finer, "What to Expect as Tillerson Travels to Moscow," National Public Radio, April 12, 2017, https://www.npr.org/2017/04/12/523534035/what-to-expect-as -tillerson-travels-to-moscow.

391. Author's notes, July 15, 2016.

392. Ibid.

393. Ibid.

394. "Democratic National Committee email leak," Wikipedia, https://en.wikipedia.org/wiki/2016 _Democratic_National_Committee_email_leak.

395. "Joint Statement from the Department of Homeland Security and Office of the Director of National Intelligence on Election Security," U.S. Department of Homeland Security, October 7, 2016, https://www.dhs.gov/news/2016/10/07/joint-statement-department-homeland-security-and-office -director-national.

396. "10 revelations from Wikileaks' hacked Clinton emails," BBC, October 27, 2016, http://www .bbc.com/news/world-us-canada-37639370.

397. David E. Sanger, "Obama Strikes Back at Russia for Election Hacking," *The New York Times*, December 29, 2016, https://www.nytimes.com/2016/12/29/us/politics/russia -election-hacking-sanctions.html.

398. Barack Obama, "Statement by the President on Actions in Response to Russian Malicious Cyber Activity and Harassment," The White House, December 29, 2016, https://obamawhitehouse .archives.gov/the-press-office/2016/12/29/statement-president-actions-response-russian-malicious -cyber-activity.

399. Peter Baker, "Trump to Sign Russia Sanctions Bill, White House Says," *The New York Times*, July 28, 2017, https://www.nytimes.com/2017/07/28/us/trump-to-sign-russia-sanctions-bill-white -house-says.html.

400. Andrew Roth, "U.S. Embassy stops issuing nonimmigrant visas to Russians as diplomatic standoff deepens," *The Washington Post*, August 21, 2017, https://www.washingtonpost.com/world /us-halts-non-immigrant-visas-in-russia-as-diplomatic-standoff-deepens/2017/08/21/90f82c18-8654 -11e7-a50f-e0d4e6ec070a_story.html?utm_term=.8988d540759f.

401. Neil MacFarquhar, "Putin, Responding to Sanctions, Orders U.S. to Cut Diplomatic Staff by 755," *The New York Times*, July 30, 2017, https://www.nytimes.com/2017/07/30/world/europe/russia -sanctions-us-diplomats-expelled.html.

Chapter 8

402. Author's notes, November 8, 2016.

403. Louis Jacobson, "Yes, Donald Trump did call climate change a Chinese hoax," Politifact, June 3, 2016, http://www.politifact.com/truth-o-meter/statements/2016/jun/03/hillary-clinton /yes-donald-trump-did-call-climate-change-chinese-h/.

404. Donald Trump, Remarks, "Transcript: Donald Trump's Victory Speech," *The New York Times*, November 9, 2016, https://www.nytimes.com/2016/11/10/us/politics/trump-speech-transcript.html.

405. Author's notes, November 8, 2016.

406. Justin Gillis, "John Kerry's Antarctica Visit Highlights a Continent, and Climate Policies, Under Threat," *The New York Times*, November 15, 2016, https://www.nytimes.com/2016/11/16/science/antarctica-john-kerry-global-warming.html.

407. John Kerry, Remarks, "Statement of Senator John F. Kerry, Nominee for Secretary of State," District of Columbia, January 24, 2013, https://2009-2017.state.gov/secretary/remarks/2013/01/203455.htm.

408. Mark Landler, "U.S. and China Reach Climate Accord After Months of Talks," *The New York Times*, November 11, 2014, https://www.nytimes.com/2014/11/12/world/asia/china-us-xi-obama-apec.html.

409. "Member States," Arctic Council, July 6, 2015, http://www.arctic-council.org/index.php/en/about-us/member-states.

410. "Kiruna," Wikipedia, https://en.wikipedia.org/wiki/Kiruna.

411. John Kerry, Remarks, "Remarks at the Arctic Council Ministerial Session," Kiruna, May 15, 2013, https://2009-2017.state.gov/secretary/remarks/2013/05/209403.htm.

412. Alan Taylor, "Svalbard: Halfway Between Norway and the North Pole," *The Atlantic*, March 8, 2016, https://www.theatlantic.com/photo/2016/03/svalbard-halfway-between-norway-and-the-north-pole/472785/.

413. "Svalbard Global Seed Vault," Wikipedia, https://en.wikipedia.org/wiki/Svalbard_Global_Seed_Vault.

414. Thomas Nilsen, "Kerry eyewitnessed melting Arctic," *The Barents Observer*, June 16, 2016, https://thebarentsobserver.com/en/arctic/2016/06/kerry-eyewitnessed-melting-arctic.

415. NBC News, interview with John Kerry, June 16, 2016. https://www.nbcnews.com/video/john-kerry-in-svalbard-to-view-effects-of-climate-change-707136067664.

416. "Jakobshavn Glacier," Wikipedia, https://en.wikipedia.org/wiki/Jakobshavn_Glacier

417. Ibid.

418. Ibid.

419. Matthew Lee, "Kerry's Arctic climate change adventure hits Greenland," *Seattle Times*, June 17, 2016, https://www.seattletimes.com/nation-world/nation-politics/kerrys-arctic-climate-change-adventure-hits-greenland/.

420. John Kerry, Remarks, "Remarks with Greenland Foreign Minister Vittus Qujaukitsoq and Danish Foreign Minister Kristian Jensen," Greenland, June 17, 2016, https://2009-2017.state.gov/secretary/remarks/2016/06/258646.htm.

421. John Kerry, Remarks, "Remarks on the U.S.-India Strategic Partnership," New Delhi, June 23, 2013, https://2009-2017.state.gov/secretary/remarks/2013/06/211013.htm.

422. Ibid.

423. John Kerry, Remarks, "Remarks at Energy Event," Islamabad, August 1, 2013, https://2009-2017.state.gov/secretary/remarks/2013/08/212617.htm.

424. Ibid.

425. John Kerry, Remarks, "Remarks at a Visit to Benoa Port," Bali, October 6, 2013, https://2009-2017.state.gov/secretary/remarks/2013/10/215155.htm.

426. "Typhoon Haiyan," Wikipedia, https://en.wikipedia.org/wiki/Typhoon_Haiyan.

427. John Kerry, Remarks, "Remarks at USAID Tacloban," Tacloban, December 18, 2013, https://2009-2017.state.gov/secretary/remarks/2013/12/218869.htm.

428. "Forests and Landscapes in Indonesia," World Resources Institute, http://www.wri.org/our-work/project/forests-and-landscapes-indonesia/climate-change-indonesia.

429. John Kerry, Remarks, "Remarks on Climate Change," Jakarta, February 16, 2014, https://2009-2017.state.gov/secretary/remarks/2014/02/221704.htm.

430. Ibid.

431. Ibid.

432. John Kerry, Remarks, "Remarks at the Montreal Protocol High-level Segment," Vienna, July 22, 2016, https://2009-2017.state.gov/secretary/remarks/2016/07/260401.html.

433. Alyssa Canobbio, "Kerry: Air conditioners as big a threat as ISIS," Fox News, July 23, 2016, http://www.foxnews.com/politics/2016/07/23/kerry-air-conditioners-as-big-threat-as-isis.html.

434. John Kerry, Remarks, "Remarks on Climate Change at COP-20," Lima, December 11, 2014, https://2009-2017.state.gov/secretary/remarks/2014/12/234969.htm.

435. Ibid.

436. John Kerry, Remarks, "Welcoming Remarks at Our Ocean Conference," District of Columbia, June 15, 2014, https://2009-2017.state.gov/secretary/remarks/2014/06/227626.htm.

437. John Kerry, Leonardo DiCaprio, Remarks, "Second Day of Our Ocean Conference," District of Columbia, June 17, 2014, https://2009-2017.state.gov/secretary/remarks/2014/06/227681.htm.

438. Senior State Department Officials, "Background Briefing on the Our Ocean Conference," U.S. Department of State, October 4, 2015, https://2009-2017.state.gov/r/pa/prs/ps/2015/10/247857.htm.

439. Office of the Spokesperson, "Updates on Commitments Made at Our Ocean 2014," October 5, 2015, https://2009-2017.state.gov/r/pa/prs/ps/2015/10/247858.htm.

440. John Kerry, Remarks, "Remarks at the Our Ocean Conference High-Level Segment," Valparaiso, October 5, 2015, https://2009-2017.state.gov/secretary/remarks/2015/10/247900.htm.

441. John Kerry, Remarks, "Welcome Remarks at the Our Ocean Conference," District of Columbia, September 15, 2016, https://2009-2017.state.gov/secretary/remarks/2016/09/261959.htm.

442. Basten Gokkon, "$10bn pledged in new commitments to protect the world's oceans," Mongabay, October 30, 2018, https://news.mongabay.com/2018/10/10bn-pledged-in-new-commitments-to-protect-the-worlds-oceans/.

443. "National Security Implications of Climate-Related Risks and a Changing Climate," July 23, 2015, Department of Defense, http://archive.defense.gov/pubs/150724-congressional-report-on-national-implications-of-climate-change.pdf?source=govdelivery.

444. "Why do militaries care about climate change?" Climate Security 101, https://climatesecurity101.org/faqs/why-do-militaries-care-about-climate-change/.

445. "Naval Station Norfolk," Wikipedia, https://en.wikipedia.org/wiki/Naval_Station_Norfolk.

446. Jeff Goodell, "John Kerry on Climate Change: The Fight of Our Time," Rolling Stone, December 1, 2015, https://www.rollingstone.com/politics/news/john-kerry-on-climate-change-the-fight-of-our-time-20151201.

447. Ibid.

448. John Kerry, Remarks, "Remarks on Climate Change and National Security," Norfolk, November 10, 2015, https://2009-2017.state.gov/secretary/remarks/2015/11/249393.htm.

449. Michael Kranish, Brian Mooney, and Nina J. Easton, John F. Kerry: The Boston Globe Biography (New York: PublicAffairs, 2013).

450. Author's notes, December 8, 2015.

451. John Kerry, Remarks, "Remarks at the Caring for Climate Business Forum," Paris, December 8, 2015, https://2009-2017.state.gov/secretary/remarks/2015/12/250472.htm.

452. Coral Davenport, "Nations Approve Landmark Climate Accord in Paris," The New York Times, December 12, 2015, https://www.nytimes.com/2015/12/13/world/europe/climate-change-accord-paris.html.

453. Ibid.

454. Charles M. Sennott, "Kerry the statesman at a crossroads in Paris," HuffPost, December 6, 2017, https://www.huffingtonpost.com/the-groundtruth-project/kerry-the-statesman-wins_b_8827762.html.

455. Michael Slezak, "World's largest marine park created in Ross Sea in Antarctica in landmark deal," The Guardian, October 27, 2016, https://www.theguardian.com/world/2016/oct/28/worlds-largest-marine-park-created-in-ross-sea-in-antarctica-in-landmark-deal.

456. John Kerry, Remarks, "On the New Marine Protected Area in Antarctica's Ross Sea," District of Columbia, October 27, 2016, https://2009-2017.state.gov/secretary/remarks/2016/10/263763.htm.

457. US Antarctic Program Briefing, October 18. 2016.

458. "Mount Erebus," Wikipedia, https://en.wikipedia.org/wiki/Mount_Erebus.

459. "Ross Ice Shelf," Wikipedia, https://en.wikipedia.org/wiki/Ross_Ice_Shelf.

460. "McMurdo Station Guide," United States Antarctic Program.

461. "Cape Royds," Wikipedia, https://en.wikipedia.org/wiki/Cape_Royds.

462. "McMurdo Dry Valleys," Wikipedia, https://en.wikipedia.org/wiki/McMurdo_Dry_Valleys.

463. "Blood Falls," Wikipedia, https://en.wikipedia.org/wiki/Blood_Falls.

464. Justin Gillis, "John Kerry's Antarctica Visit Highlights a Continent, and Climate Policies, Under Threat," *The New York Times*, November 15, 2016, https://www.nytimes.com/2016/11/16/science/antarctica-john-kerry-global-warming.html.

465. John Kerry, Remarks, "On the New Marine Protected Area in Antarctica's Ross Sea," District of Columbia, October 27, 2016, https://2009-2017.state.gov/secretary/remarks/2016/11/264635.htm.

466. John Kerry, Remarks, "Remarks at Meet and Greet with the Staff of McMurdo Station," Anarctica, November 11, 2016, https://2009-2017.state.gov/secretary/remarks/2016/11/264262.htm.

467. John Kerry, Remarks, "Press Availability with New Zealand Prime Minister John Key," Wellington, November 13, 2016, https://2009-2017.state.gov/secretary/remarks/2016/11/264266.htm.

468. Ibid.

Chapter 9

469. Rex W. Tillerson, Remarks, "Farewell Remarks to the Department," District of Columbia, March 22, 2018, https://www.state.gov/secretary/20172018tillerson/remarks/2018/03/279466.htm.

470. John Kerry, Remarks, "On the Nomination of Rex Tillerson," District of Columbia, December 13, 2016, https://2009-2017.state.gov/secretary/remarks/2016/12/265187.htm.

471. Brennan Weiss, "'His mustache is a problem': Trump reportedly soured on John Bolton for a top Cabinet position because of his looks," *Business Insider*, January 3, 2018, http://www.businessinsider.com/john-bolton-mustache-cost-him-trump-cabinet-post-fire-and-fury-claims-2018-1.

472. Ibid.

473. Michael D. Shear and Maggie Haberman, "Rex Tillerson, Exxon C.E.O., Chosen as Secretary of State," *The New York Times*, December 12, 2016, https://www.nytimes.com/2016/12/12/us/politics/rex-tillerson-secretary-of-state-trump.html.

474. Julian Borger, "Rex Tillerson: 'I didn't want this job ... my wife told me I'm supposed to do this,'" *The Guardian*, March 22, 2017, https://www.theguardian.com/us-news/2017/mar/22/rex-tillerson-i-didnt-want-this-job.

475. Phil Mattingly, Jim Acosta and Stephen Collinson, "Trump pick ExxonMobil CEO Tillerson as choice for secretary of state," *CNN*, December 13, 2016, https://www.cnn.com/2016/12/12/politics/donald-trump-rex-tillerson-secretary-of-state-exxonmobil-ceo/index.html.

476. Rex W. Tillerson, Remarks, "Welcome Remarks to Employees," District of Columbia, February 2, 2017, https://www.state.gov/secretary/20172018tillerson/remarks/2017/02/267401.htm.

477. Ibid.

478. Gardiner Harris, "Rex Tillerson Is Confirmed as Secretary of State Amid Record Opposition," *The New York Times*, February 1, 2017, https://www.nytimes.com/2017/02/01/us/politics/rex-tillerson-secretary-of-state-confirmed.html.

479. Josh Rogin, "The State Department's entire senior administrative team just resigned," *The Washington Post*, January 26, 2017, https://www.washingtonpost.com/news/josh-rogin/wp/2017/01/26/the-state-departments-entire-senior-management-team-just-resigned/?postshare=2371485449363292&utm_term=.38ed25944fd8.

480. Ibid.

481. Ibid.

482. Charles S. Clark, "State Department Loses Top Management Team in Trump's First Week," *Government Executive*, January 26, 2017, https://www.govexec.com/management/2017/01/state-department-loses-top-management-team-trumps-first-week/134904/.

483. Josh Rogin, "The State Department just broke a promise to minority and female recruits," *The Washington Post*, June 13, 2017, https://www.washingtonpost.com/opinions/global-opinions/the-state-department-just-broke-a-promise-to-minority-and-female-recruits/2017/06/18/cd1f9d44-52b9-11e7-b064-828ba60fbb98_story.html?utm_term=.5e797882b0ca.

484. Mark Landler, "State Dept. Officials Should Quit if They Disagree with Trump, White House Warns," *The New York Times*, January 31, 2017, https://www.nytimes.com/2017/01/31/us/politics/sean-spicer-state-dept-travel-ban.html.

485. Rex W. Tillerson, Remarks, "Welcome Remarks to Employees," District of Columbia, February 2, 2017, https://www.state.gov/secretary/20172018tillerson/remarks/2017/02/267401.htm.

486. Ibid.

487. Maggie Haberman, Jonathan Weisman and Eric Lichtblau, "Trump Overrules Tillerson, Rejecting Elliott Abrams for Deputy Secretary of State," *The New York Times*, Feburary 10, 2017, https://www.nytimes.com/2017/02/10/us/politics/trump-wall-21-billion-dollars.html.

488. Julian Borger, "Rex Tillerson: 'I didn't want this job … my wife told me I'm supposed to do this,'" *The Guardian*, March 22, 2017, https://www.theguardian.com/us-news/2017/mar/22/rex-tillerson-i-didnt-want-this-job.

489. Carol Morello and Anne Gearan, "In first month of Trump presidency, State Department has been sidelined," *The Washington Post*, February 22, 2017, https://www.washingtonpost.com/world/national-security/in-first-month-of-trump-presidency-state-department-has-been-sidelined/2017/02/22/cc170cd2-f924-11e6-be05-1a3817ac21a5_story.html?noredirect=on&postshare=1341487863162329&utm_term=.3cab5d336315.

490. Ibid.

491. Anne Gearan and Carol Morello, "Secretary of State Rex Tillerson spends his first weeks isolated from an anxious bureaucracy," *The Washington Post*, March 30, 2017, https://www.washingtonpost.com/world/national-security/secretary-of-state-rex-tillerson-spends-his-first-weeks-isolated-from-an-anxious-bureaucracy/2017/03/30/bdf8ec86-155f-11e7-ada0-1489b735b3a3_story.html?utm_term=.f819dfa296c7.

492. Ibid.

493. Robbie Gramer, Dan De Luce, and Colum Lynch, "How the Trump Administration Broke the State Department," *Foreign Policy*, July 31, 2017, https://foreignpolicy.com/2017/07/31/how-the-trump-administration-broke-the-state-department/.

494. Rex W. Tillerson, Remarks, "Remarks to U.S. Department of State Employees," District of Columbia, May 3, 2017, https://www.state.gov/remarks-to-u-s-department-of-state-employees/.

495. David E. Sanger, Gardiner Harris, and Mark Landler, "Where Trump Zigs, Tillerson Zags, Putting Him at Odds with White House," *The New York Times*, June 25, 2017, https://www.nytimes.com/2017/06/25/world/americas/rex-tillerson-american-diplomacy.html.

496. Ibid.

497. Ibid.

498. Jon Lee Anderson, "The Diplomat Who Quit the Trump Administration," *The New Yorker*, May 21, 2018, https://www.newyorker.com/magazine/2018/05/28/the-diplomat-who-quit-the-trump-administration.

499. Robbie Gramer, Dan De Luce, and Colum Lynch, "How the Trump Administration Broke the State Department," *Foreign Policy*, July 31, 2017, https://foreignpolicy.com/2017/07/31/how-the-trump-administration-broke-the-state-department/.

500. Carol E. Lee, Kristen Welker, Stephanie Ruhle and Dafna Linzer, "Tillerson's Fury at Trump Required an Intervention from Pence," NBC News, October 4, 2017, https://www.nbcnews.com/politics/white-house/tillerson-s-fury-trump-required-intervention-pence-n806451.

501. Rex W. Tillerson, Remarks, "Remarks at a Press Availability," District of Columbia, October 4, 2017, https://www.state.gov/remarks-at-a-press-availability-4/.

502. Ibid.

503. Rex W. Tillerson, Remarks, "Interview with Jake Tapper of CNN," District of Columbia, October 15, 2017, https://www.state.gov/interview-with-jake-tapper-of-cnn/.

504. Ibid.

505. Gardiner Harris, "Diplomats Sound the Alarm as They Are Pushed Out in Droves," *The New York Times*, November 24, 2017, https://www.nytimes.com/2017/11/24/us/politics/state-department-tillerson.html.

506. Gardiner Harris, "Trump Rejects Reports That His Top Diplomat Is Departing," *The New York Times*, December 1, 2017, https://www.nytimes.com/2017/12/01/us/politics/tillerson-state-departure-reports-laughable.html?smid=tw-share.

507. Margaret Brennan, "Rex Tillerson Opens Up in Rare, Wide-Ranging Interview," CBS News, February 18, 2018, https://www.cbsnews.com/news/rex-tillerson-secretary-of-state-60-minutes-interview/.

508. Ibid.

509. Julie Hirschfeld Davis, Sheryl Gay Stolberg and Thomas Kaplan, "Trump Alarms Lawmakers with Disparaging Words for Haiti and Africa," *The New York Times*, January 11, 2018, https://www.nytimes.com/2018/01/11/us/politics/trump-shithole-countries.html?module=inline.

510. Mike Pompeo and John J. Sullivan, Remarks, "Welcome Remarks to Employees," District of Columbia, May 1, 2018, https://www.state.gov/secretary/remarks/2018/05/281365.htm.

511. Ed Sanora, "Mike Pompeo Full Interview with Chris Wallace—Fox News Sunday," YouTube, May 13, 2018, https://www.youtube.com/watch?v=hQjQG8pnuXg.

512. Melanie Arter, "Rex Tillerson: 'Under the Right Conditions,' US Could Stay in Paris Accord," CNS News, September 18, 2017, https://www.cnsnews.com/news/article/melanie-arter/rex-tillerson-under-right-conditions-us-could-stay-paris-accord.

513. Michael C. Bender and Felicia Schwartz, "Rex Tillerson Is Out as Secretary of State; Donald Trump Taps Mike Pompeo," *The Wall Street Journal*, March 13, 2018, https://www.wsj.com/articles/rex-tillerson-is-out-as-secretary-of-state-donald-trump-taps-mike-pompeo-1520978116.

514. Bob Dreyfuss, "Tillerson Ousted by Trump: State Department Goes from Bad to Worse," *Rolling Stone*, March 13, 2018, https://www.rollingstone.com/politics/politics-features/tillerson-ousted-by-trump-state-department-goes-from-bad-to-worse-199102/.

515. Nahal Toosi, "Pompeo asks Clinton for advice as he preps for confirmation battle," *Politico*, April 10, 2018, https://www.politico.com/story/2018/04/10/pompeo-hearing-state-clinton-512155.

516. Ashley Parker, Philip Rucker, John Hudson and Carol D. Leonnig, "Trump ousts Tillerson, will replace him as secretary of state with CIA chief Pompeo," *The Washington Post*, March 13, 2018, https://www.washingtonpost.com/politics/trump-ousts-tillerson-will-replace-him-as-secretary-of-state-with-cia-chief-pompeo/2018/03/13/30f34eea-26ba-11e8-b79d-f3d931db7f68_story.html?utm_term=.e2777cb878ed.

517. Glen Johnson, "End of Iran deal: Shredding diplomacy for spite, not gain," *The Boston Globe*, May 8, 2018, https://www.bostonglobe.com/opinion/2018/05/08/end-iran-deal-shredding-diplomacy-for-spite-not-gain/Ow97SNGe2bXT0QoTlZGlRO/story.html.

518. Jill R. Russell, "With rifle and bibliography: General Mattis on professional reading," *Strife*, May 7, 2013, http://www.strifeblog.org/2013/05/07/with-rifle-and-bibliography-general-mattis-on-professional-reading/.

519. "Saudi Arabia Visa Information," ItsEasy Passport and Visa, https://www.itseasy.com/visa-expediting/saudi-arabia/.

520. "Do US citizens buy property in China, as much as Chinese citizens buy property in the US?" Quora, https://www.quora.com/Do-US-citizens-buy-property-in-China-as-much-as-Chinese-citizens-buy-property-in-the-US.

521. Matt Viser, "John Kerry back at home, but not for very long," *The Boston Globe*, June 14, 2015, https://www.bostonglobe.com/news/politics/2015/06/13/john-kerry-reflects-his-bicycle-accident -exclusive-globe-interview/nRK32wk1YCJ15Mmd4tcoJJ/story.html.

Epilogue

522. Barack Obama, Remarks, "Remarks by the President at Nomination of Senator John Kerry as Secretary of State," District of Columbia, December 21, 2012, https://obamawhitehouse.archives.gov /the-press-office/2012/12/21/remarks-president-nomination-senator-john-kerry-secretary-state.

523. Author's recollection, January 1, 1998.

524. Author's recollection, June 2001.

525. Author's notes, January 15, 2013.

526. Ibid.

527. Author's recollection, January 16, 2013.

Acknowledgments

528. Adam Nagourney, "Kerry to Undergo Surgery for Prostate Cancer Today," *The New York Times*, February 12, 2003, http://www.nytimes.com/2003/02/12/us/kerry-to-undergo-surgery-for -prostate-cancer-today.html.

529. Amie Parnes, "Kerry aid gave boss a loyal proposition," *Politico*, http://www.politico.com /politicopros/davidwade.

ABOUT THE AUTHOR

GLEN JOHNSON COVERED FIVE presidential elections over three decades reporting for *The Boston Globe*, the Associated Press, a string of local newspapers, and the historic City News Bureau of Chicago. He served as US deputy assistant secretary of State for strategic communications from 2013 to 2017 under an appointment by President Barack Obama, and took over 100,000 photos of Secretary Kerry during their international travels. Johnson proudly graduated from Lawrence University in Appleton, Wisconsin. He now lives outside Boston.